100% Perfect Girl

Vol. 1

WANN

NETCOMICS

100% Perfect Girl Vol. 1
Story and Art by Wann

English translation rights in USA,
Canada, UK, NZ, Australia arranged by
Ecomix Media Company
395-21 Seogyo-dong, Mapo-gu, Seoul, Korea 121-840
info@ecomixmedia.com

- Produced by Ecomix Media Company
- Translator Jennifer Park
- Graphic Designers Hyekyoung Choi, Eunsook Lee
- Cover Designer purj
- Editor Jeffrey Tompkins
- Managing Editor Soyoung Jung
- President & Publisher Heewoon Chung

NETCOMICS

P.O. Box 16484, Jersey City, NJ 07306
info@netcomics.com
www.NETCOMICS.com

ISBN: 978-1-60009-216-9

First printing: February 2007
10 9 8 7 6 5 4 3 2 1
Printed in Korea

100% Perfect Girl

Vol. 1

WANN

Author's Words

Manhwagas are usually a species of a rebellious disposition.
This human being, Wann, is no exception. When she wraps up a series she tends to plan a new book that's at least a tiny bit different, instead of working on something in the same genre. I have nothing to say if you attack me with "Well, it's still the same old romantic drama!"
To be honest, I'm not a die-hard fan of the Cinderella story. There are so many stories that are a lot like it, as you well know. But, a great work is... how should I put it... It definitely has some kind of charm--like the way it touches your deepest heart's desire! Or it sends down a wave of electricity somewhere...! Or it makes your heart pound so much that you can't fall asleep at night.
But such work is very hard to find.
So I went all out and decided to write my own Cinderella story, one suited exactly to my taste. Was that almost ten years ago...? It was a story I started writing entirely for my own enjoyment, without intending to release it as my work. For ten years, I wrote alone, read alone, and went crazy over it alone....
At least this one reader was very happy. But now, I think I will enjoy it with you.
When I thought that I could finally draw with the tip of my pen the world I'd only imagined in my head, I couldn't stand waiting anymore. After all, I have managed to make quite a few drawings along the way, I've been drawing *manhwa* for quite a while now, and I've become more shameless.
If you are a reader who's basically thought of my books as "not so bad," I'm sure you will find *100% Perfect Girl* to be the height of Wann's world of romance. (Argh... there goes my baseless self-confidence again.)
But because the author isn't as talented, she might have ended up creating an inferior work.
I still want to drown myself in the world of Jay and Jarte, and paw my way around it to my heart's content.
Now then, I present you with *100% Perfect Girl.*

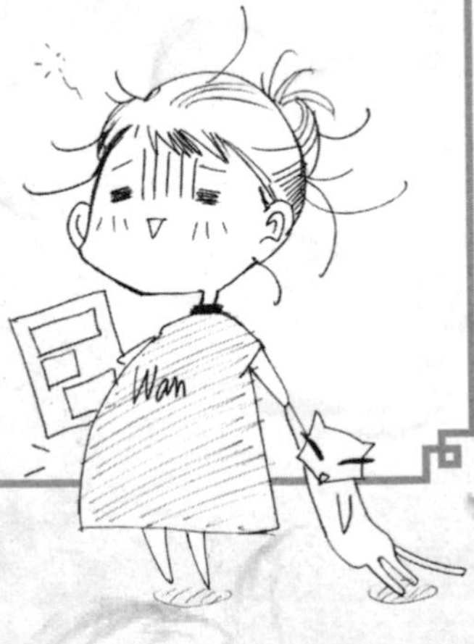
Wan

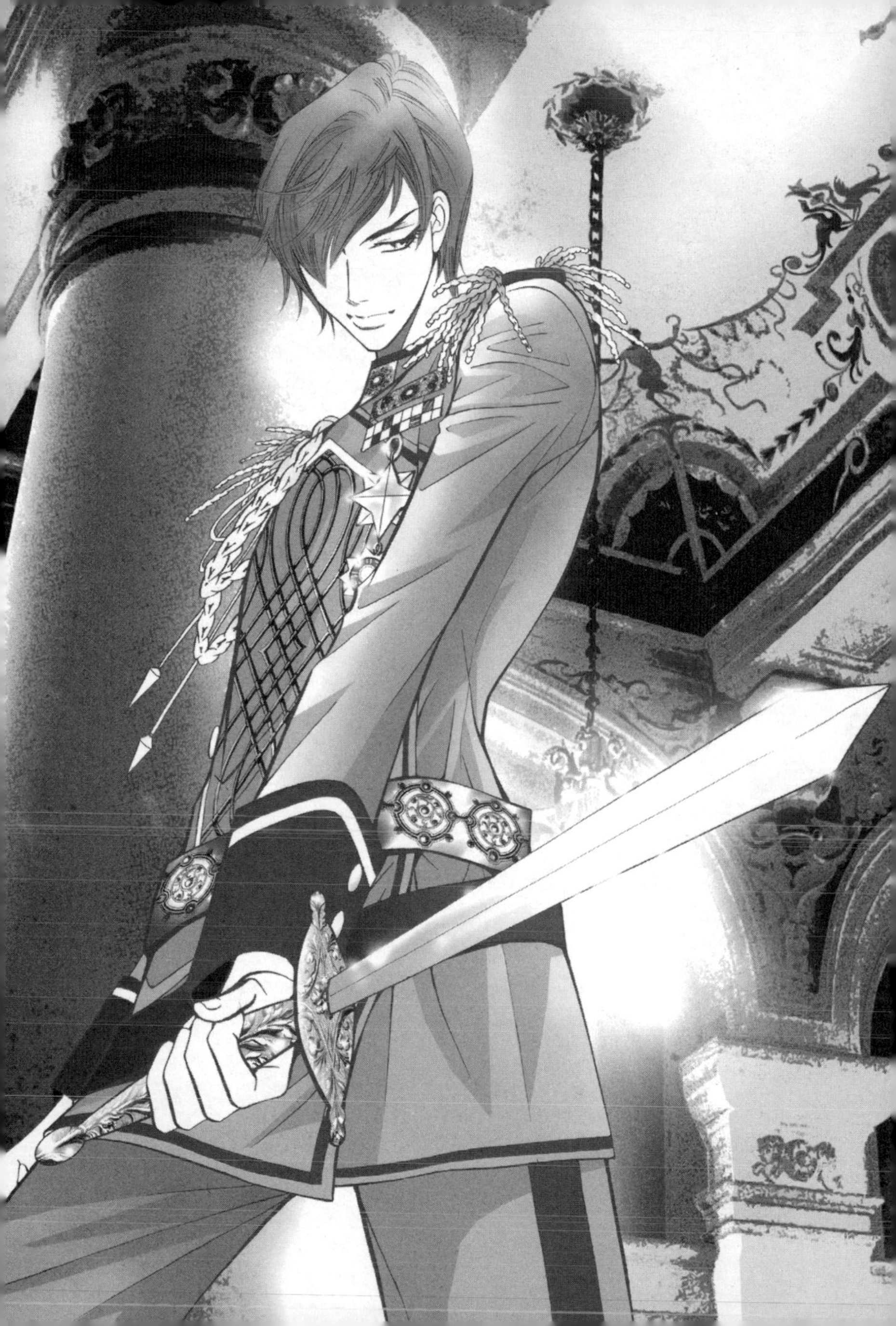

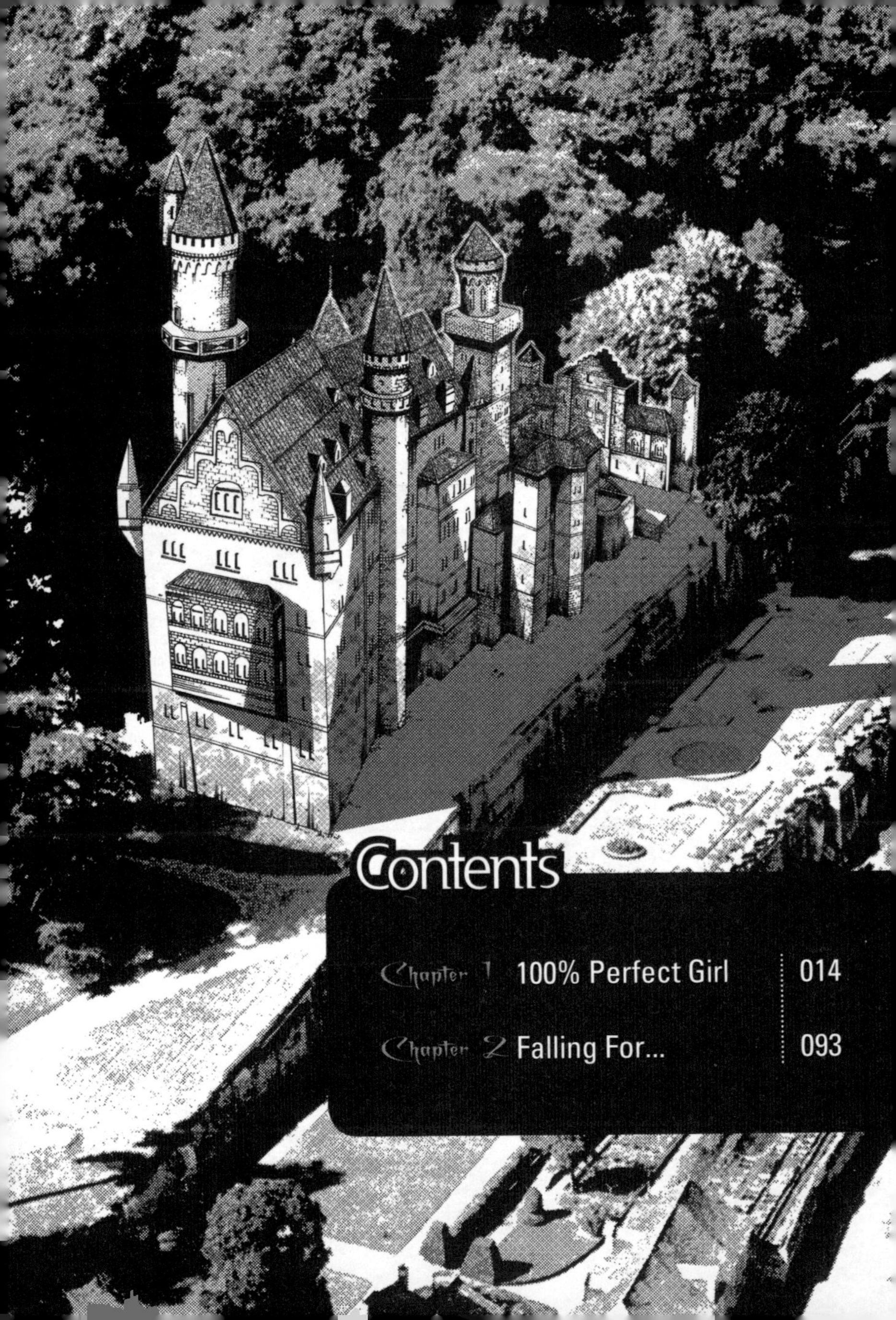

Contents

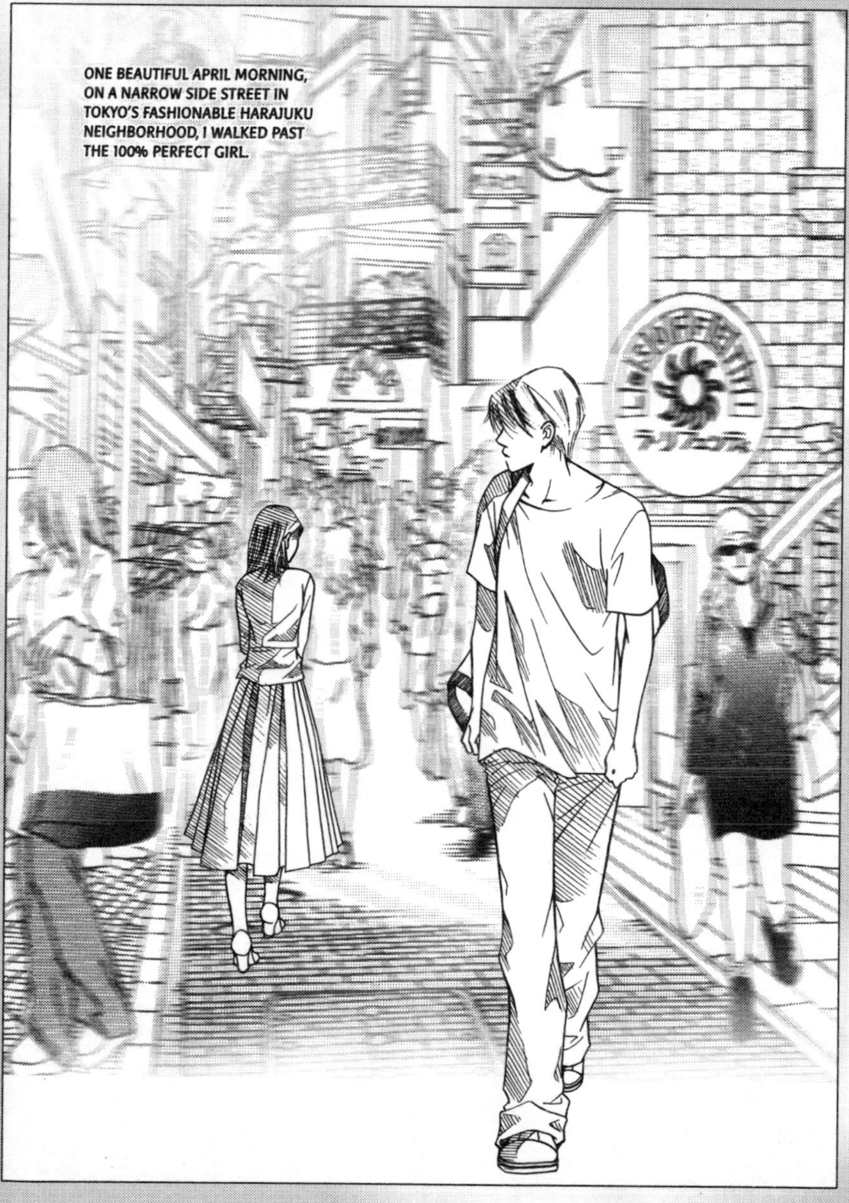
ONE BEAUTIFUL APRIL MORNING, ON A NARROW SIDE STREET IN TOKYO'S FASHIONABLE HARAJUKU NEIGHBORHOOD, I WALKED PAST THE 100% PERFECT GIRL.

TELL YOU THE TRUTH, SHE'S NOT THAT GOOD-LOOKING.

SHE DOESN'T STAND OUT IN ANY WAY.

...BUT STILL, I KNOW FROM FIFTY YARDS AWAY:

SHE'S THE 100% PERFECT GIRL FOR ME.

THE MOMENT I SEE HER, THERE'S A RUMBLING IN MY CHEST, AND MY MOUTH IS AS DRY AS A DESERT.

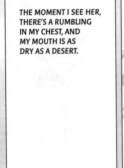

MAYBE YOU HAVE YOUR OWN PARTICULAR FAVORITE TYPE OF GIRL-ONE WITH SLIM ANKLES, SAY, OR BIG EYES, OR GRACEFUL FINGERS, OR YOU'RE DRAWN FOR NO GOOD REASON TO GIRLS WHO TAKE THEIR TIME WITH EVERY MEAL.

BUT NO ONE CAN INSIST THAT HIS 100% PERFECT GIRL CORRESPOND TO SOME PRECONCEIVED TYPE.

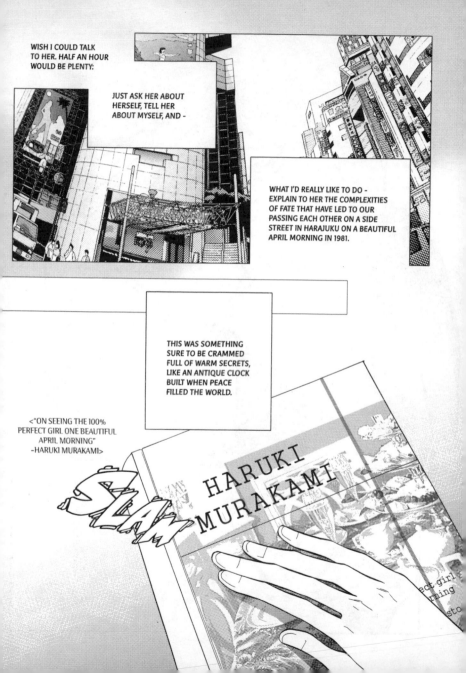

WISH I COULD TALK TO HER. HALF AN HOUR WOULD BE PLENTY:

JUST ASK HER ABOUT HERSELF, TELL HER ABOUT MYSELF, AND -

WHAT I'D REALLY LIKE TO DO - EXPLAIN TO HER THE COMPLEXITIES OF FATE THAT HAVE LED TO OUR PASSING EACH OTHER ON A SIDE STREET IN HARAJUKU ON A BEAUTIFUL APRIL MORNING IN 1981.

THIS WAS SOMETHING SURE TO BE CRAMMED FULL OF WARM SECRETS, LIKE AN ANTIQUE CLOCK BUILT WHEN PEACE FILLED THE WORLD.

<"ON SEEING THE 100% PERFECT GIRL ONE BEAUTIFUL APRIL MORNING" -HARUKI MURAKAMI>

SLAM

HARUKI MURAKAMI

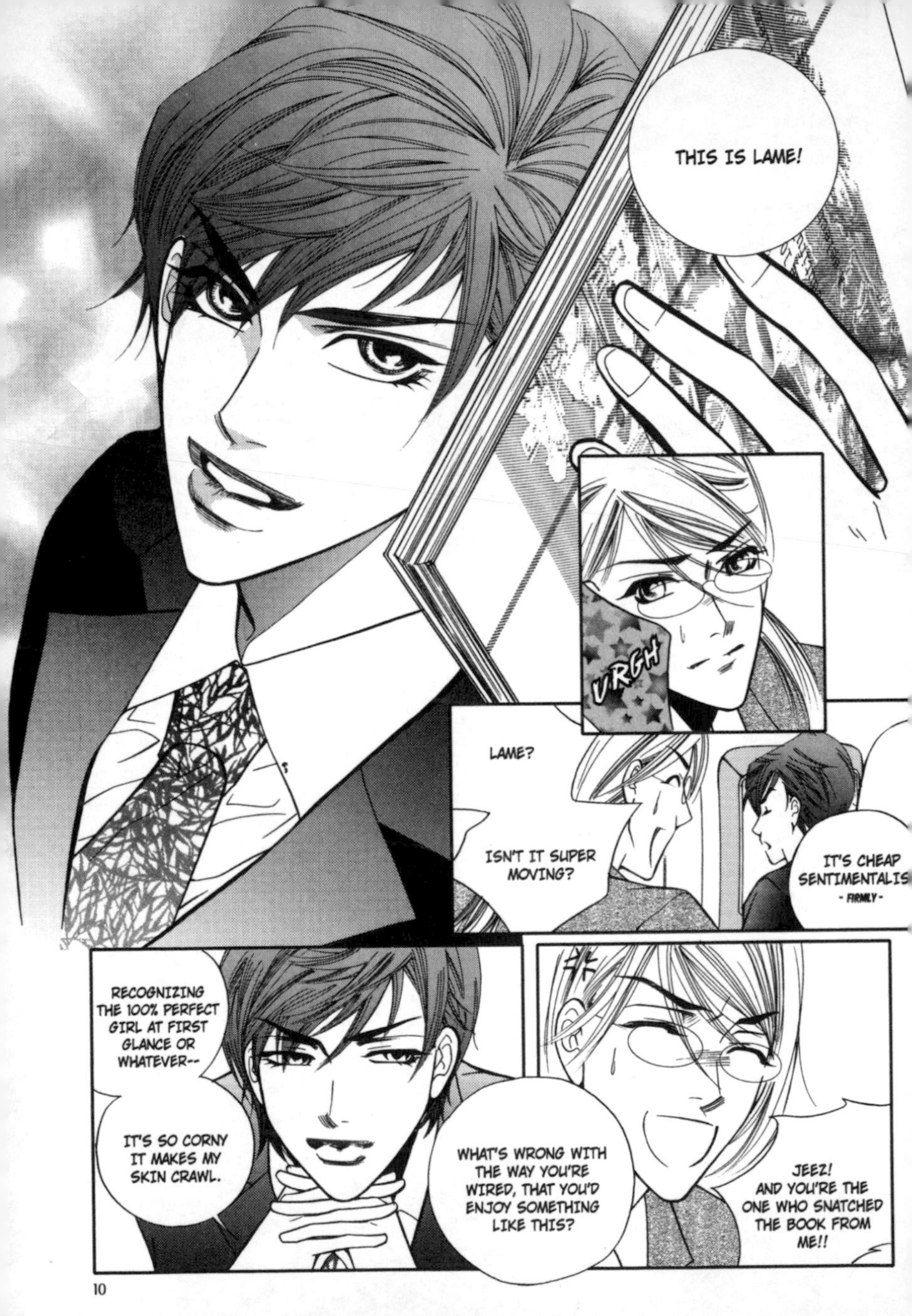
THIS IS LAME!
URGH
LAME?
ISN'T IT SUPER MOVING?
IT'S CHEAP SENTIMENTALIS
- FIRMLY -
RECOGNIZING THE 100% PERFECT GIRL AT FIRST GLANCE OR WHATEVER--
IT'S SO CORNY IT MAKES MY SKIN CRAWL.
WHAT'S WRONG WITH THE WAY YOU'RE WIRED, THAT YOU'D ENJOY SOMETHING LIKE THIS?
JEEZ! AND YOU'RE THE ONE WHO SNATCHED THE BOOK FROM ME!!

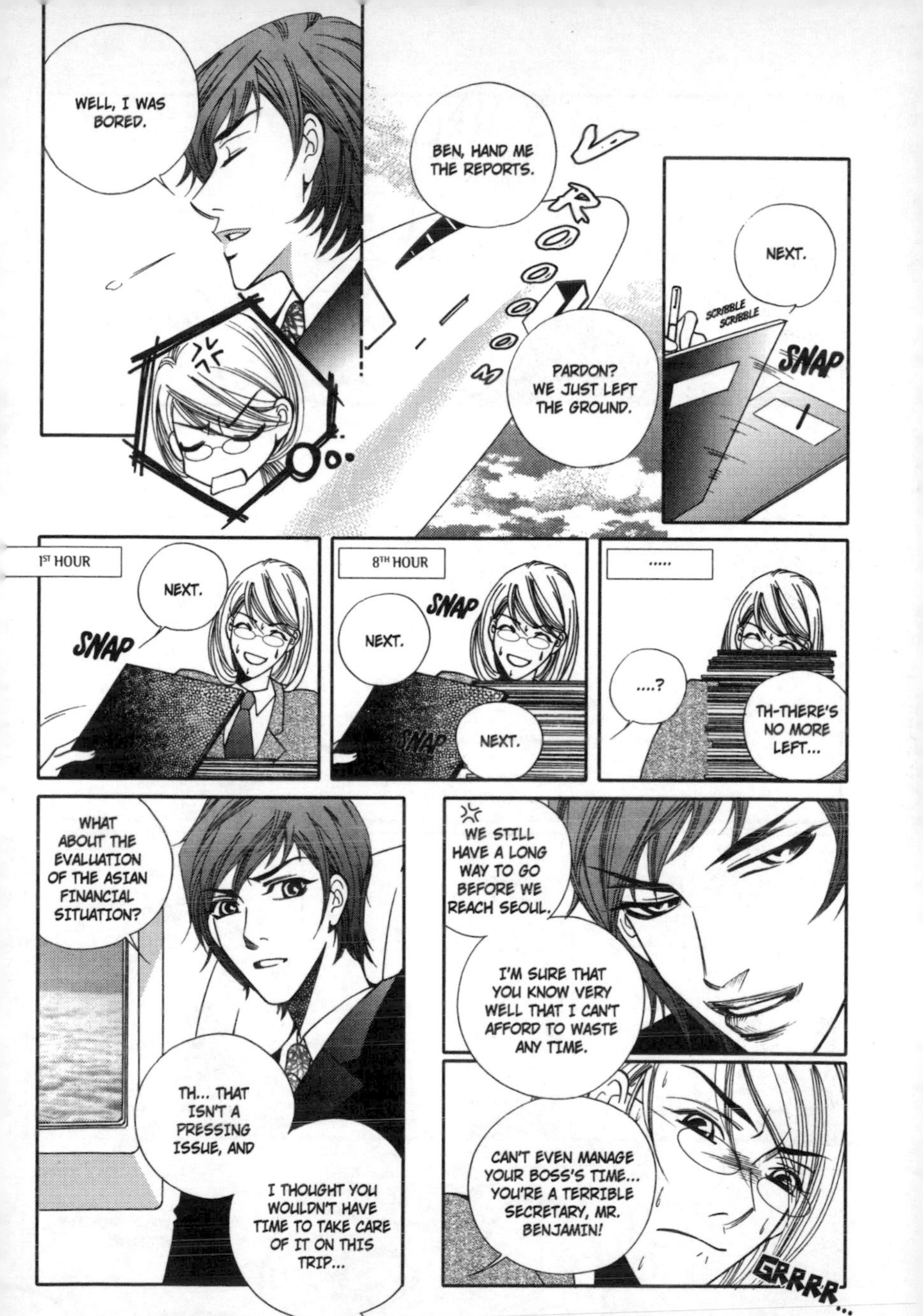
WELL, I WAS BORED.
BEN, HAND ME THE REPORTS.
VROOOOOOM
PARDON? WE JUST LEFT THE GROUND.
NEXT.
SCRIBBLE SCRIBBLE
SNAP
1ST HOUR
NEXT.
SNAP
8TH HOUR
SNAP
NEXT.
SNAP
NEXT.
.....
....?
TH-THERE'S NO MORE LEFT...
WHAT ABOUT THE EVALUATION OF THE ASIAN FINANCIAL SITUATION?
TH... THAT ISN'T A PRESSING ISSUE, AND
I THOUGHT YOU WOULDN'T HAVE TIME TO TAKE CARE OF IT ON THIS TRIP...
WE STILL HAVE A LONG WAY TO GO BEFORE WE REACH SEOUL.
I'M SURE THAT YOU KNOW VERY WELL THAT I CAN'T AFFORD TO WASTE ANY TIME.
CAN'T EVEN MANAGE YOUR BOSS'S TIME... YOU'RE A TERRIBLE SECRETARY, MR. BENJAMIN!
GRRRR...

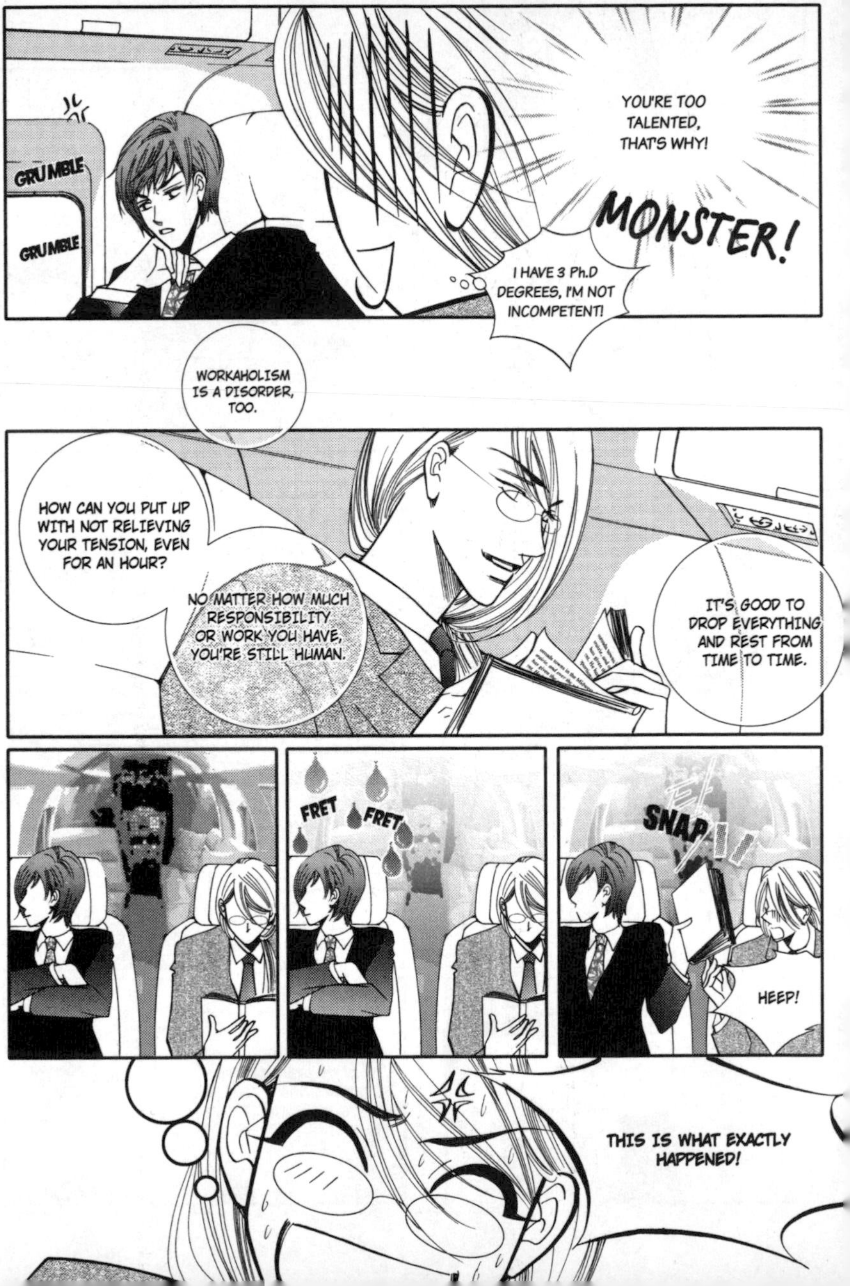
GRUMBLE
GRUMBLE
YOU'RE TOO TALENTED, THAT'S WHY!
MONSTER!
I HAVE 3 Ph.D DEGREES, I'M NOT INCOMPETENT!
WORKAHOLISM IS A DISORDER, TOO.
HOW CAN YOU PUT UP WITH NOT RELIEVING YOUR TENSION, EVEN FOR AN HOUR?
NO MATTER HOW MUCH RESPONSIBILITY OR WORK YOU HAVE, YOU'RE STILL HUMAN.
IT'S GOOD TO DROP EVERYTHING AND REST FROM TIME TO TIME.
FRET
FRET
SNAP!!
HEEP!
THIS IS WHAT EXACTLY HAPPENED!

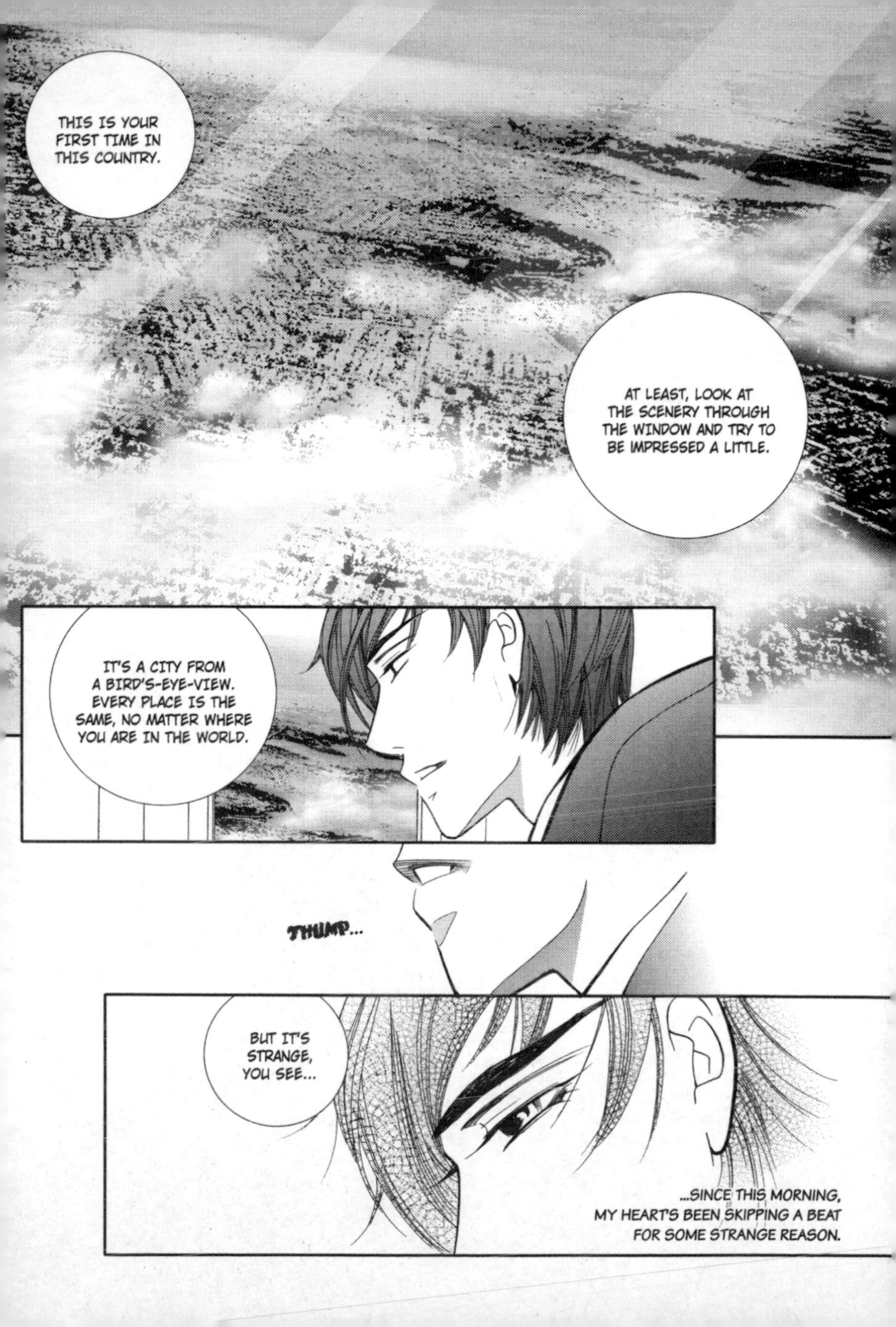
THIS IS YOUR FIRST TIME IN THIS COUNTRY.
AT LEAST, LOOK AT THE SCENERY THROUGH THE WINDOW AND TRY TO BE IMPRESSED A LITTLE.
IT'S A CITY FROM A BIRD'S-EYE-VIEW. EVERY PLACE IS THE SAME, NO MATTER WHERE YOU ARE IN THE WORLD.
THUMP...
BUT IT'S STRANGE, YOU SEE...
...SINCE THIS MORNING, MY HEART'S BEEN SKIPPING A BEAT FOR SOME STRANGE REASON.

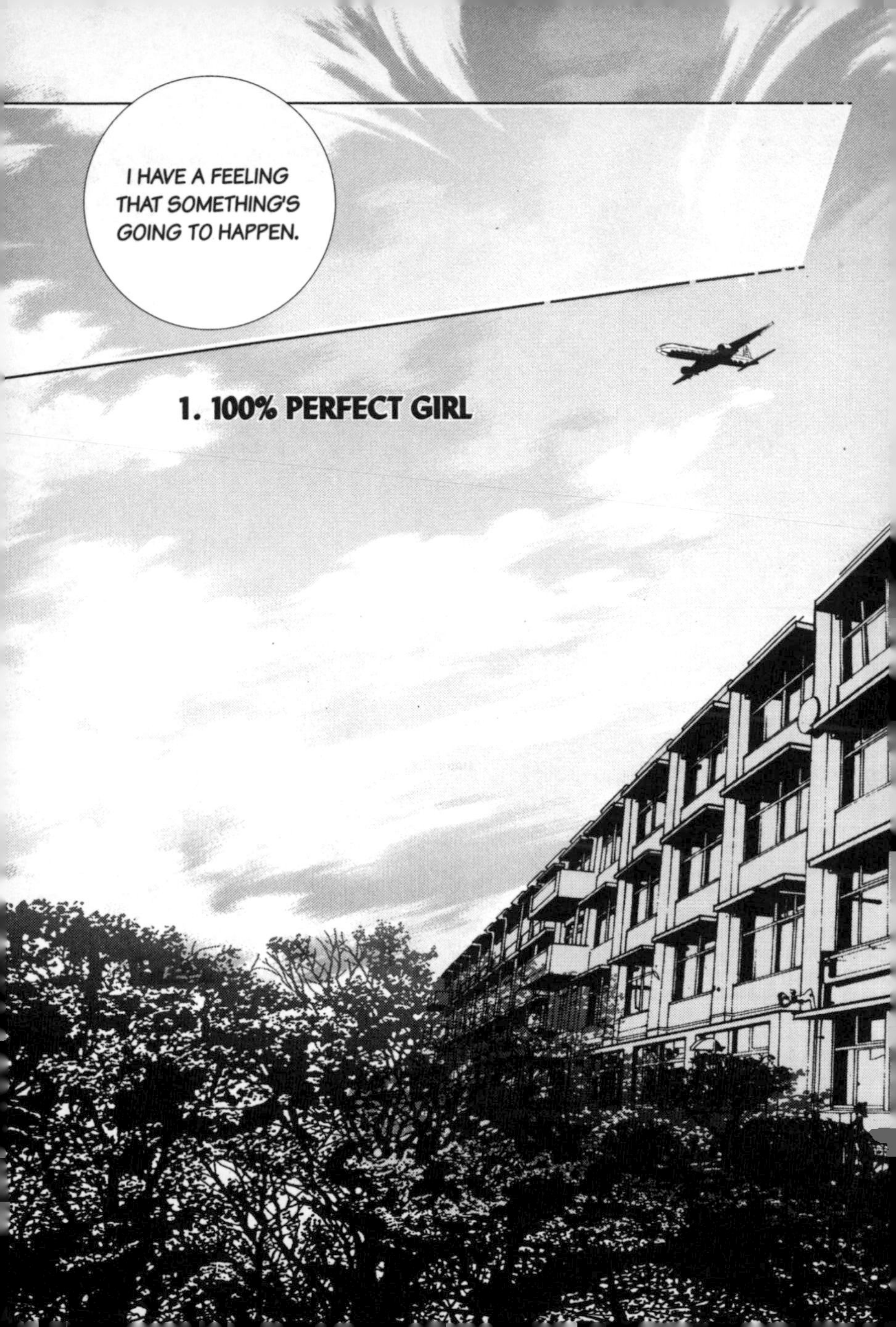
I HAVE A FEELING THAT SOMETHING'S GOING TO HAPPEN.
1. 100% PERFECT GIRL

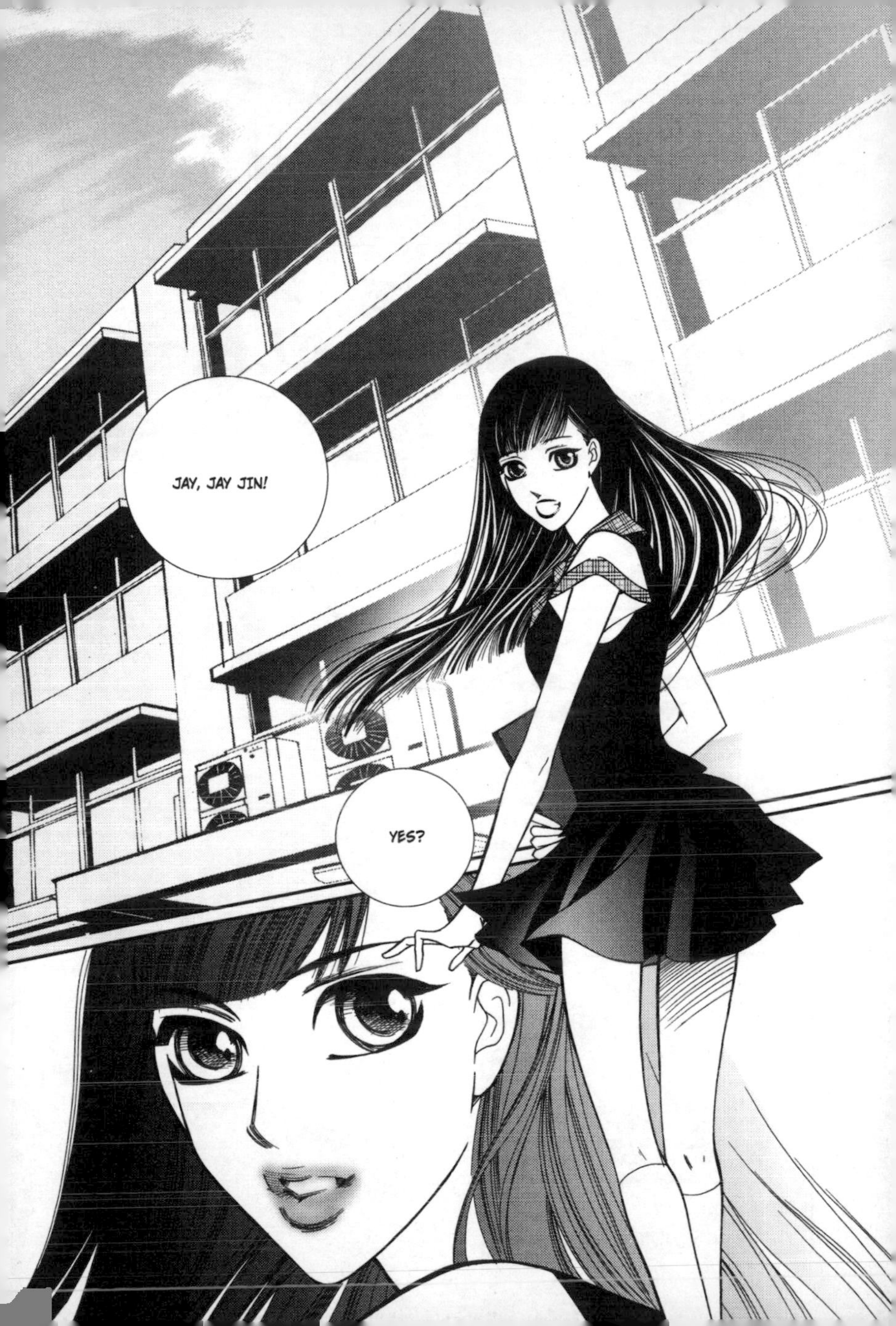
JAY, JAY JIN!
YES?

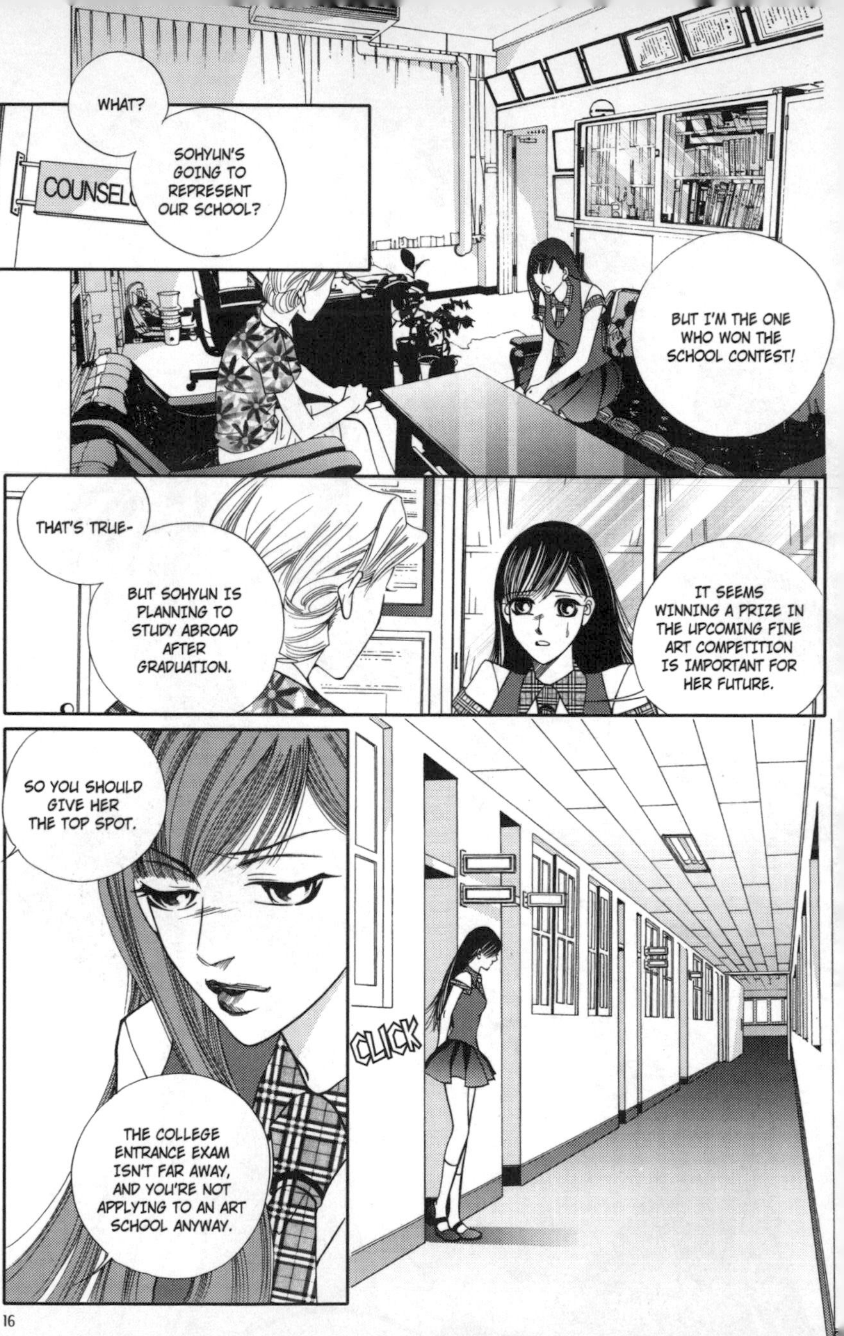

COUNSEL
WHAT?
SOHYUN'S GOING TO REPRESENT OUR SCHOOL?
BUT I'M THE ONE WHO WON THE SCHOOL CONTEST!
THAT'S TRUE-
BUT SOHYUN IS PLANNING TO STUDY ABROAD AFTER GRADUATION.
IT SEEMS WINNING A PRIZE IN THE UPCOMING FINE ART COMPETITION IS IMPORTANT FOR HER FUTURE.
SO YOU SHOULD GIVE HER THE TOP SPOT.
THE COLLEGE ENTRANCE EXAM ISN'T FAR AWAY, AND YOU'RE NOT APPLYING TO AN ART SCHOOL ANYWAY.
CLICK

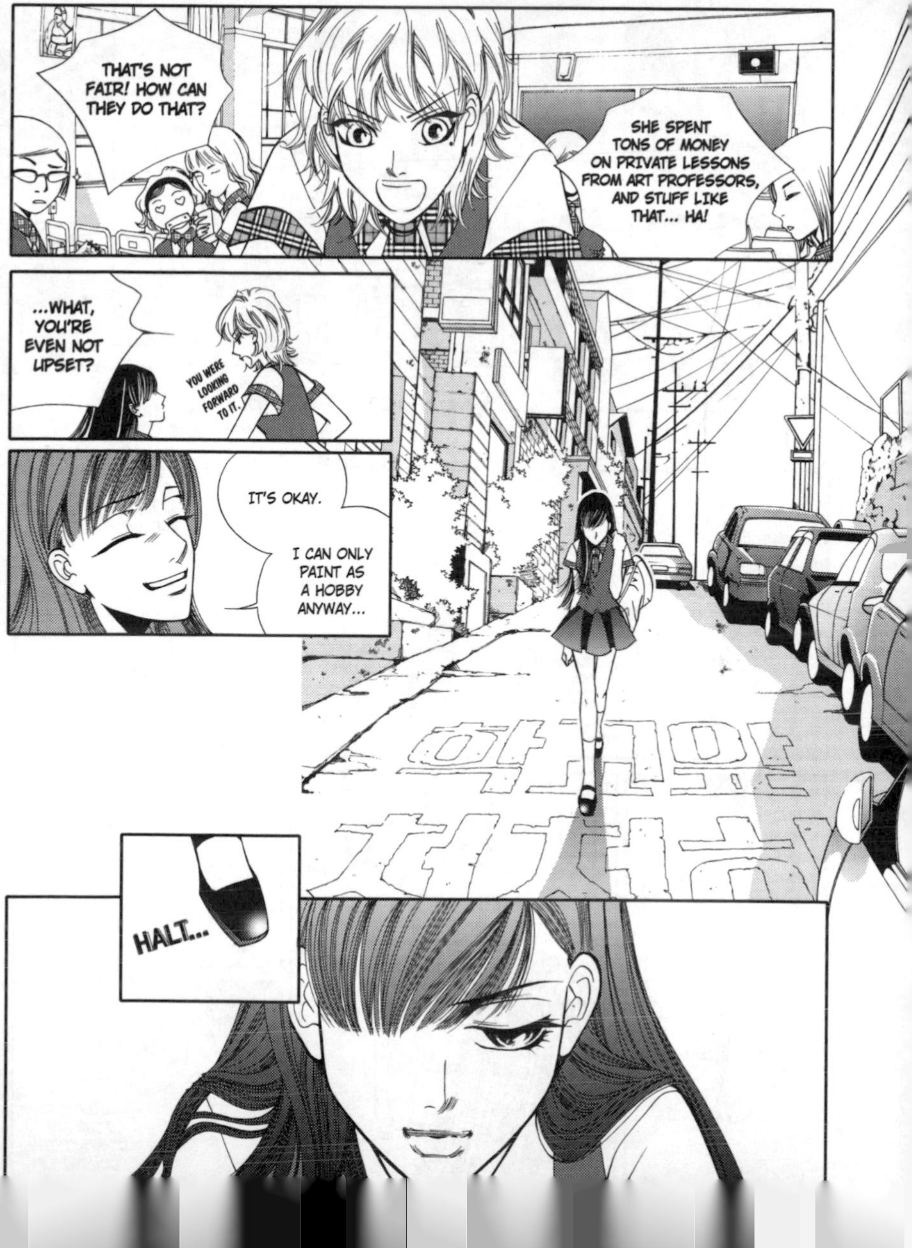
THAT'S NOT FAIR! HOW CAN THEY DO THAT?
SHE SPENT TONS OF MONEY ON PRIVATE LESSONS FROM ART PROFESSORS, AND STUFF LIKE THAT... HA!
...WHAT, YOU'RE EVEN NOT UPSET?
YOU WERE LOOKING FORWARD TO IT.
IT'S OKAY.
I CAN ONLY PAINT AS A HOBBY ANYWAY...
HALT...

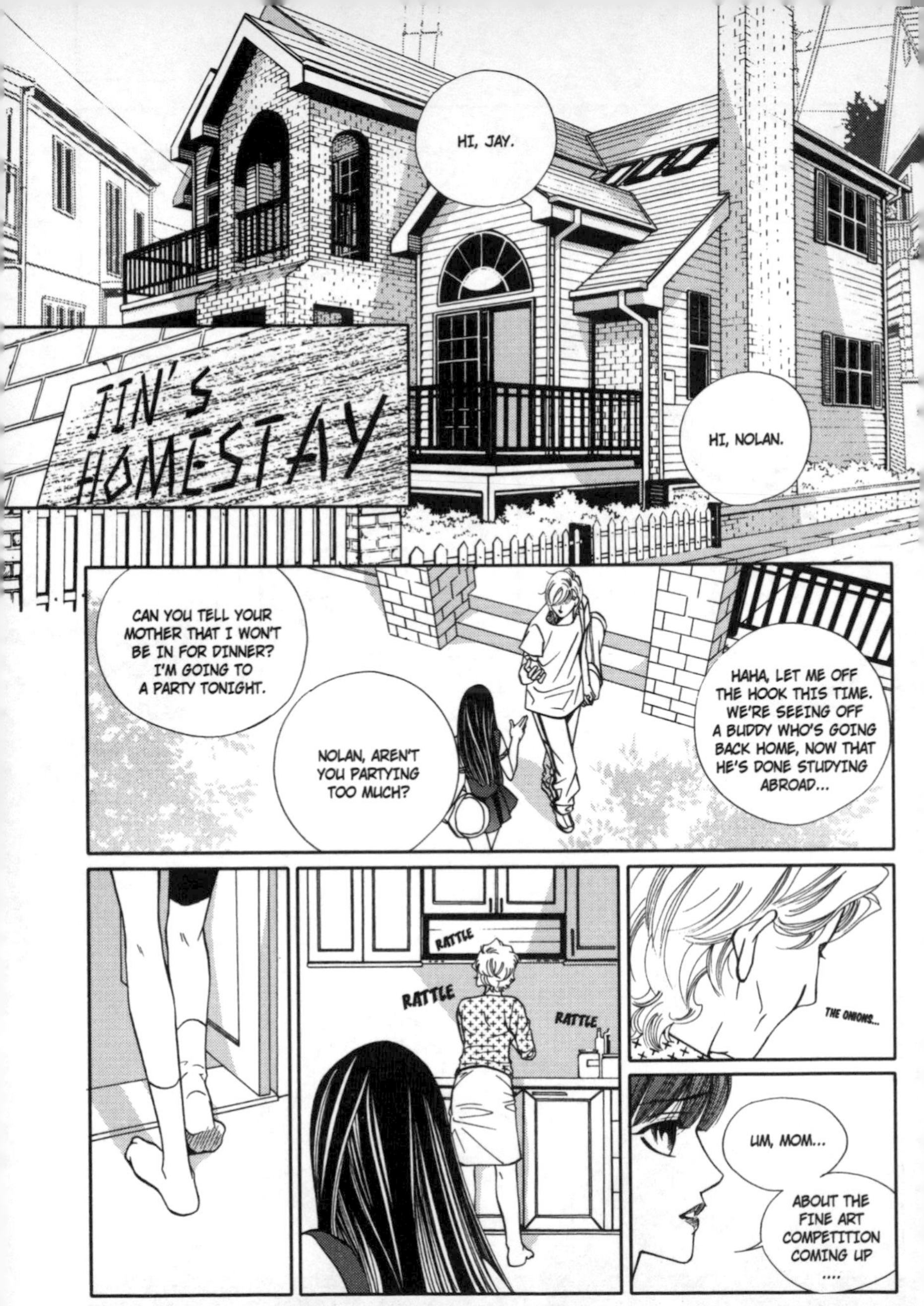
JIN'S HOMESTAY
HI, JAY.
HI, NOLAN.
CAN YOU TELL YOUR MOTHER THAT I WON'T BE IN FOR DINNER? I'M GOING TO A PARTY TONIGHT.
NOLAN, AREN'T YOU PARTYING TOO MUCH?
HAHA, LET ME OFF THE HOOK THIS TIME. WE'RE SEEING OFF A BUDDY WHO'S GOING BACK HOME, NOW THAT HE'S DONE STUDYING ABROAD...
RATTLE
RATTLE
RATTLE
THE ONIONS...
UM, MOM...
ABOUT THE FINE ART COMPETITION COMING UP ....

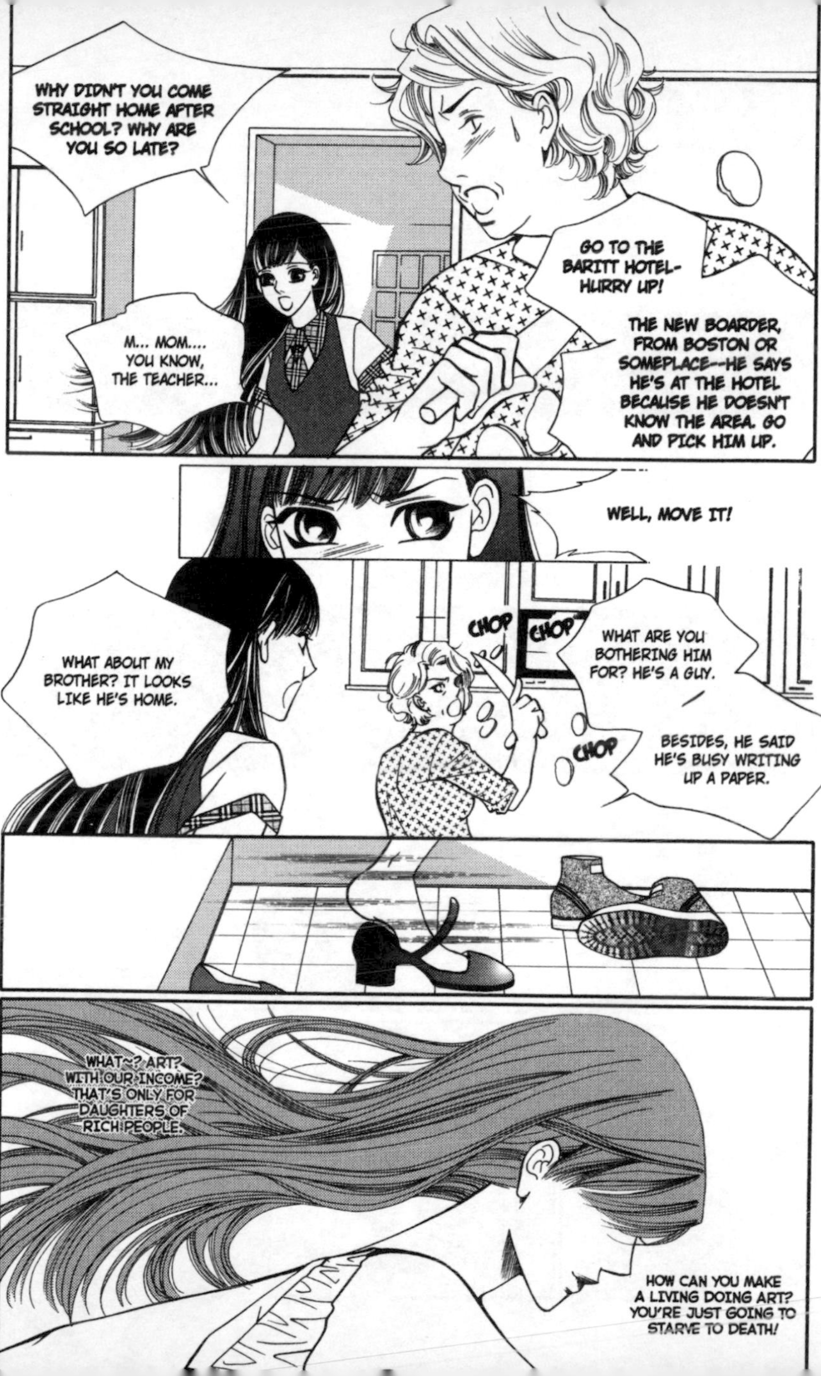
WHY DIDN'T YOU COME STRAIGHT HOME AFTER SCHOOL? WHY ARE YOU SO LATE?
M... MOM.... YOU KNOW, THE TEACHER...
GO TO THE BARITT HOTEL-HURRY UP!
THE NEW BOARDER, FROM BOSTON OR SOMEPLACE--HE SAYS HE'S AT THE HOTEL BECAUSE HE DOESN'T KNOW THE AREA. GO AND PICK HIM UP.
WELL, MOVE IT!
WHAT ABOUT MY BROTHER? IT LOOKS LIKE HE'S HOME.
CHOP
CHOP
WHAT ARE YOU BOTHERING HIM FOR? HE'S A GUY.
CHOP
BESIDES, HE SAID HE'S BUSY WRITING UP A PAPER.
WHAT~? ART? WITH OUR INCOME? THAT'S ONLY FOR DAUGHTERS OF RICH PEOPLE.
HOW CAN YOU MAKE A LIVING DOING ART? YOU'RE JUST GOING TO STARVE TO DEATH!

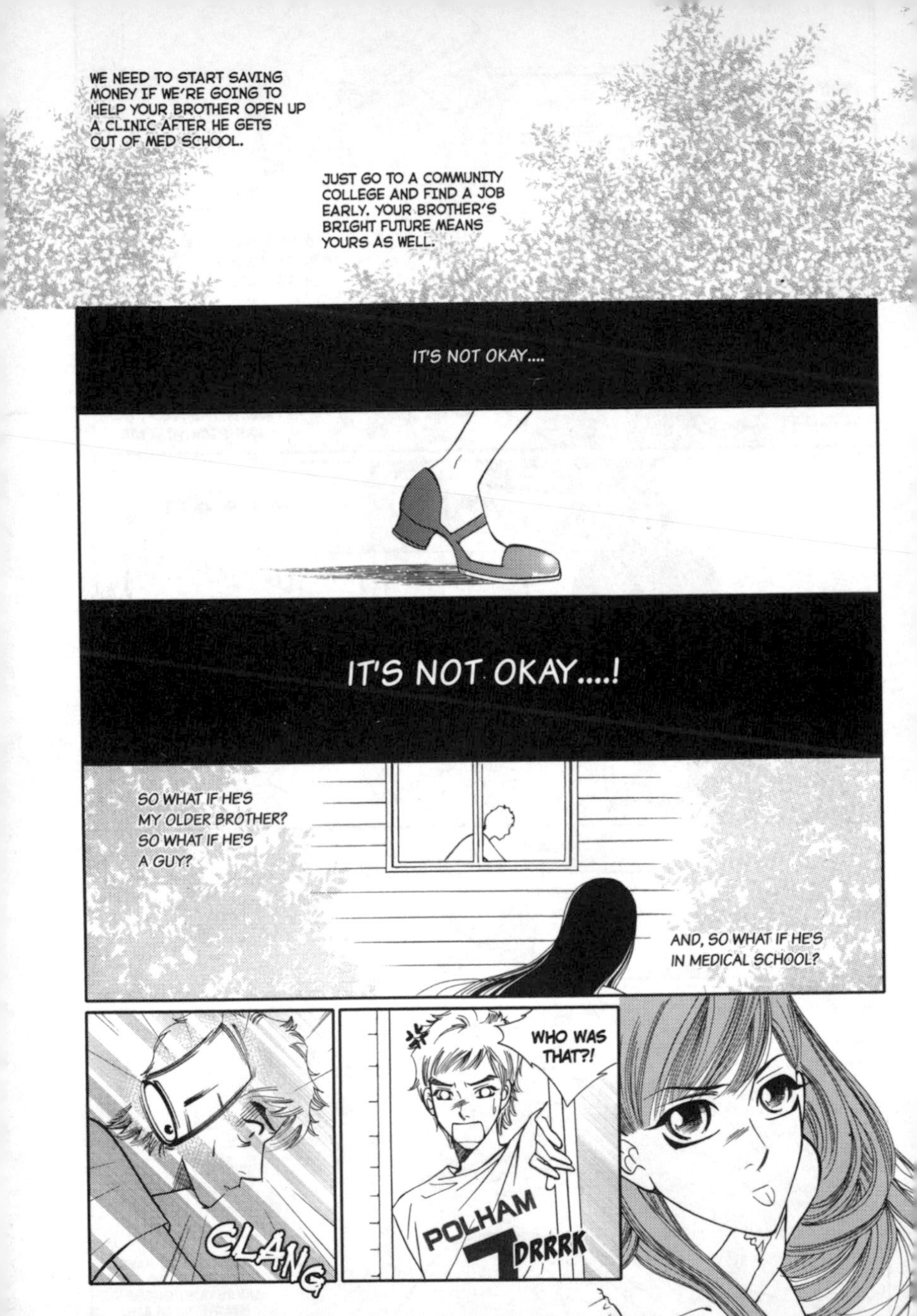
WE NEED TO START SAVING MONEY IF WE'RE GOING TO HELP YOUR BROTHER OPEN UP A CLINIC AFTER HE GETS OUT OF MED SCHOOL.
JUST GO TO A COMMUNITY COLLEGE AND FIND A JOB EARLY. YOUR BROTHER'S BRIGHT FUTURE MEANS YOURS AS WELL.
IT'S NOT OKAY....
IT'S NOT OKAY....!
SO WHAT IF HE'S MY OLDER BROTHER? SO WHAT IF HE'S A GUY?
AND, SO WHAT IF HE'S IN MEDICAL SCHOOL?
CLANG
WHO WAS THAT?!
POLHAM
DRRRK

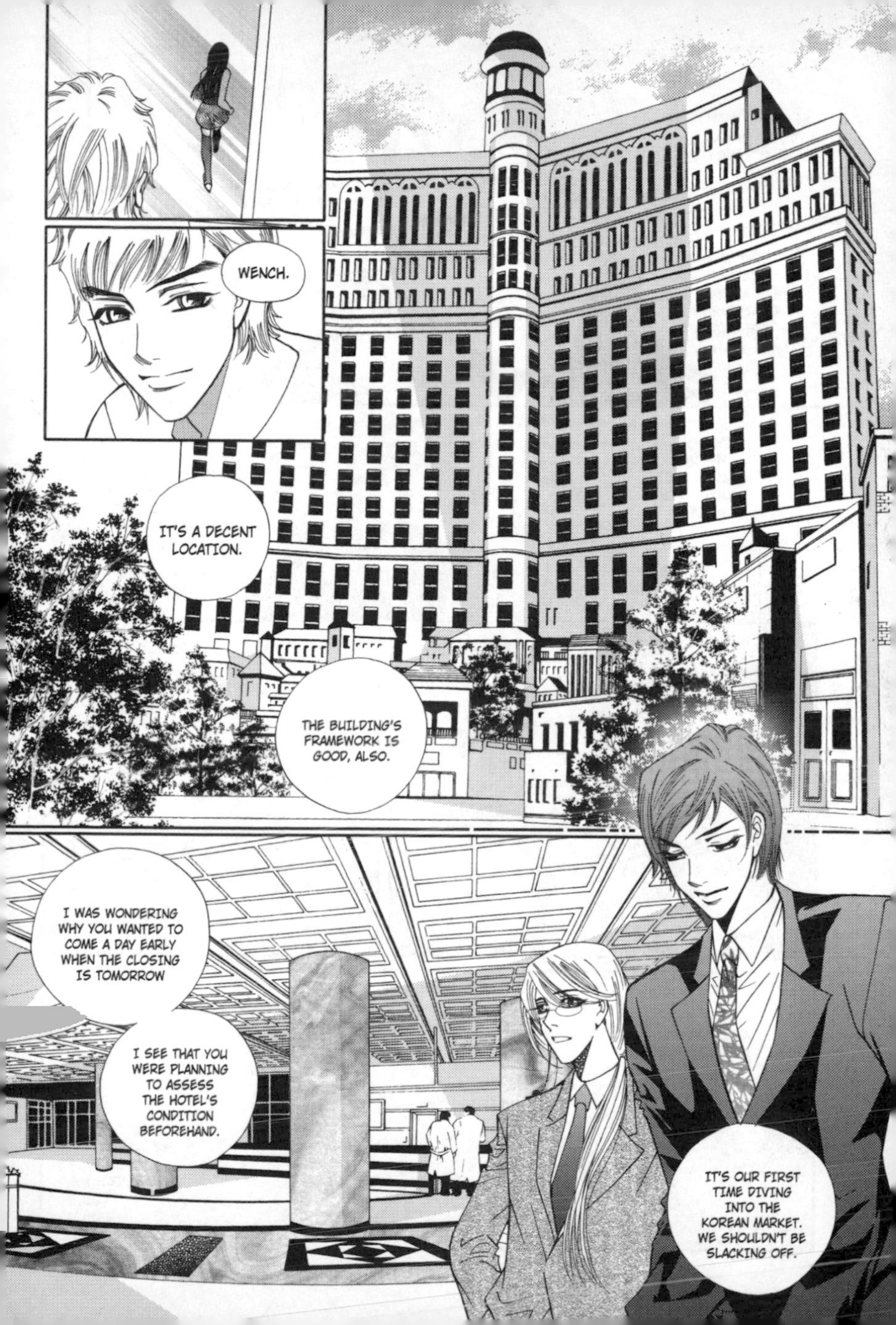
WENCH.
IT'S A DECENT LOCATION.
THE BUILDING'S FRAMEWORK IS GOOD, ALSO.
I WAS WONDERING WHY YOU WANTED TO COME A DAY EARLY WHEN THE CLOSING IS TOMORROW
I SEE THAT YOU WERE PLANNING TO ASSESS THE HOTEL'S CONDITION BEFOREHAND.
IT'S OUR FIRST TIME DIVING INTO THE KOREAN MARKET. WE SHOULDN'T BE SLACKING OFF.

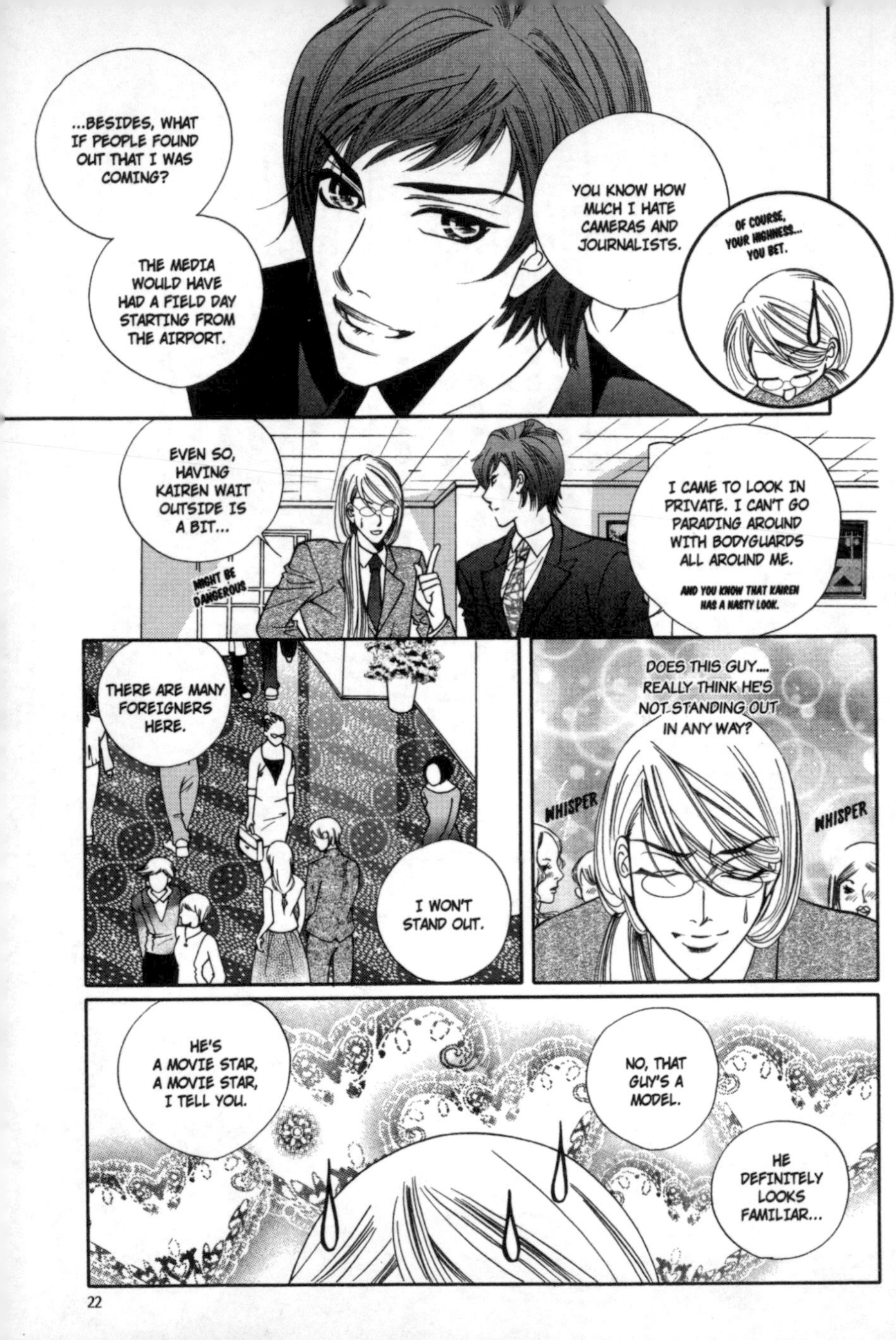
...BESIDES, WHAT IF PEOPLE FOUND OUT THAT I WAS COMING?
THE MEDIA WOULD HAVE HAD A FIELD DAY STARTING FROM THE AIRPORT.
YOU KNOW HOW MUCH I HATE CAMERAS AND JOURNALISTS.
OF COURSE, YOUR HIGHNESS... YOU BET.
EVEN SO, HAVING KAIREN WAIT OUTSIDE IS A BIT...
MIGHT BE DANGEROUS
I CAME TO LOOK IN PRIVATE. I CAN'T GO PARADING AROUND WITH BODYGUARDS ALL AROUND ME.
AND YOU KNOW THAT KAIREN HAS A NASTY LOOK.
THERE ARE MANY FOREIGNERS HERE.
I WON'T STAND OUT.
DOES THIS GUY.... REALLY THINK HE'S NOT STANDING OUT IN ANY WAY?
WHISPER
WHISPER
HE'S A MOVIE STAR, A MOVIE STAR, I TELL YOU.
NO, THAT GUY'S A MODEL.
HE DEFINITELY LOOKS FAMILIAR...

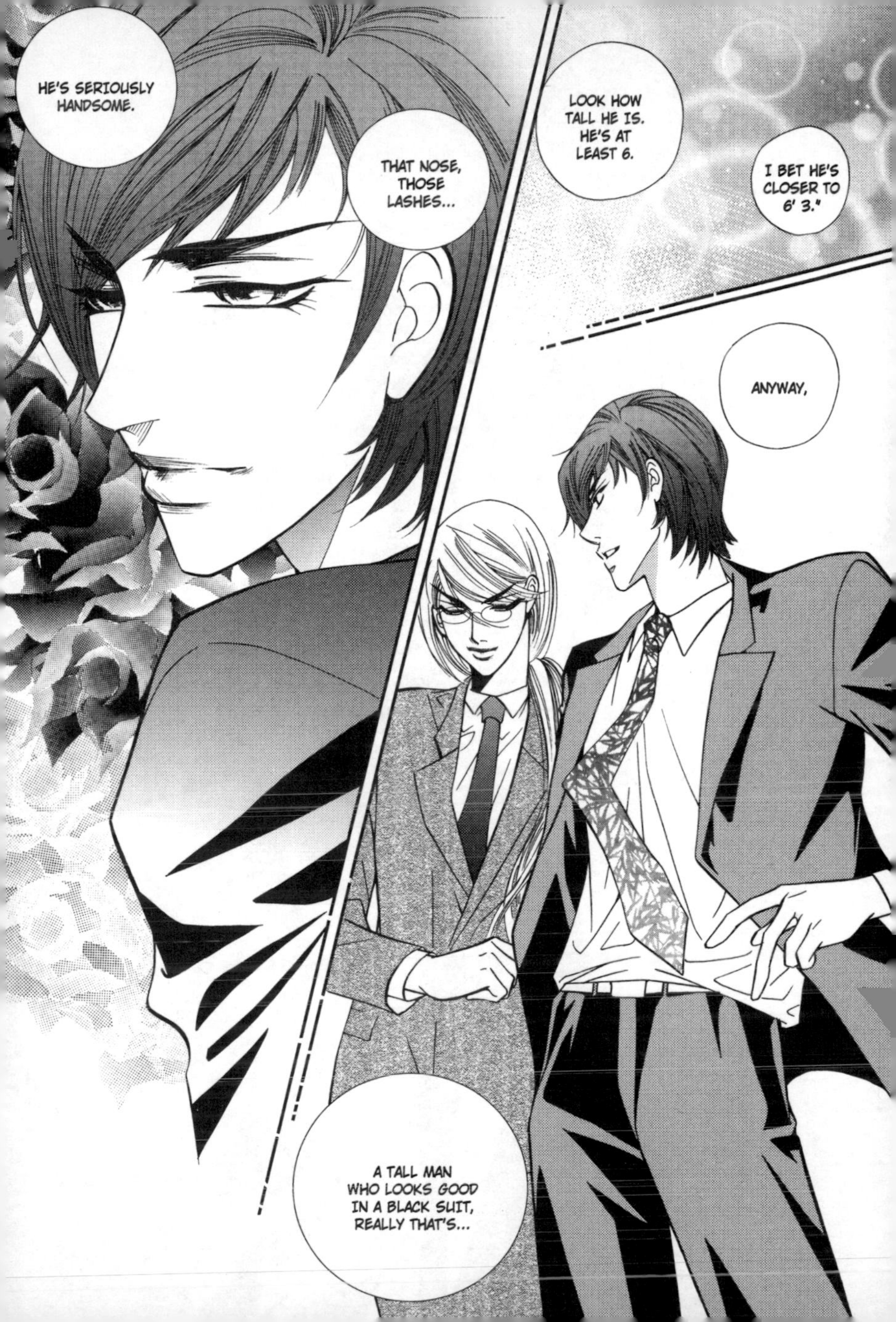
HE'S SERIOUSLY HANDSOME.
THAT NOSE, THOSE LASHES...
LOOK HOW TALL HE IS. HE'S AT LEAST 6.
I BET HE'S CLOSER TO 6' 3."
ANYWAY,
A TALL MAN WHO LOOKS GOOD IN A BLACK SUIT, REALLY THAT'S...

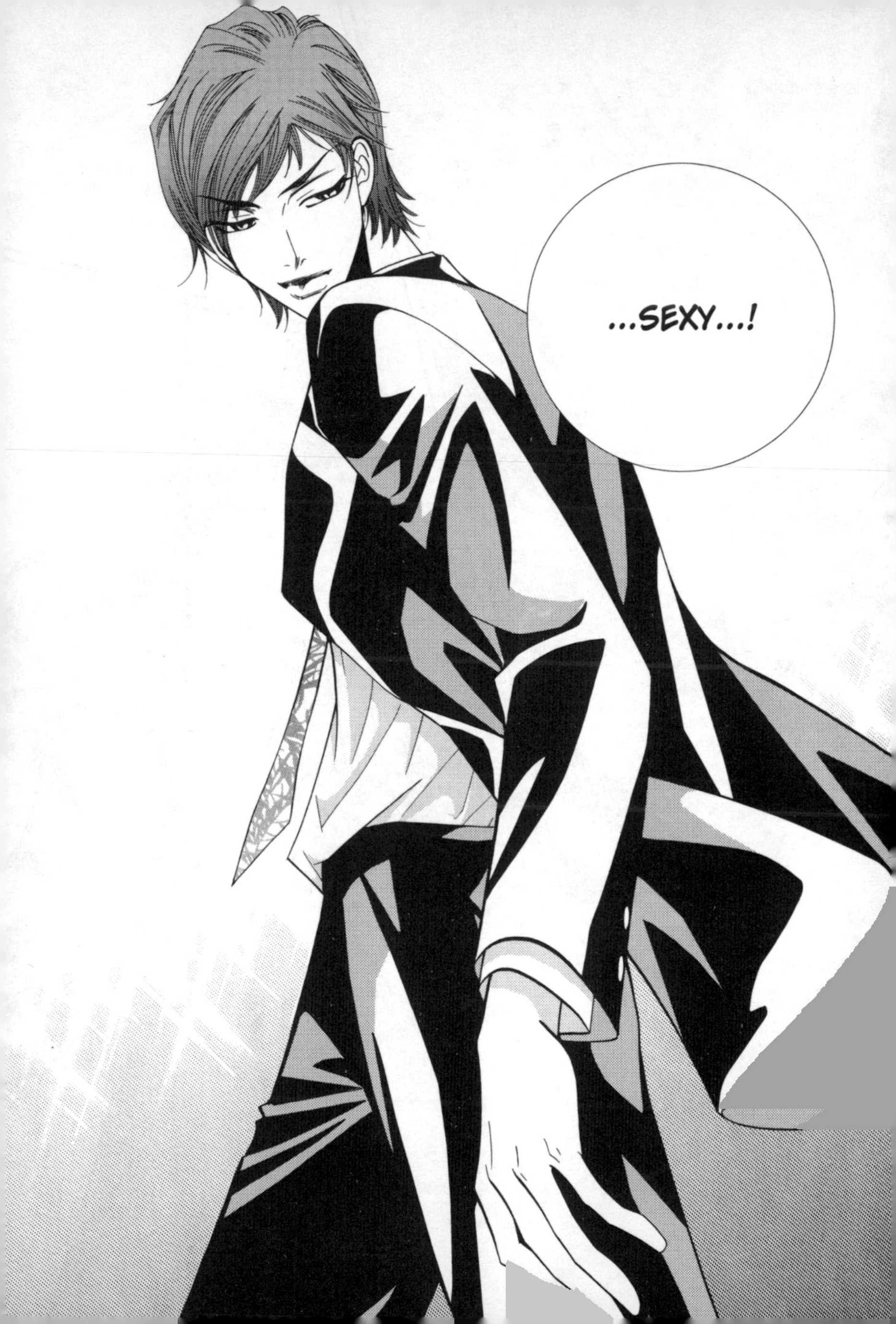
...SEXY...!

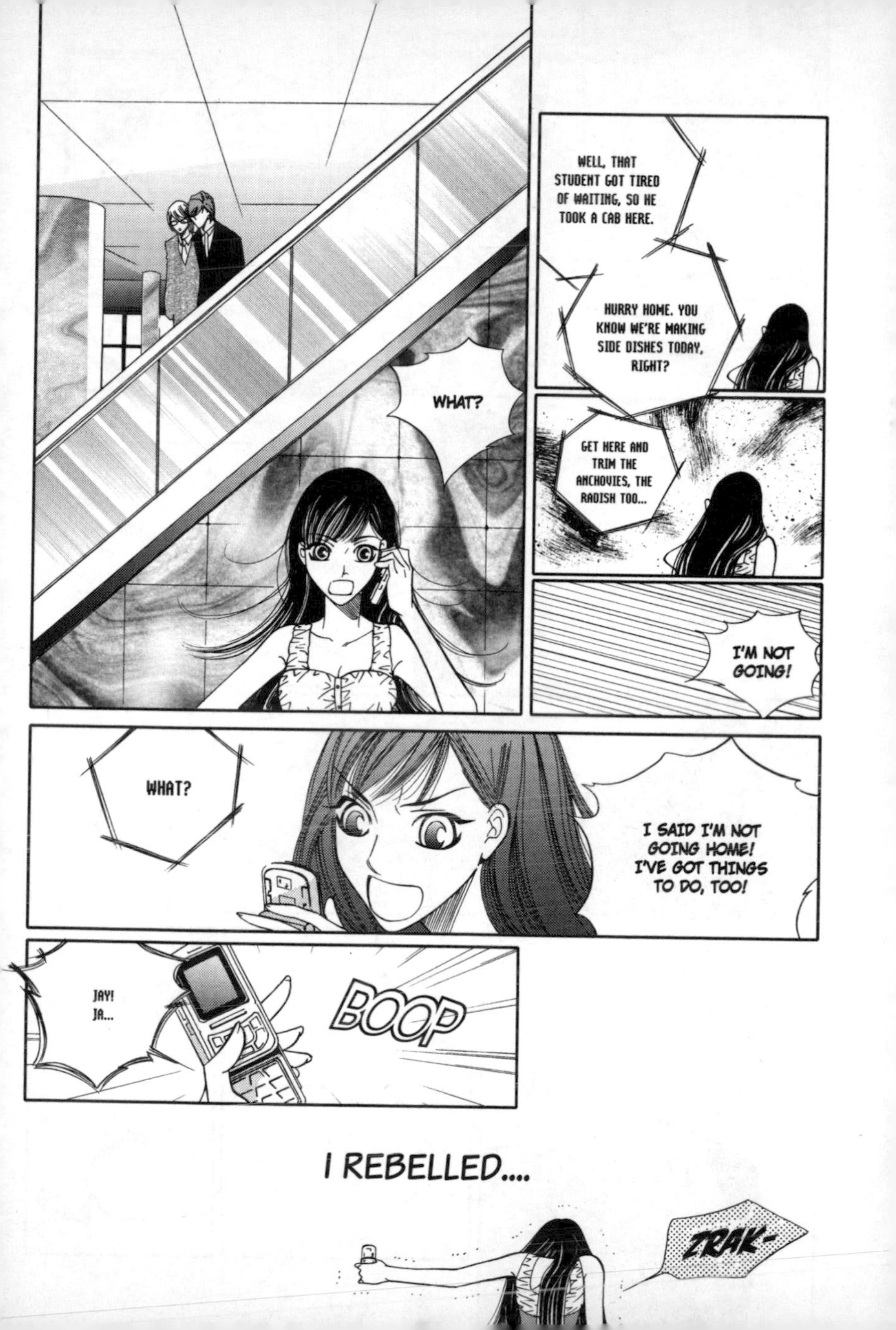
WHAT?
WELL, THAT STUDENT GOT TIRED OF WAITING, SO HE TOOK A CAB HERE.
HURRY HOME. YOU KNOW WE'RE MAKING SIDE DISHES TODAY, RIGHT?
GET HERE AND TRIM THE ANCHOVIES, THE RADISH TOO...
I'M NOT GOING!
WHAT?
I SAID I'M NOT GOING HOME! I'VE GOT THINGS TO DO, TOO!
JAY! JA...
BOOP
I REBELLED....
ZRAK-

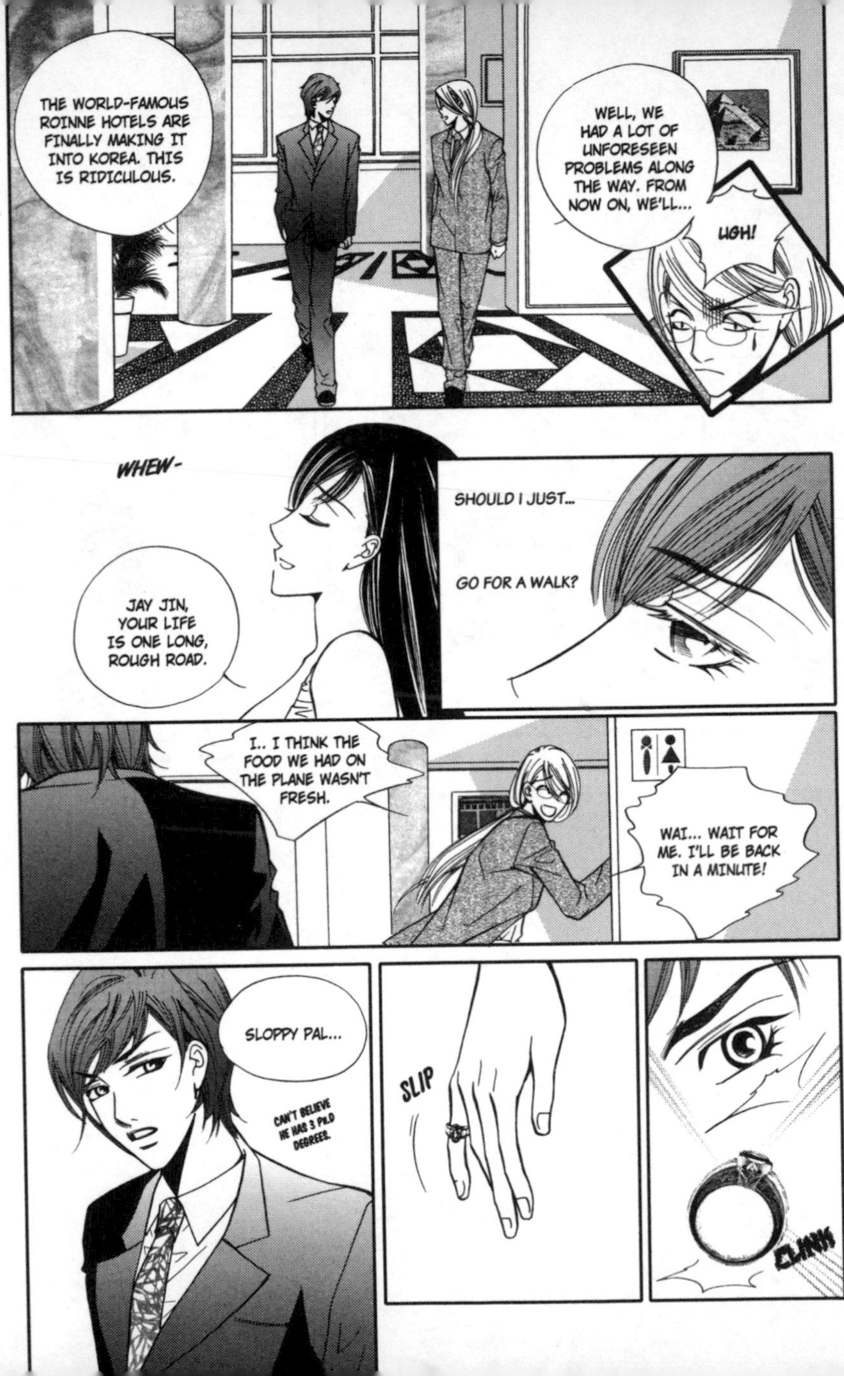
THE WORLD-FAMOUS ROINNE HOTELS ARE FINALLY MAKING IT INTO KOREA. THIS IS RIDICULOUS.
WELL, WE HAD A LOT OF UNFORESEEN PROBLEMS ALONG THE WAY. FROM NOW ON, WE'LL...
UGH!
WHEW-
JAY JIN, YOUR LIFE IS ONE LONG, ROUGH ROAD.
SHOULD I JUST...
GO FOR A WALK?
I.. I THINK THE FOOD WE HAD ON THE PLANE WASN'T FRESH.
WAI... WAIT FOR ME. I'LL BE BACK IN A MINUTE!
SLOPPY PAL...
CAN'T BELIEVE HE HAS 3 PH.D DEGREES.
SLIP
CLINK

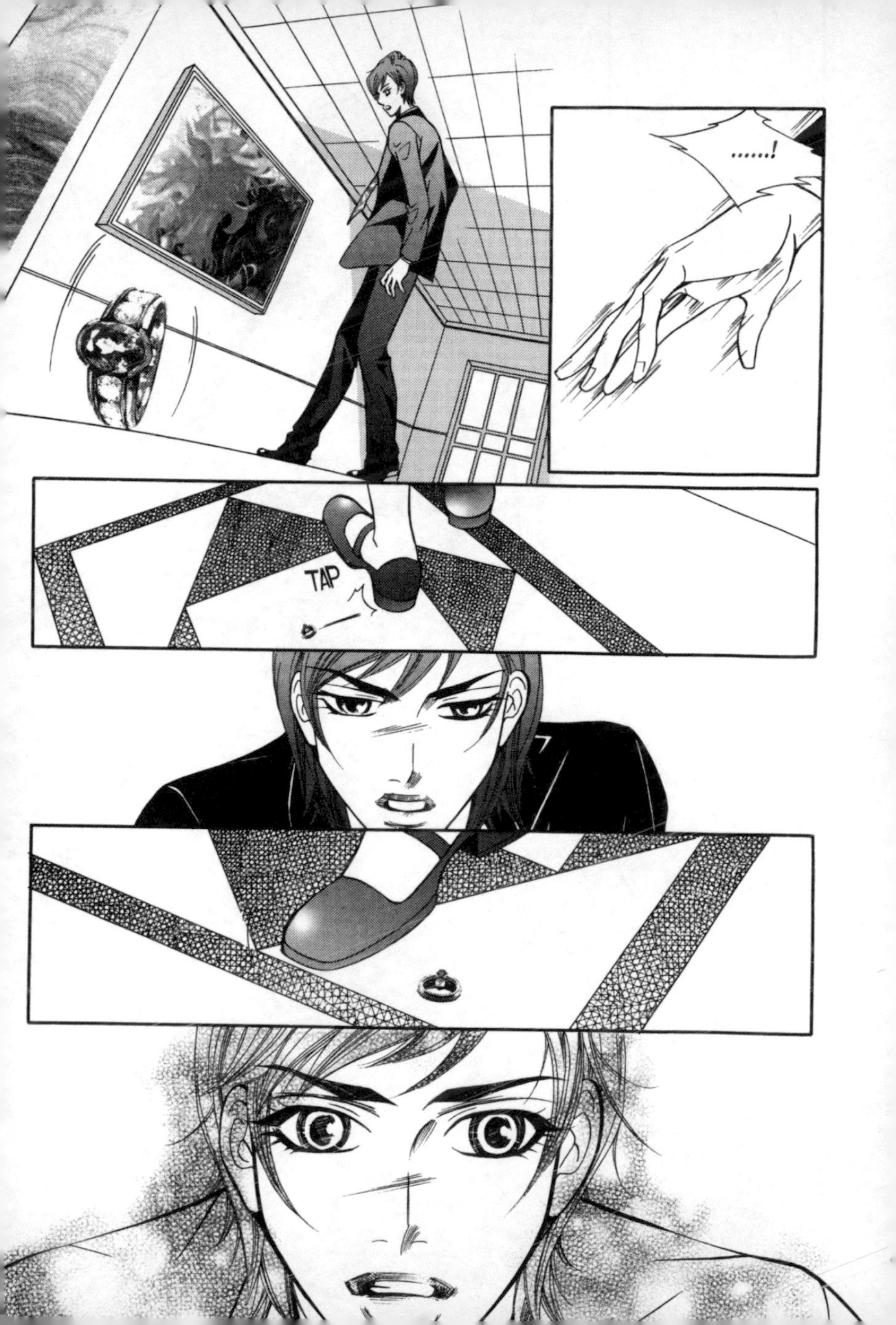
......!
TAP

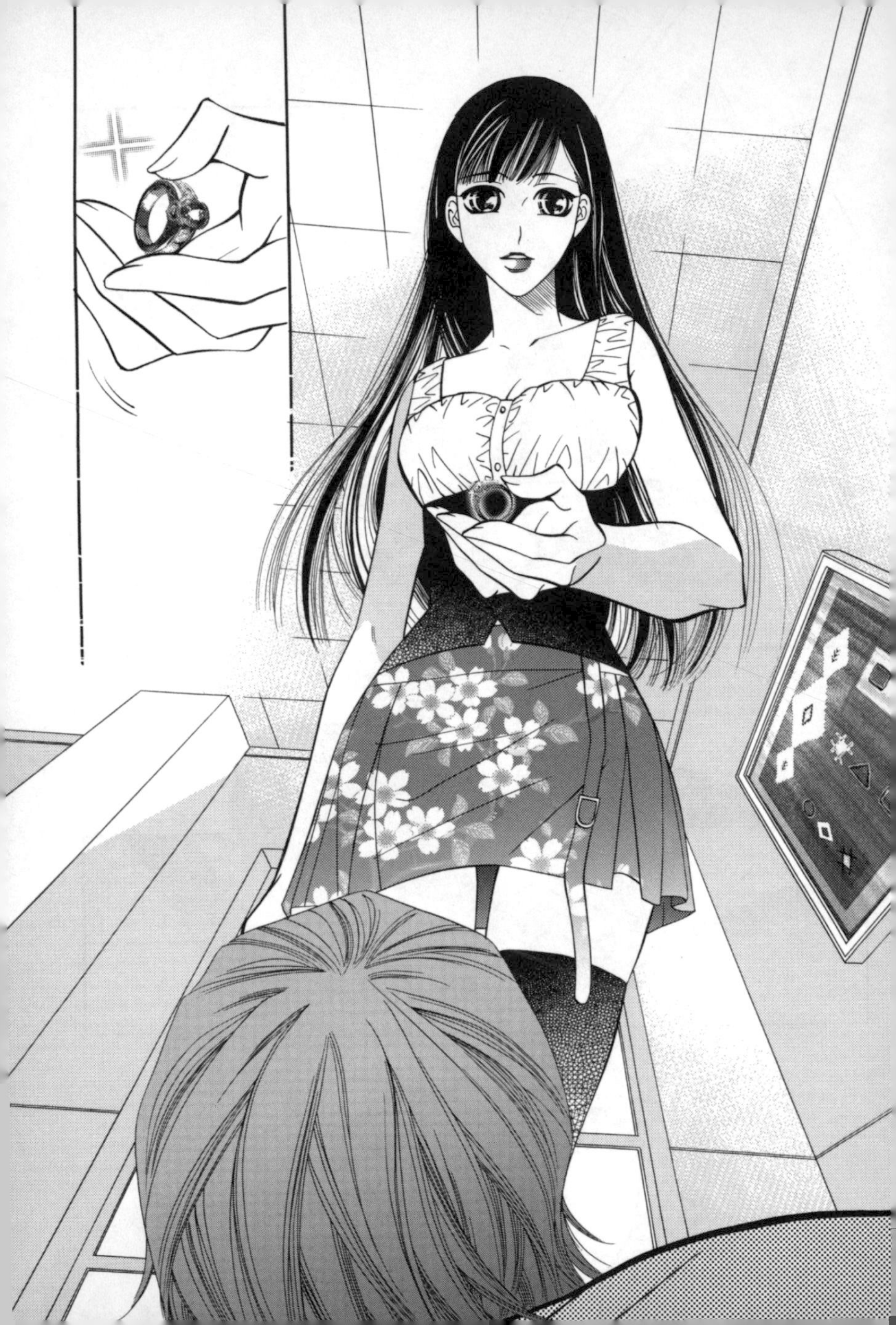

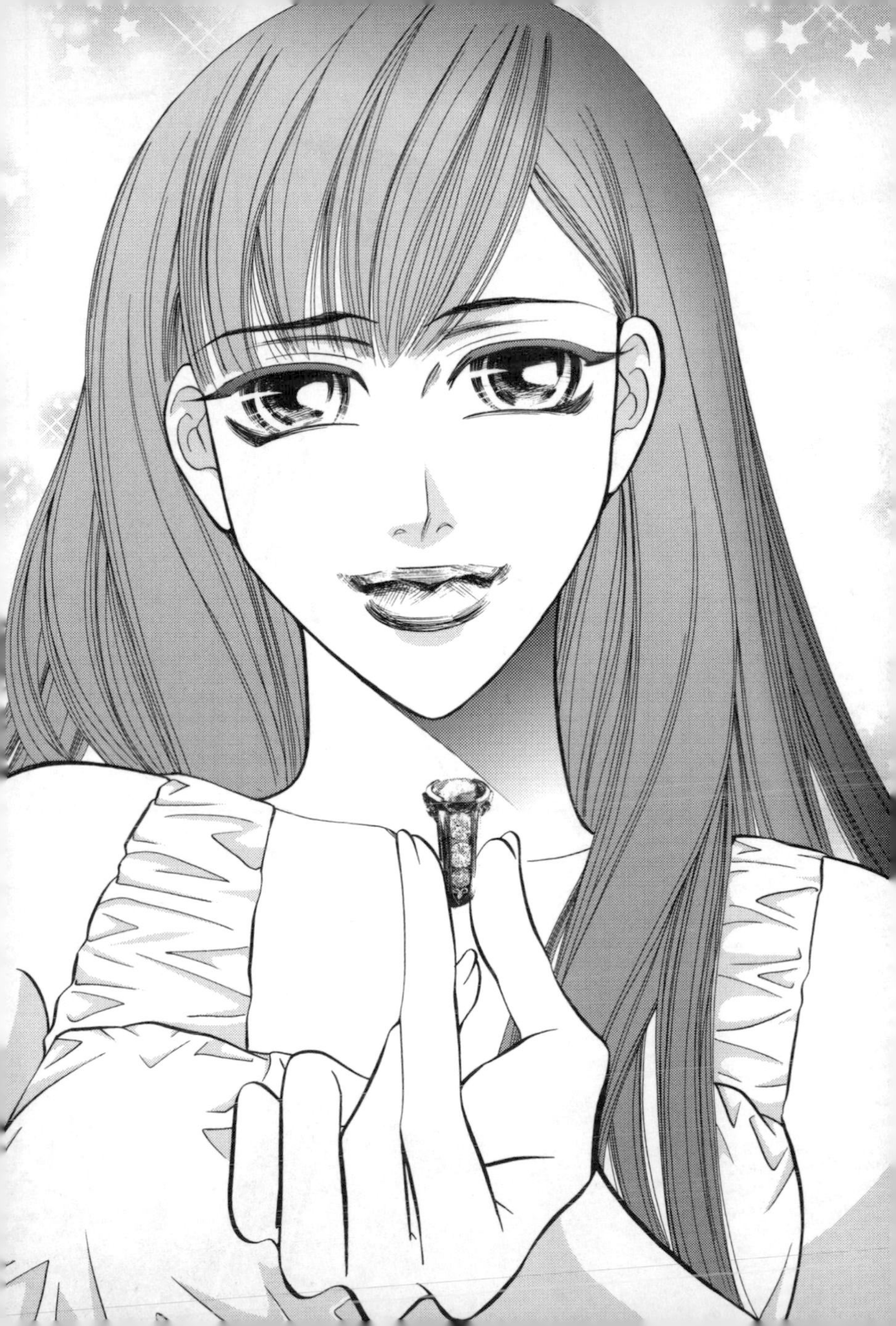

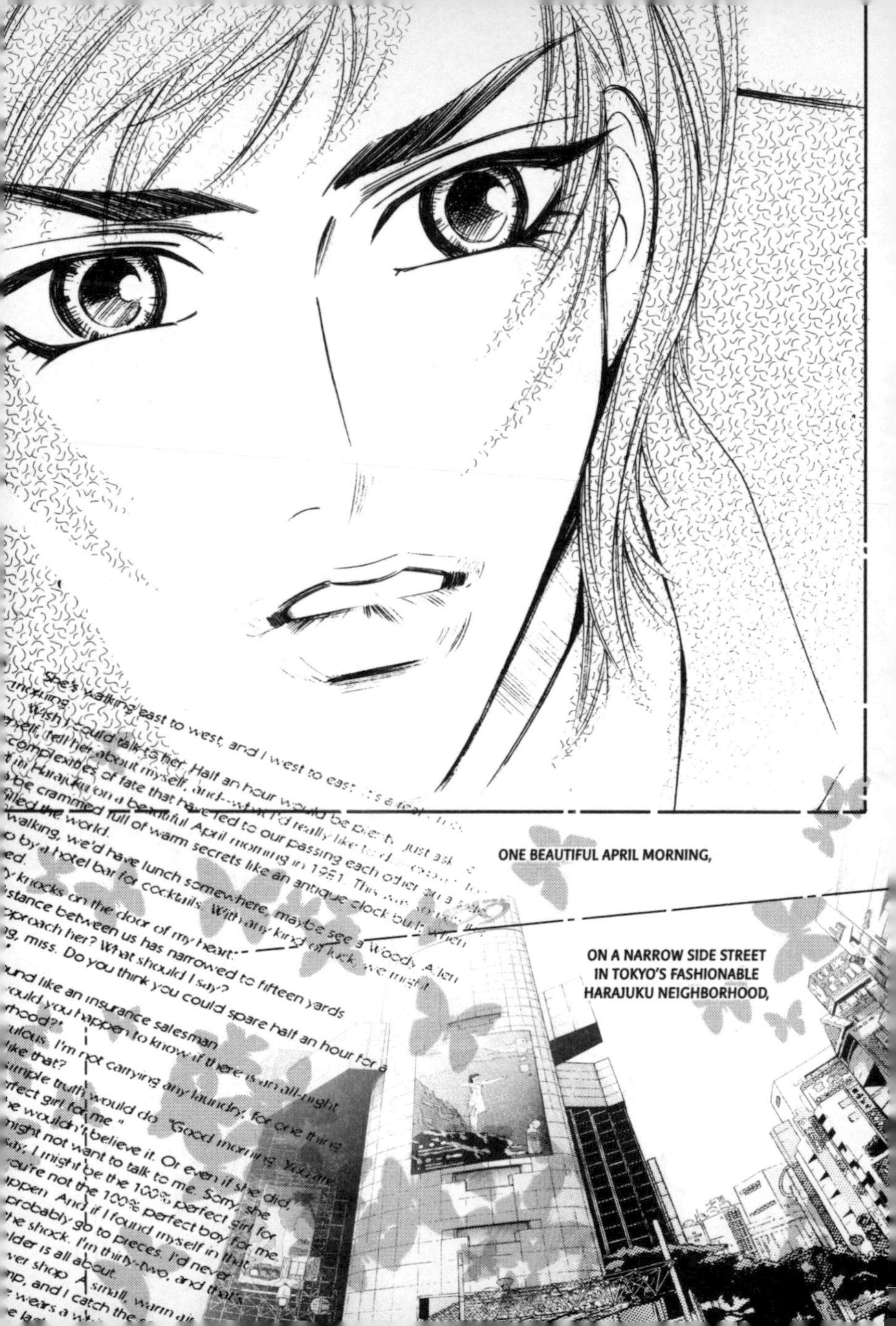
ONE BEAUTIFUL APRIL MORNING,
ON A NARROW SIDE STREET IN TOKYO'S FASHIONABLE HARAJUKU NEIGHBORHOOD,

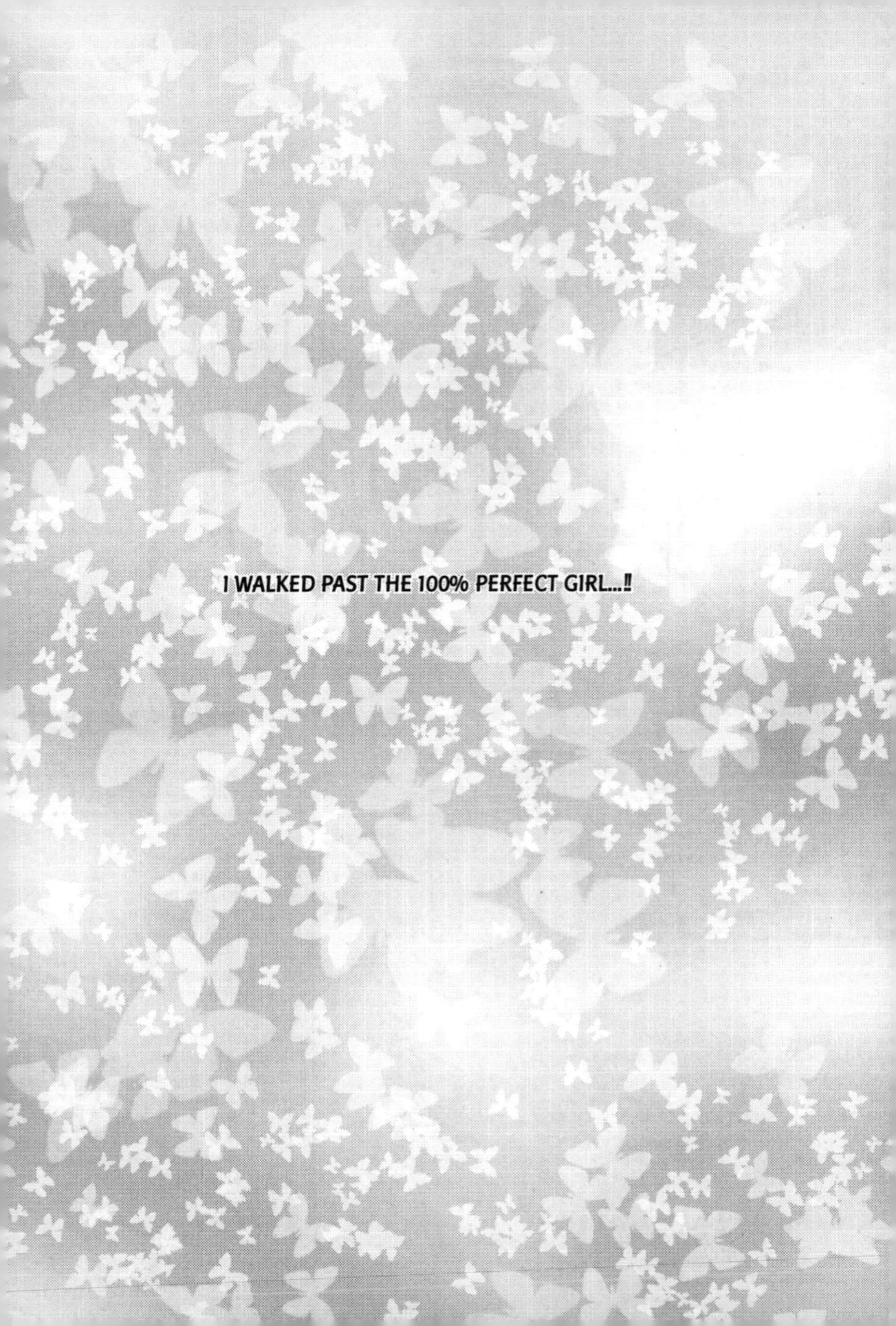
I WALKED PAST THE 100% PERFECT GIRL...!!

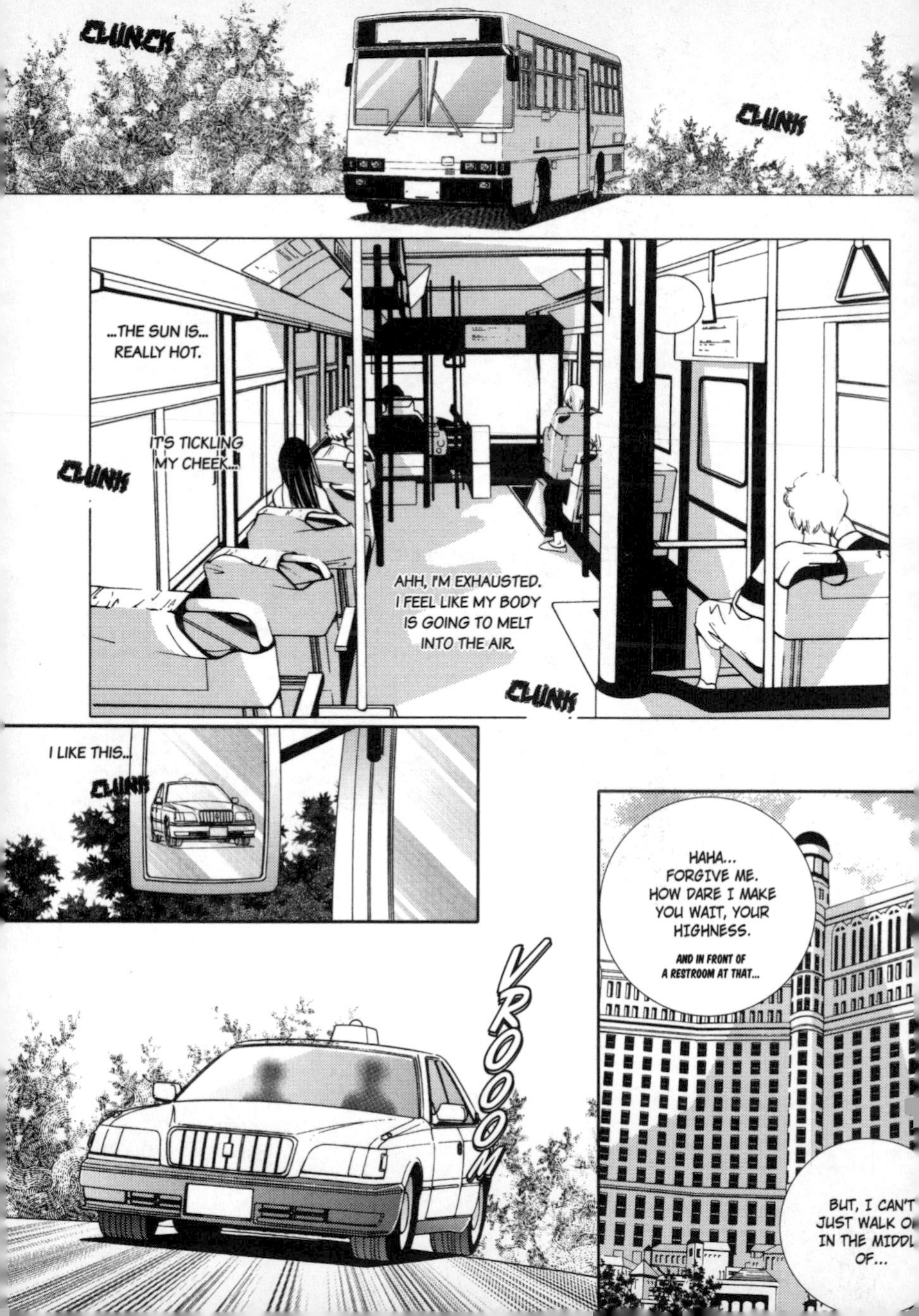
CLUNCK
CLUNK
...THE SUN IS... REALLY HOT.
IT'S TICKLING MY CHEEK...
CLUNK
AHH, I'M EXHAUSTED. I FEEL LIKE MY BODY IS GOING TO MELT INTO THE AIR.
CLUNK
I LIKE THIS...
CLUNK
HAHA... FORGIVE ME. HOW DARE I MAKE YOU WAIT, YOUR HIGHNESS.
AND IN FRONT OF A RESTROOM AT THAT...
VROOOOM
BUT, I CAN'T JUST WALK O IN THE MIDDL OF...

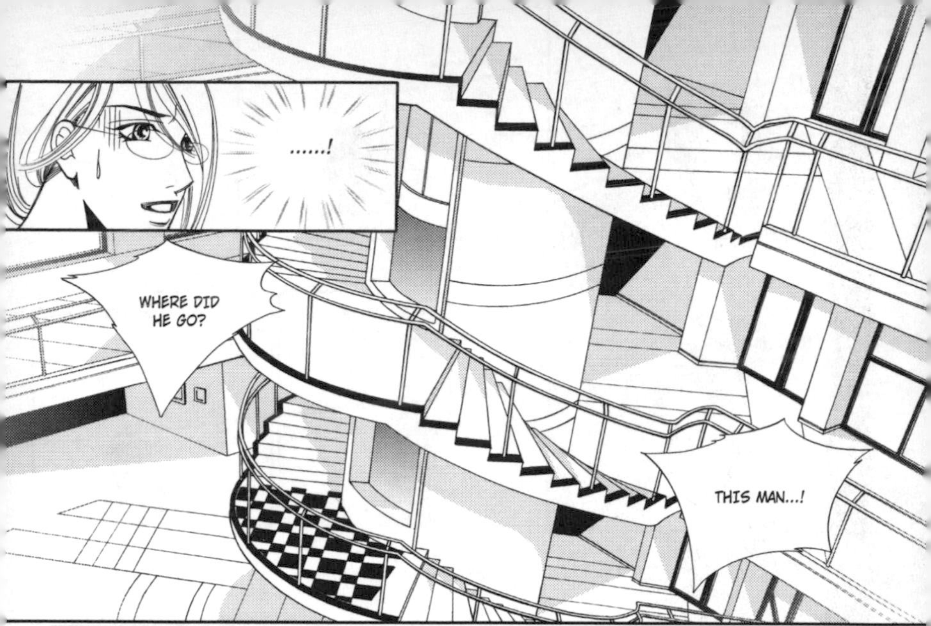
......!
WHERE DID HE GO?
THIS MAN...!
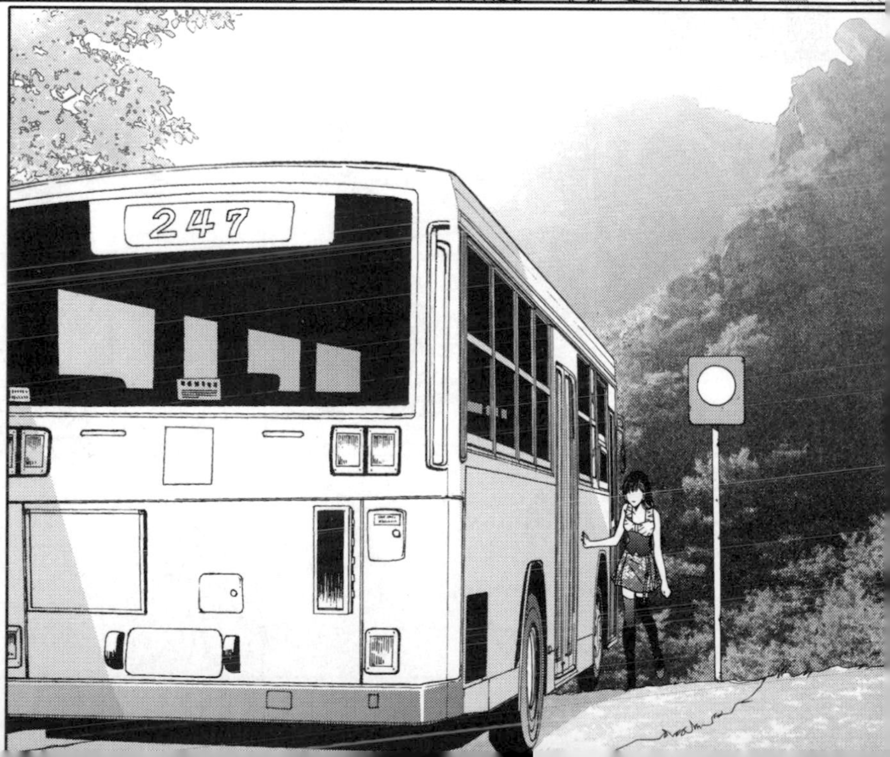
247

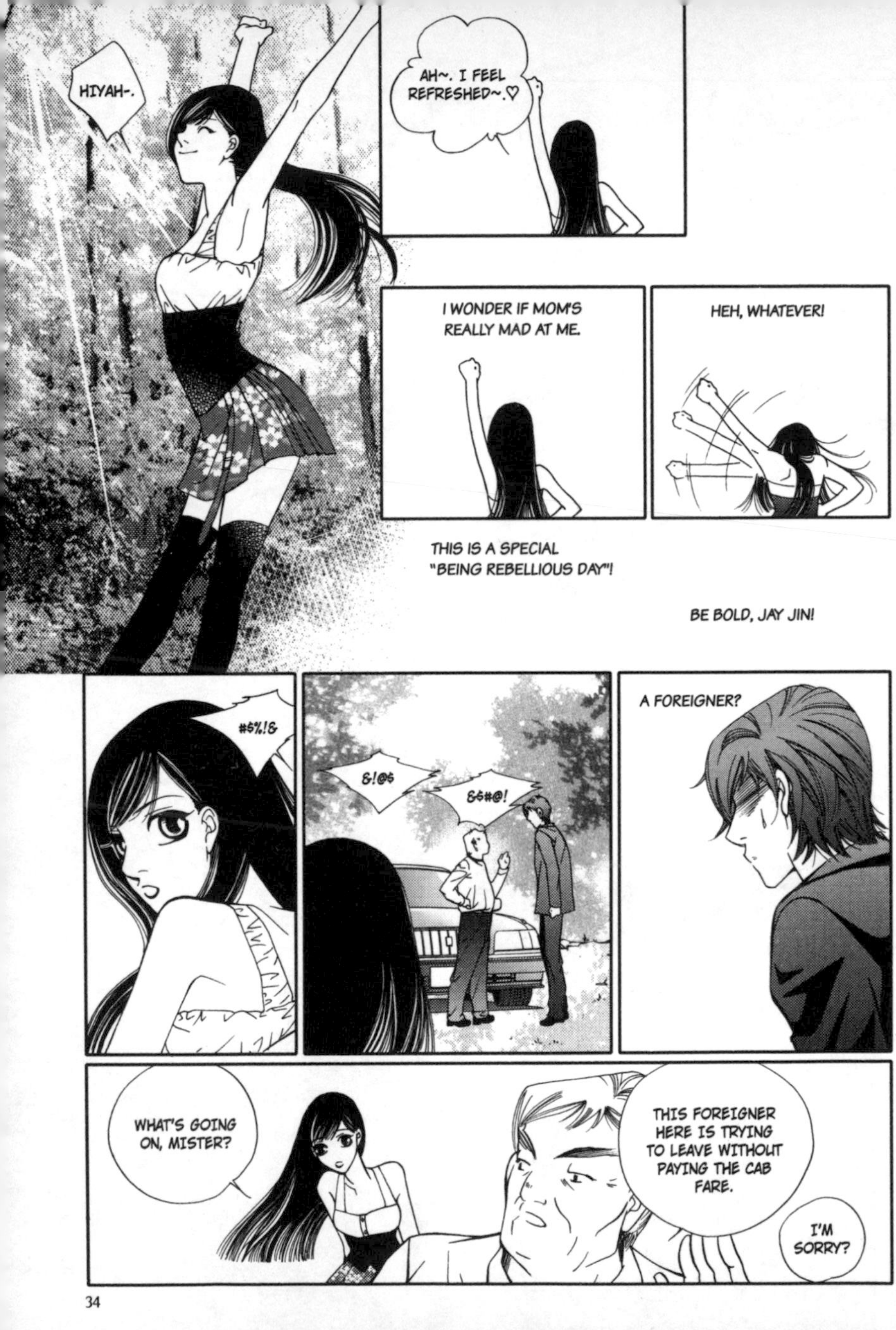
HIYAH-.
AH~. I FEEL REFRESHED~.♡
I WONDER IF MOM'S REALLY MAD AT ME.
HEH, WHATEVER!
THIS IS A SPECIAL "BEING REBELLIOUS DAY"!
BE BOLD, JAY JIN!
#$%!&
&!@$
&$#@!
A FOREIGNER?
WHAT'S GOING ON, MISTER?
THIS FOREIGNER HERE IS TRYING TO LEAVE WITHOUT PAYING THE CAB FARE.
I'M SORRY?

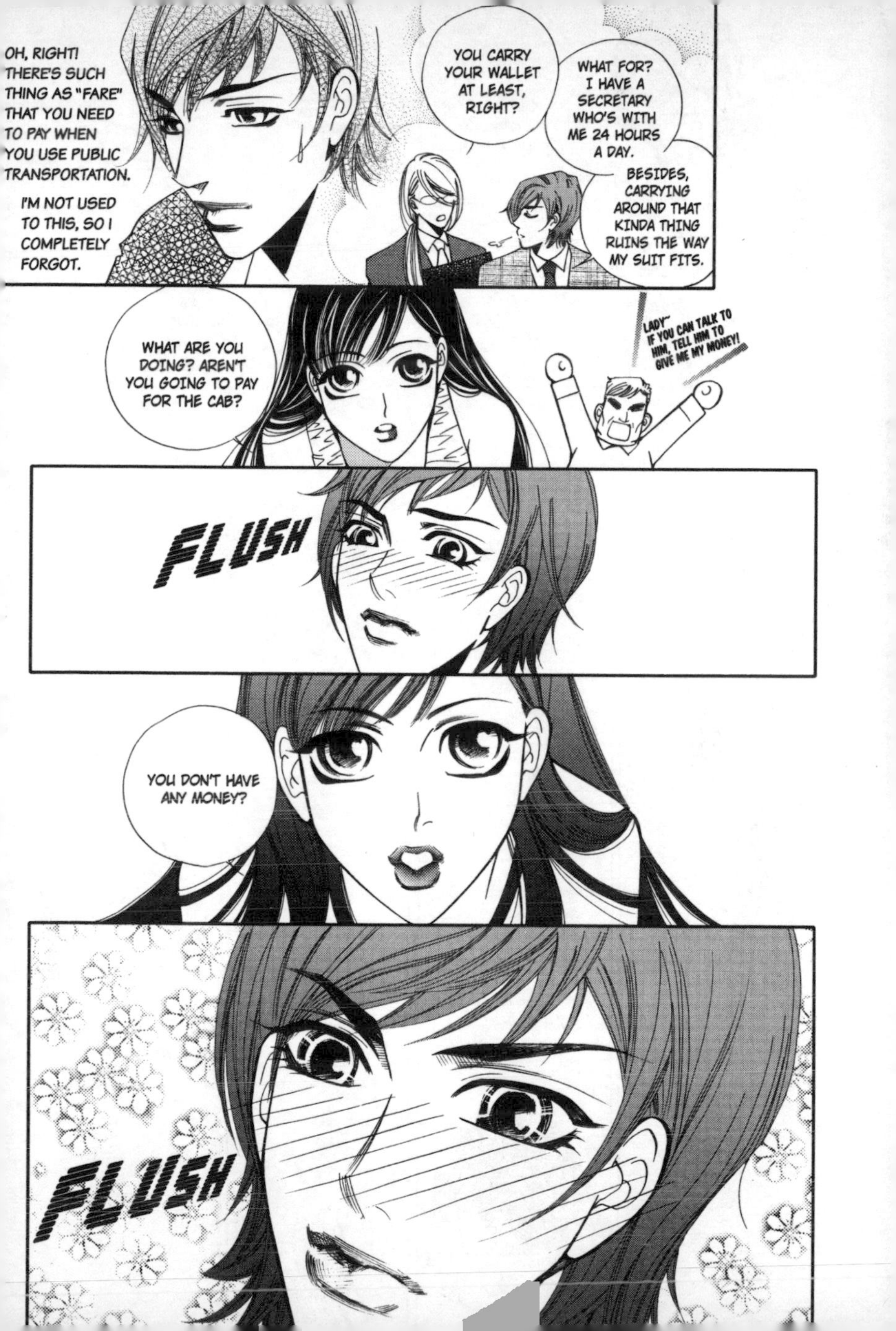
OH, RIGHT! THERE'S SUCH THING AS "FARE" THAT YOU NEED TO PAY WHEN YOU USE PUBLIC TRANSPORTATION.
I'M NOT USED TO THIS, SO I COMPLETELY FORGOT.
YOU CARRY YOUR WALLET AT LEAST, RIGHT?
WHAT FOR? I HAVE A SECRETARY WHO'S WITH ME 24 HOURS A DAY.
BESIDES, CARRYING AROUND THAT KINDA THING RUINS THE WAY MY SUIT FITS.
WHAT ARE YOU DOING? AREN'T YOU GOING TO PAY FOR THE CAB?
LADY~ IF YOU CAN TALK TO HIM, TELL HIM TO GIVE ME MY MONEY!
FLUSH
YOU DON'T HAVE ANY MONEY?
FLUSH

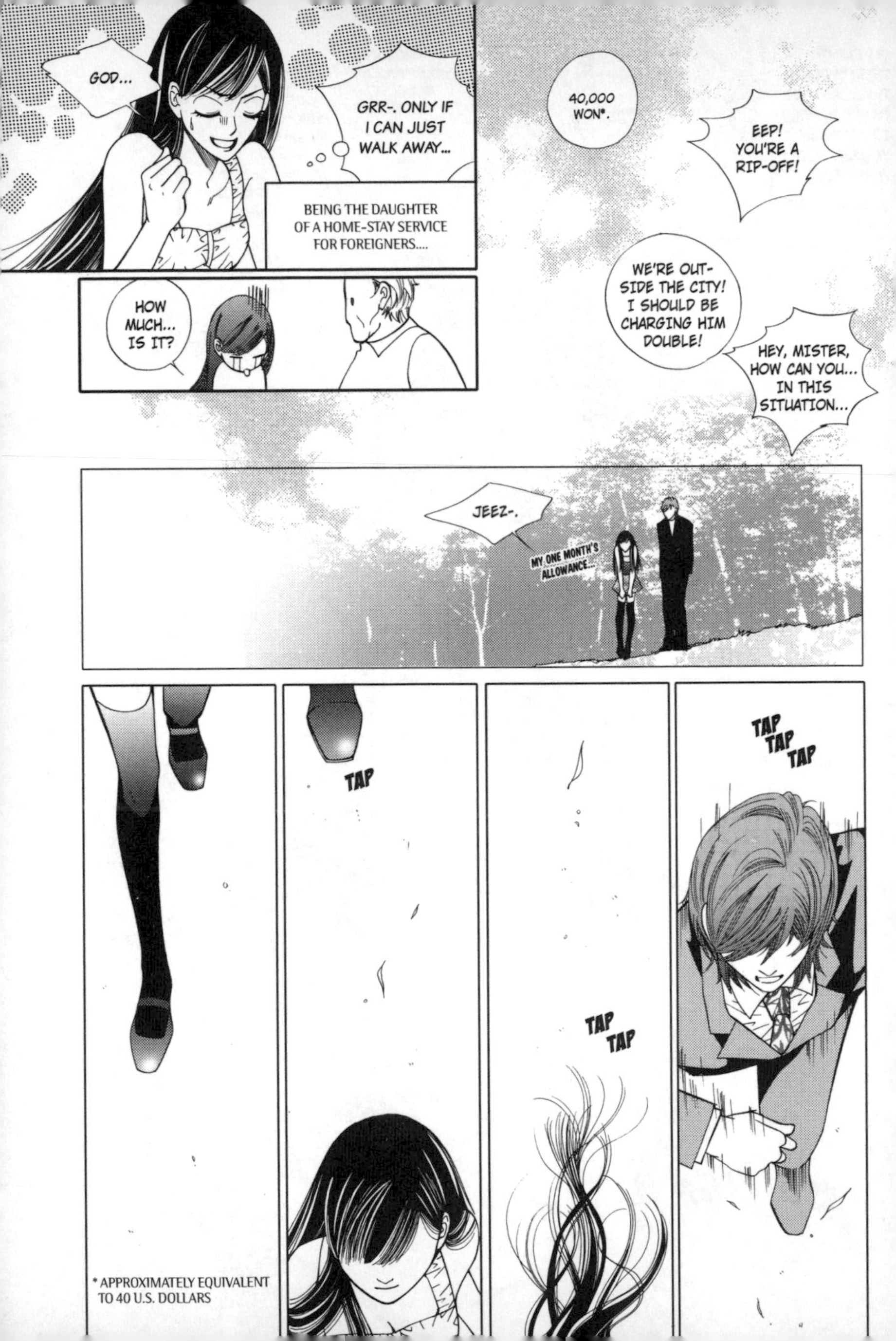
GOD...
GRR-. ONLY IF I CAN JUST WALK AWAY...
BEING THE DAUGHTER OF A HOME-STAY SERVICE FOR FOREIGNERS....
HOW MUCH... IS IT?
40,000 WON*.
EEP! YOU'RE A RIP-OFF!
WE'RE OUT-SIDE THE CITY! I SHOULD BE CHARGING HIM DOUBLE!
HEY, MISTER, HOW CAN YOU... IN THIS SITUATION...
JEEZ-.
MY ONE MONTH'S ALLOWANCE...
TAP
TAP TAP
TAP TAP TAP
* APPROXIMATELY EQUIVALENT TO 40 U.S. DOLLARS

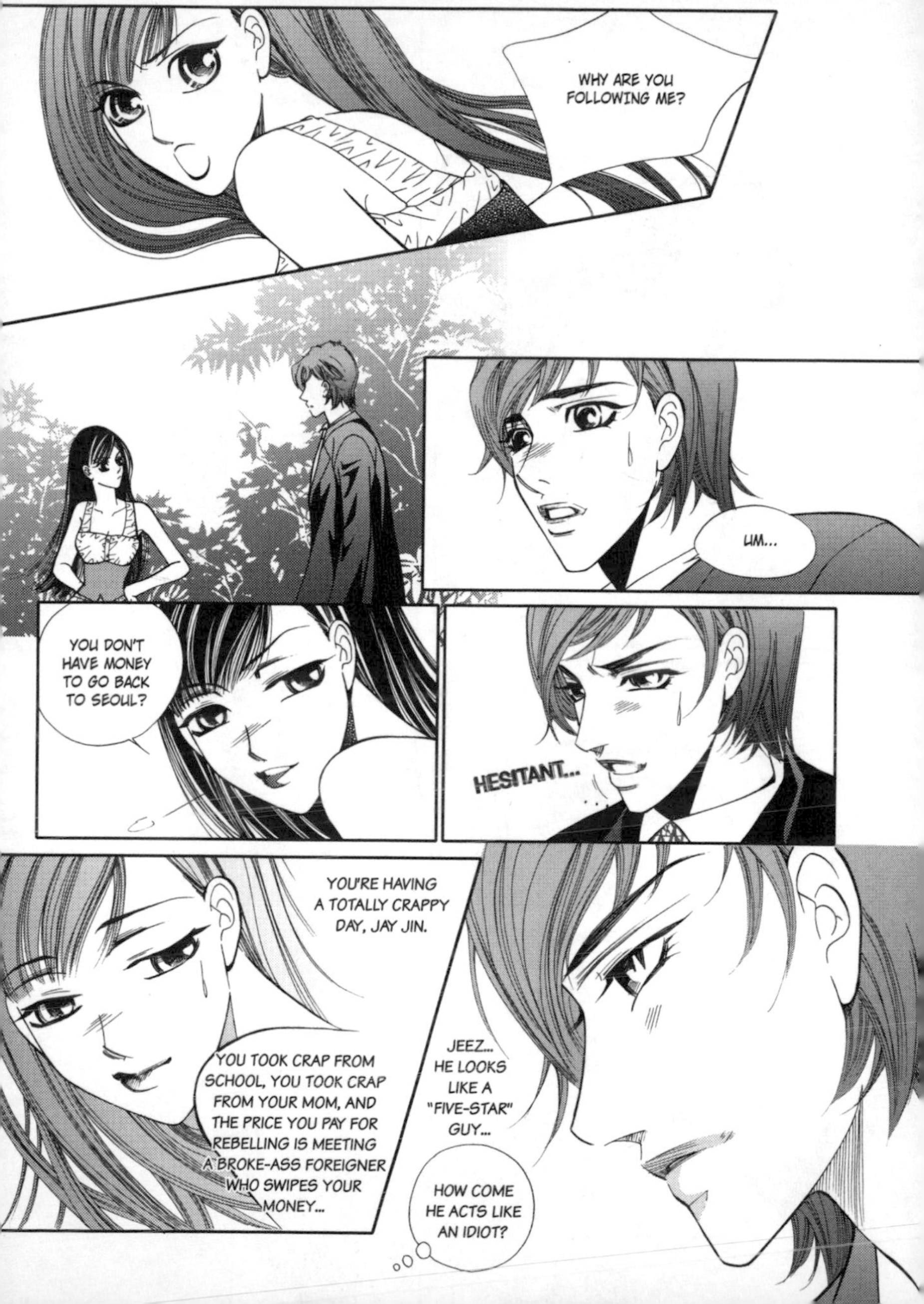
WHY ARE YOU FOLLOWING ME?
UM...
YOU DON'T HAVE MONEY TO GO BACK TO SEOUL?
HESITANT...
YOU'RE HAVING A TOTALLY CRAPPY DAY, JAY JIN.
YOU TOOK CRAP FROM SCHOOL, YOU TOOK CRAP FROM YOUR MOM, AND THE PRICE YOU PAY FOR REBELLING IS MEETING A BROKE-ASS FOREIGNER WHO SWIPES YOUR MONEY...
JEEZ... HE LOOKS LIKE A "FIVE-STAR" GUY...
HOW COME HE ACTS LIKE AN IDIOT?

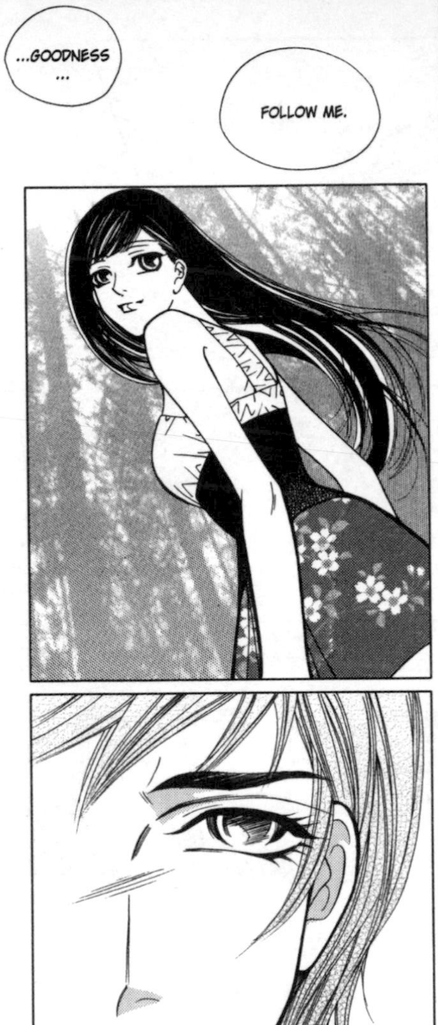
...GOODNESS ...
FOLLOW ME.

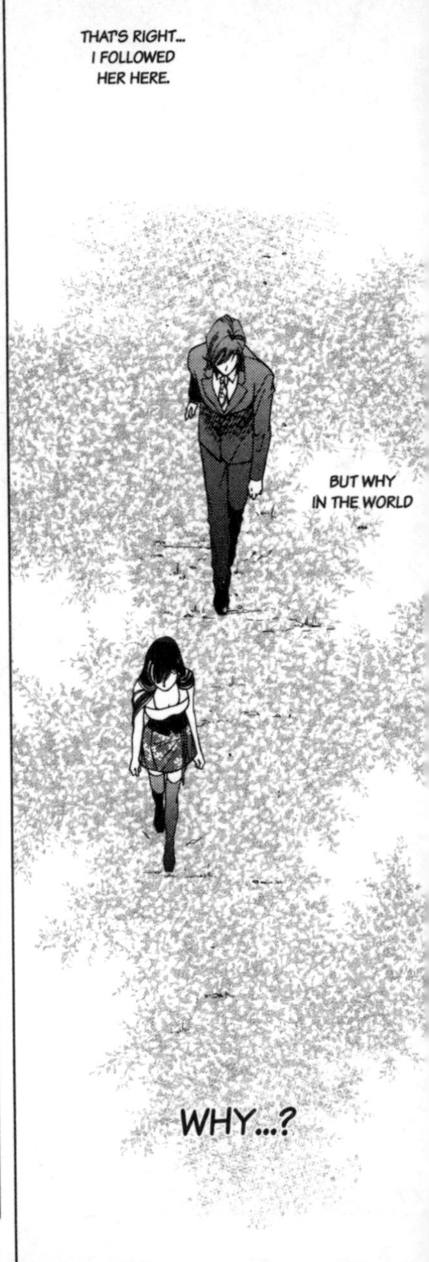
THAT'S RIGHT... I FOLLOWED HER HERE.
BUT WHY IN THE WORLD
WHY...?

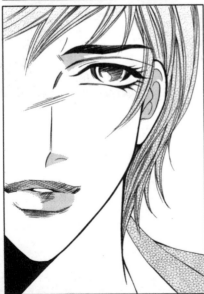

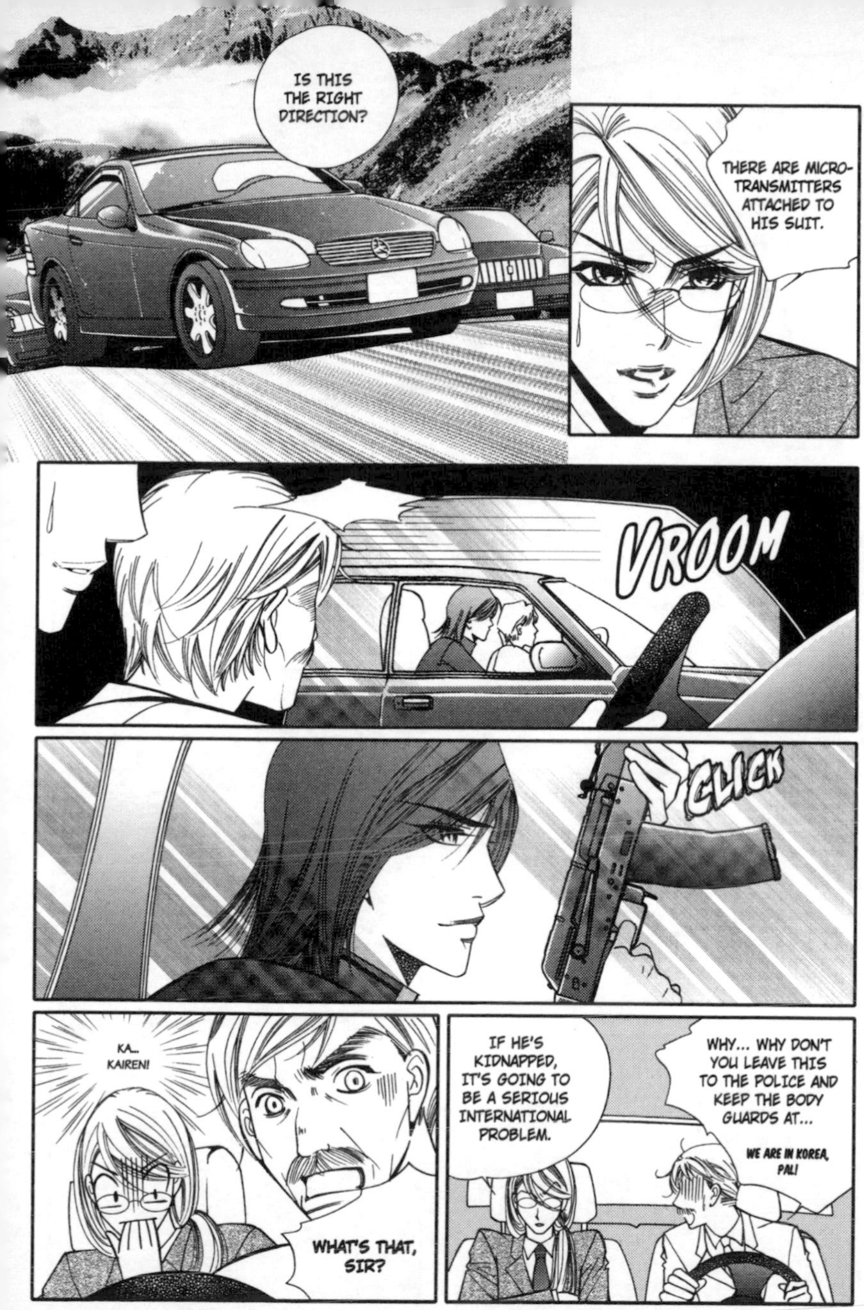
IS THIS THE RIGHT DIRECTION?
THERE ARE MICRO-TRANSMITTERS ATTACHED TO HIS SUIT.
VROOM
CLICK
KA... KAIREN!
WHAT'S THAT, SIR?
IF HE'S KIDNAPPED, IT'S GOING TO BE A SERIOUS INTERNATIONAL PROBLEM.
WHY... WHY DON'T YOU LEAVE THIS TO THE POLICE AND KEEP THE BODY GUARDS AT...
WE ARE IN KOREA, PAL!

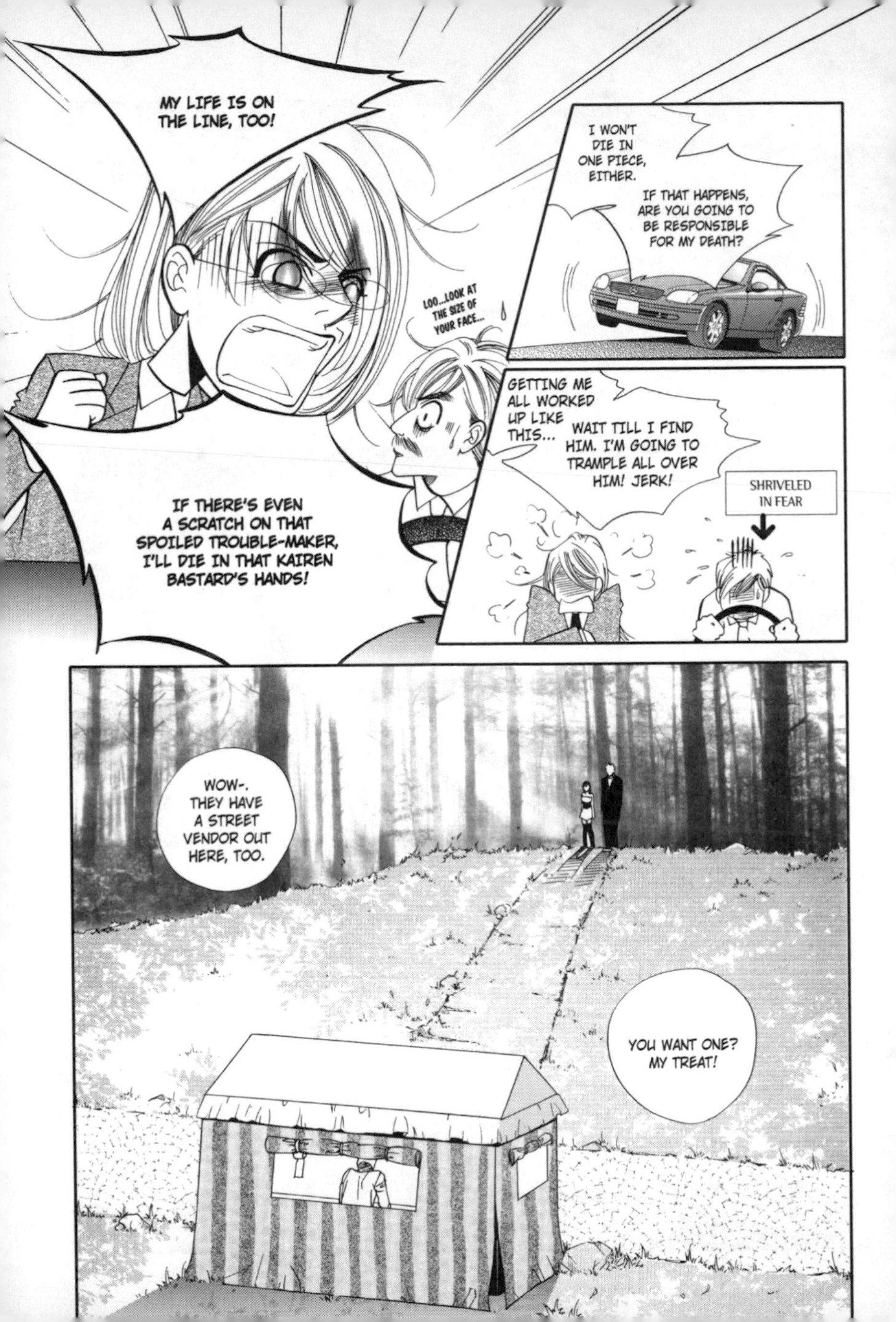
MY LIFE IS ON THE LINE, TOO!
LOO...LOOK AT THE SIZE OF YOUR FACE...
IF THERE'S EVEN A SCRATCH ON THAT SPOILED TROUBLE-MAKER, I'LL DIE IN THAT KAIREN BASTARD'S HANDS!
I WON'T DIE IN ONE PIECE, EITHER.
IF THAT HAPPENS, ARE YOU GOING TO BE RESPONSIBLE FOR MY DEATH?
GETTING ME ALL WORKED UP LIKE THIS...
WAIT TILL I FIND HIM. I'M GOING TO TRAMPLE ALL OVER HIM! JERK!
SHRIVELED IN FEAR
WOW-. THEY HAVE A STREET VENDOR OUT HERE, TOO.
YOU WANT ONE? MY TREAT!

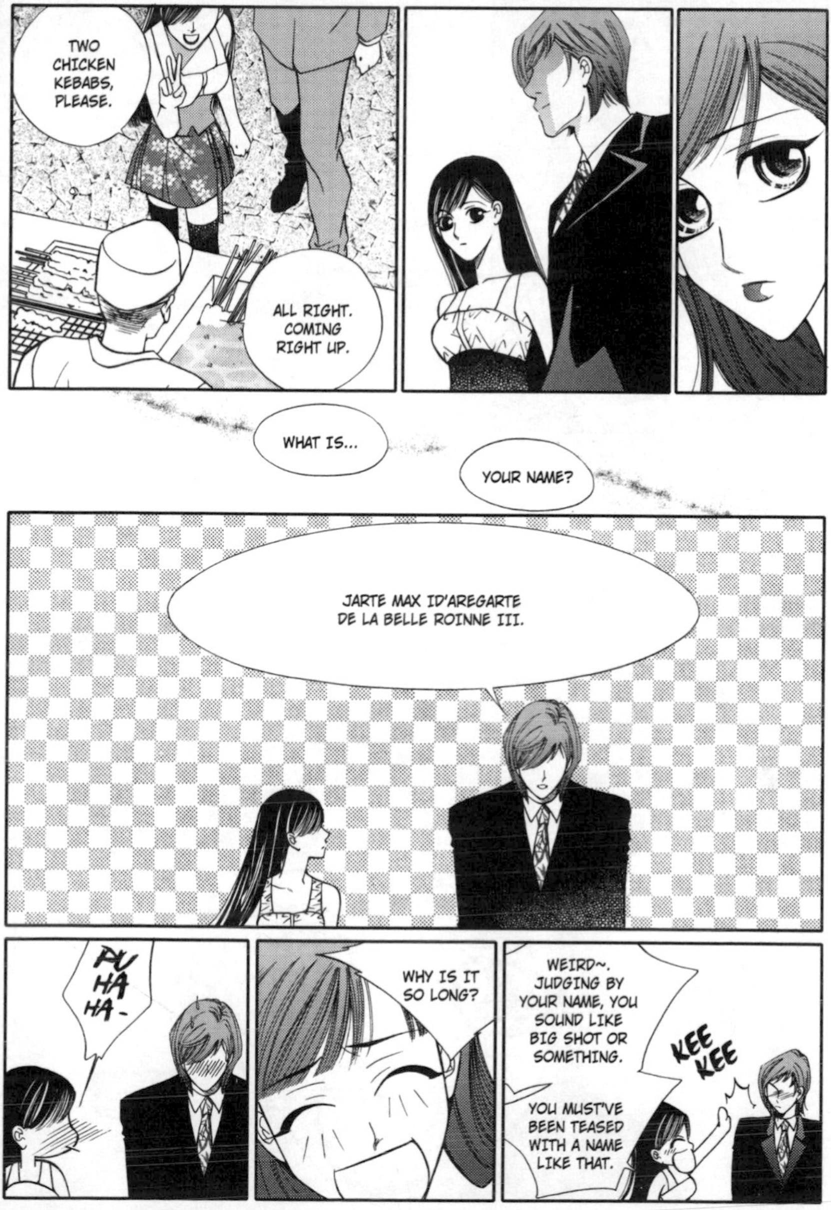
TWO CHICKEN KEBABS, PLEASE.
ALL RIGHT. COMING RIGHT UP.
WHAT IS...
YOUR NAME?
JARTE MAX ID'AREGARTE DE LA BELLE ROINNE III.
PU HA HA-
WHY IS IT SO LONG?
WEIRD~. JUDGING BY YOUR NAME, YOU SOUND LIKE BIG SHOT OR SOMETHING.
KEE KEE
YOU MUST'VE BEEN TEASED WITH A NAME LIKE THAT.

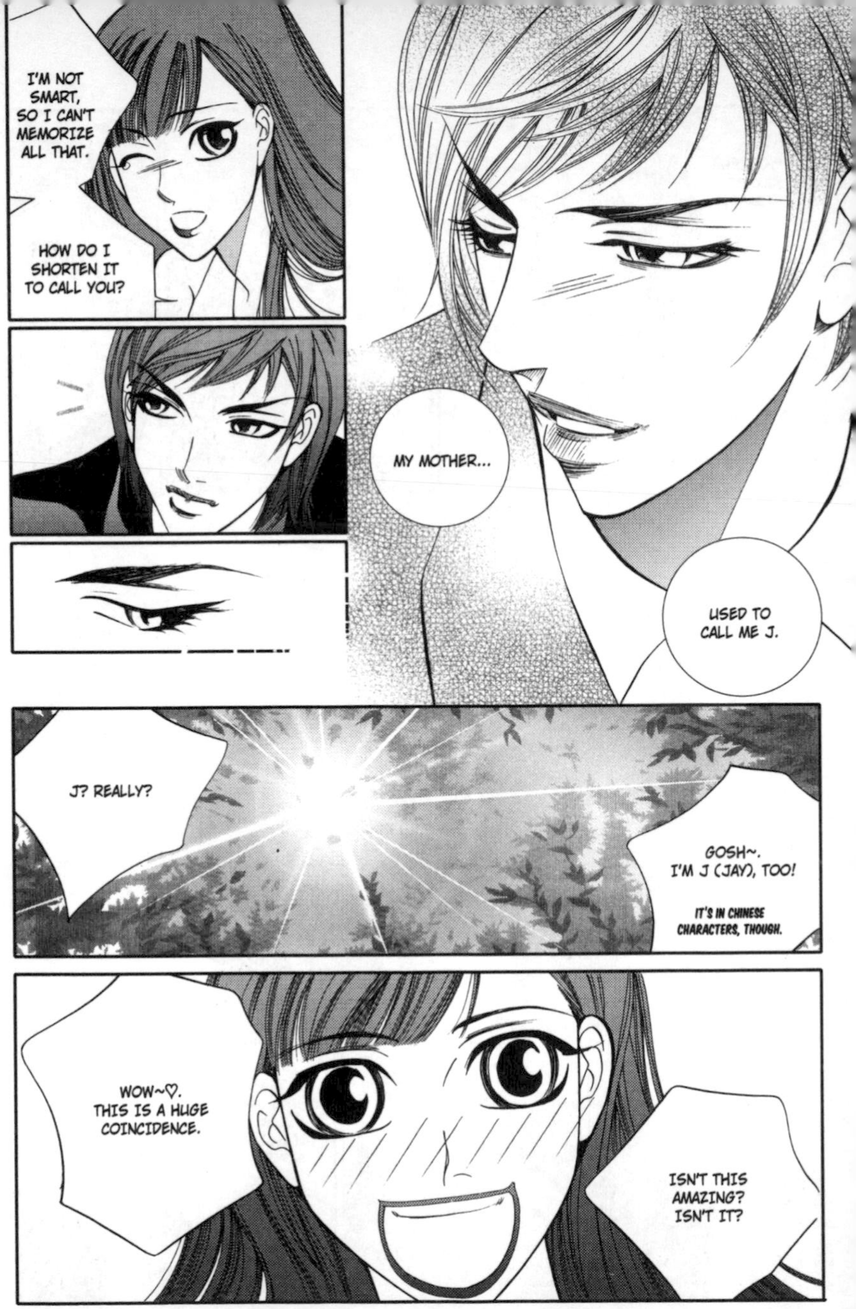
I'M NOT SMART, SO I CAN'T MEMORIZE ALL THAT.
HOW DO I SHORTEN IT TO CALL YOU?
MY MOTHER...
USED TO CALL ME J.
J? REALLY?
GOSH~. I'M J (JAY), TOO!
IT'S IN CHINESE CHARACTERS, THOUGH.
WOW~♡. THIS IS A HUGE COINCIDENCE.
ISN'T THIS AMAZING? ISN'T IT?

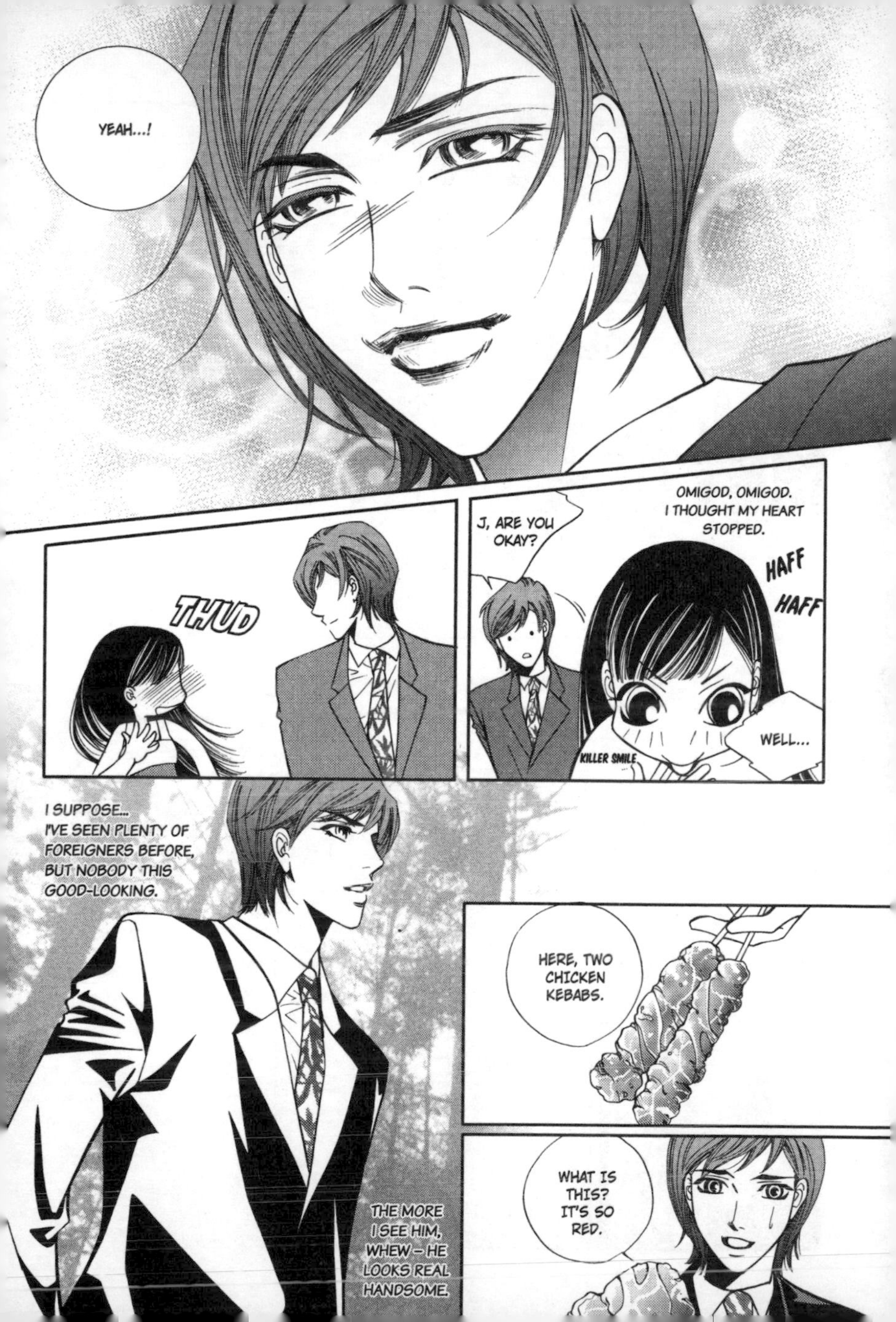
YEAH...!
THUD
J, ARE YOU OKAY?
OMIGOD, OMIGOD. I THOUGHT MY HEART STOPPED.
HAFF
HAFF
KILLER SMILE
WELL...
I SUPPOSE... I'VE SEEN PLENTY OF FOREIGNERS BEFORE, BUT NOBODY THIS GOOD-LOOKING.
THE MORE I SEE HIM, WHEW – HE LOOKS REAL HANDSOME.
HERE, TWO CHICKEN KEBABS.
WHAT IS THIS? IT'S SO RED.

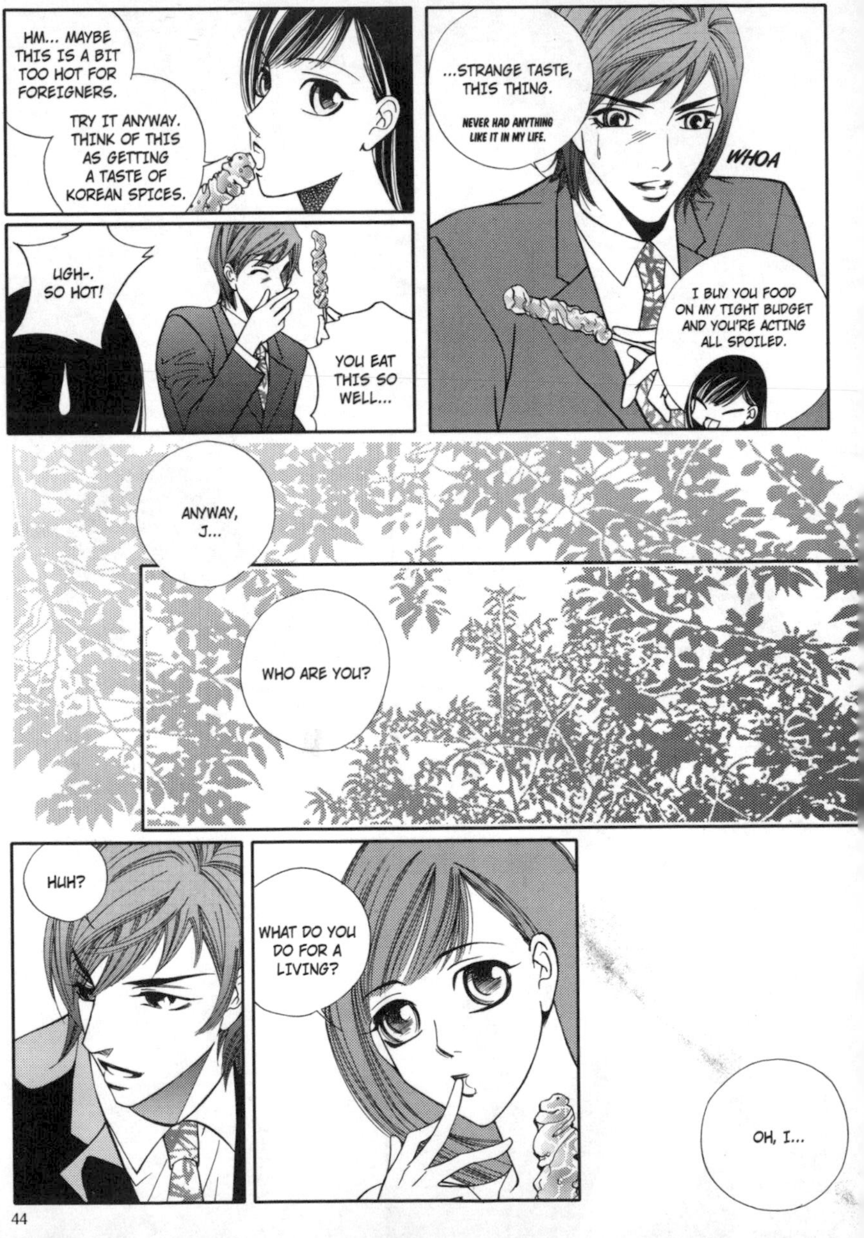
HM... MAYBE THIS IS A BIT TOO HOT FOR FOREIGNERS.
TRY IT ANYWAY. THINK OF THIS AS GETTING A TASTE OF KOREAN SPICES.
UGH-. SO HOT!
YOU EAT THIS SO WELL...
...STRANGE TASTE, THIS THING.
NEVER HAD ANYTHING LIKE IT IN MY LIFE.
WHOA
I BUY YOU FOOD ON MY TIGHT BUDGET AND YOU'RE ACTING ALL SPOILED.
ANYWAY, J...
WHO ARE YOU?
HUH?
WHAT DO YOU DO FOR A LIVING?
OH, I...

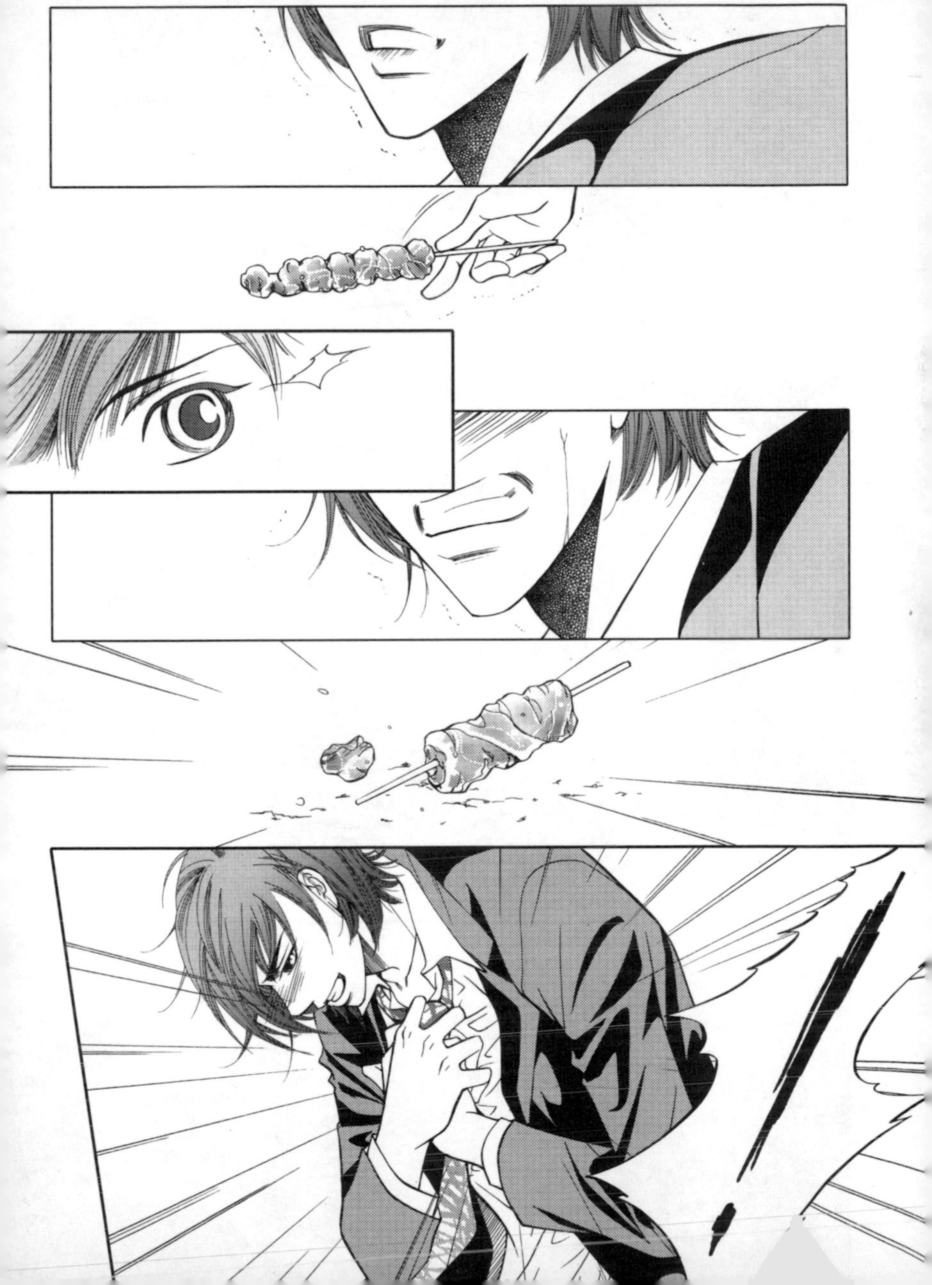

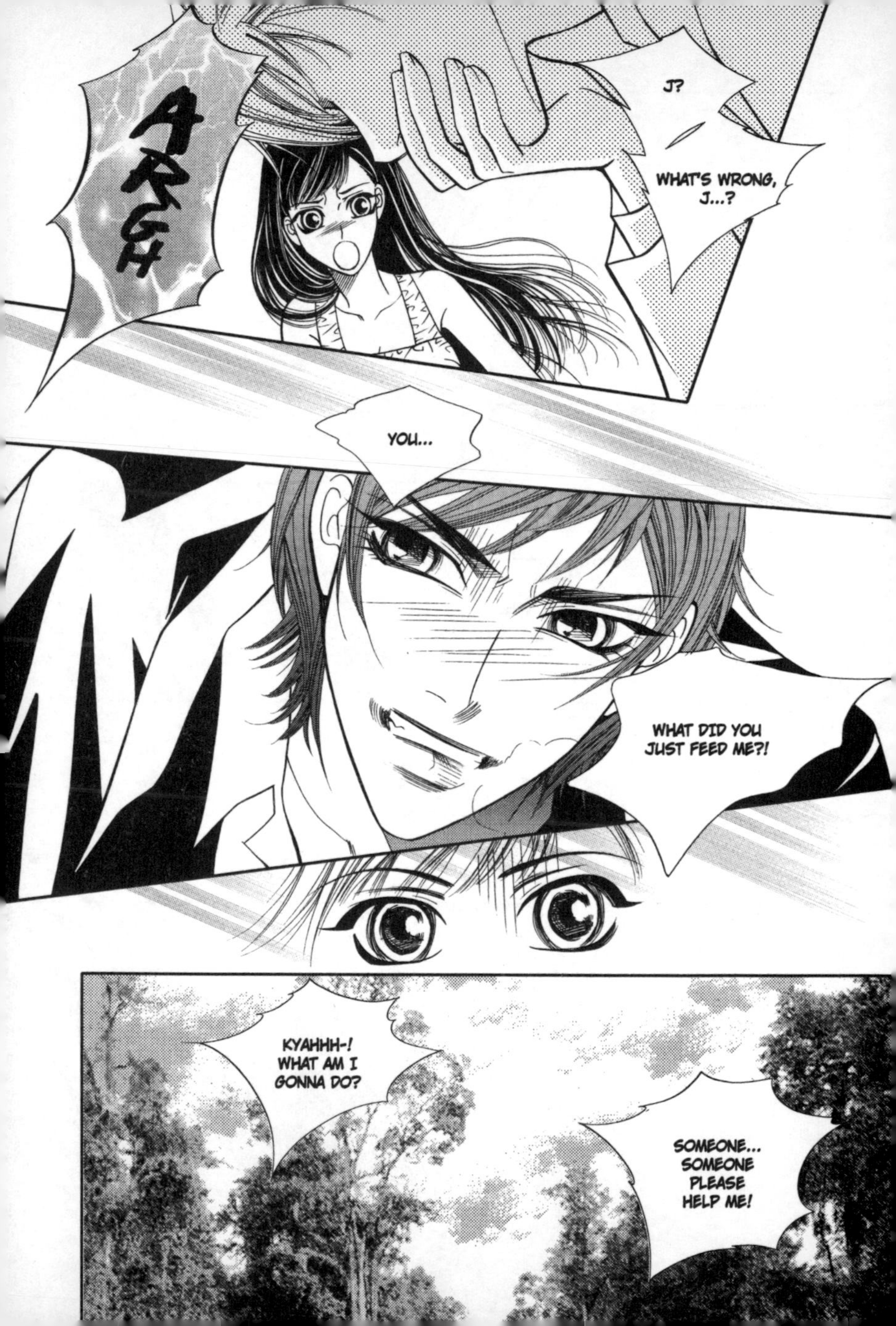
ARGH
J?
WHAT'S WRONG, J...?
YOU...
WHAT DID YOU JUST FEED ME?!
KYAHHH-! WHAT AM I GONNA DO?
SOMEONE... SOMEONE PLEASE HELP ME!

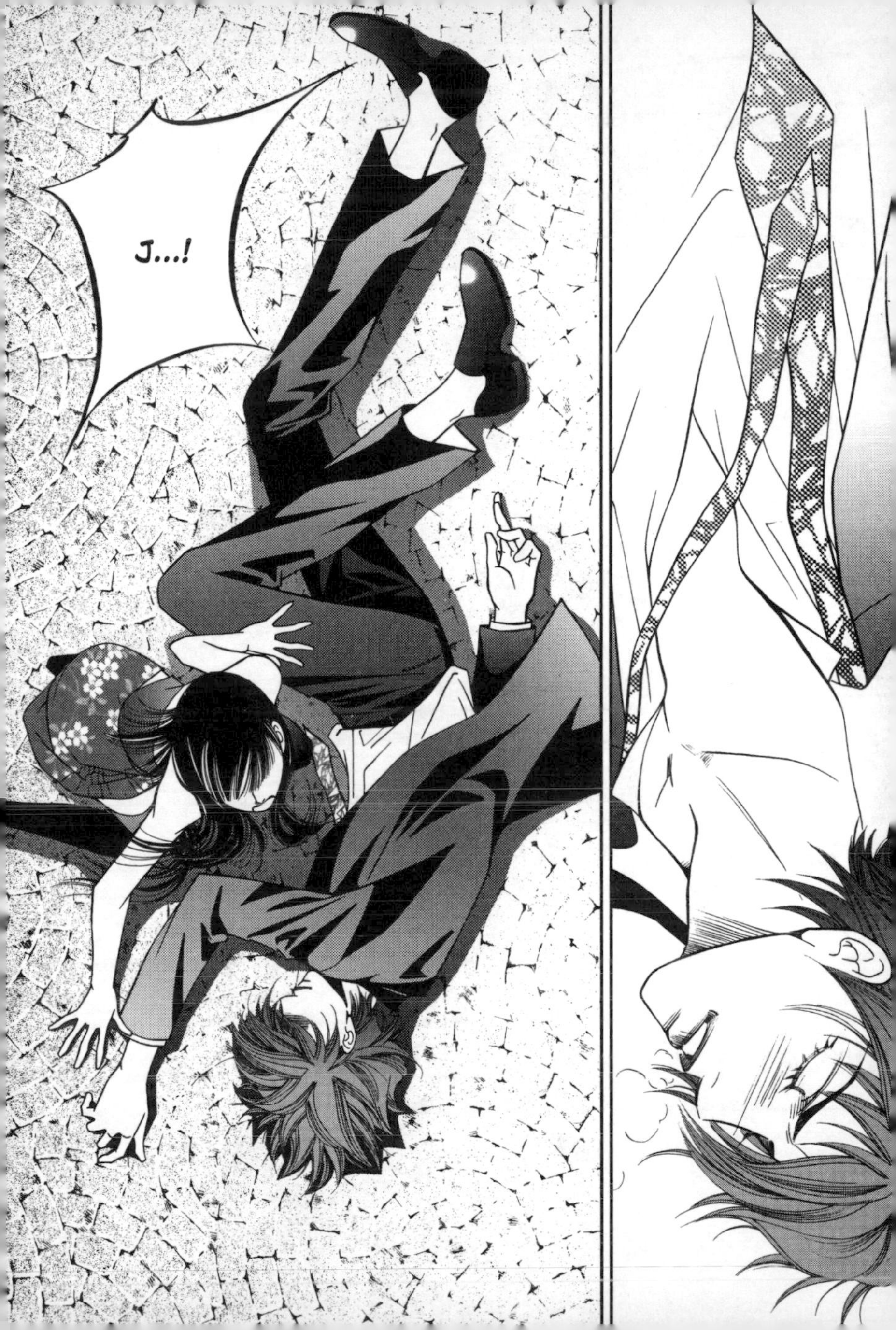
J...!

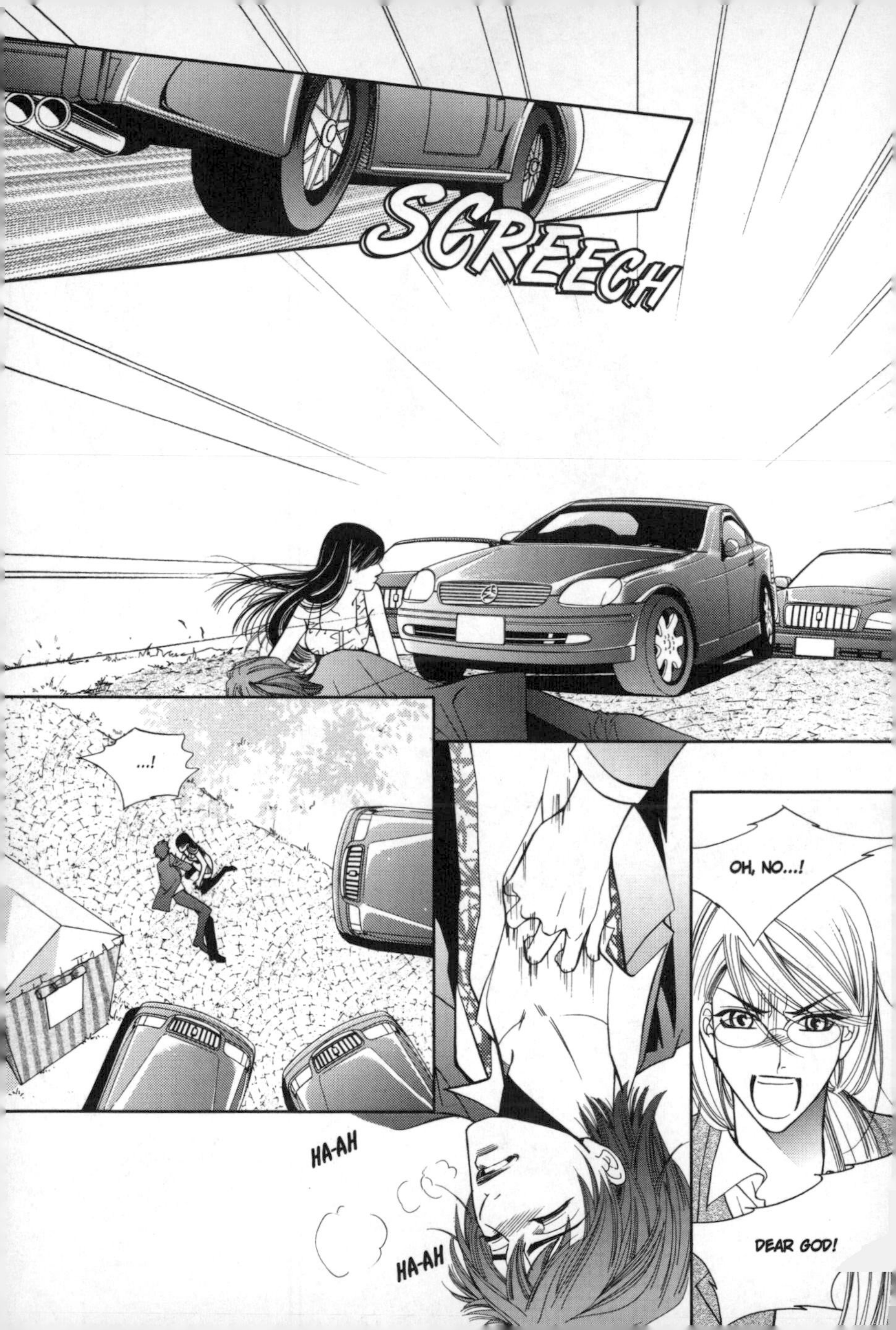
SCREECH
...!
OH, NO...!
HA-AH
HA-AH
DEAR GOD!

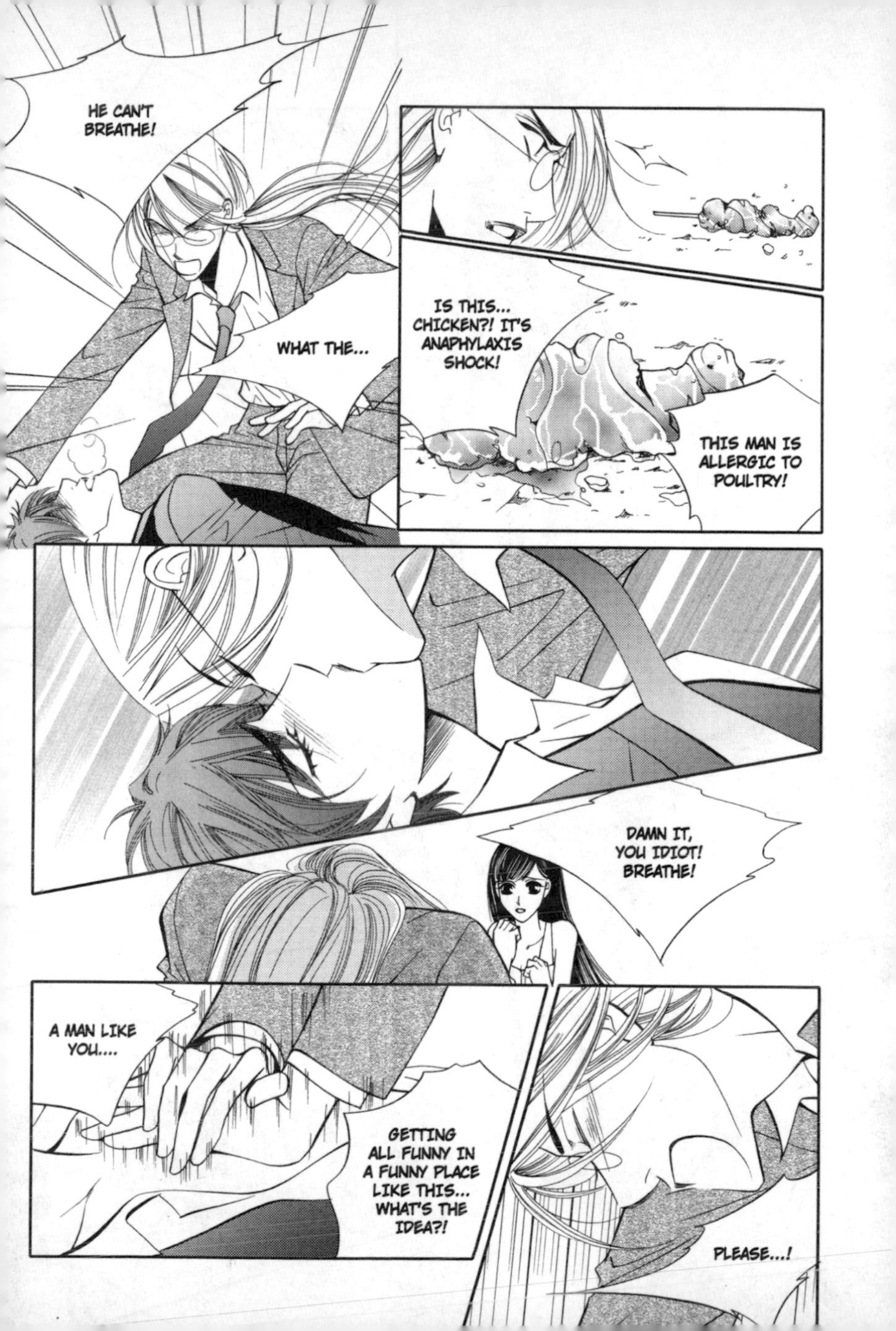
HE CAN'T BREATHE!
WHAT THE...
IS THIS... CHICKEN?! IT'S ANAPHYLAXIS SHOCK!
THIS MAN IS ALLERGIC TO POULTRY!
DAMN IT, YOU IDIOT! BREATHE!
A MAN LIKE YOU....
GETTING ALL FUNNY IN A FUNNY PLACE LIKE THIS... WHAT'S THE IDEA?!
PLEASE...!

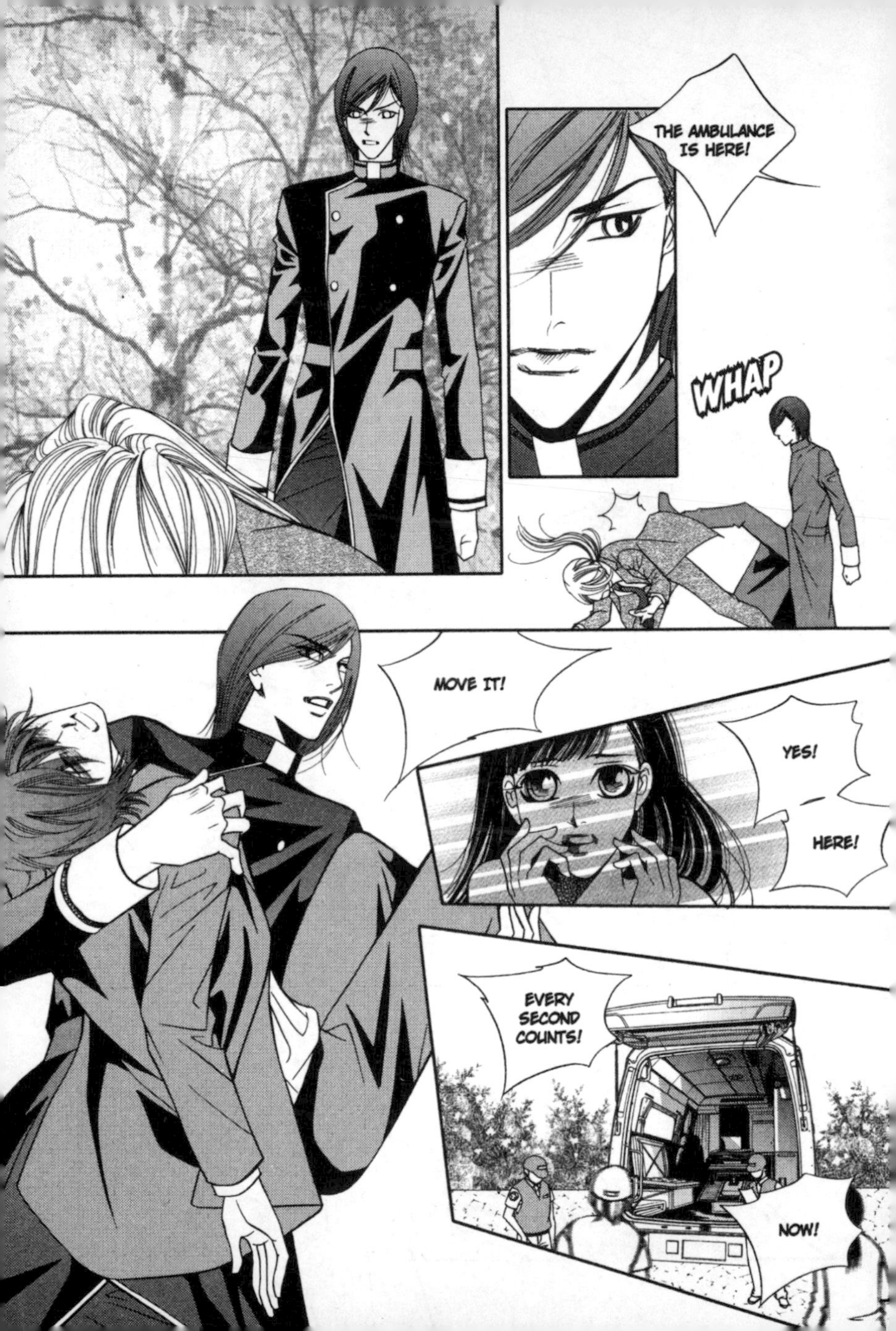
THE AMBULANCE IS HERE!
WHAP
MOVE IT!
YES!
HERE!
EVERY SECOND COUNTS!
NOW!

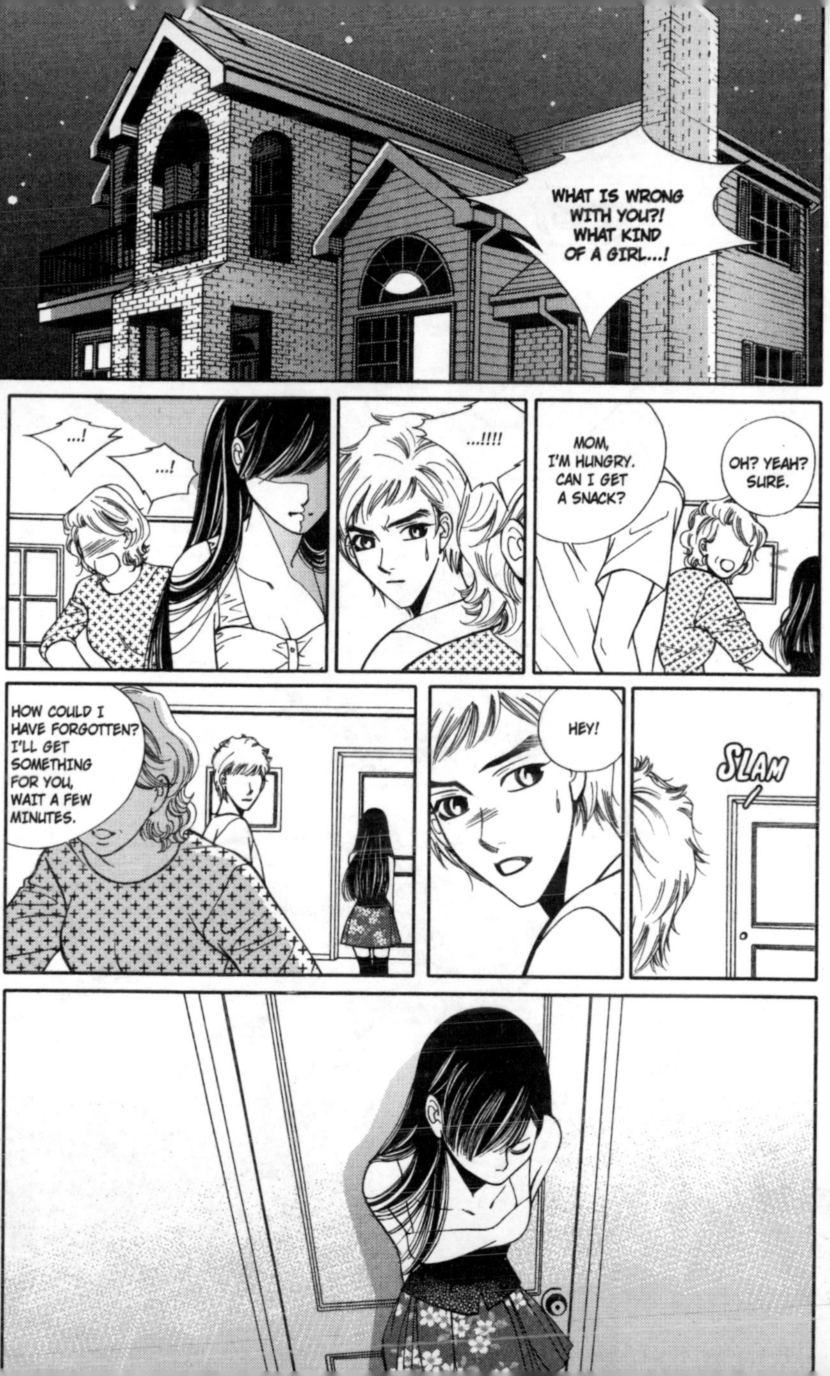
WHAT IS WRONG WITH YOU?! WHAT KIND OF A GIRL...!
...!
...!
...!!!!
MOM, I'M HUNGRY. CAN I GET A SNACK?
OH? YEAH? SURE.
HOW COULD I HAVE FORGOTTEN? I'LL GET SOMETHING FOR YOU, WAIT A FEW MINUTES.
HEY!
SLAM

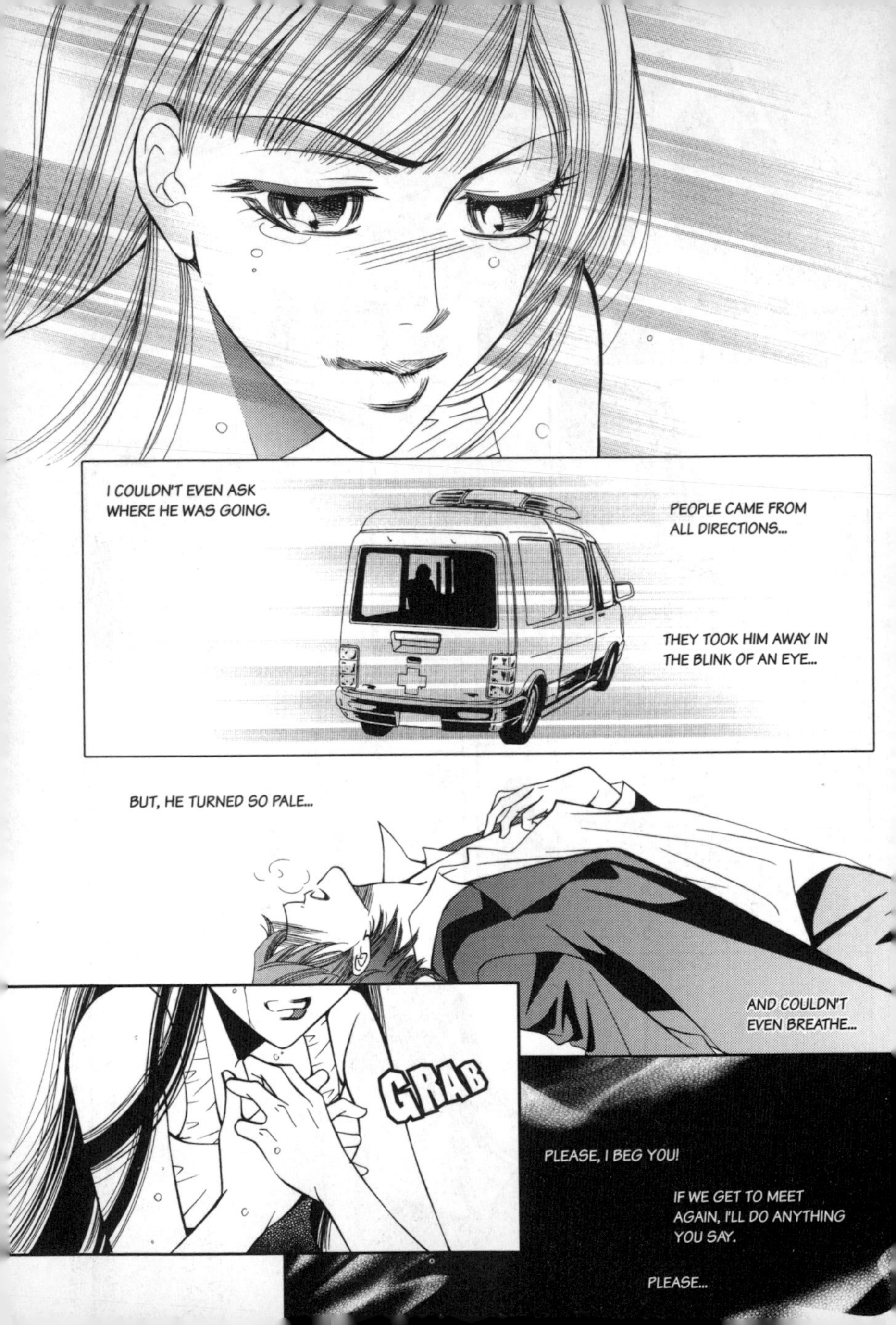
I COULDN'T EVEN ASK WHERE HE WAS GOING.
PEOPLE CAME FROM ALL DIRECTIONS...
THEY TOOK HIM AWAY IN THE BLINK OF AN EYE...
BUT, HE TURNED SO PALE...
AND COULDN'T EVEN BREATHE...
GRAB
PLEASE, I BEG YOU!
IF WE GET TO MEET AGAIN, I'LL DO ANYTHING YOU SAY.
PLEASE...

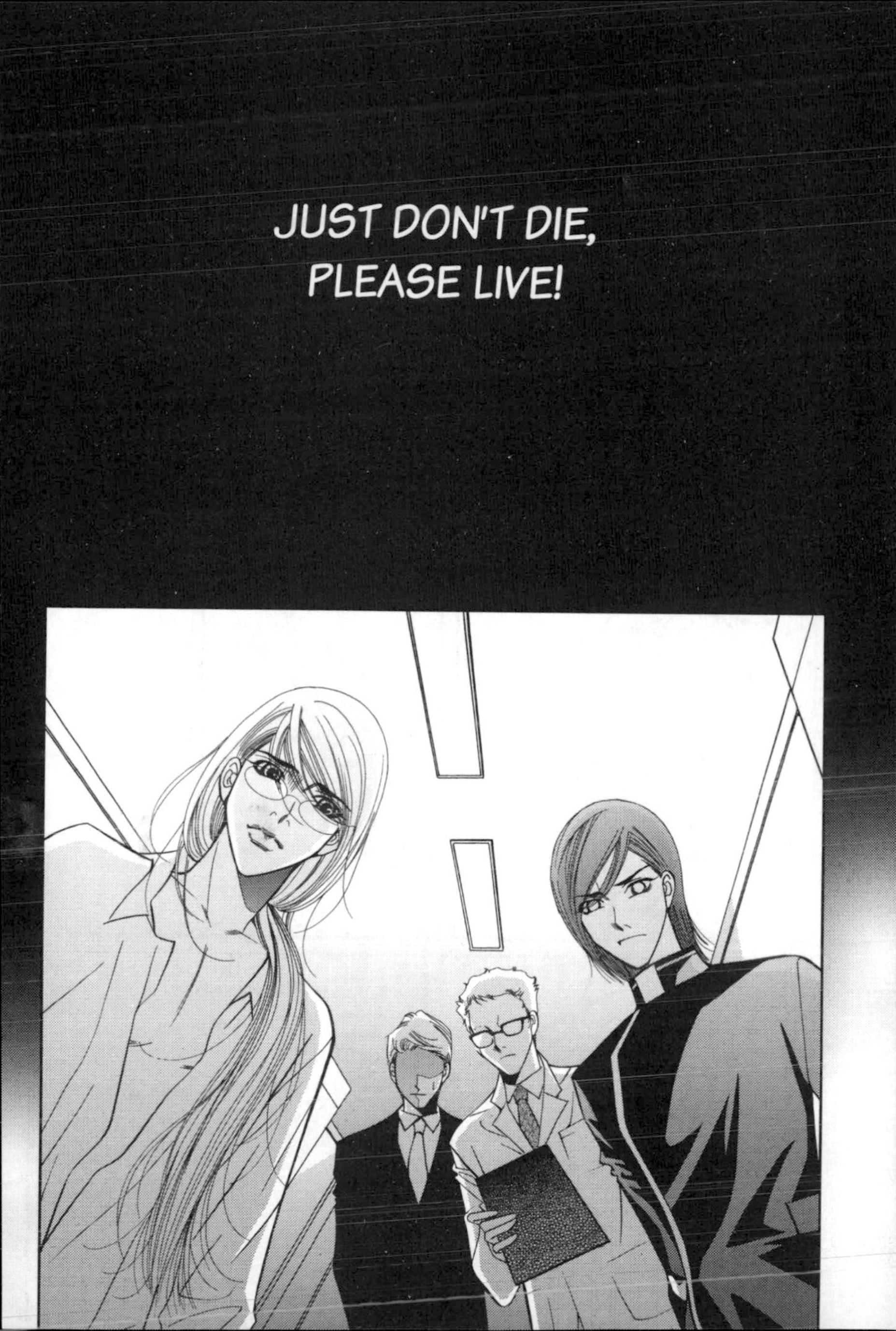
JUST DON'T DIE, PLEASE LIVE!

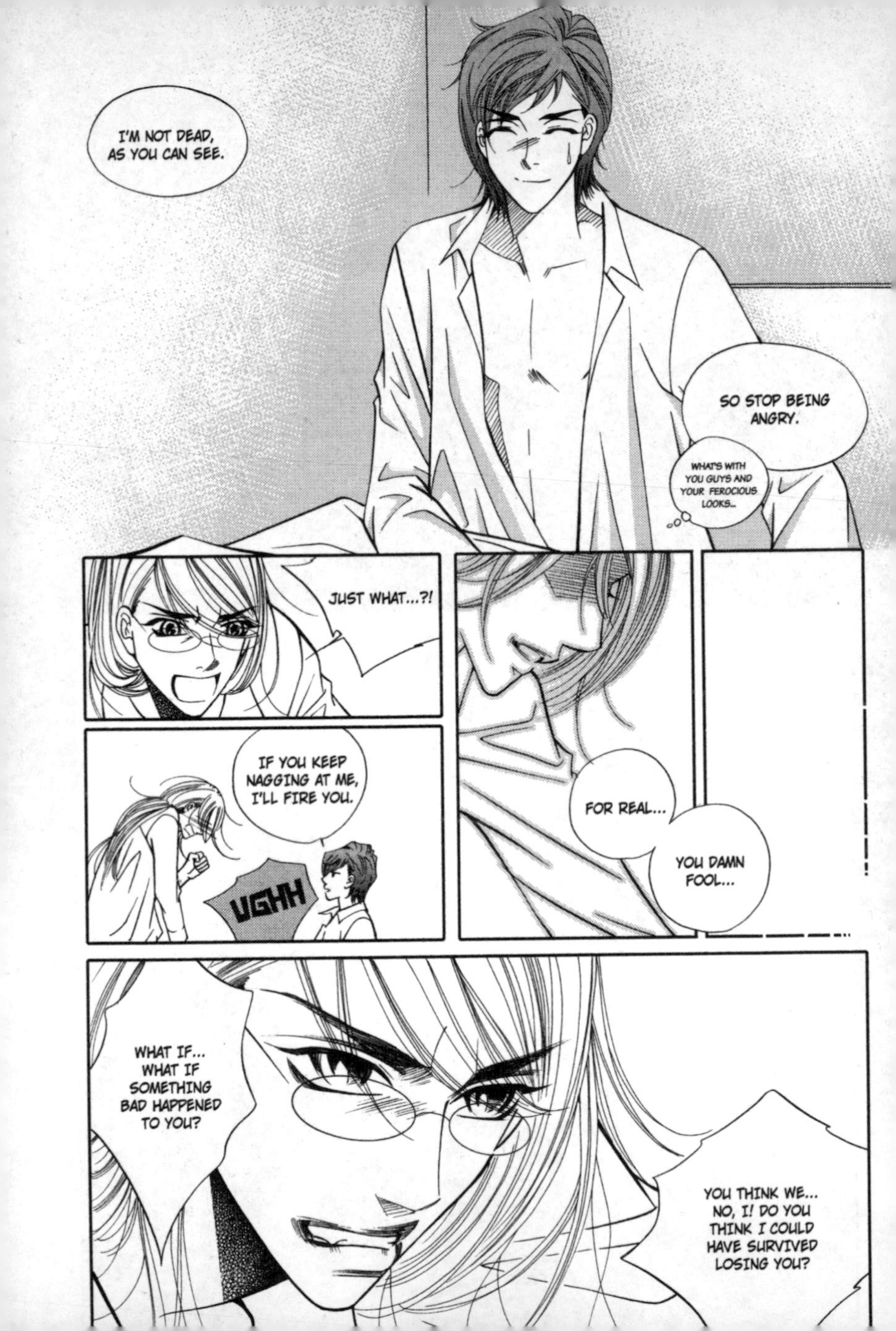
I'M NOT DEAD, AS YOU CAN SEE.
SO STOP BEING ANGRY.
WHAT'S WITH YOU GUYS AND YOUR FEROCIOUS LOOKS...
JUST WHAT...?!
IF YOU KEEP NAGGING AT ME, I'LL FIRE YOU.
UGHH
FOR REAL...
YOU DAMN FOOL...
WHAT IF... WHAT IF SOMETHING BAD HAPPENED TO YOU?
YOU THINK WE... NO, I! DO YOU THINK I COULD HAVE SURVIVED LOSING YOU?

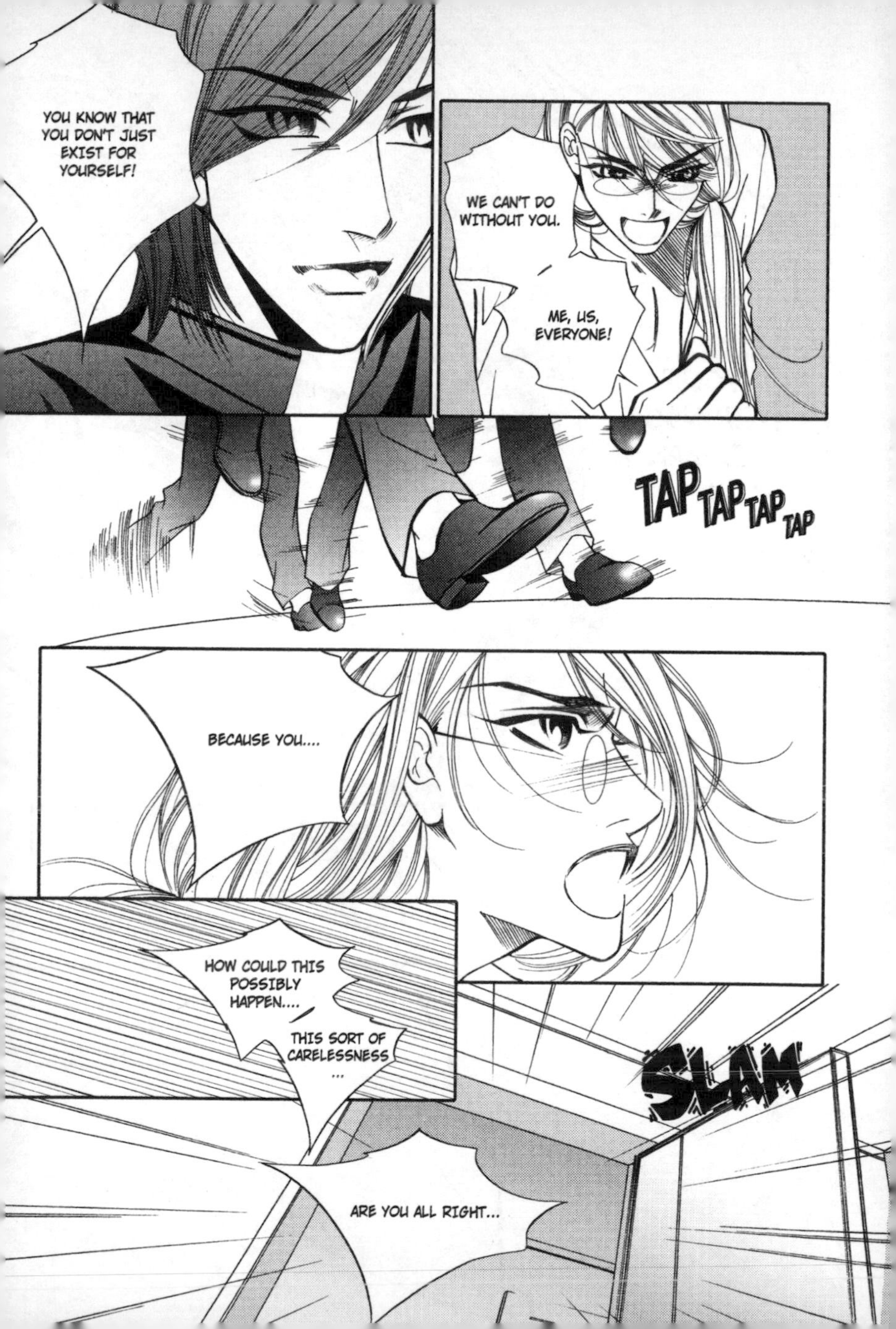
YOU KNOW THAT YOU DON'T JUST EXIST FOR YOURSELF!
WE CAN'T DO WITHOUT YOU.
ME, US, EVERYONE!
TAP TAP TAP TAP
BECAUSE YOU....
HOW COULD THIS POSSIBLY HAPPEN....
THIS SORT OF CARELESSNESS ...
SLAM
ARE YOU ALL RIGHT...

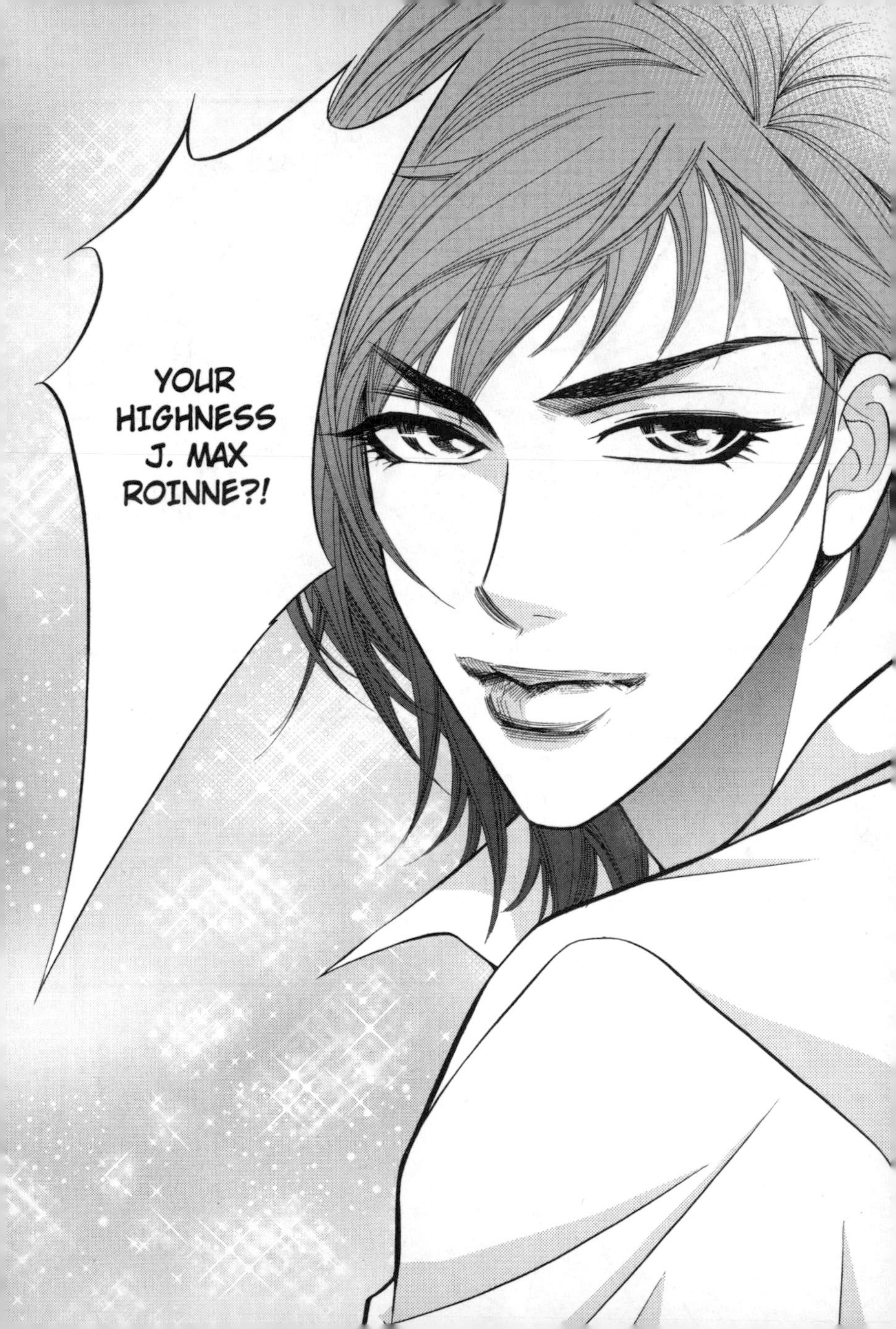
YOUR HIGHNESS J. MAX ROINNE?!

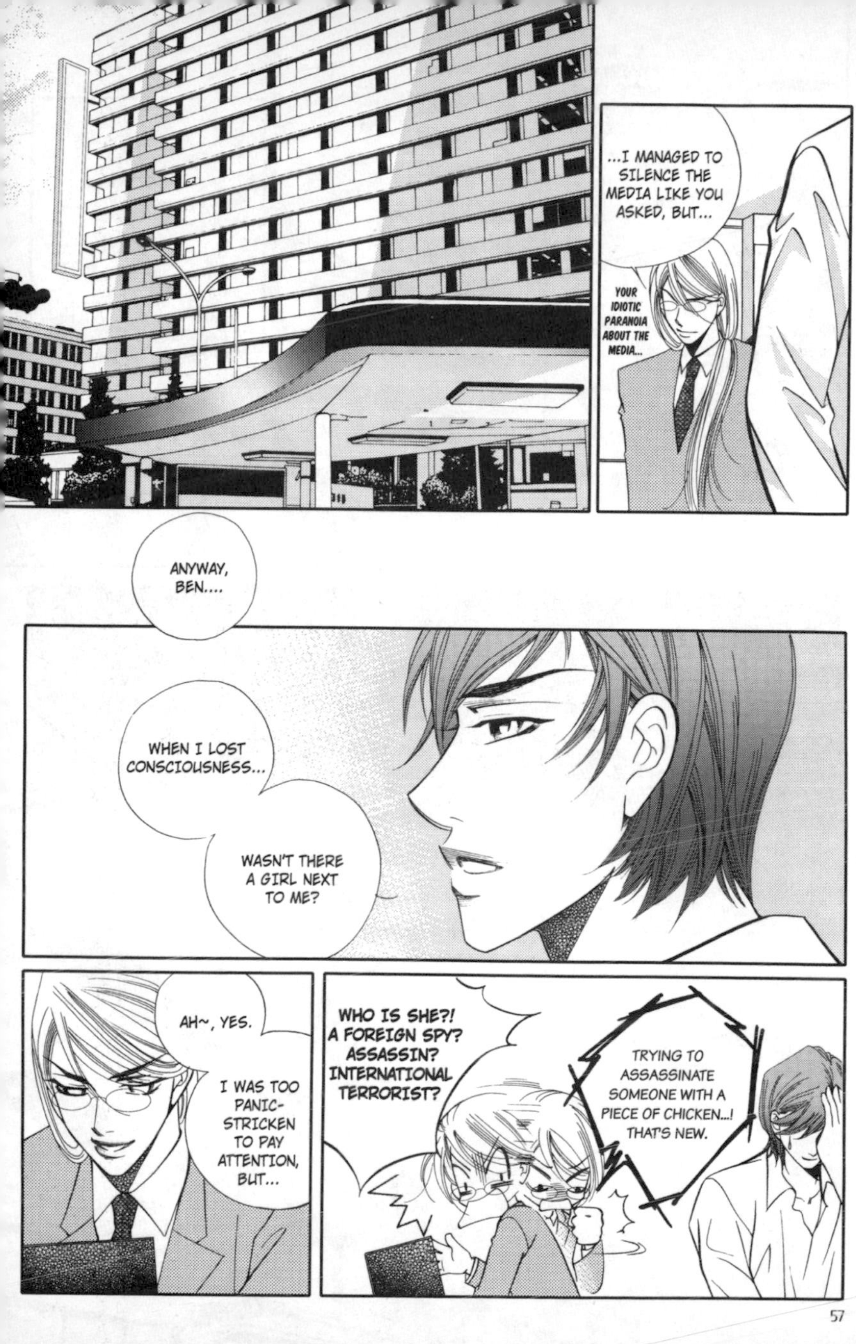
...I MANAGED TO SILENCE THE MEDIA LIKE YOU ASKED, BUT...
YOUR IDIOTIC PARANOIA ABOUT THE MEDIA...
ANYWAY, BEN....
WHEN I LOST CONSCIOUSNESS...
WASN'T THERE A GIRL NEXT TO ME?
AH~, YES.
I WAS TOO PANIC-STRICKEN TO PAY ATTENTION, BUT...
WHO IS SHE?! A FOREIGN SPY? ASSASSIN? INTERNATIONAL TERRORIST?
TRYING TO ASSASSINATE SOMEONE WITH A PIECE OF CHICKEN...! THAT'S NEW.

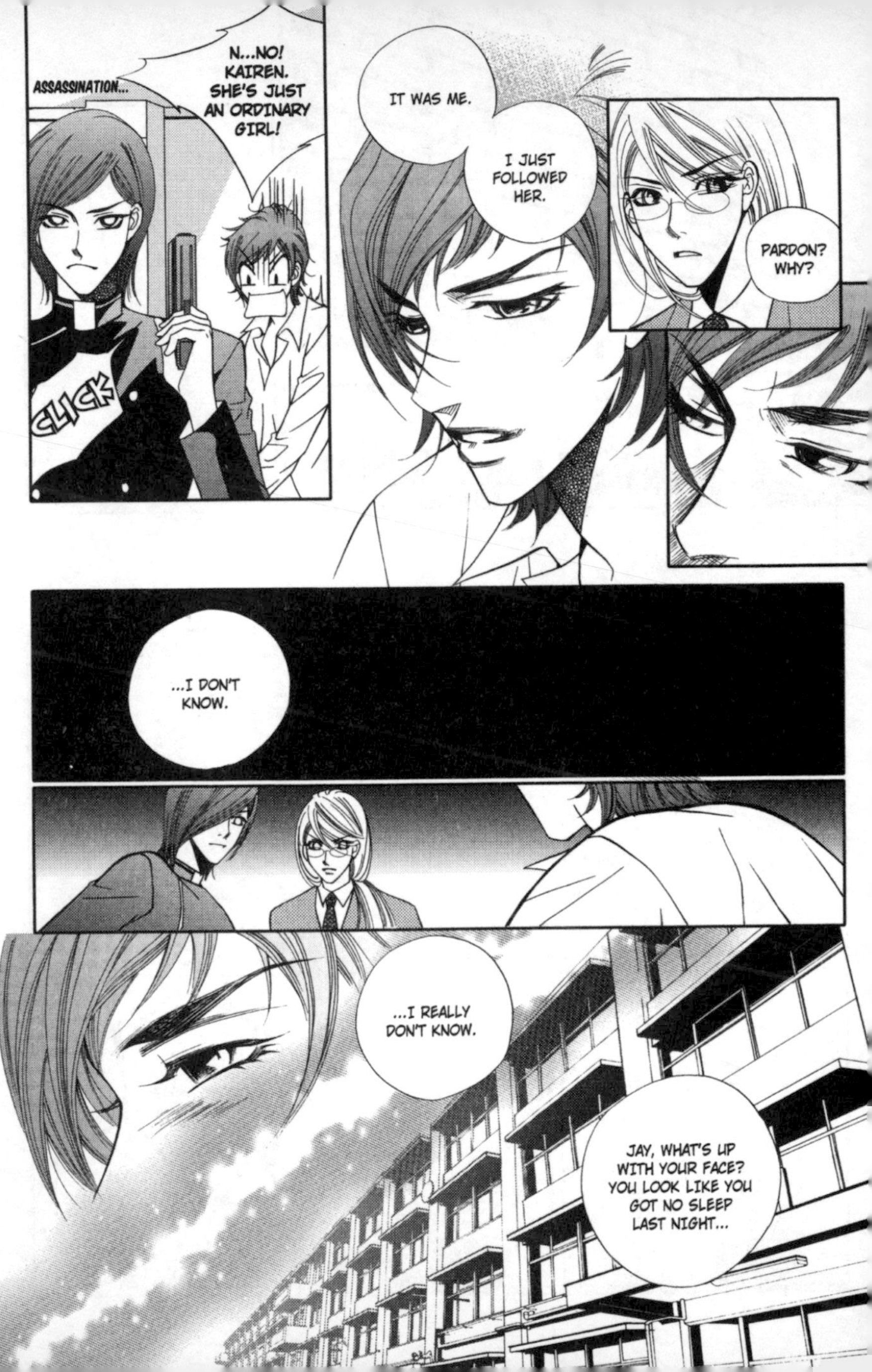
ASSASSINATION...
N...NO! KAIREN. SHE'S JUST AN ORDINARY GIRL!
CLICK
IT WAS ME.
I JUST FOLLOWED HER.
PARDON? WHY?
...I DON'T KNOW.
...I REALLY DON'T KNOW.
JAY, WHAT'S UP WITH YOUR FACE? YOU LOOK LIKE YOU GOT NO SLEEP LAST NIGHT...

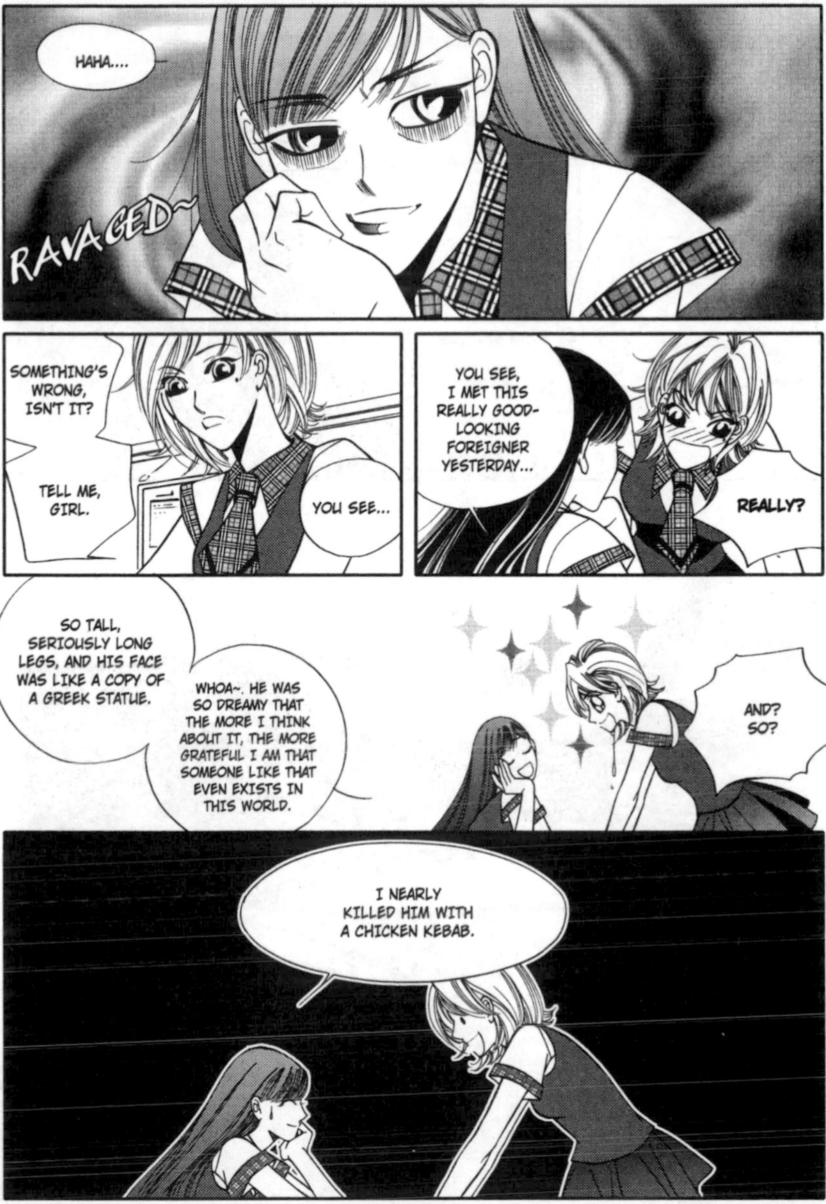
HAHA....
RAVAGED~
SOMETHING'S WRONG, ISN'T IT?
TELL ME, GIRL.
YOU SEE...
YOU SEE, I MET THIS REALLY GOOD-LOOKING FOREIGNER YESTERDAY...
REALLY?
SO TALL, SERIOUSLY LONG LEGS, AND HIS FACE WAS LIKE A COPY OF A GREEK STATUE.
WHOA~. HE WAS SO DREAMY THAT THE MORE I THINK ABOUT IT, THE MORE GRATEFUL I AM THAT SOMEONE LIKE THAT EVEN EXISTS IN THIS WORLD.
AND? SO?
I NEARLY KILLED HIM WITH A CHICKEN KEBAB.

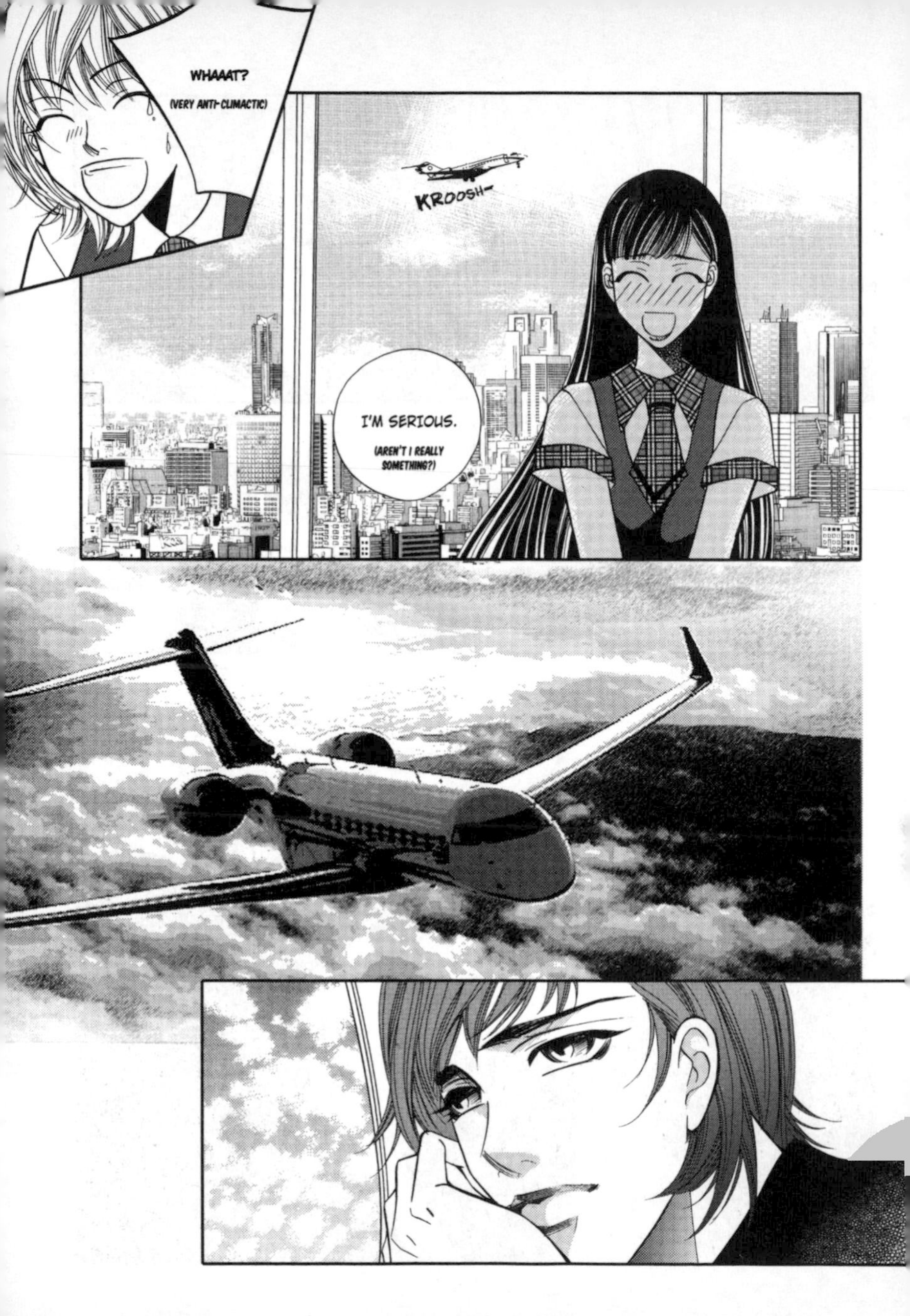
WHAAAT?
(VERY ANTI-CLIMACTIC)
KROOSH-
I'M SERIOUS.
(AREN'T I REALLY SOMETHING?)

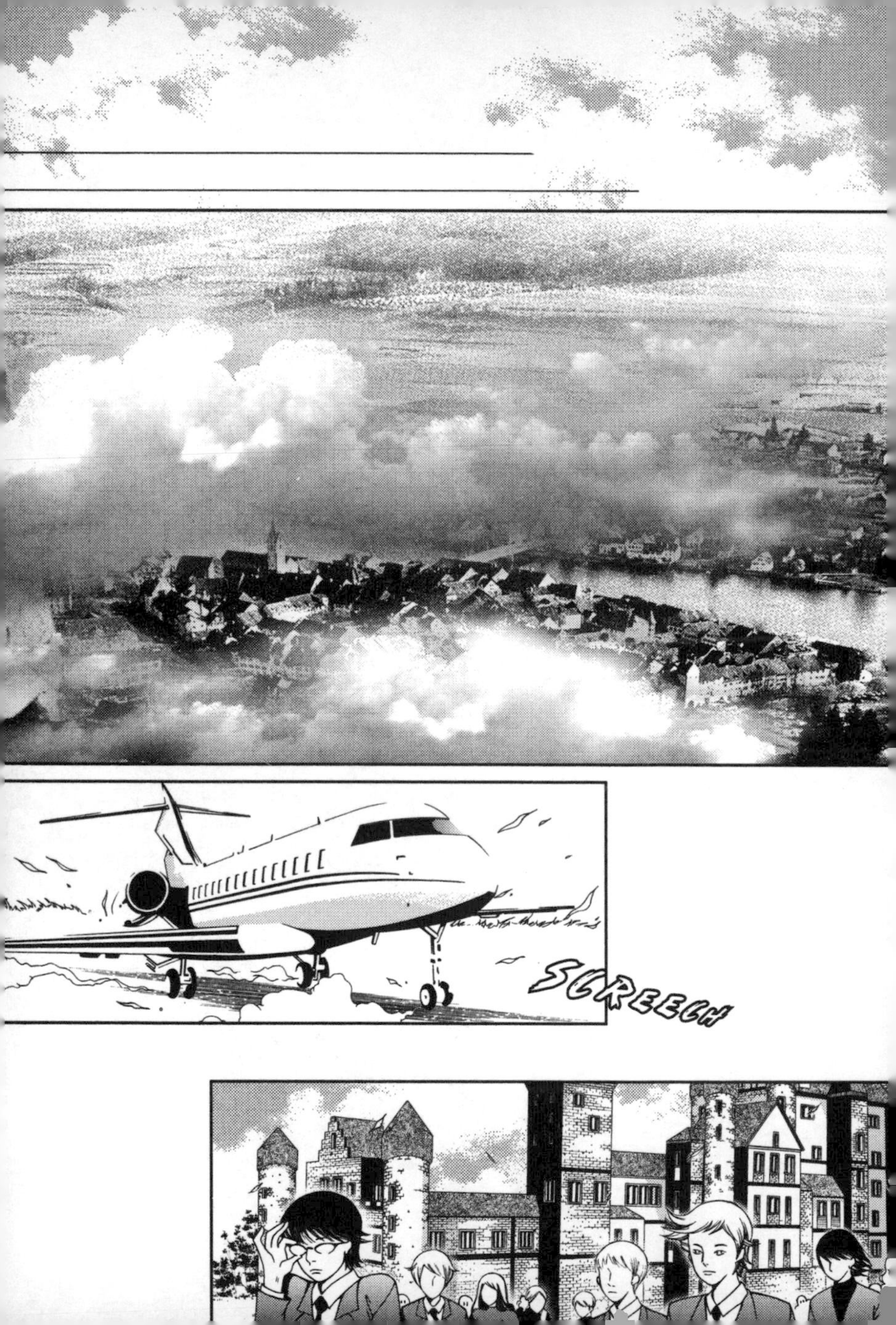
SCREECH

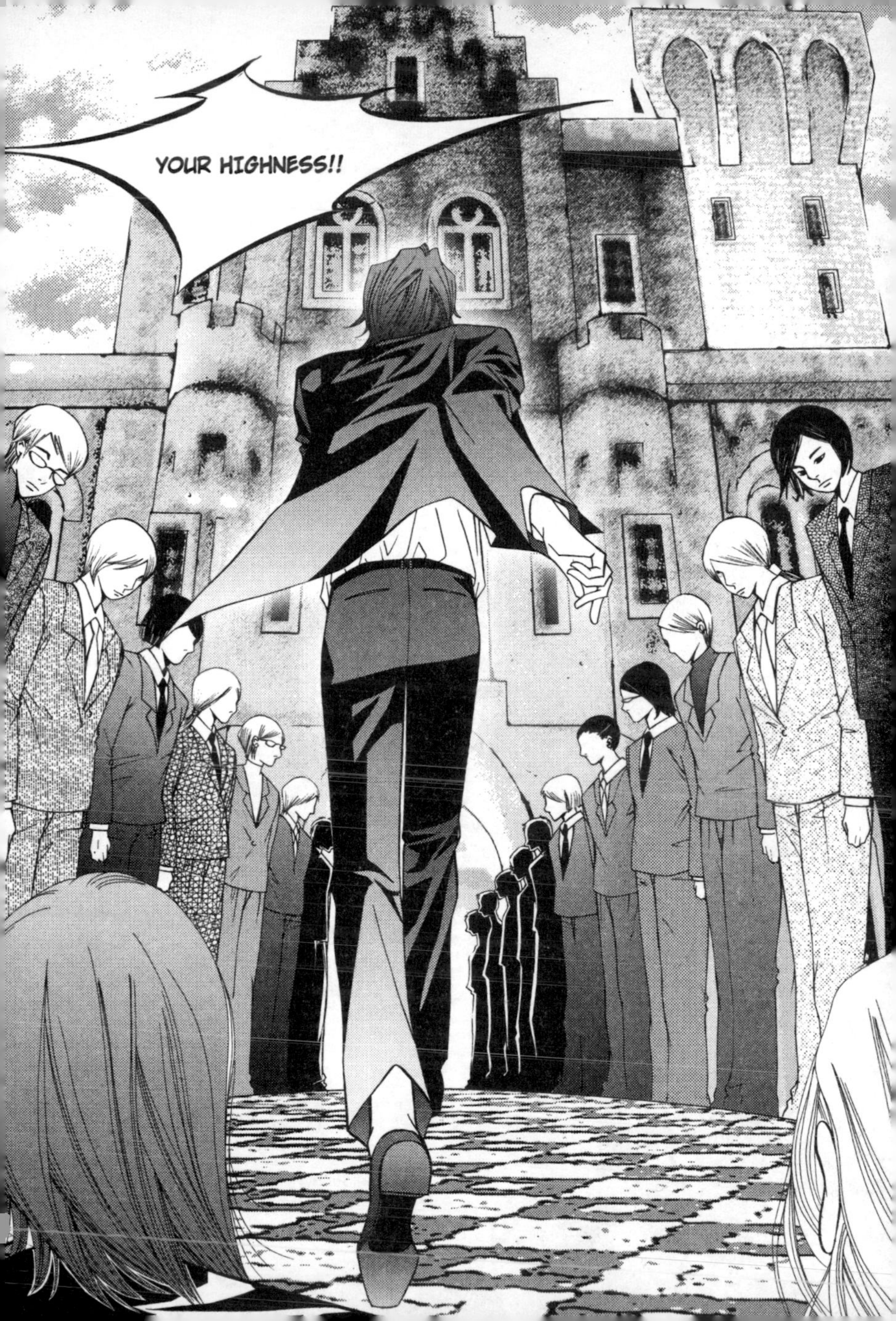
YOUR HIGHNESS!!

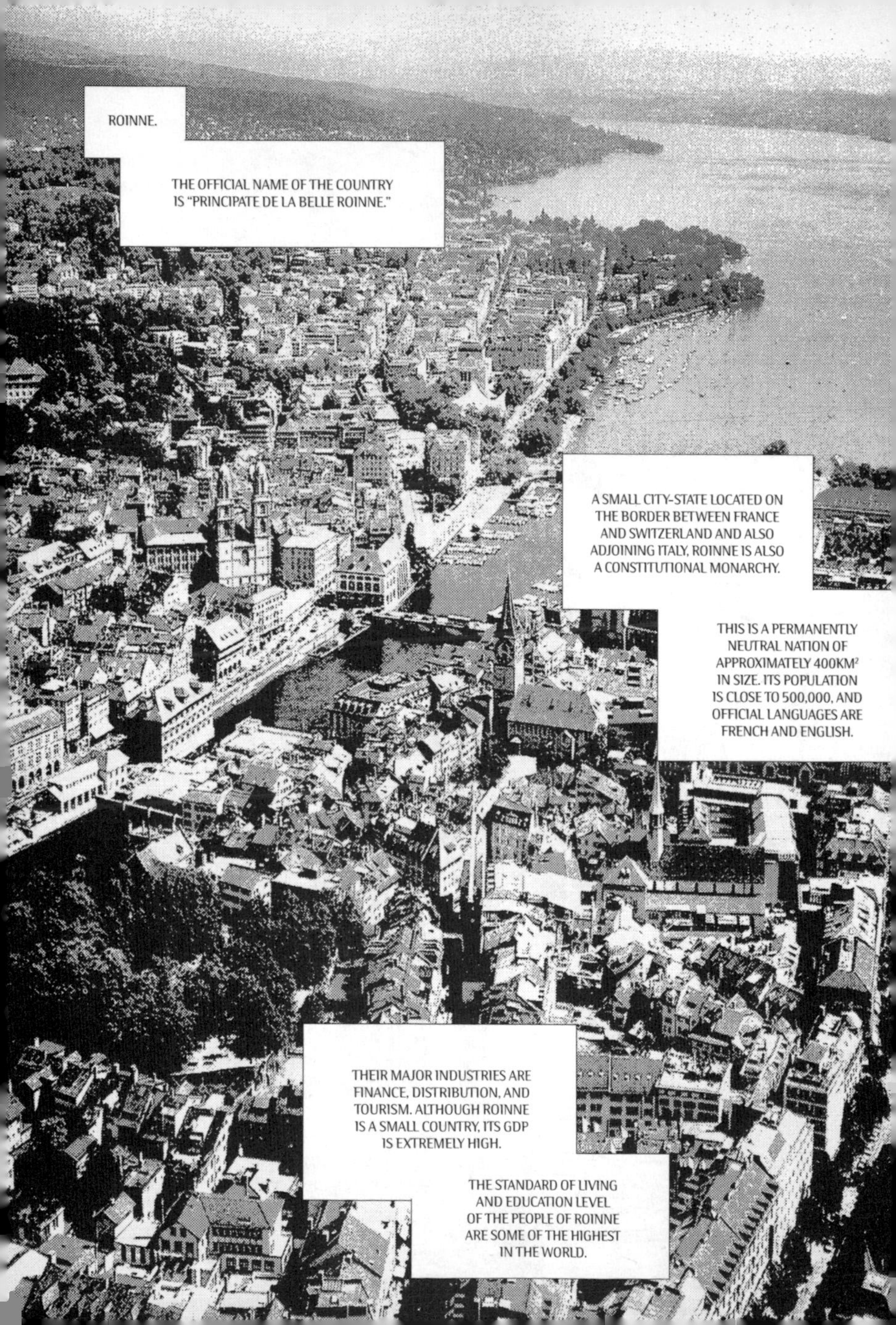
ROINNE.
THE OFFICIAL NAME OF THE COUNTRY IS "PRINCIPATE DE LA BELLE ROINNE."
A SMALL CITY-STATE LOCATED ON THE BORDER BETWEEN FRANCE AND SWITZERLAND AND ALSO ADJOINING ITALY, ROINNE IS ALSO A CONSTITUTIONAL MONARCHY.
THIS IS A PERMANENTLY NEUTRAL NATION OF APPROXIMATELY 400KM² IN SIZE. ITS POPULATION IS CLOSE TO 500,000, AND OFFICIAL LANGUAGES ARE FRENCH AND ENGLISH.
THEIR MAJOR INDUSTRIES ARE FINANCE, DISTRIBUTION, AND TOURISM. ALTHOUGH ROINNE IS A SMALL COUNTRY, ITS GDP IS EXTREMELY HIGH.
THE STANDARD OF LIVING AND EDUCATION LEVEL OF THE PEOPLE OF ROINNE ARE SOME OF THE HIGHEST IN THE WORLD.

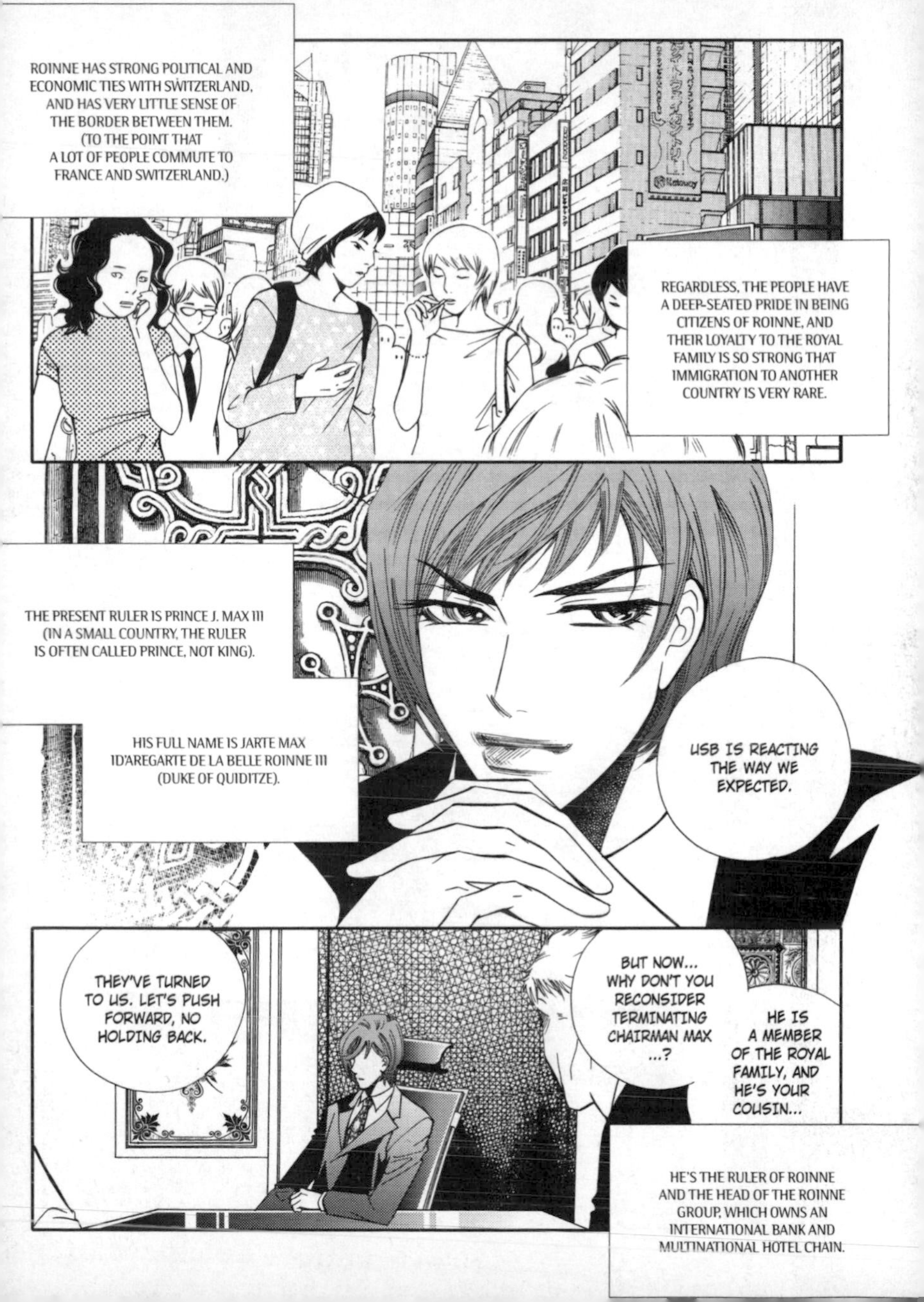
ROINNE HAS STRONG POLITICAL AND ECONOMIC TIES WITH SWITZERLAND, AND HAS VERY LITTLE SENSE OF THE BORDER BETWEEN THEM. (TO THE POINT THAT A LOT OF PEOPLE COMMUTE TO FRANCE AND SWITZERLAND.)
REGARDLESS, THE PEOPLE HAVE A DEEP-SEATED PRIDE IN BEING CITIZENS OF ROINNE, AND THEIR LOYALTY TO THE ROYAL FAMILY IS SO STRONG THAT IMMIGRATION TO ANOTHER COUNTRY IS VERY RARE.
THE PRESENT RULER IS PRINCE J. MAX III (IN A SMALL COUNTRY, THE RULER IS OFTEN CALLED PRINCE, NOT KING).
HIS FULL NAME IS JARTE MAX ID'AREGARTE DE LA BELLE ROINNE III (DUKE OF QUIDITZE).
USB IS REACTING THE WAY WE EXPECTED.
THEY'VE TURNED TO US. LET'S PUSH FORWARD, NO HOLDING BACK.
BUT NOW... WHY DON'T YOU RECONSIDER TERMINATING CHAIRMAN MAX ...?
HE IS A MEMBER OF THE ROYAL FAMILY, AND HE'S YOUR COUSIN...
HE'S THE RULER OF ROINNE AND THE HEAD OF THE ROINNE GROUP, WHICH OWNS AN INTERNATIONAL BANK AND MULTINATIONAL HOTEL CHAIN.

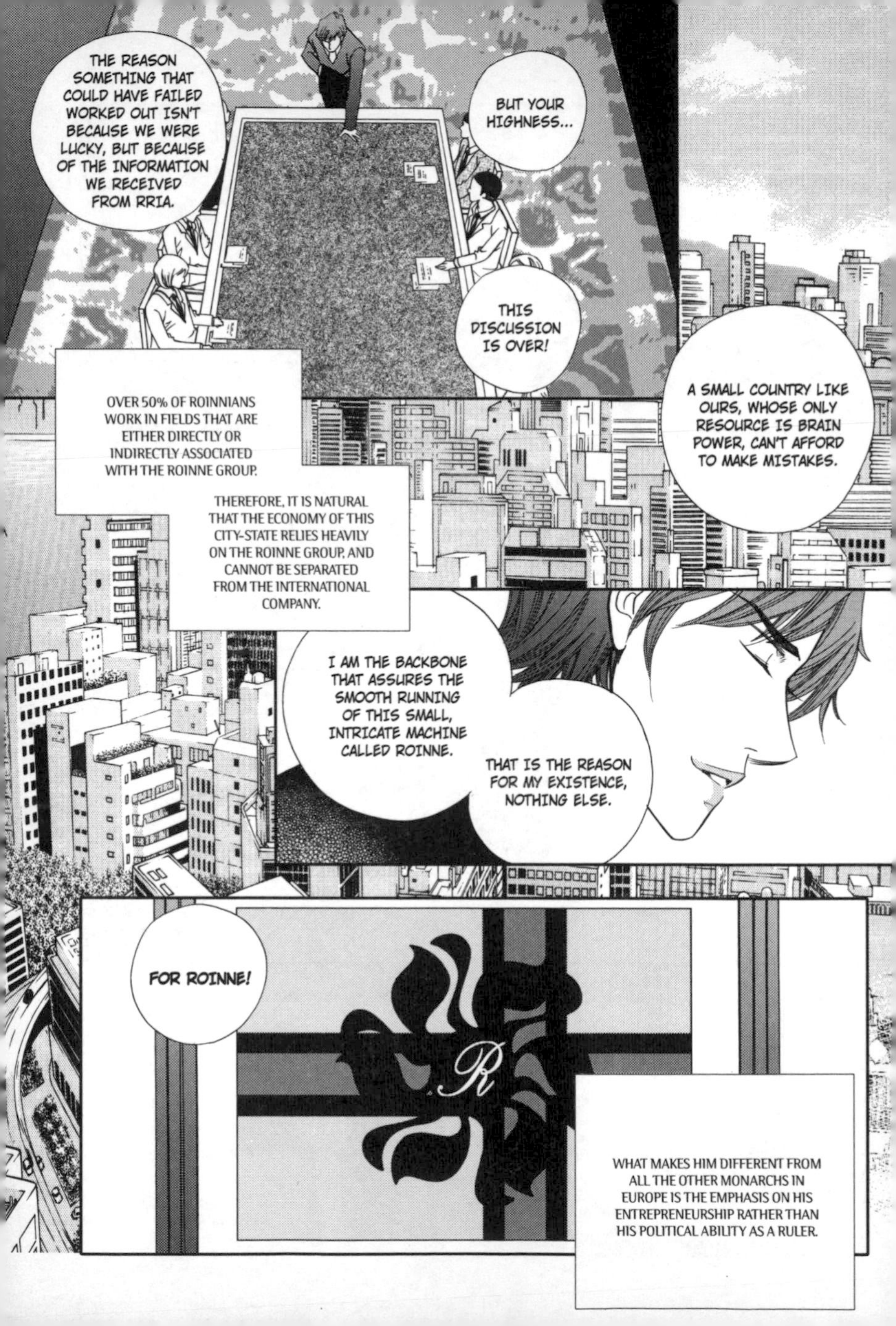
THE REASON SOMETHING THAT COULD HAVE FAILED WORKED OUT ISN'T BECAUSE WE WERE LUCKY, BUT BECAUSE OF THE INFORMATION WE RECEIVED FROM RRIA.
BUT YOUR HIGHNESS...
THIS DISCUSSION IS OVER!
A SMALL COUNTRY LIKE OURS, WHOSE ONLY RESOURCE IS BRAIN POWER, CAN'T AFFORD TO MAKE MISTAKES.
OVER 50% OF ROINNIANS WORK IN FIELDS THAT ARE EITHER DIRECTLY OR INDIRECTLY ASSOCIATED WITH THE ROINNE GROUP.
THEREFORE, IT IS NATURAL THAT THE ECONOMY OF THIS CITY-STATE RELIES HEAVILY ON THE ROINNE GROUP, AND CANNOT BE SEPARATED FROM THE INTERNATIONAL COMPANY.
I AM THE BACKBONE THAT ASSURES THE SMOOTH RUNNING OF THIS SMALL, INTRICATE MACHINE CALLED ROINNE.
THAT IS THE REASON FOR MY EXISTENCE, NOTHING ELSE.
FOR ROINNE!
WHAT MAKES HIM DIFFERENT FROM ALL THE OTHER MONARCHS IN EUROPE IS THE EMPHASIS ON HIS ENTREPRENEURSHIP RATHER THAN HIS POLITICAL ABILITY AS A RULER.

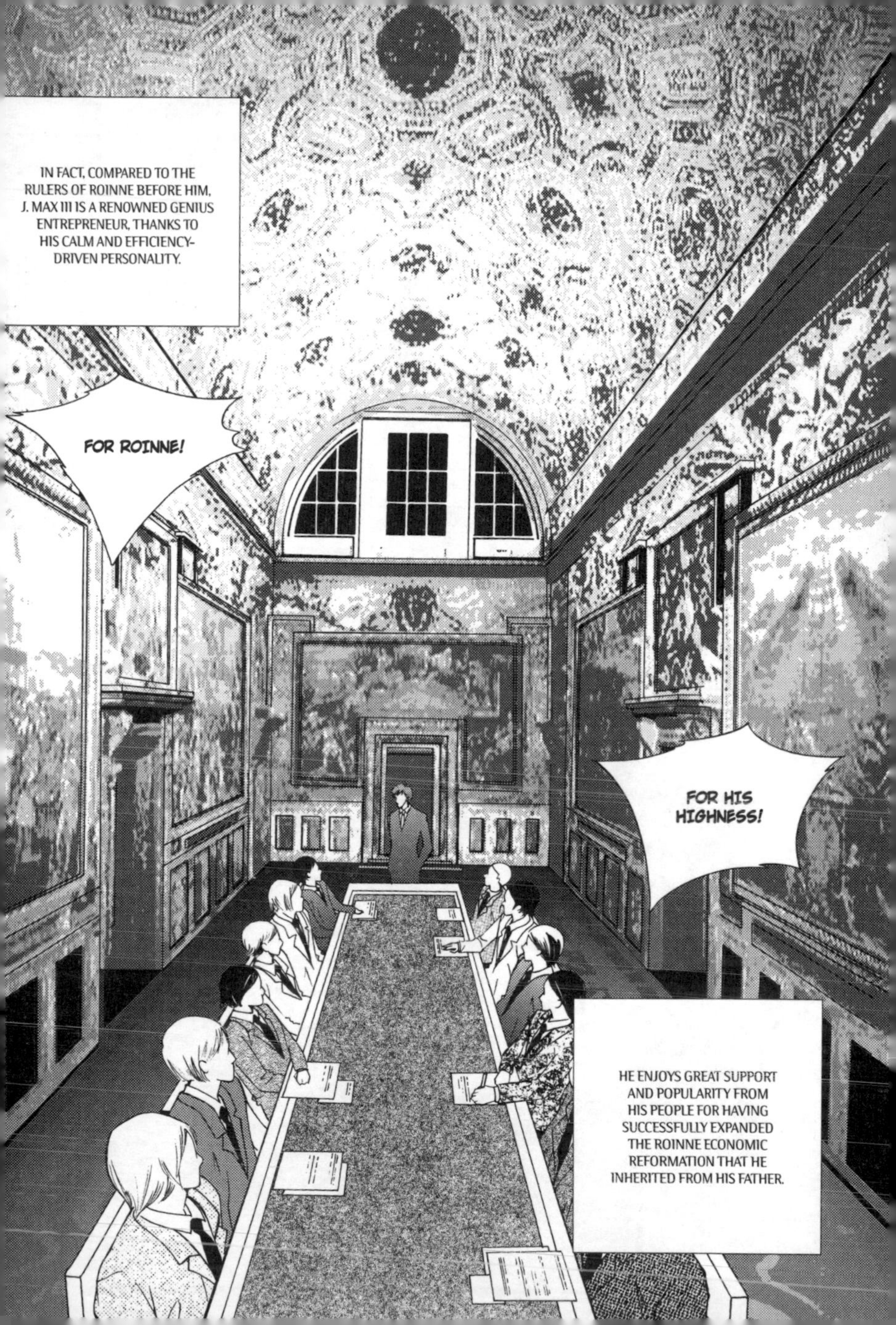

IN FACT, COMPARED TO THE RULERS OF ROINNE BEFORE HIM, J. MAX III IS A RENOWNED GENIUS ENTREPRENEUR, THANKS TO HIS CALM AND EFFICIENCY-DRIVEN PERSONALITY.
FOR ROINNE!
FOR HIS HIGHNESS!
HE ENJOYS GREAT SUPPORT AND POPULARITY FROM HIS PEOPLE FOR HAVING SUCCESSFULLY EXPANDED THE ROINNE ECONOMIC REFORMATION THAT HE INHERITED FROM HIS FATHER.

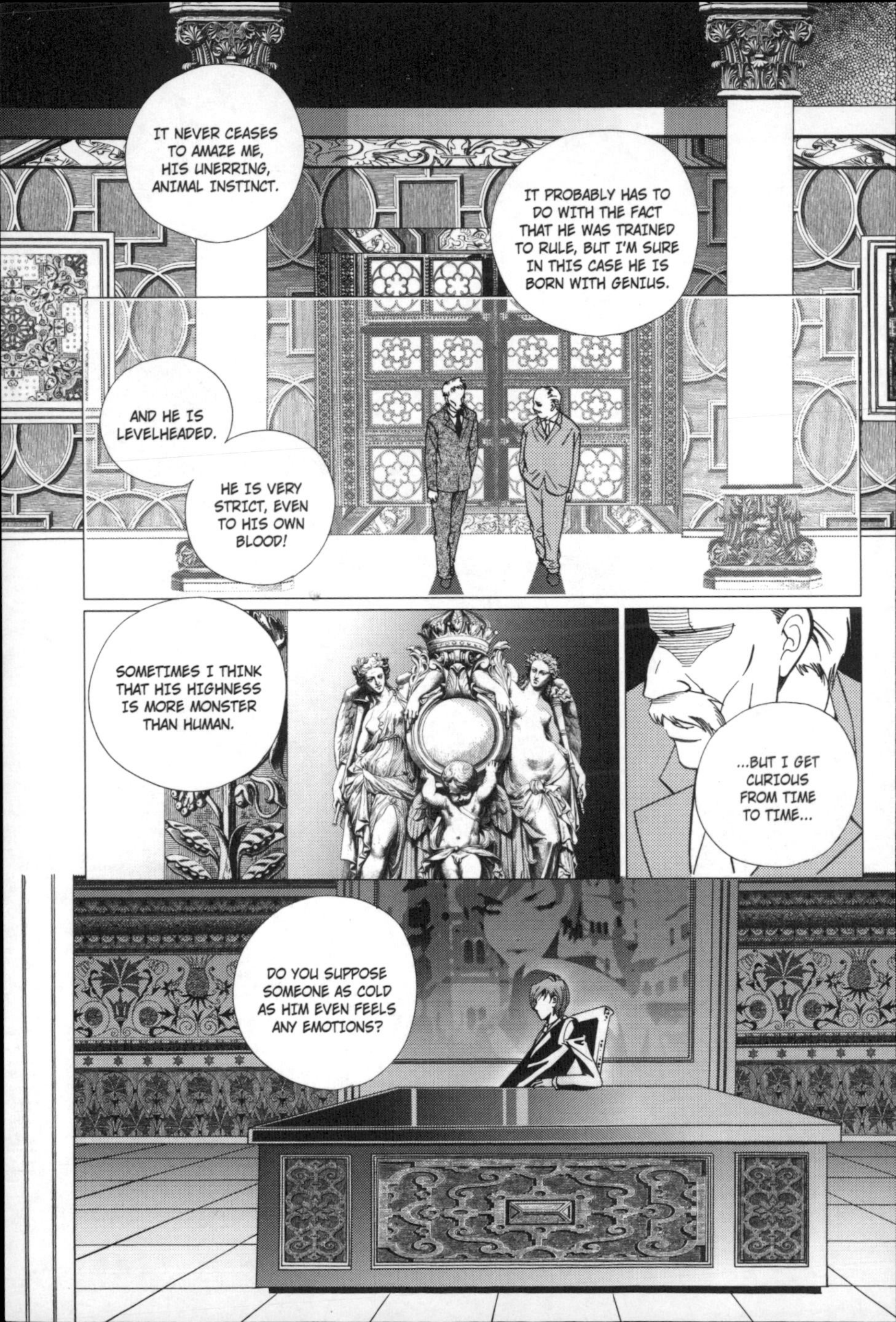
IT NEVER CEASES TO AMAZE ME, HIS UNERRING, ANIMAL INSTINCT.
IT PROBABLY HAS TO DO WITH THE FACT THAT HE WAS TRAINED TO RULE, BUT I'M SURE IN THIS CASE HE IS BORN WITH GENIUS.
AND HE IS LEVELHEADED.
HE IS VERY STRICT, EVEN TO HIS OWN BLOOD!
SOMETIMES I THINK THAT HIS HIGHNESS IS MORE MONSTER THAN HUMAN.
...BUT I GET CURIOUS FROM TIME TO TIME...
DO YOU SUPPOSE SOMEONE AS COLD AS HIM EVEN FEELS ANY EMOTIONS?

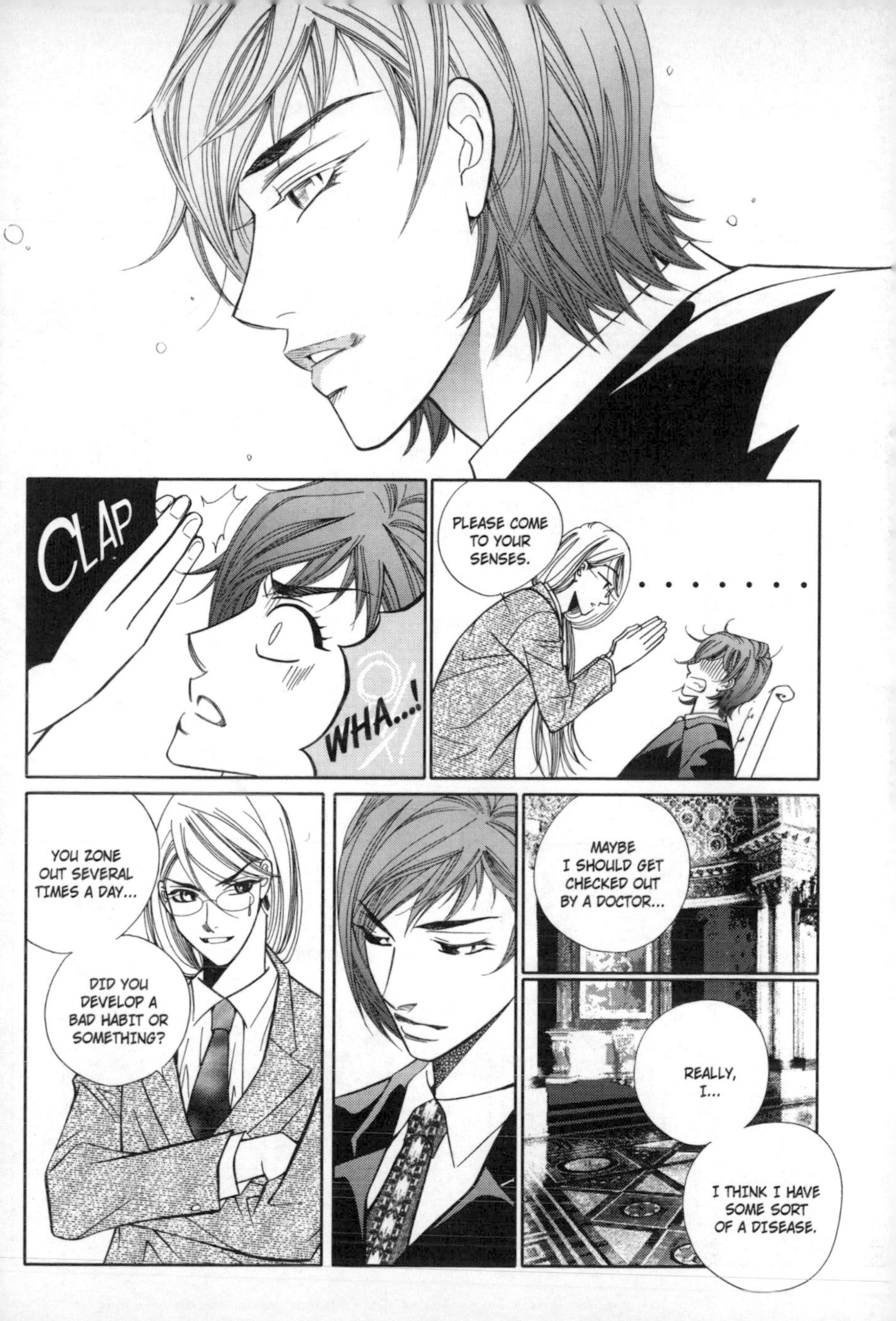
CLAP
WHA...!
PLEASE COME TO YOUR SENSES.
....
YOU ZONE OUT SEVERAL TIMES A DAY...
DID YOU DEVELOP A BAD HABIT OR SOMETHING?
MAYBE I SHOULD GET CHECKED OUT BY A DOCTOR...
REALLY, I...
I THINK I HAVE SOME SORT OF A DISEASE.

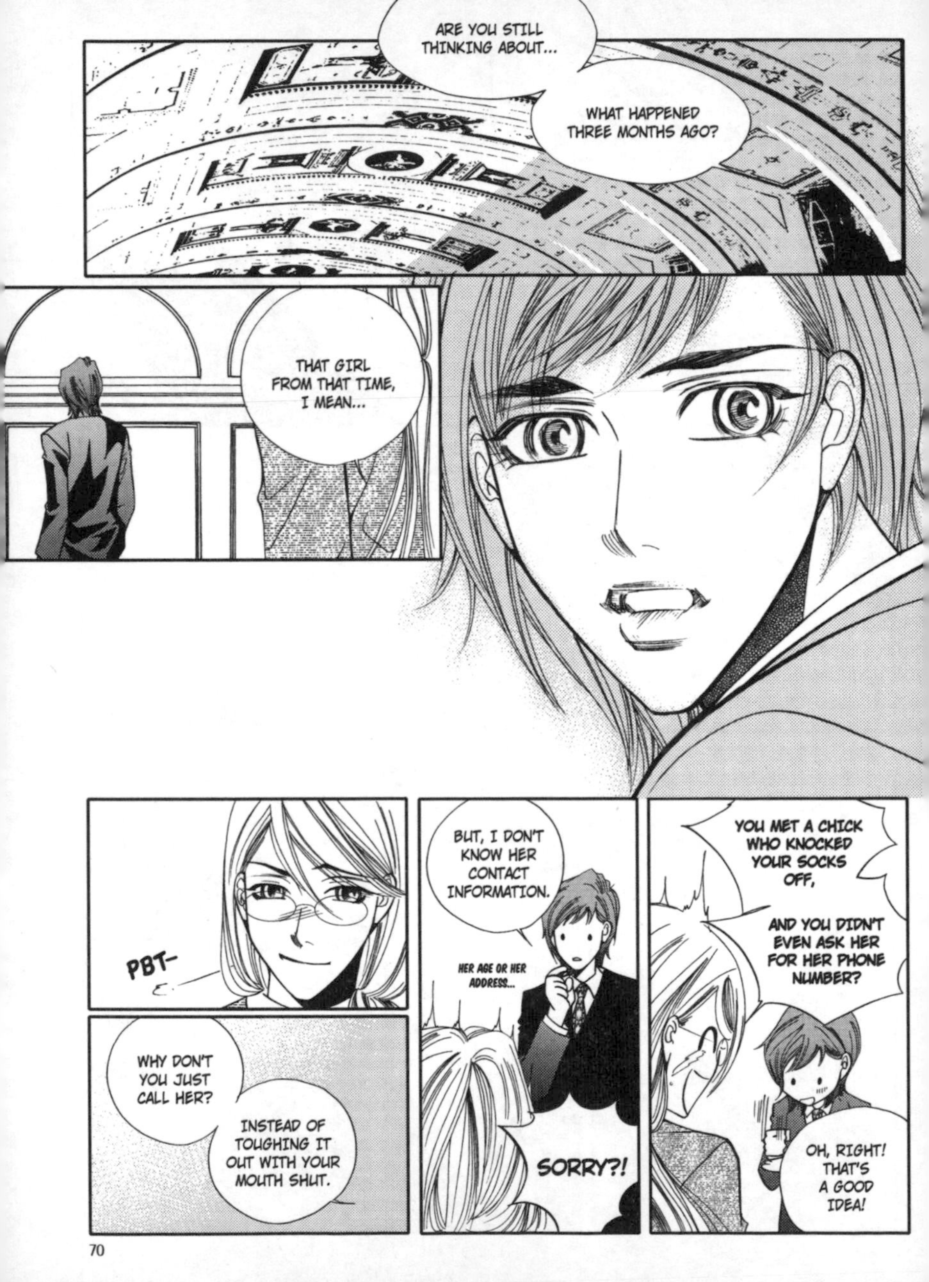
ARE YOU STILL THINKING ABOUT...
WHAT HAPPENED THREE MONTHS AGO?
THAT GIRL FROM THAT TIME, I MEAN...
YOU MET A CHICK WHO KNOCKED YOUR SOCKS OFF,
AND YOU DIDN'T EVEN ASK HER FOR HER PHONE NUMBER?
OH, RIGHT! THAT'S A GOOD IDEA!
BUT, I DON'T KNOW HER CONTACT INFORMATION.
HER AGE OR HER ADDRESS...
SORRY?!
PBT-
WHY DON'T YOU JUST CALL HER?
INSTEAD OF TOUGHING IT OUT WITH YOUR MOUTH SHUT.

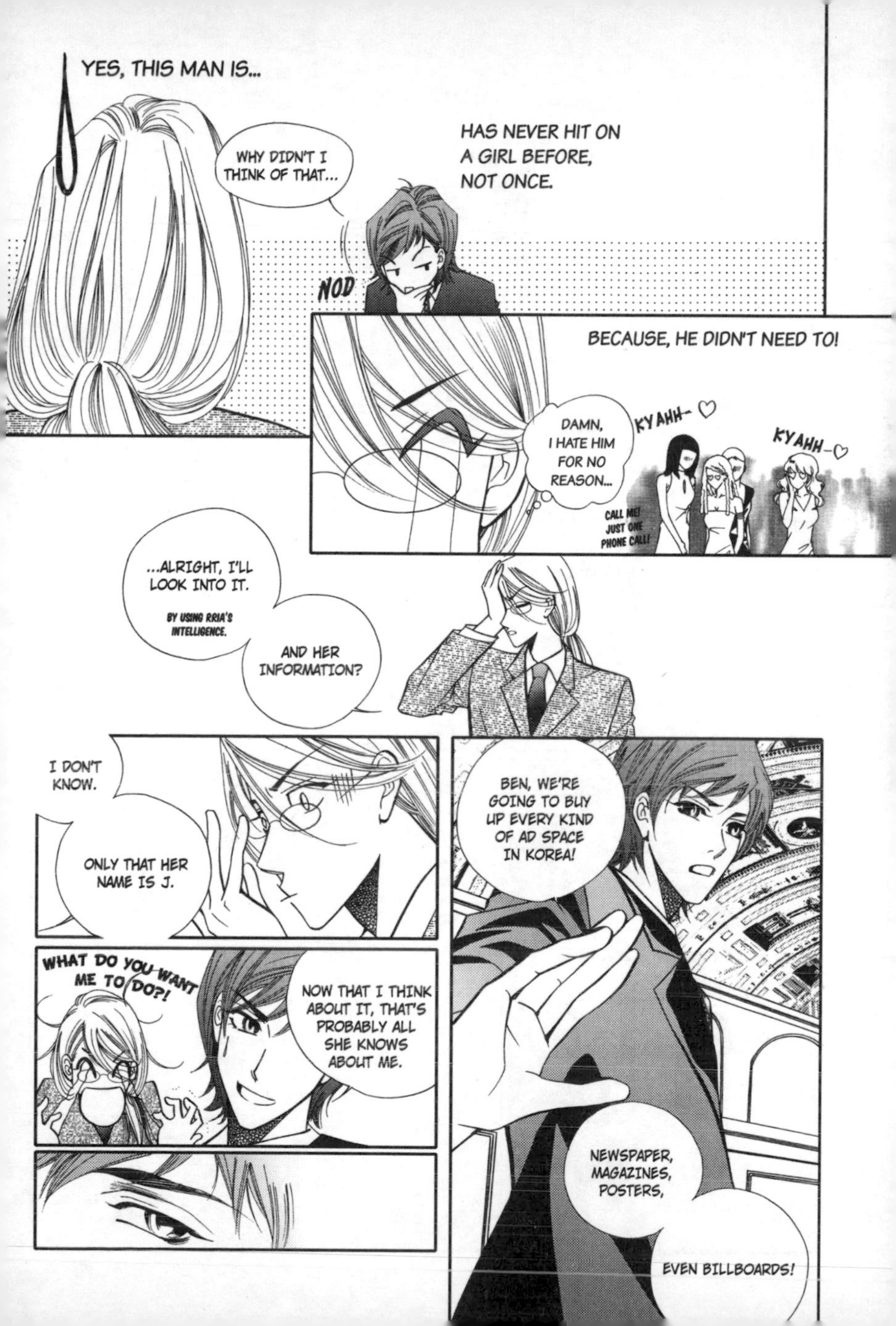

YES, THIS MAN IS...
WHY DIDN'T I THINK OF THAT...
HAS NEVER HIT ON A GIRL BEFORE, NOT ONCE.
NOD
BECAUSE, HE DIDN'T NEED TO!
DAMN, I HATE HIM FOR NO REASON...
KYAHH-♡
KYAHH-♡
CALL ME! JUST ONE PHONE CALL!
...ALRIGHT, I'LL LOOK INTO IT.
BY USING RRIA'S INTELLIGENCE.
AND HER INFORMATION?
I DON'T KNOW.
ONLY THAT HER NAME IS J.
WHAT DO YOU WANT ME TO DO?!
NOW THAT I THINK ABOUT IT, THAT'S PROBABLY ALL SHE KNOWS ABOUT ME.
BEN, WE'RE GOING TO BUY UP EVERY KIND OF AD SPACE IN KOREA!
NEWSPAPER, MAGAZINES, POSTERS,
EVEN BILLBOARDS!

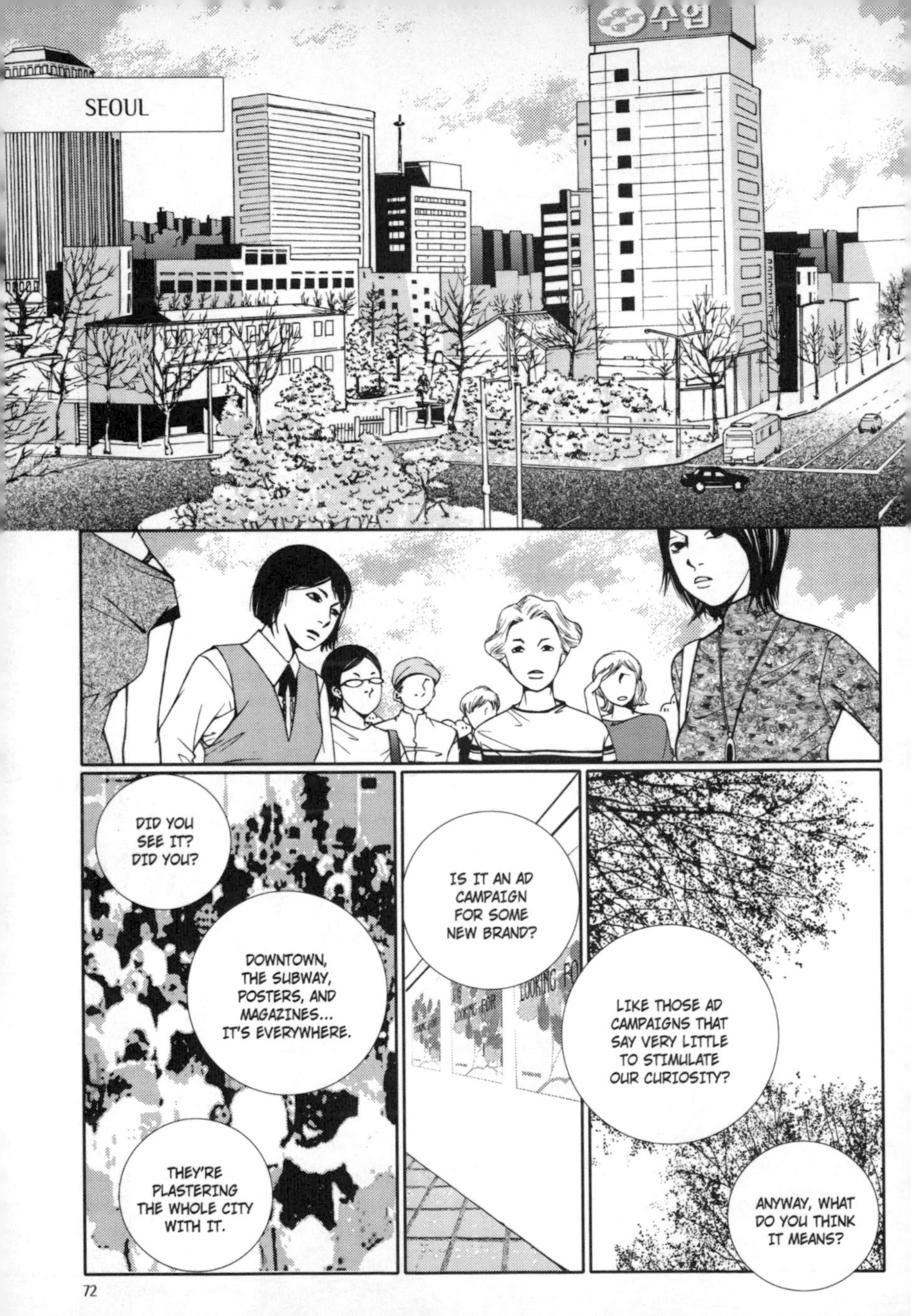
SEOUL
수협
DID YOU SEE IT? DID YOU?
DOWNTOWN, THE SUBWAY, POSTERS, AND MAGAZINES... IT'S EVERYWHERE.
THEY'RE PLASTERING THE WHOLE CITY WITH IT.
IS IT AN AD CAMPAIGN FOR SOME NEW BRAND?
LIKE THOSE AD CAMPAIGNS THAT SAY VERY LITTLE TO STIMULATE OUR CURIOSITY?
ANYWAY, WHAT DO YOU THINK IT MEANS?

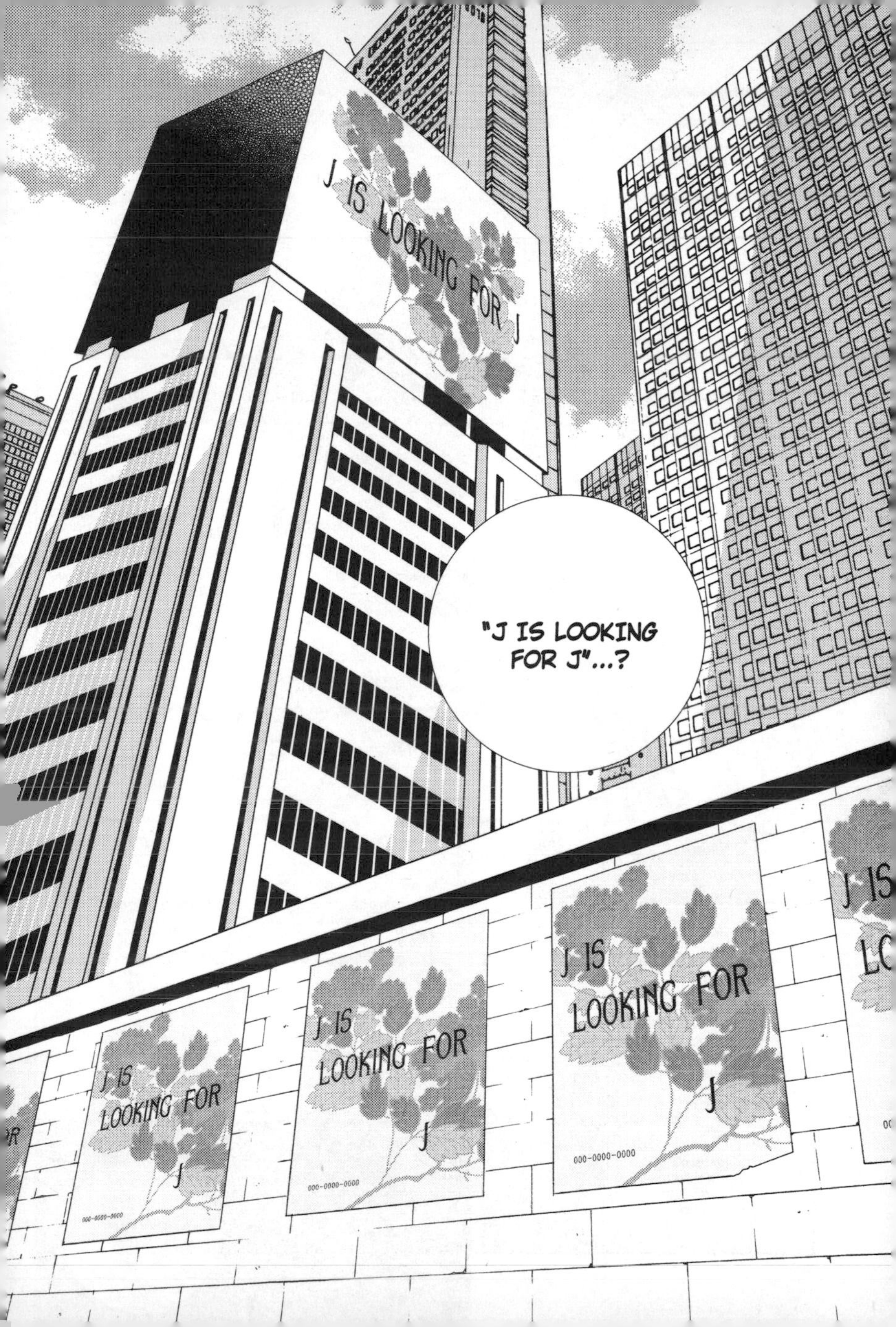
J IS LOOKING FOR J
"J IS LOOKING FOR J"...?
J IS LOOKING FOR J
J IS LOOKING FOR J
000-0000-0000
J IS LOOKING FOR J
000-0000-0000

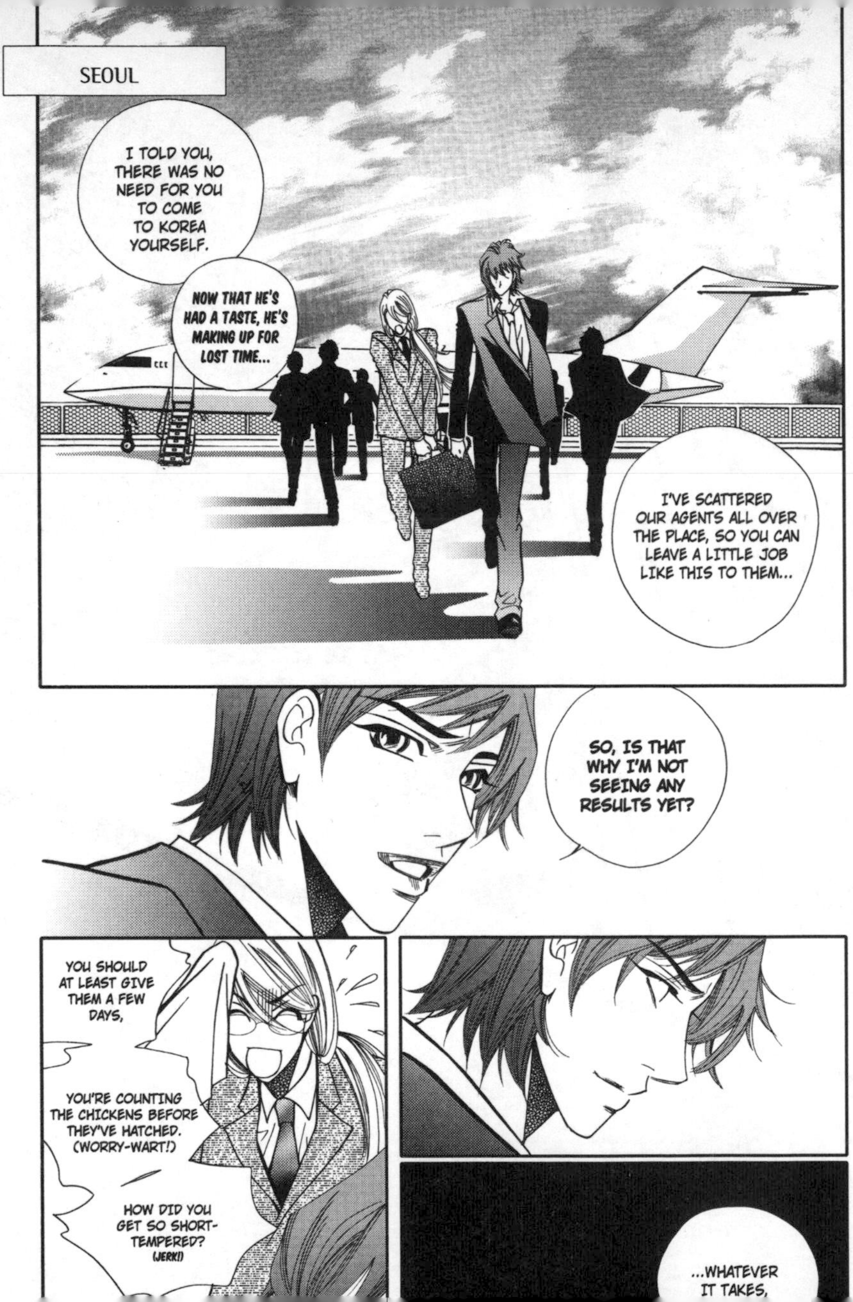
SEOUL
I TOLD YOU, THERE WAS NO NEED FOR YOU TO COME TO KOREA YOURSELF.
NOW THAT HE'S HAD A TASTE, HE'S MAKING UP FOR LOST TIME...
I'VE SCATTERED OUR AGENTS ALL OVER THE PLACE, SO YOU CAN LEAVE A LITTLE JOB LIKE THIS TO THEM...
SO, IS THAT WHY I'M NOT SEEING ANY RESULTS YET?
YOU SHOULD AT LEAST GIVE THEM A FEW DAYS,
YOU'RE COUNTING THE CHICKENS BEFORE THEY'VE HATCHED. (WORRY-WART!)
HOW DID YOU GET SO SHORT-TEMPERED?
(JERK!)
...WHATEVER IT TAKES,

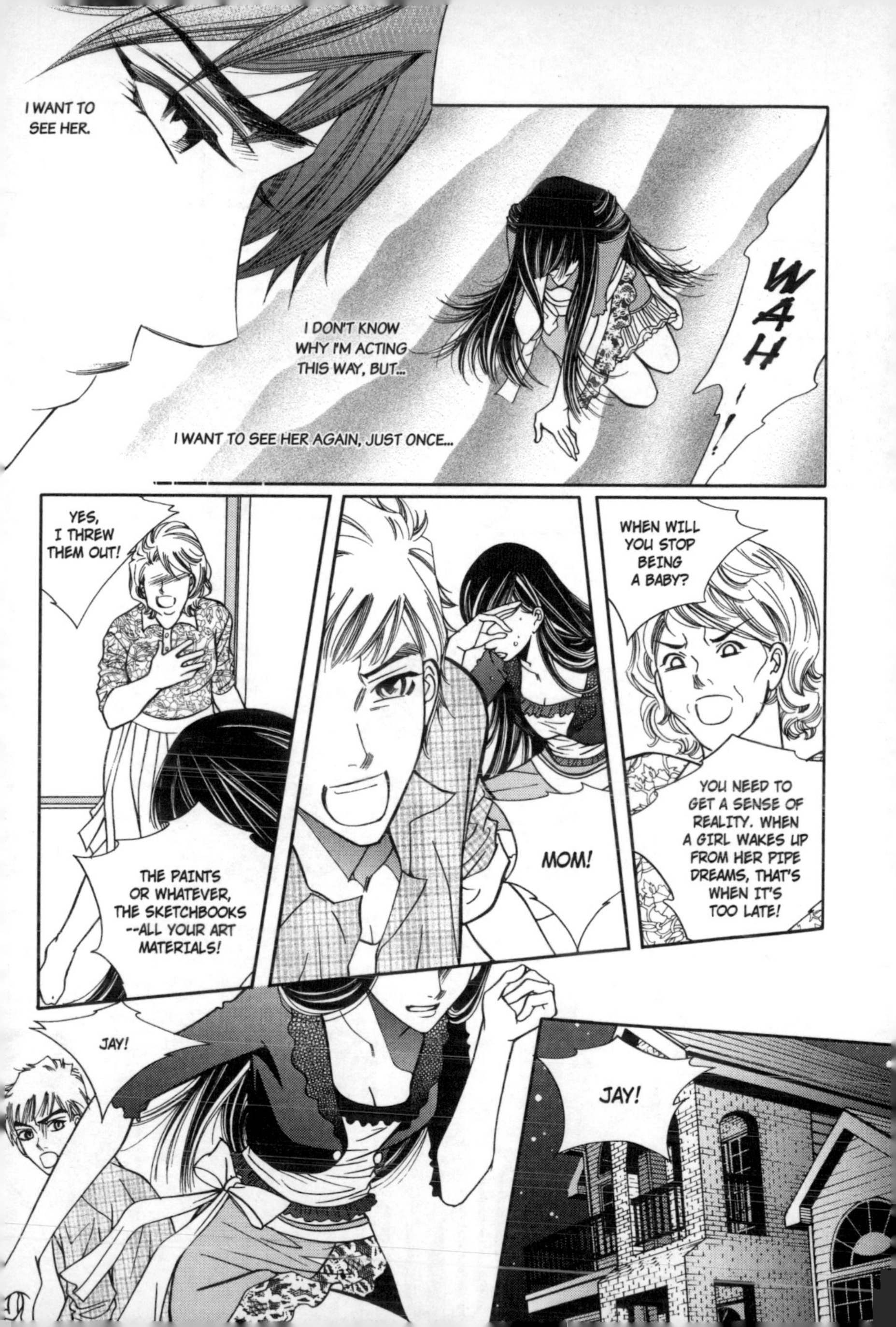
I WANT TO SEE HER.
I DON'T KNOW WHY I'M ACTING THIS WAY, BUT...
I WANT TO SEE HER AGAIN, JUST ONCE...
WAH!!
YES, I THREW THEM OUT!
THE PAINTS OR WHATEVER, THE SKETCHBOOKS --ALL YOUR ART MATERIALS!
MOM!
WHEN WILL YOU STOP BEING A BABY?
YOU NEED TO GET A SENSE OF REALITY. WHEN A GIRL WAKES UP FROM HER PIPE DREAMS, THAT'S WHEN IT'S TOO LATE!
JAY!
JAY!

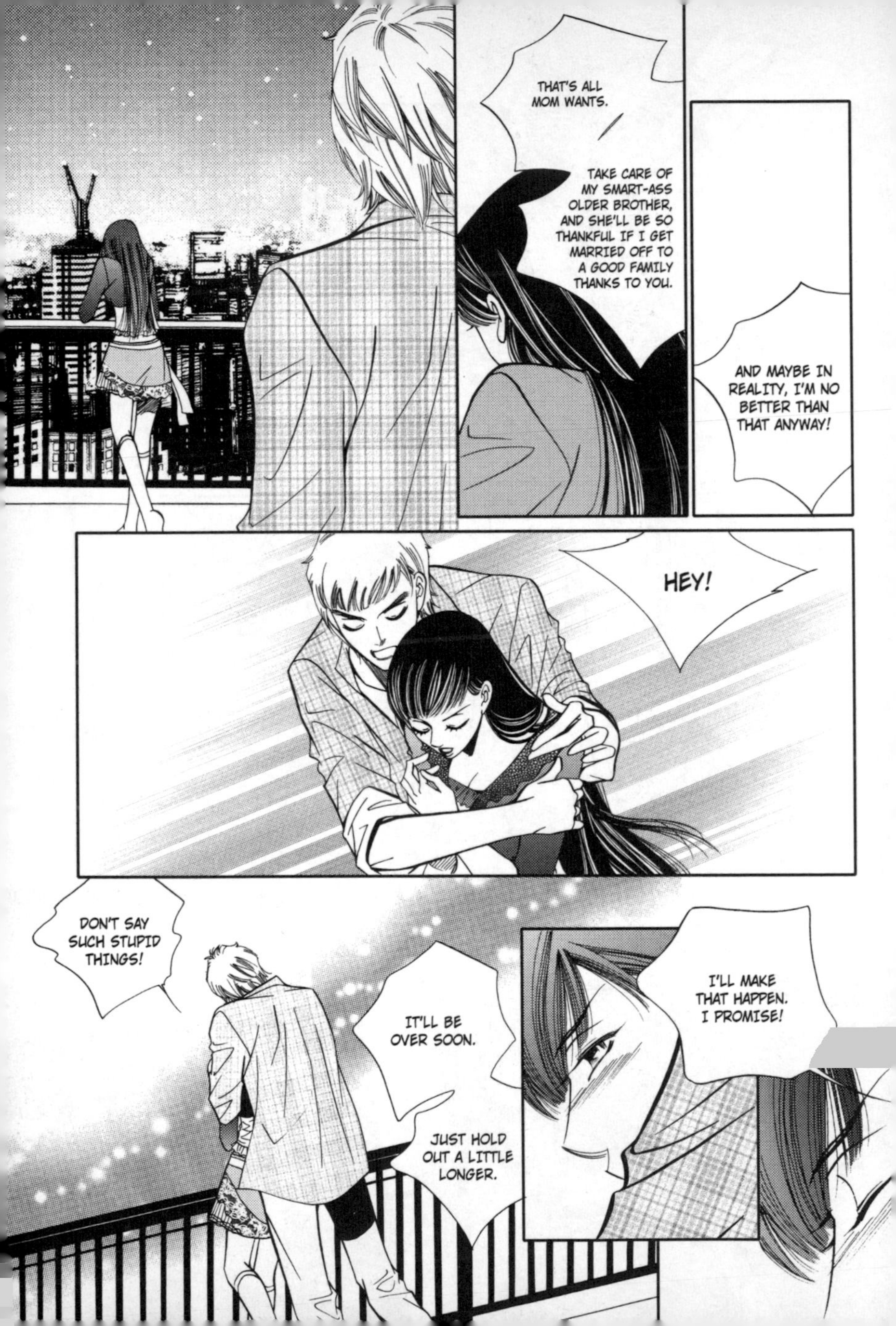
THAT'S ALL MOM WANTS.
TAKE CARE OF MY SMART-ASS OLDER BROTHER, AND SHE'LL BE SO THANKFUL IF I GET MARRIED OFF TO A GOOD FAMILY THANKS TO YOU.
AND MAYBE IN REALITY, I'M NO BETTER THAN THAT ANYWAY!
HEY!
DON'T SAY SUCH STUPID THINGS!
IT'LL BE OVER SOON.
JUST HOLD OUT A LITTLE LONGER.
I'LL MAKE THAT HAPPEN. I PROMISE!

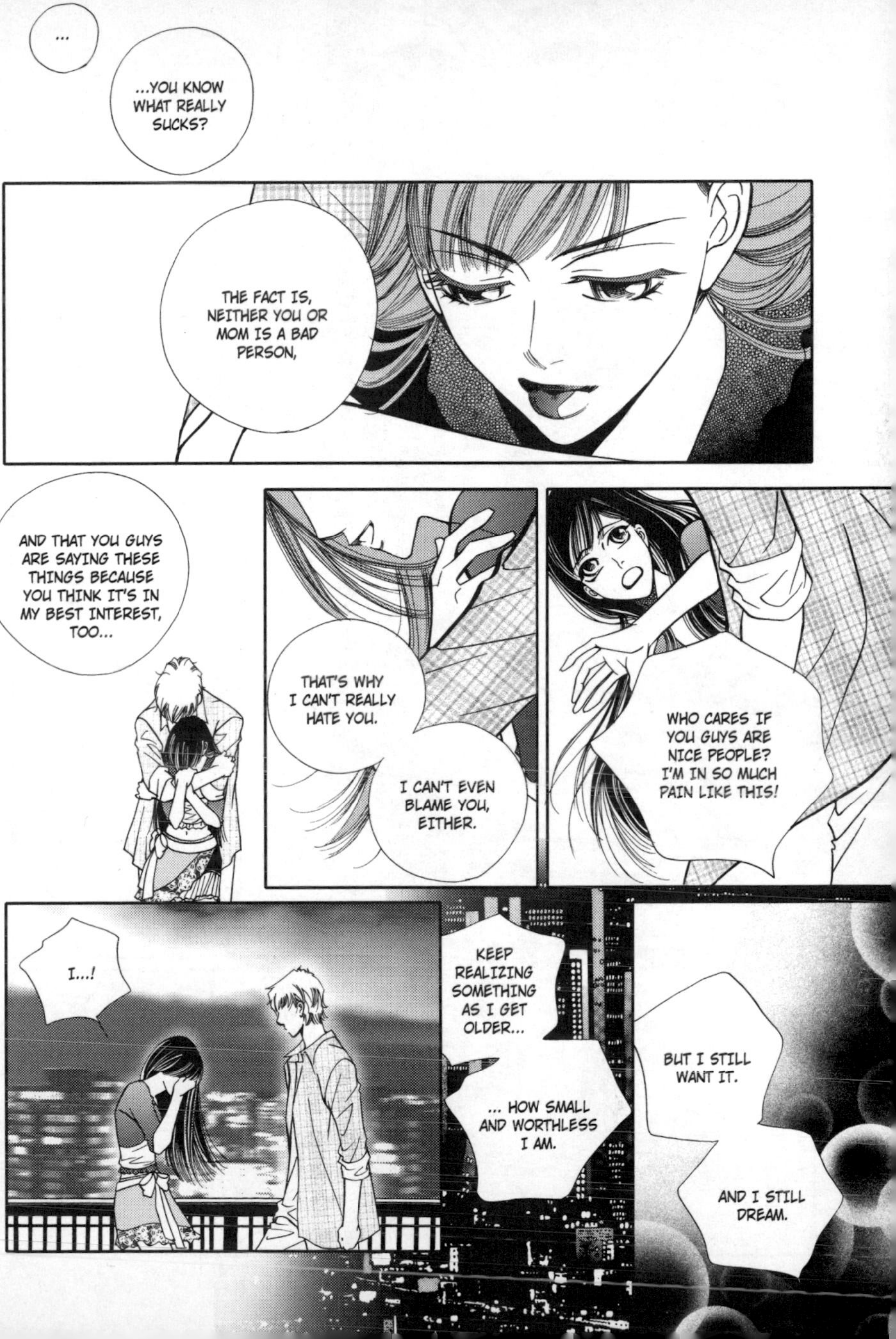
...
...YOU KNOW WHAT REALLY SUCKS?
THE FACT IS, NEITHER YOU OR MOM IS A BAD PERSON,
AND THAT YOU GUYS ARE SAYING THESE THINGS BECAUSE YOU THINK IT'S IN MY BEST INTEREST, TOO...
THAT'S WHY I CAN'T REALLY HATE YOU.
I CAN'T EVEN BLAME YOU, EITHER.
WHO CARES IF YOU GUYS ARE NICE PEOPLE? I'M IN SO MUCH PAIN LIKE THIS!
I...!
KEEP REALIZING SOMETHING AS I GET OLDER...
... HOW SMALL AND WORTHLESS I AM.
BUT I STILL WANT IT.
AND I STILL DREAM.

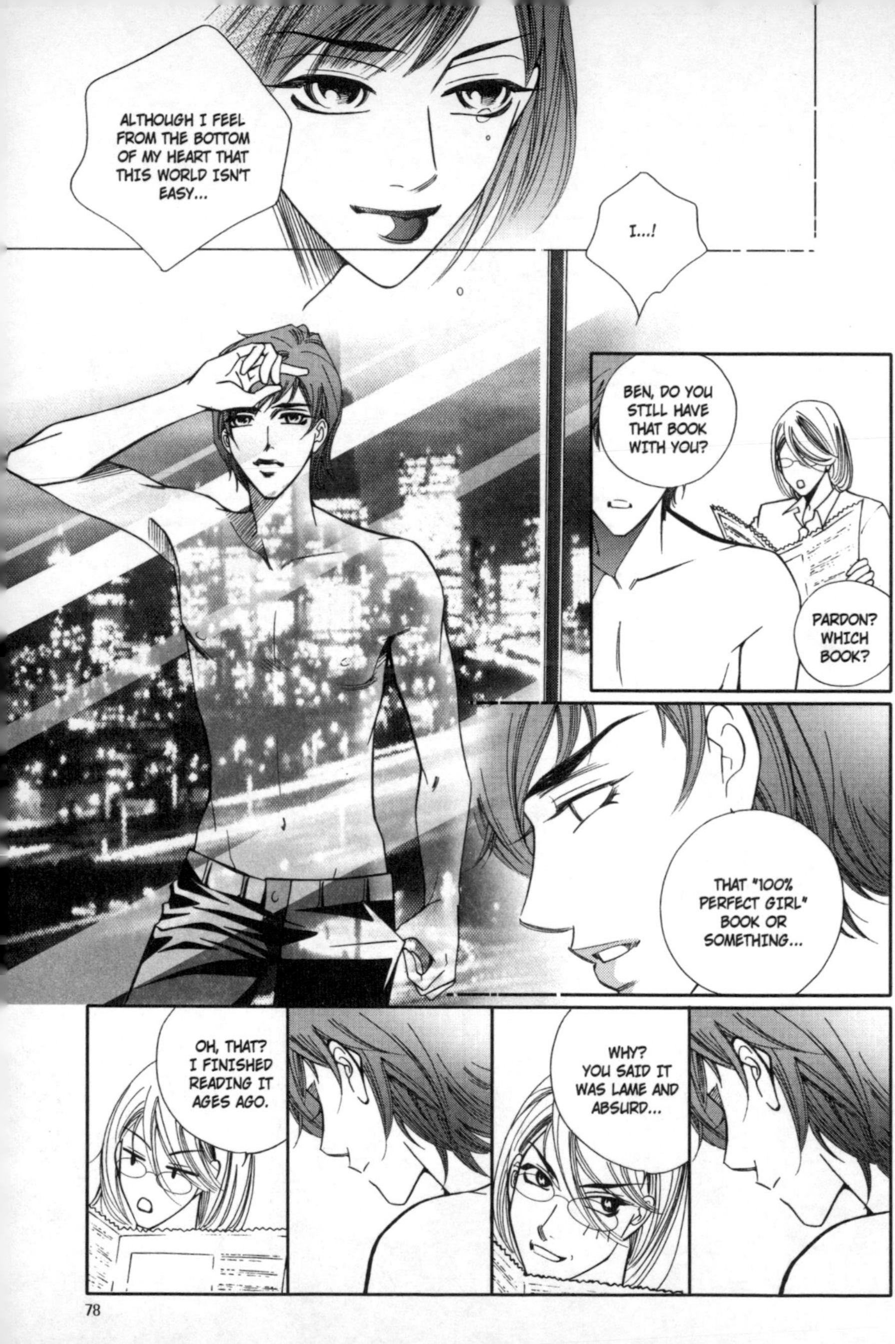
ALTHOUGH I FEEL FROM THE BOTTOM OF MY HEART THAT THIS WORLD ISN'T EASY...
I...!
BEN, DO YOU STILL HAVE THAT BOOK WITH YOU?
PARDON? WHICH BOOK?
THAT "100% PERFECT GIRL" BOOK OR SOMETHING...
OH, THAT? I FINISHED READING IT AGES AGO.
WHY? YOU SAID IT WAS LAME AND ABSURD...

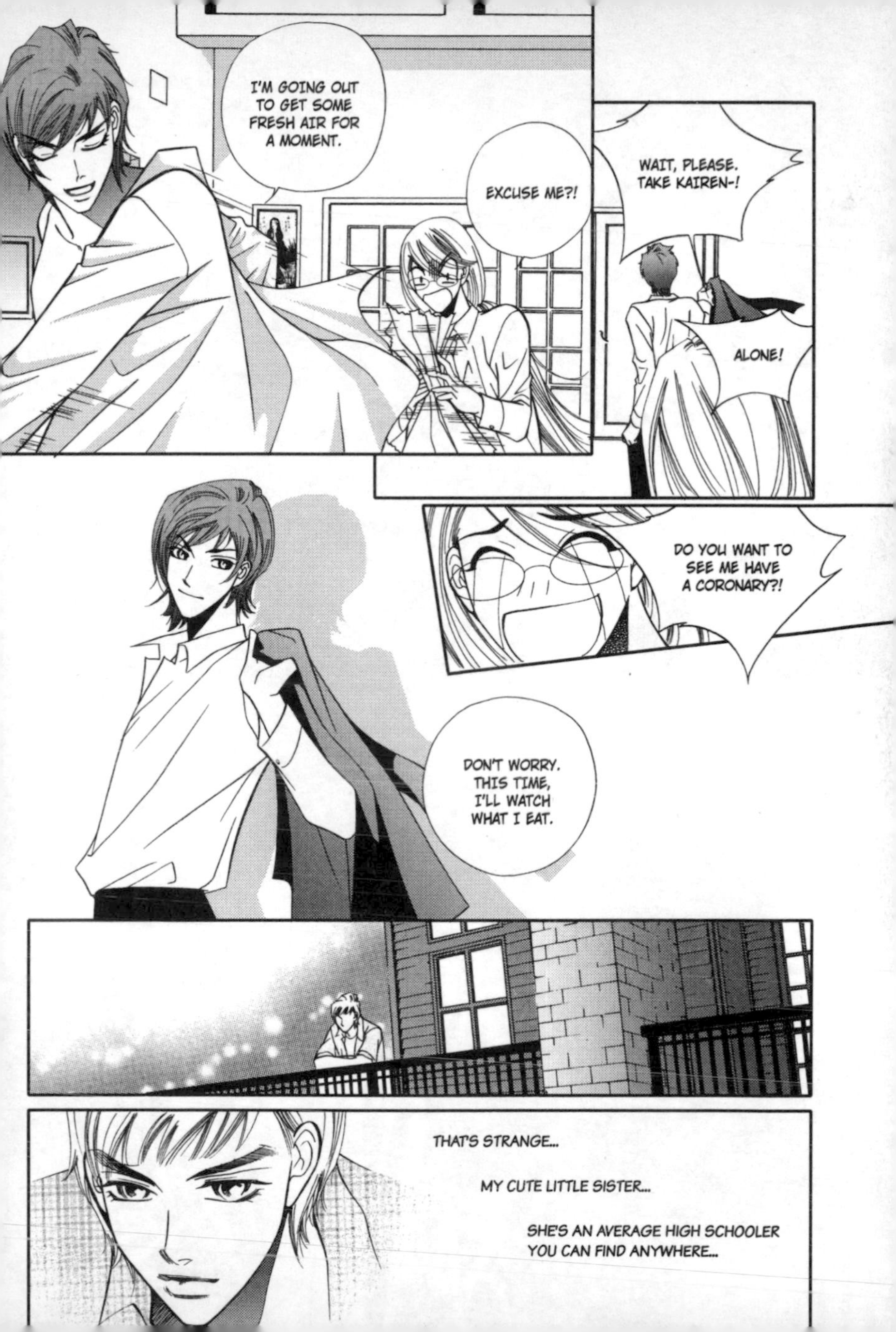
I'M GOING OUT TO GET SOME FRESH AIR FOR A MOMENT.
EXCUSE ME?!
WAIT, PLEASE. TAKE KAIREN-!
ALONE!
DON'T WORRY. THIS TIME, I'LL WATCH WHAT I EAT.
DO YOU WANT TO SEE ME HAVE A CORONARY?!
THAT'S STRANGE...
MY CUTE LITTLE SISTER...
SHE'S AN AVERAGE HIGH SCHOOLER YOU CAN FIND ANYWHERE...

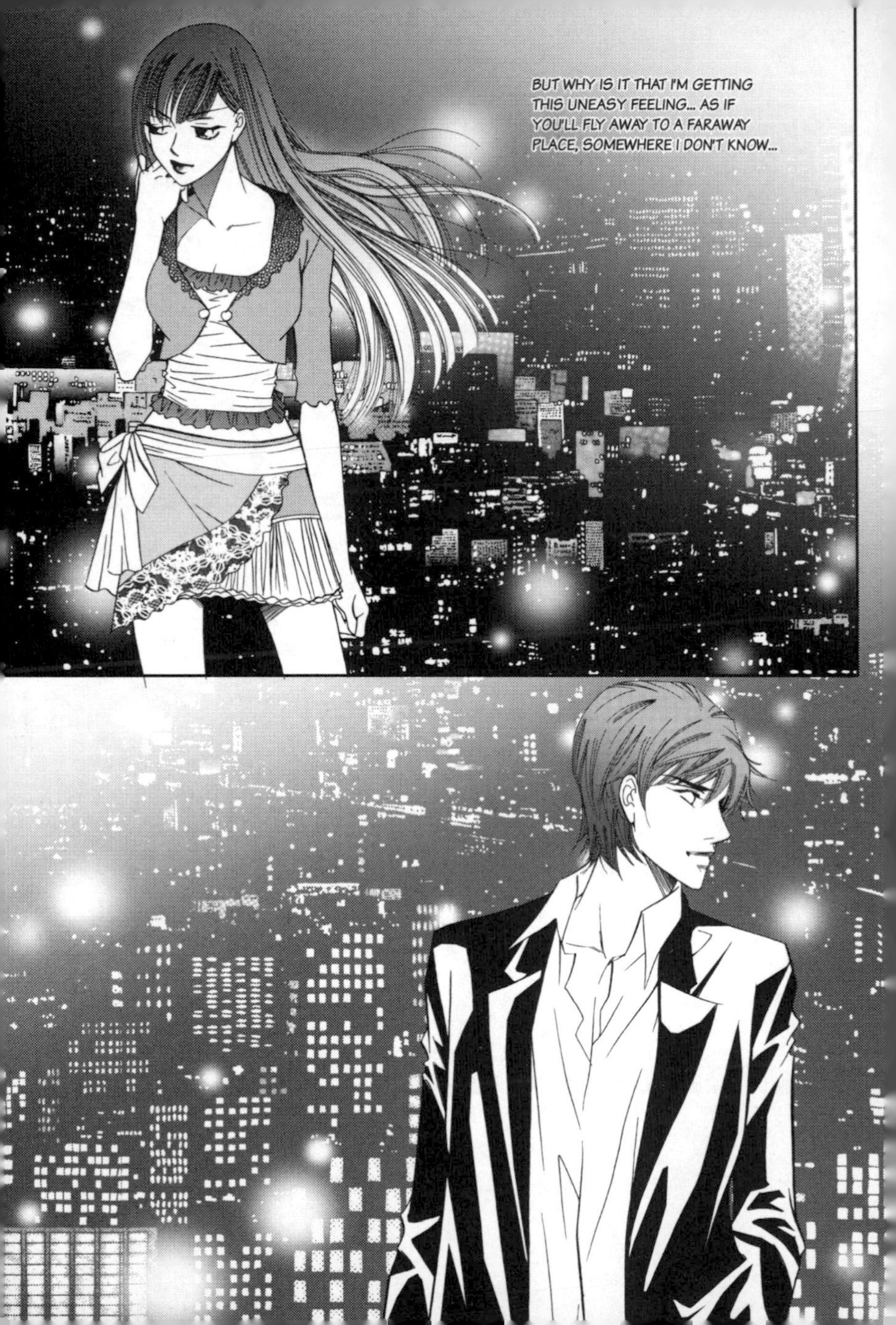
BUT WHY IS IT THAT I'M GETTING THIS UNEASY FEELING... AS IF YOU'LL FLY AWAY TO A FARAWAY PLACE, SOMEWHERE I DON'T KNOW...

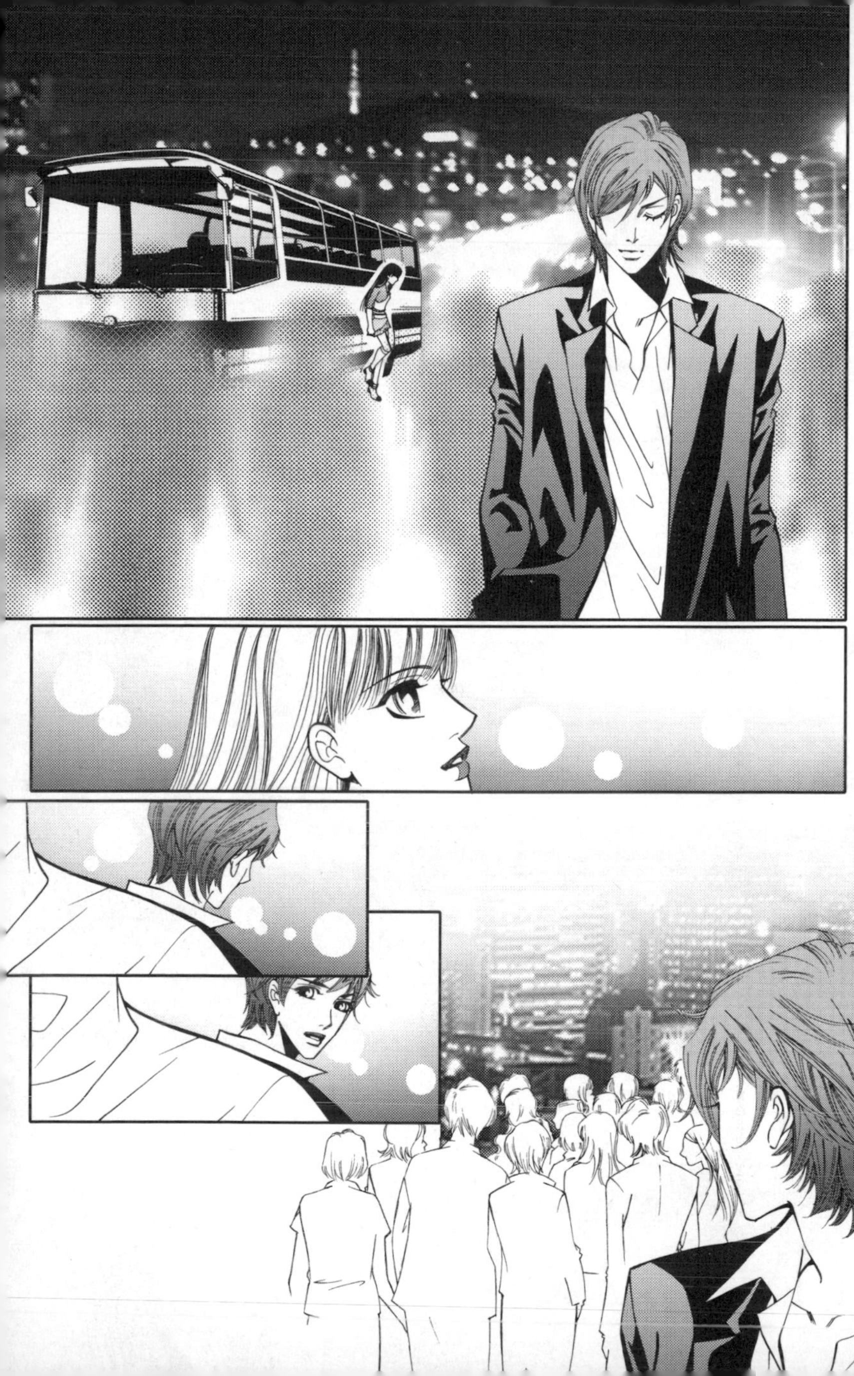

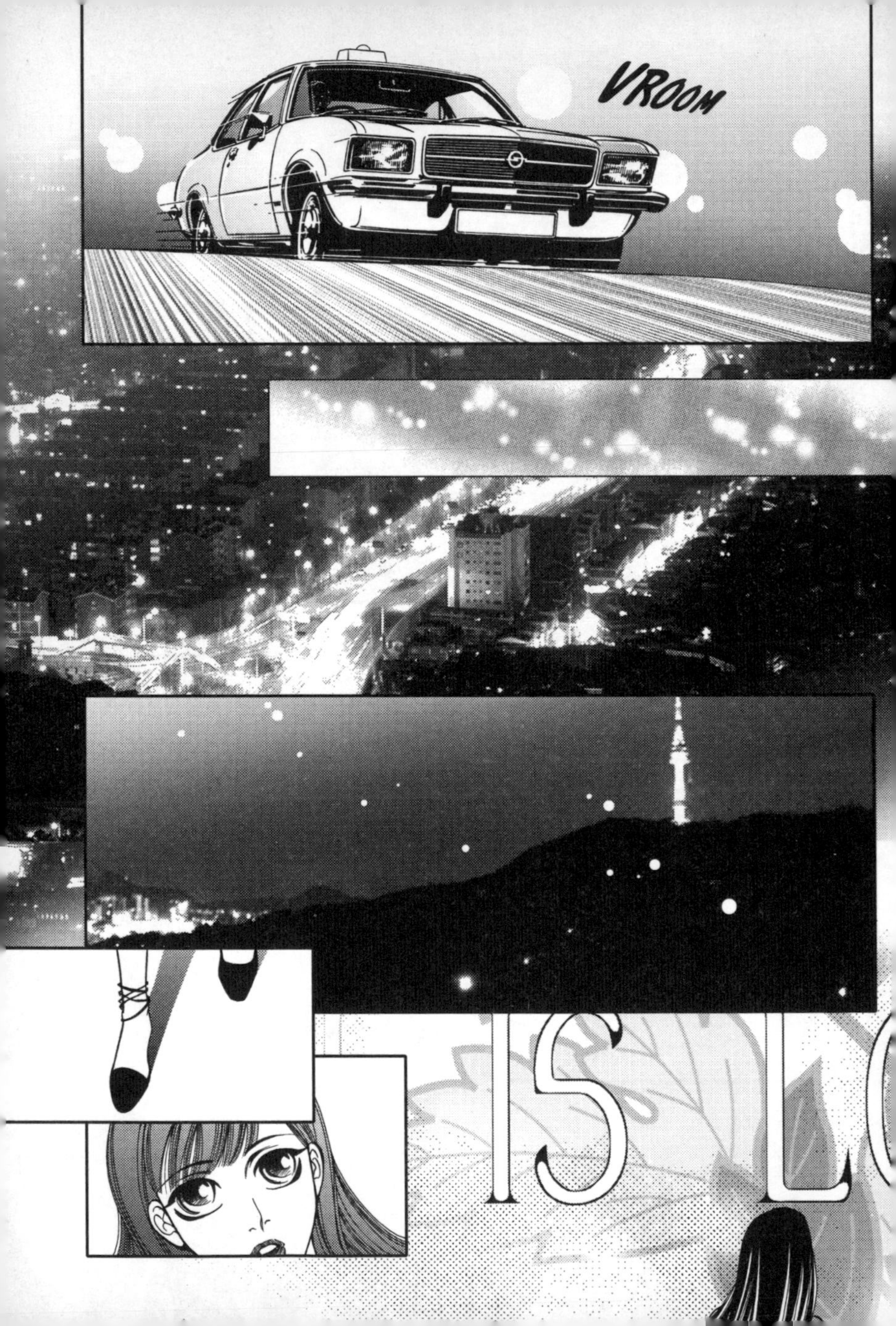
VROOM

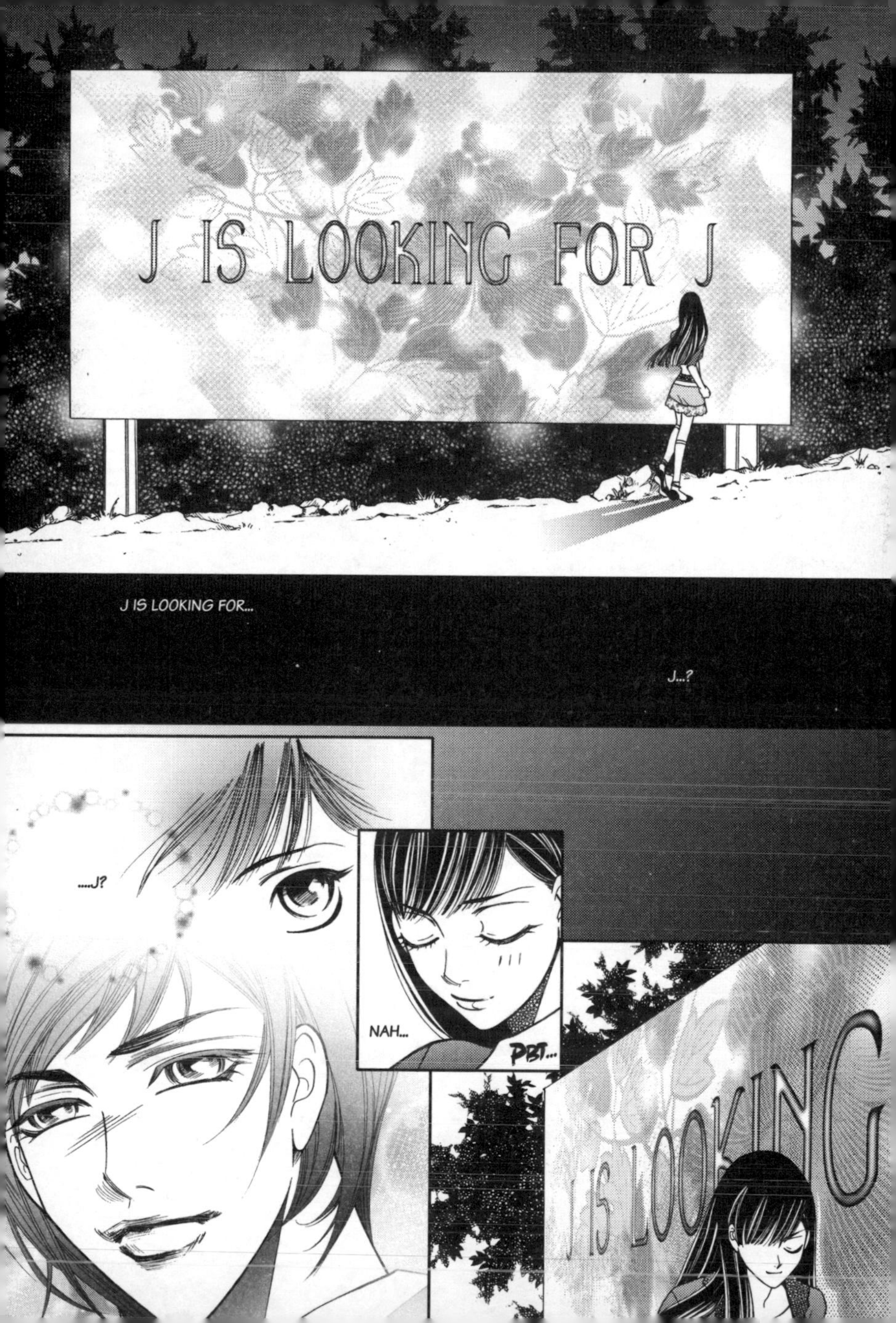

J IS LOOKING FOR J
J IS LOOKING FOR...
J...?
....J?
NAH...
PBT...
J IS LOOKING

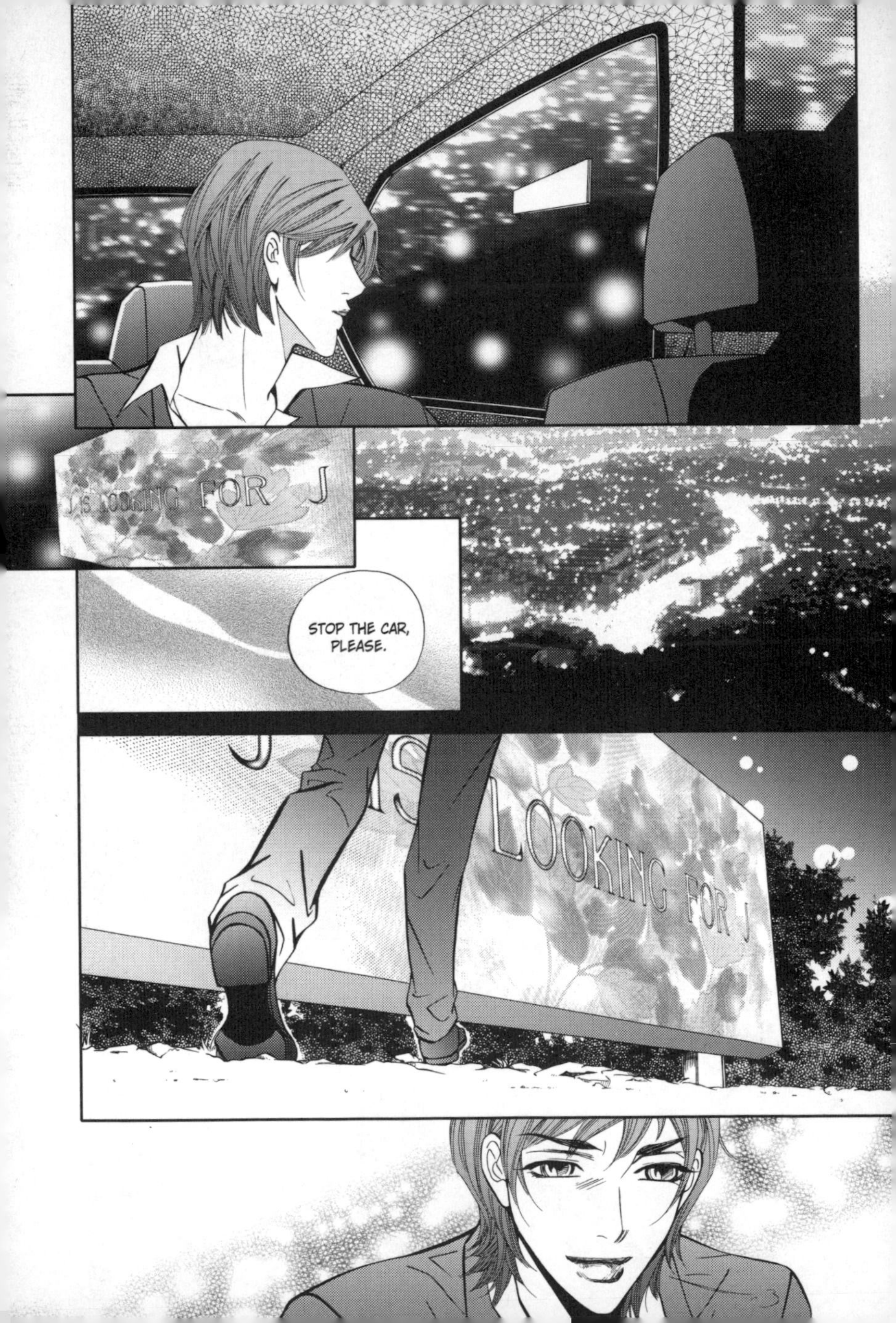
J IS LOOKING FOR J
STOP THE CAR, PLEASE.
LOOKING FOR J

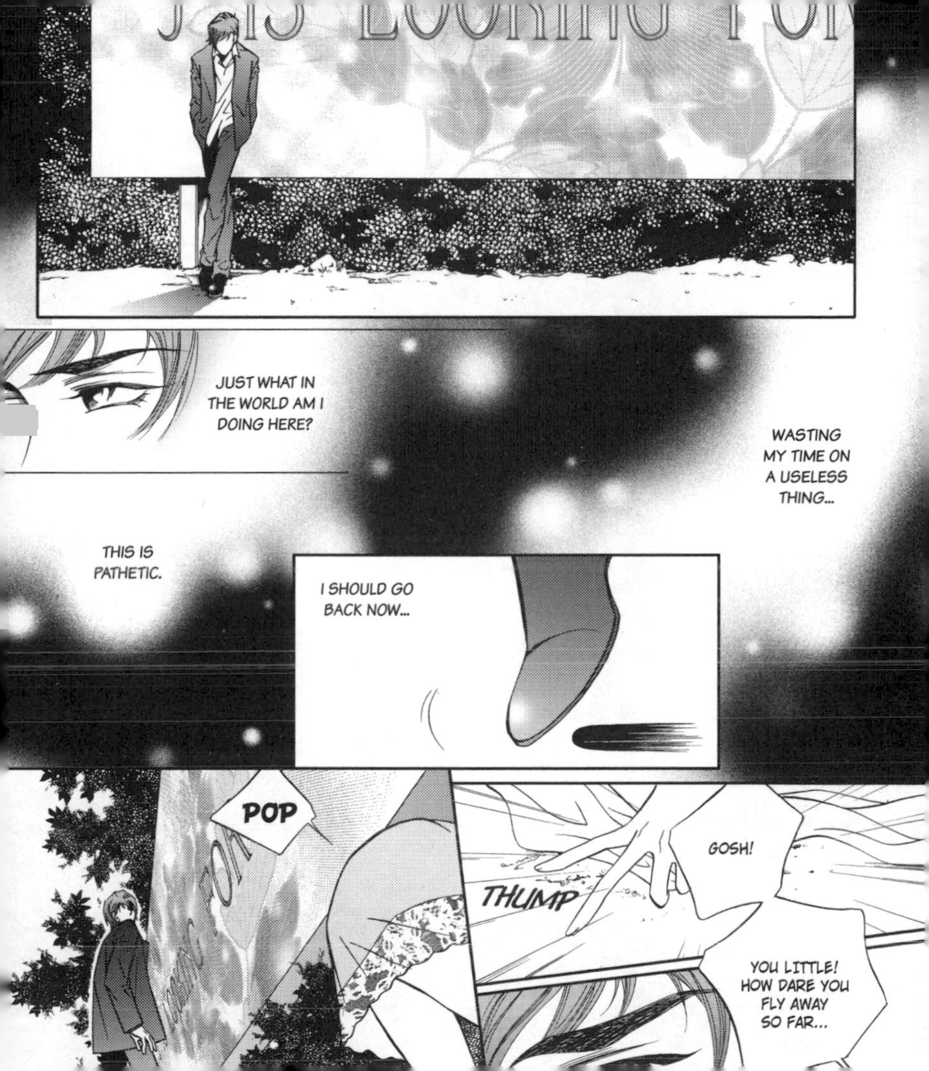

JUST WHAT IN THE WORLD AM I DOING HERE?
WASTING MY TIME ON A USELESS THING...
THIS IS PATHETIC.
I SHOULD GO BACK NOW...
POP
THUMP
GOSH!
YOU LITTLE! HOW DARE YOU FLY AWAY SO FAR...

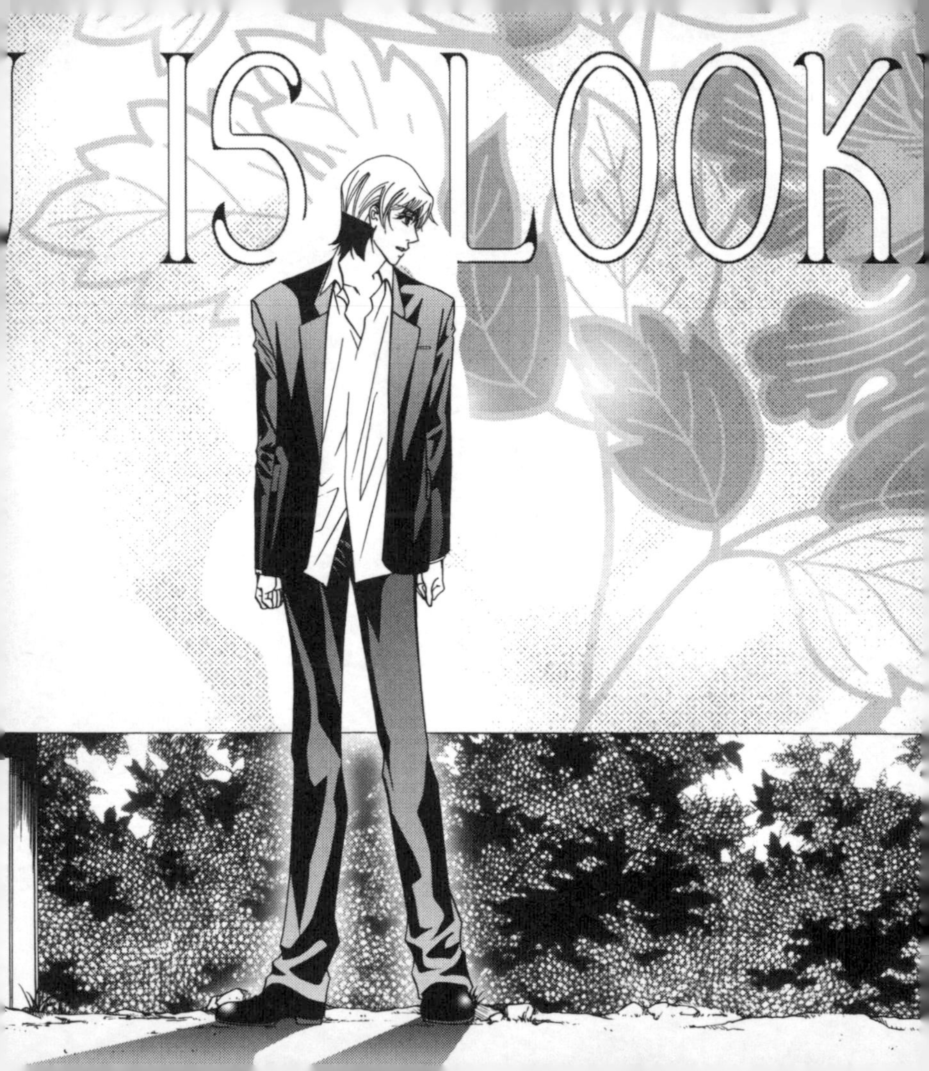
IS LOOK

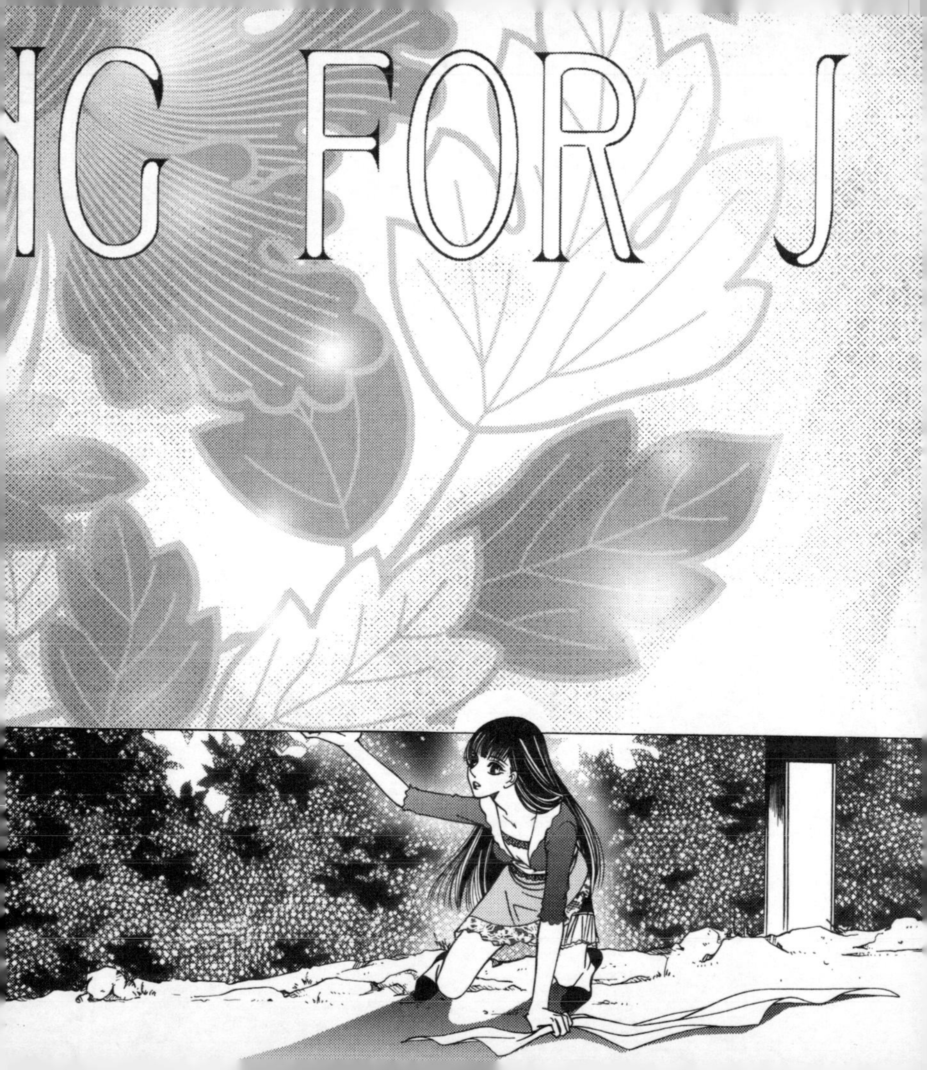
G FOR J

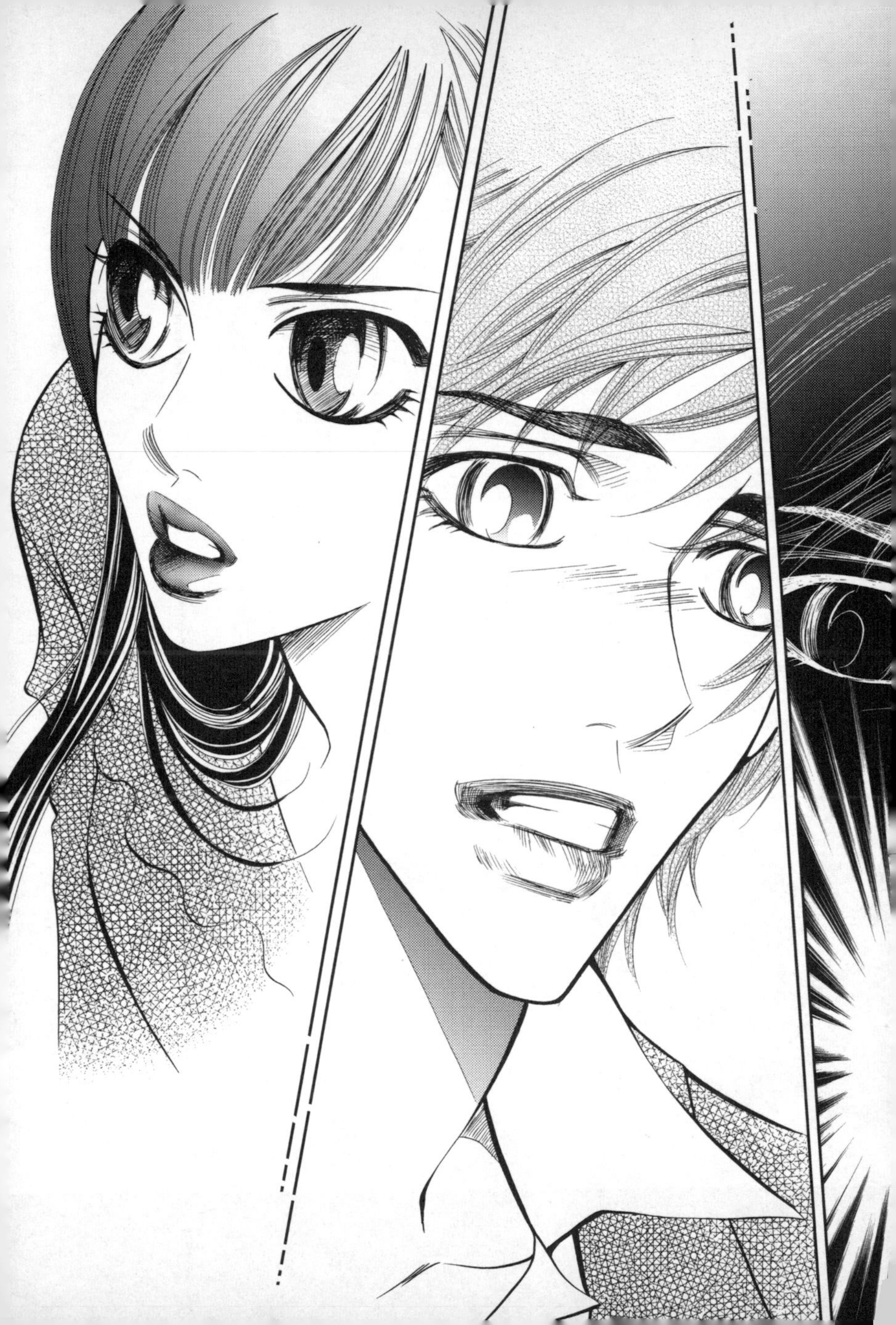

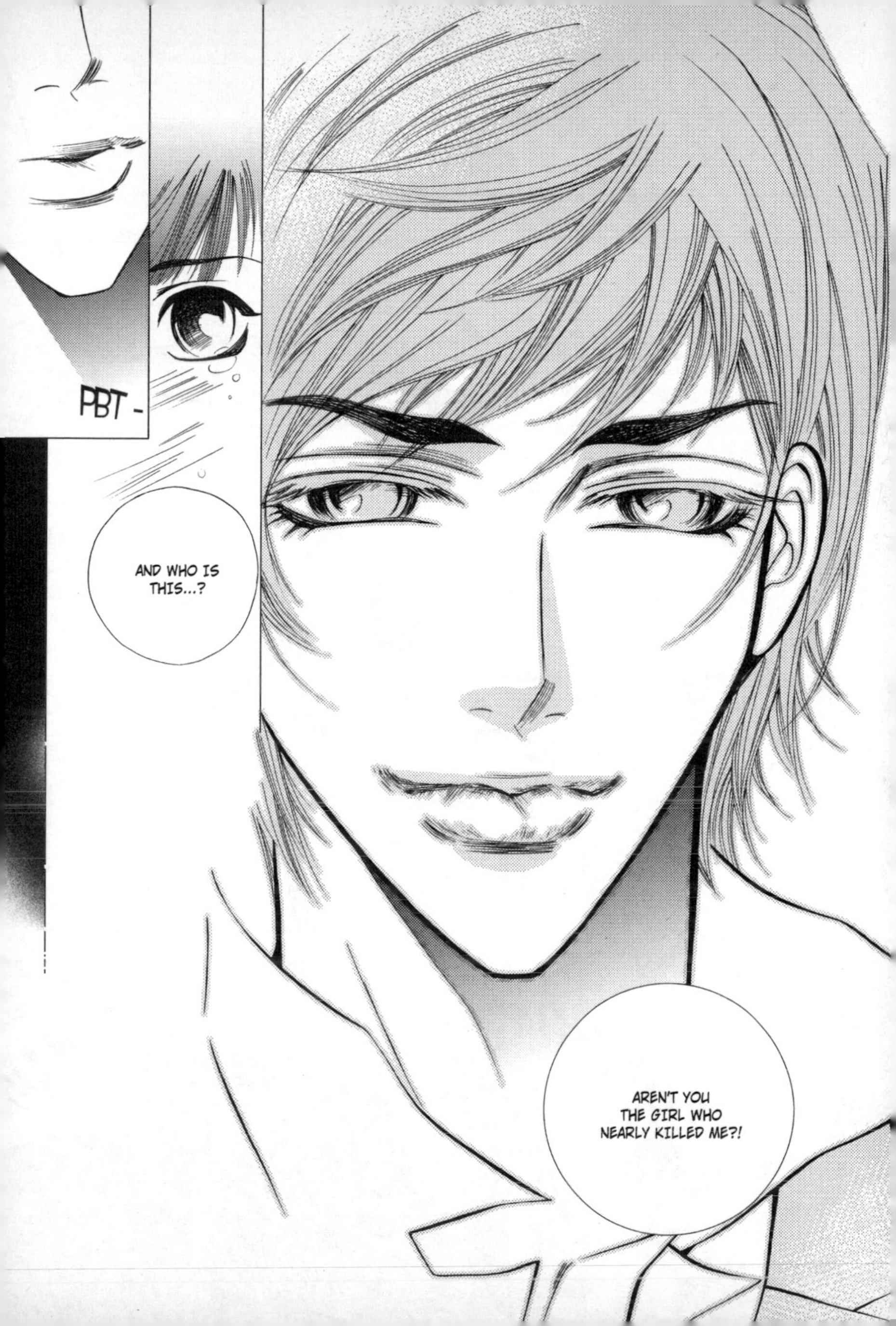
PBT -
AND WHO IS THIS...?
AREN'T YOU THE GIRL WHO NEARLY KILLED ME?!

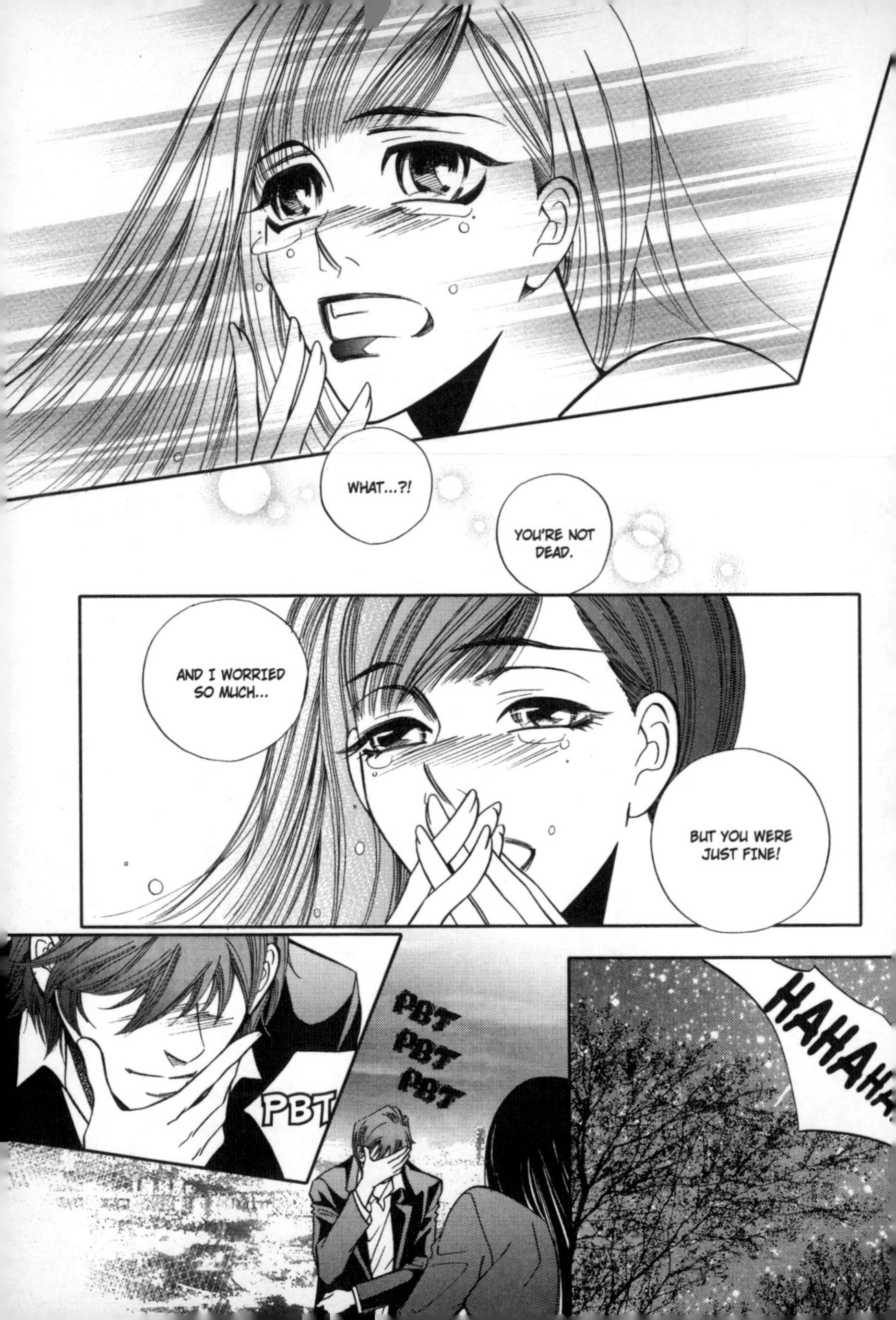
WHAT...?!
YOU'RE NOT DEAD.
AND I WORRIED SO MUCH...
BUT YOU WERE JUST FINE!
PBT
PBT
PBT
PBT
HAHAHA

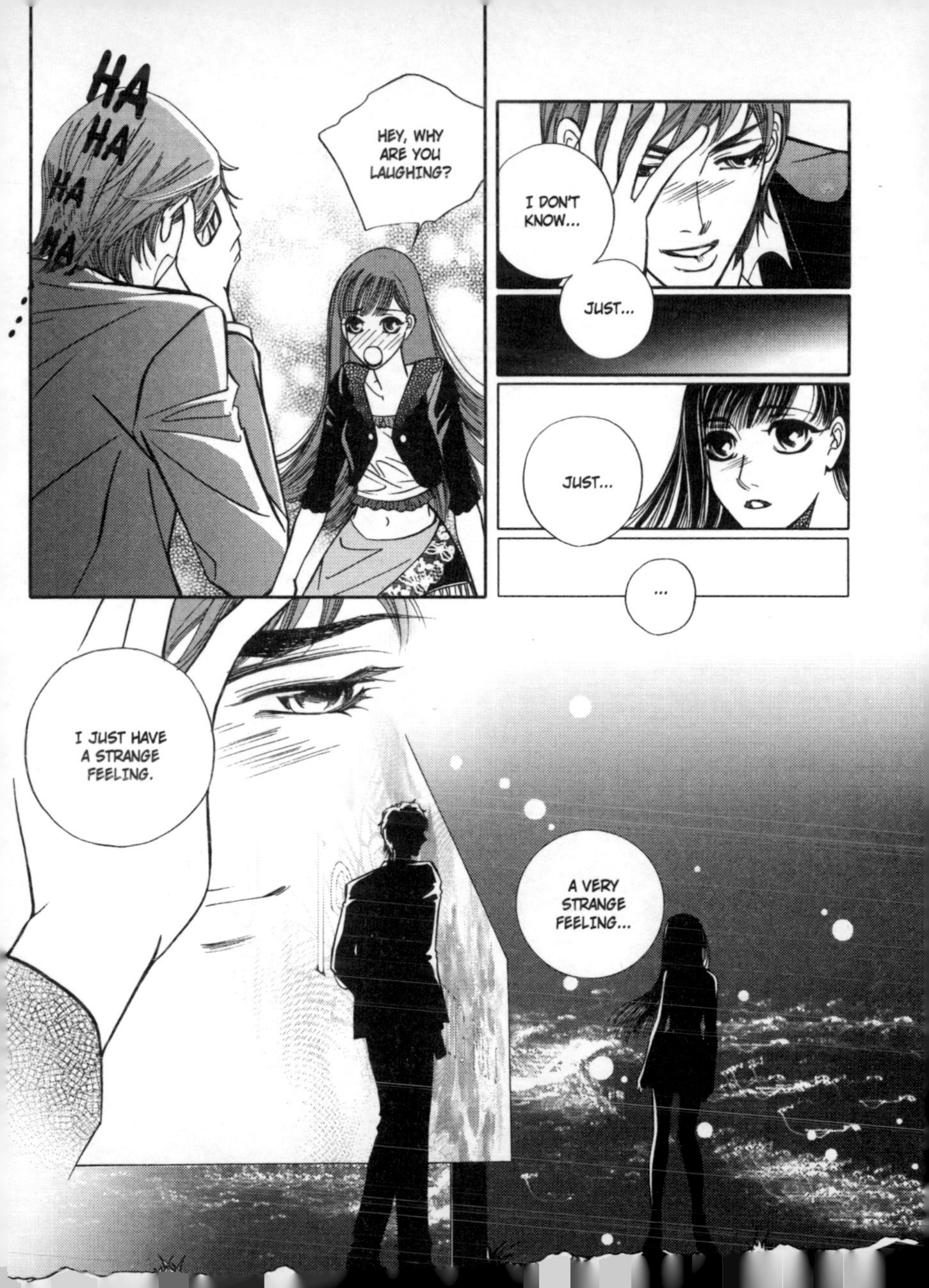
HA HA HA HA
HEY, WHY ARE YOU LAUGHING?
I DON'T KNOW...
JUST...
JUST...
...
I JUST HAVE A STRANGE FEELING.
A VERY STRANGE FEELING...

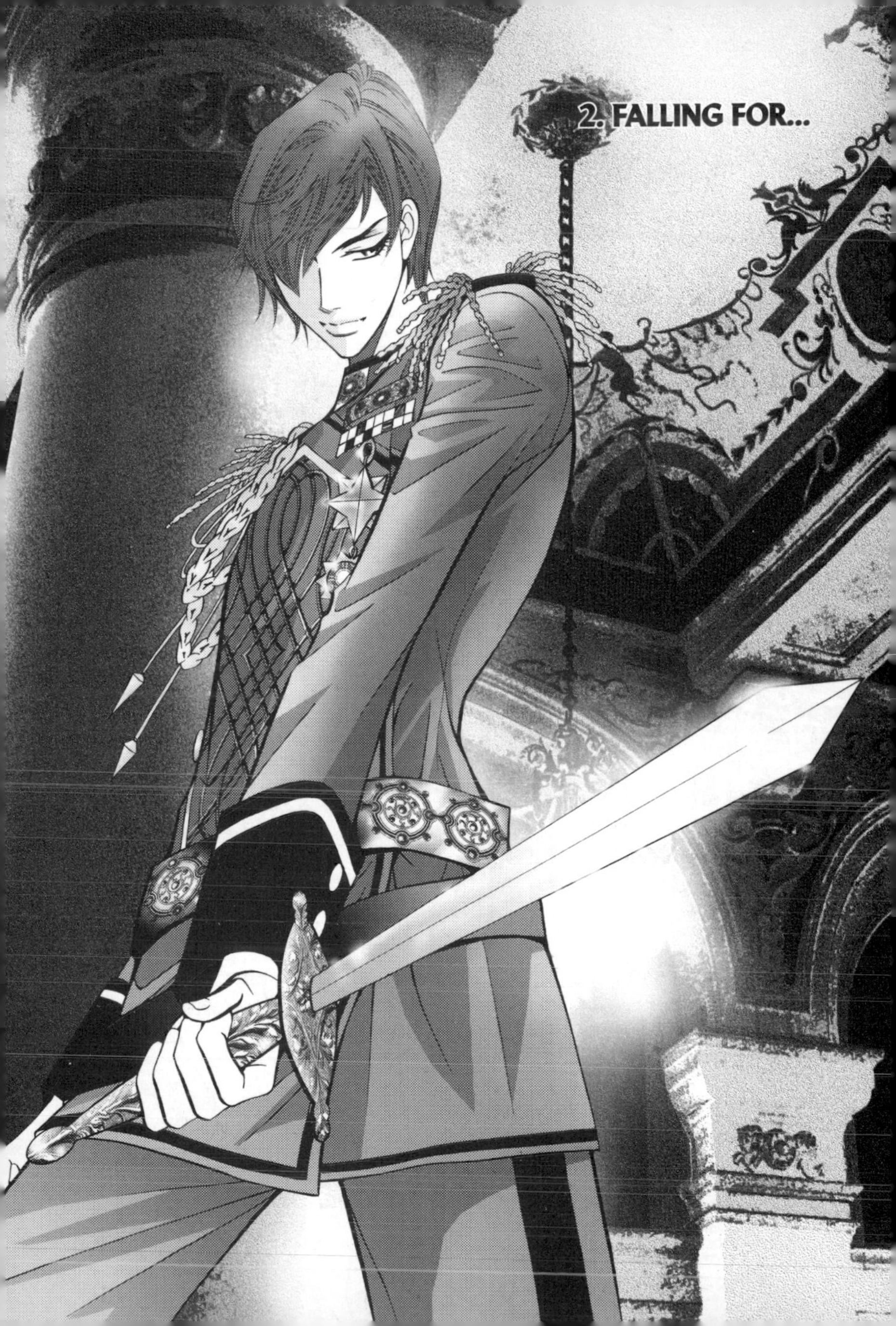
2. FALLING FOR...

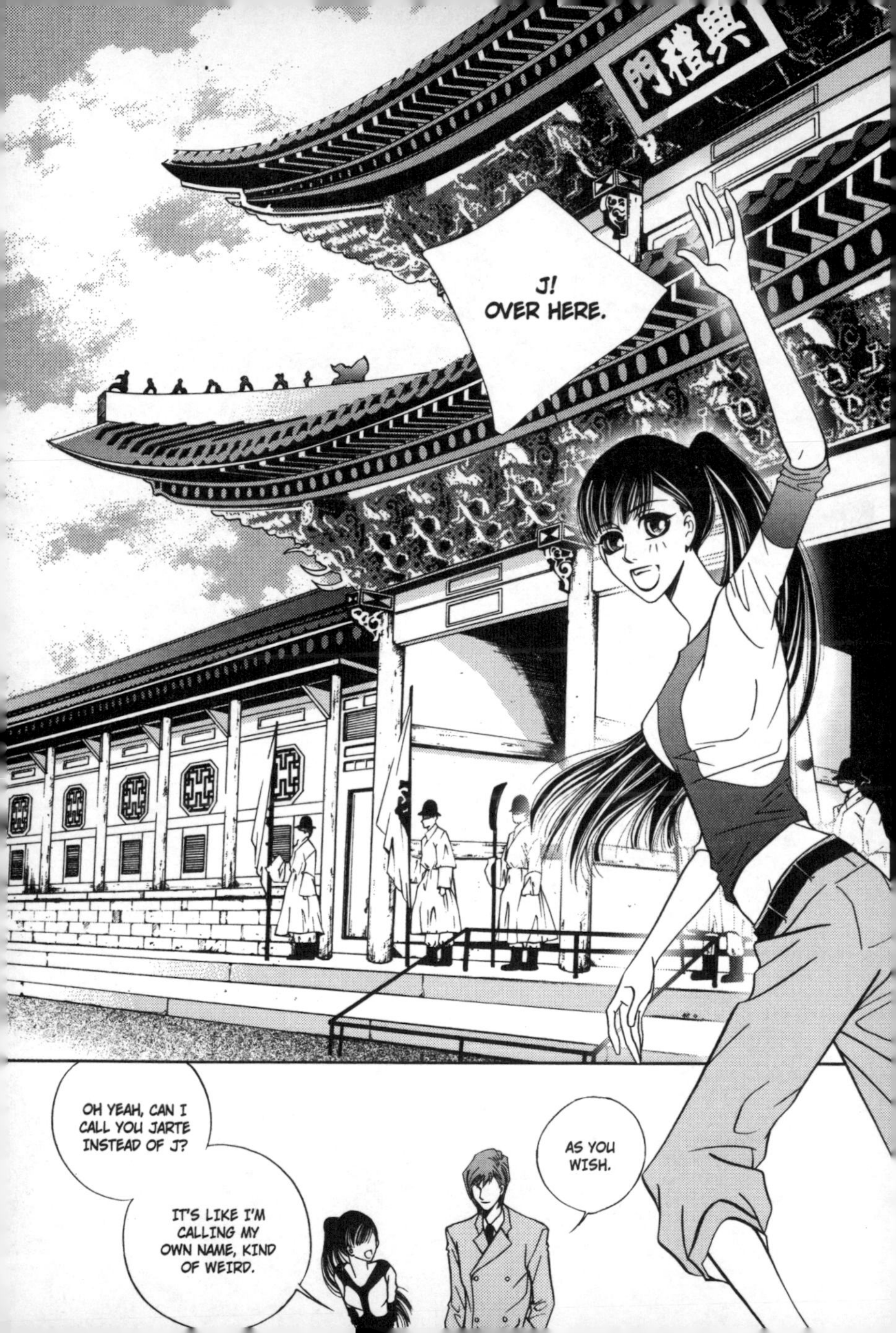
興禮門
J! OVER HERE.
OH YEAH, CAN I CALL YOU JARTE INSTEAD OF J?
IT'S LIKE I'M CALLING MY OWN NAME, KIND OF WEIRD.
AS YOU WISH.

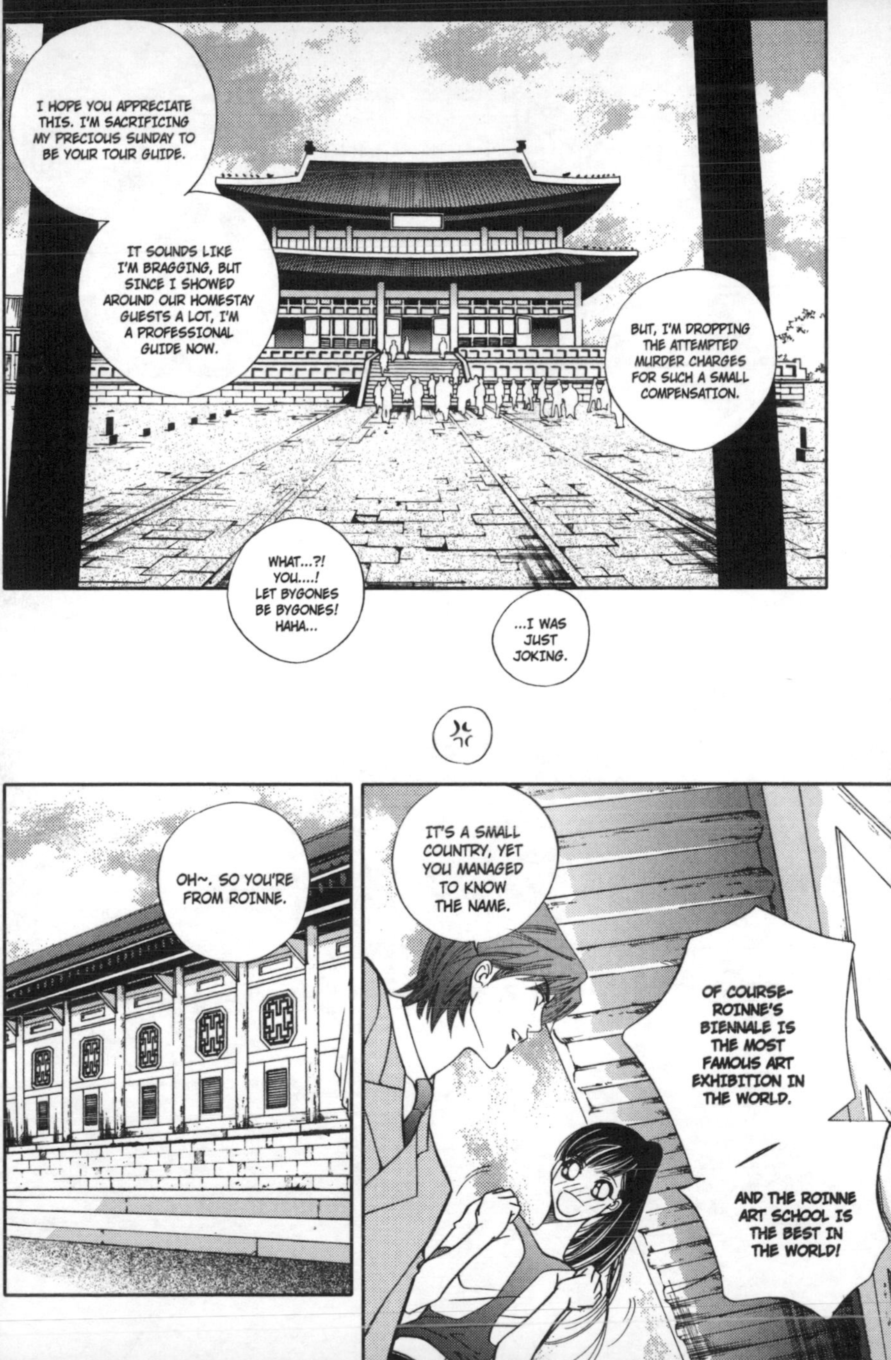
I HOPE YOU APPRECIATE THIS. I'M SACRIFICING MY PRECIOUS SUNDAY TO BE YOUR TOUR GUIDE.
IT SOUNDS LIKE I'M BRAGGING, BUT SINCE I SHOWED AROUND OUR HOMESTAY GUESTS A LOT, I'M A PROFESSIONAL GUIDE NOW.
BUT, I'M DROPPING THE ATTEMPTED MURDER CHARGES FOR SUCH A SMALL COMPENSATION.
WHAT...?! YOU....! LET BYGONES BE BYGONES! HAHA...
...I WAS JUST JOKING.
OH~. SO YOU'RE FROM ROINNE.
IT'S A SMALL COUNTRY, YET YOU MANAGED TO KNOW THE NAME.
OF COURSE- ROINNE'S BIENNALE IS THE MOST FAMOUS ART EXHIBITION IN THE WORLD.
AND THE ROINNE ART SCHOOL IS THE BEST IN THE WORLD!

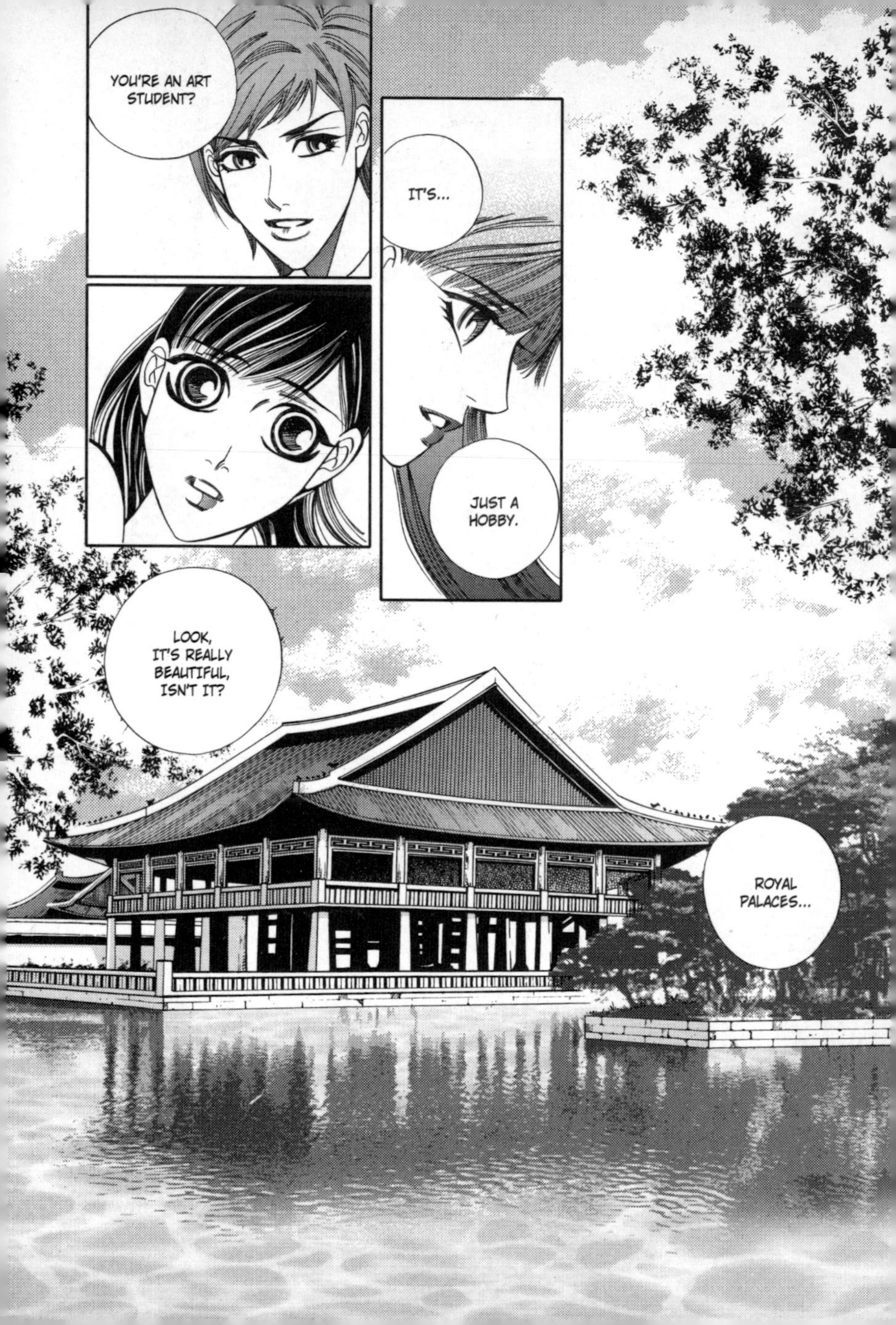
YOU'RE AN ART STUDENT?
IT'S...
JUST A HOBBY.
LOOK, IT'S REALLY BEAUTIFUL, ISN'T IT?
ROYAL PALACES...

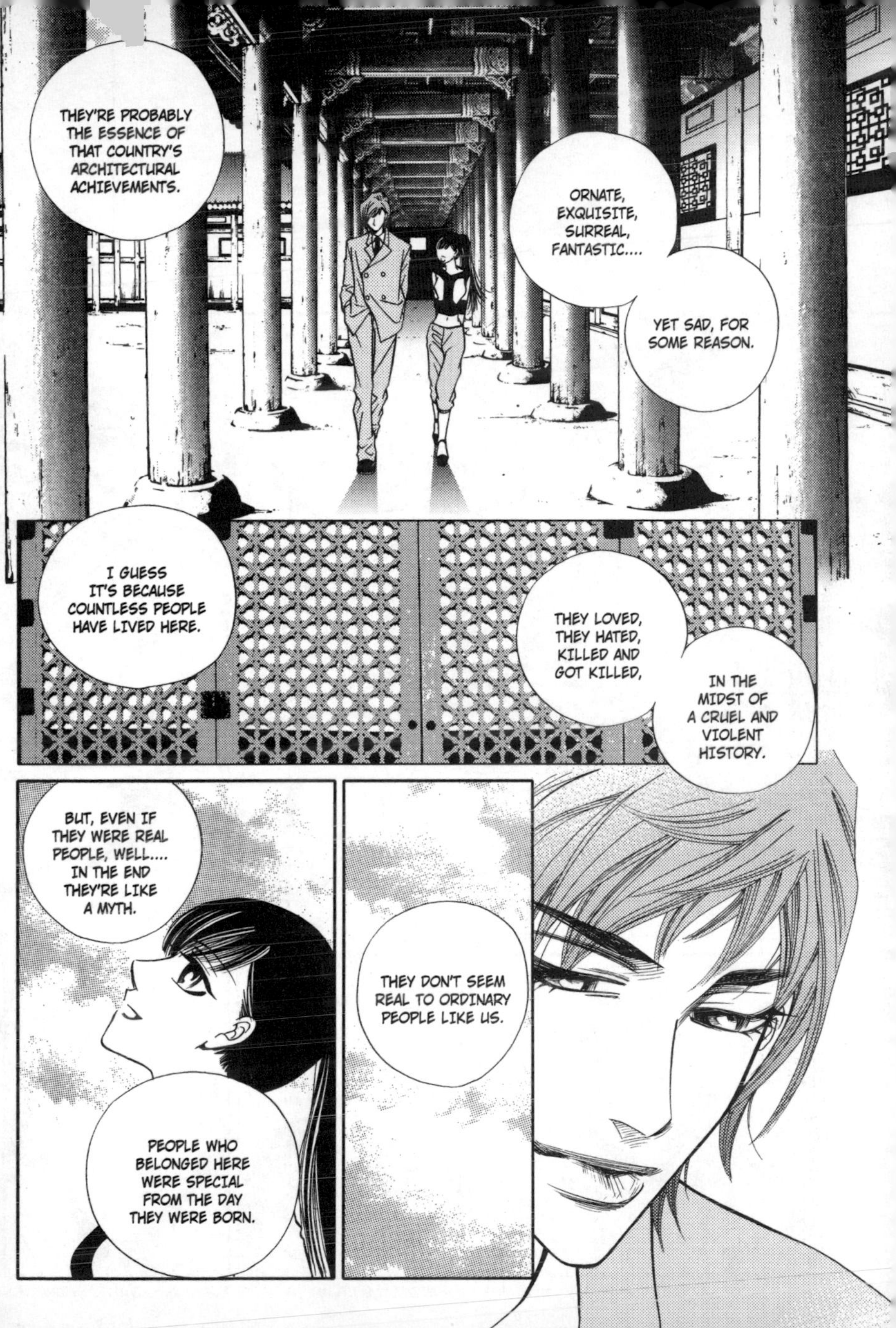
THEY'RE PROBABLY THE ESSENCE OF THAT COUNTRY'S ARCHITECTURAL ACHIEVEMENTS.
ORNATE, EXQUISITE, SURREAL, FANTASTIC....
YET SAD, FOR SOME REASON.
I GUESS IT'S BECAUSE COUNTLESS PEOPLE HAVE LIVED HERE.
THEY LOVED, THEY HATED, KILLED AND GOT KILLED,
IN THE MIDST OF A CRUEL AND VIOLENT HISTORY.
BUT, EVEN IF THEY WERE REAL PEOPLE, WELL.... IN THE END THEY'RE LIKE A MYTH.
PEOPLE WHO BELONGED HERE WERE SPECIAL FROM THE DAY THEY WERE BORN.
THEY DON'T SEEM REAL TO ORDINARY PEOPLE LIKE US.

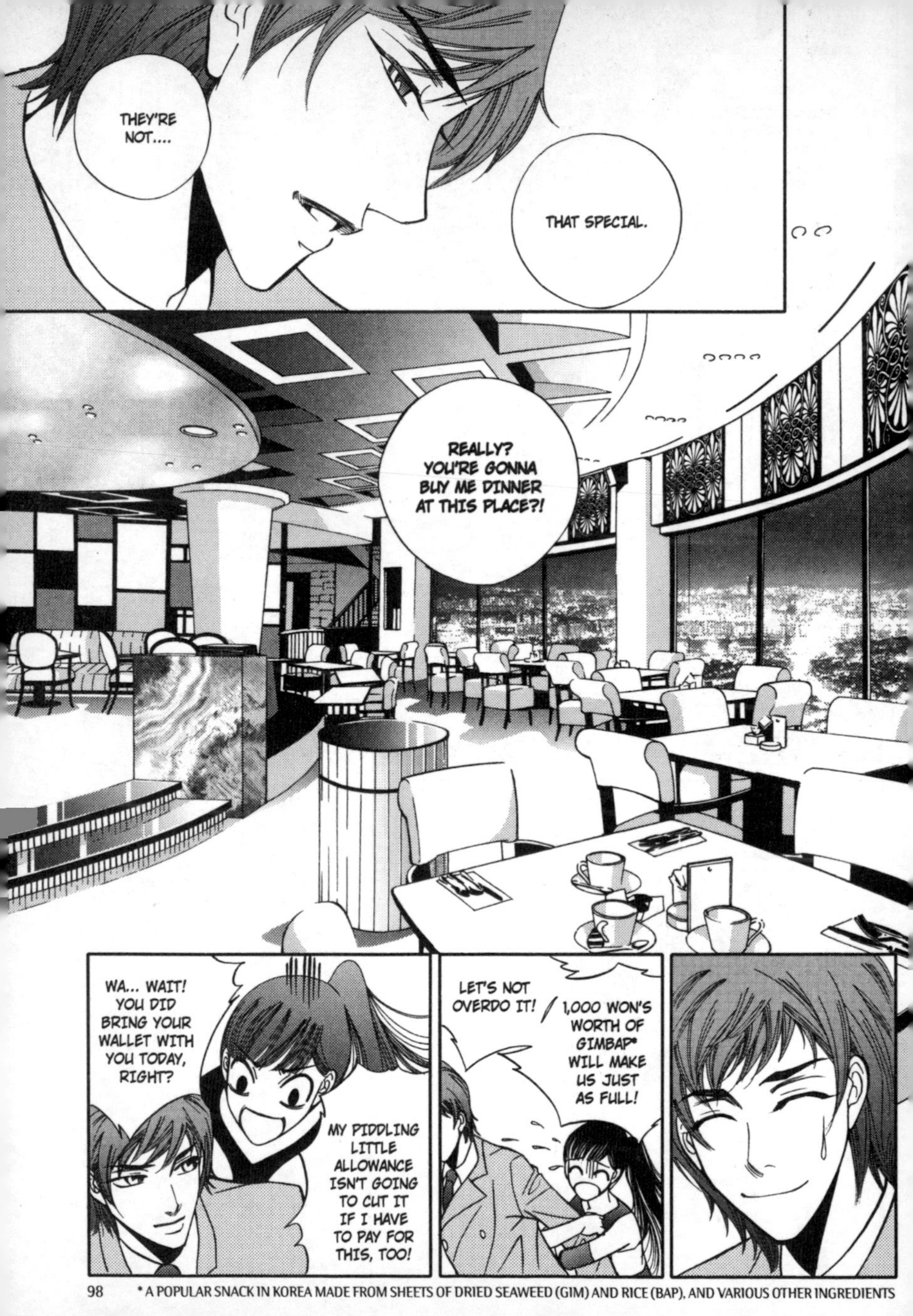
THEY'RE NOT....
THAT SPECIAL.
REALLY? YOU'RE GONNA BUY ME DINNER AT THIS PLACE?!
WA... WAIT! YOU DID BRING YOUR WALLET WITH YOU TODAY, RIGHT?
MY PIDDLING LITTLE ALLOWANCE ISN'T GOING TO CUT IT IF I HAVE TO PAY FOR THIS, TOO!
LET'S NOT OVERDO IT!
1,000 WON'S WORTH OF GIMBAP* WILL MAKE US JUST AS FULL!

* A POPULAR SNACK IN KOREA MADE FROM SHEETS OF DRIED SEAWEED (GIM) AND RICE (BAP), AND VARIOUS OTHER INGREDIENTS

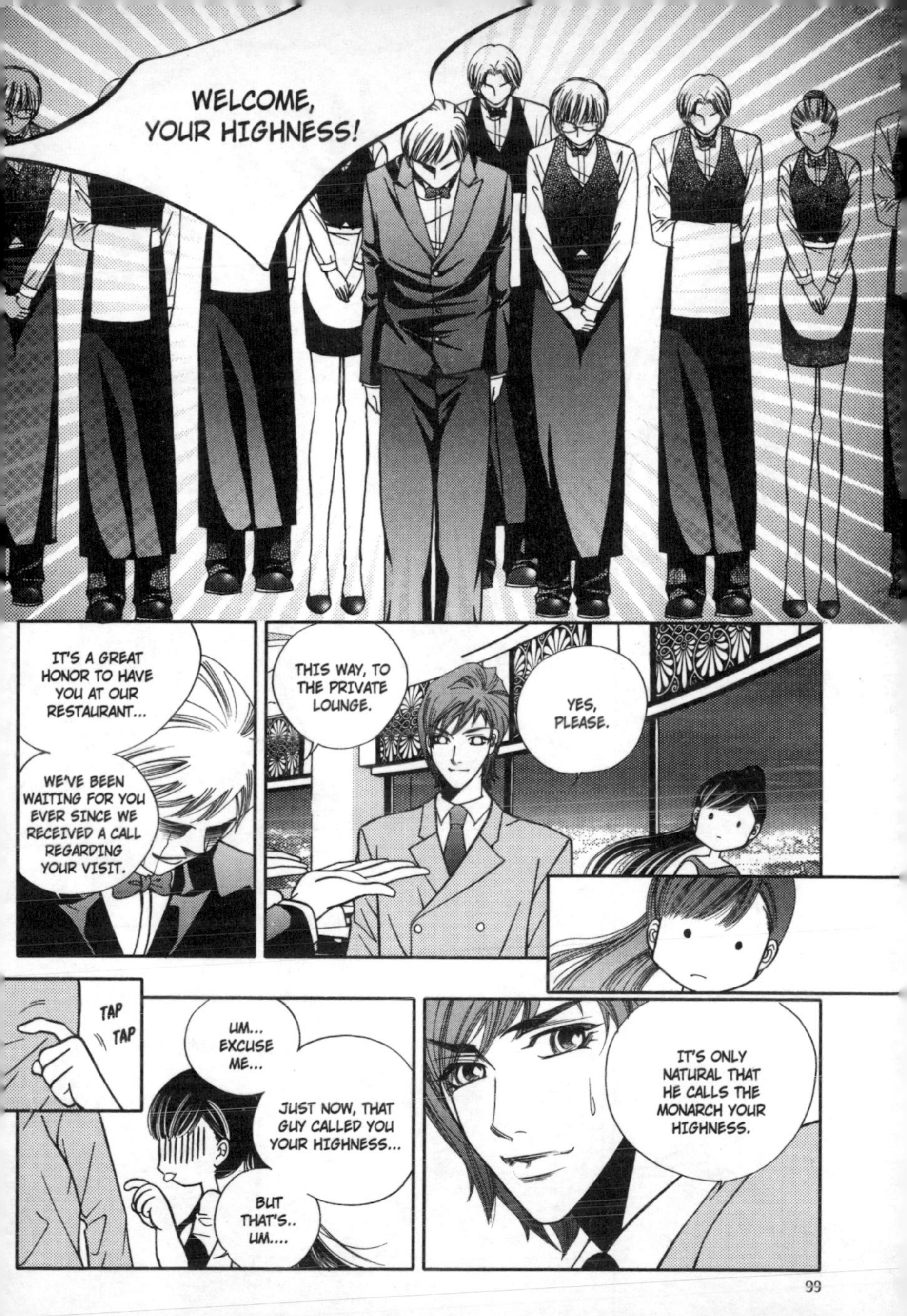
WELCOME, YOUR HIGHNESS!
IT'S A GREAT HONOR TO HAVE YOU AT OUR RESTAURANT...
WE'VE BEEN WAITING FOR YOU EVER SINCE WE RECEIVED A CALL REGARDING YOUR VISIT.
THIS WAY, TO THE PRIVATE LOUNGE.
YES, PLEASE.
TAP TAP
UM... EXCUSE ME...
JUST NOW, THAT GUY CALLED YOU YOUR HIGHNESS...
BUT THAT'S.. UM....
IT'S ONLY NATURAL THAT HE CALLS THE MONARCH YOUR HIGHNESS.

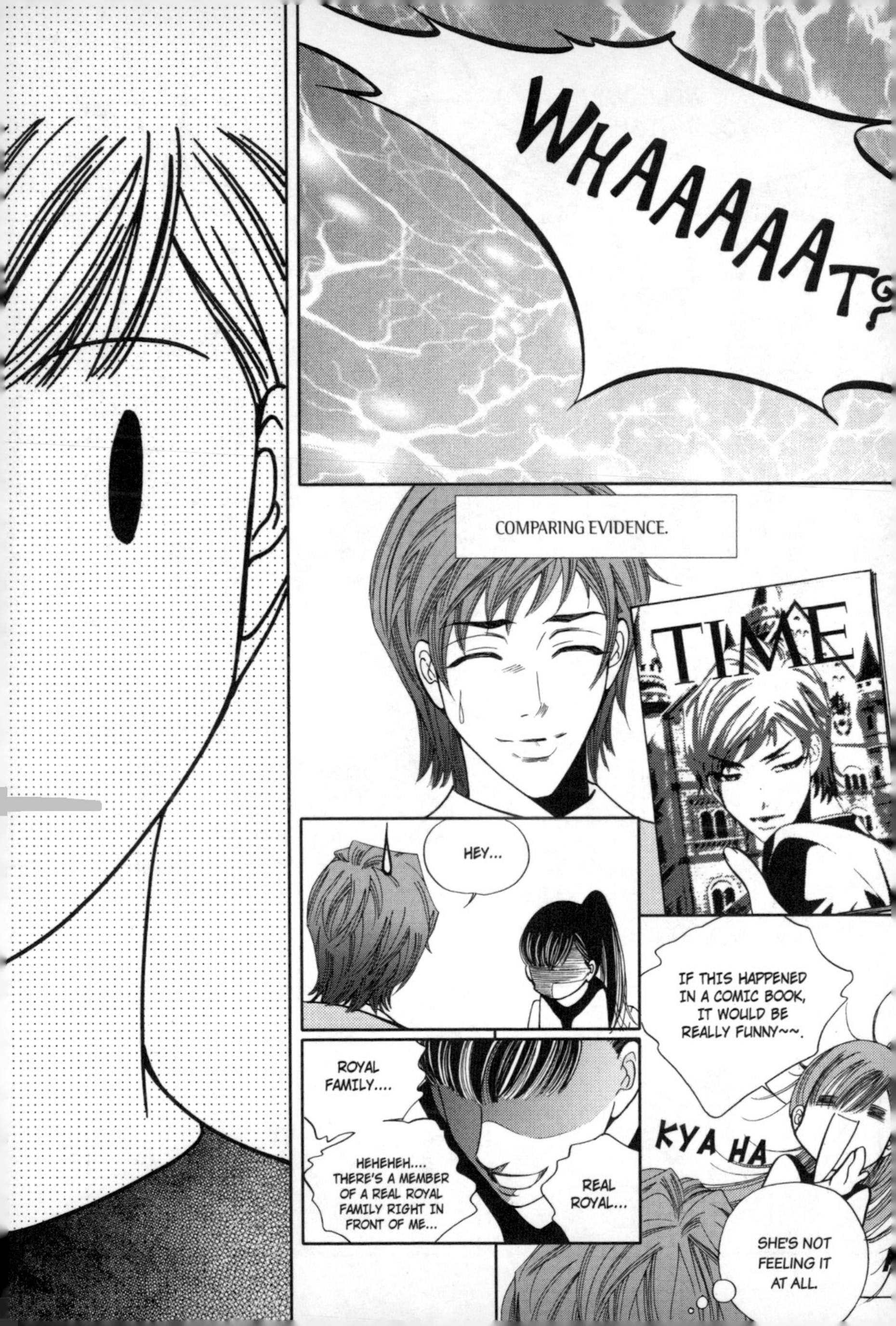
WHAAAAAT?!
COMPARING EVIDENCE.
TIME
HEY...
IF THIS HAPPENED IN A COMIC BOOK, IT WOULD BE REALLY FUNNY~~.
ROYAL FAMILY....
HEHEHEH.... THERE'S A MEMBER OF A REAL ROYAL FAMILY RIGHT IN FRONT OF ME...
REAL ROYAL...
KYA HA
SHE'S NOT FEELING IT AT ALL.

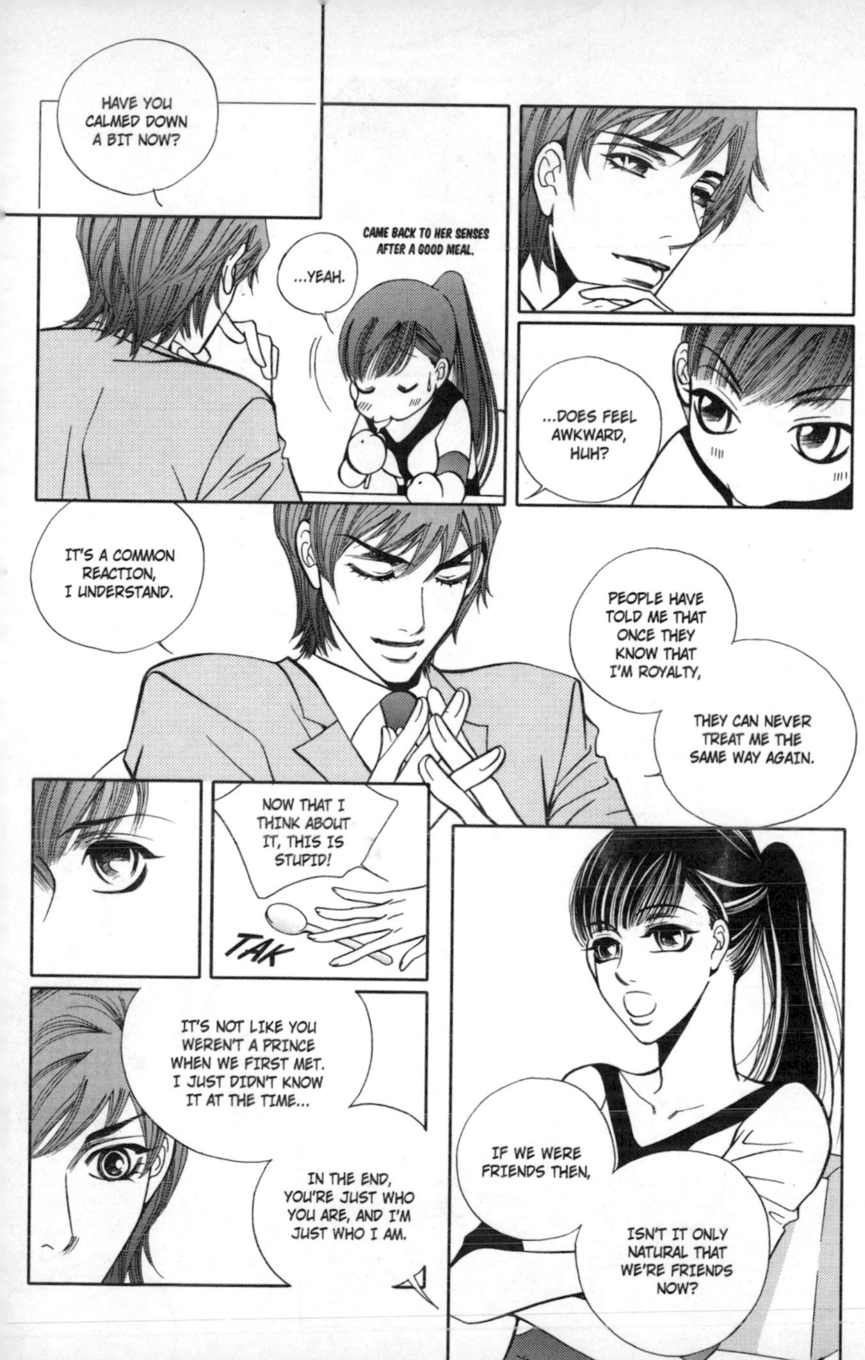
HAVE YOU CALMED DOWN A BIT NOW?
CAME BACK TO HER SENSES AFTER A GOOD MEAL.
...YEAH.
...DOES FEEL AWKWARD, HUH?
IT'S A COMMON REACTION, I UNDERSTAND.
PEOPLE HAVE TOLD ME THAT ONCE THEY KNOW THAT I'M ROYALTY,
THEY CAN NEVER TREAT ME THE SAME WAY AGAIN.
NOW THAT I THINK ABOUT IT, THIS IS STUPID!
TAK
IT'S NOT LIKE YOU WEREN'T A PRINCE WHEN WE FIRST MET. I JUST DIDN'T KNOW IT AT THE TIME...
IN THE END, YOU'RE JUST WHO YOU ARE, AND I'M JUST WHO I AM.
IF WE WERE FRIENDS THEN,
ISN'T IT ONLY NATURAL THAT WE'RE FRIENDS NOW?

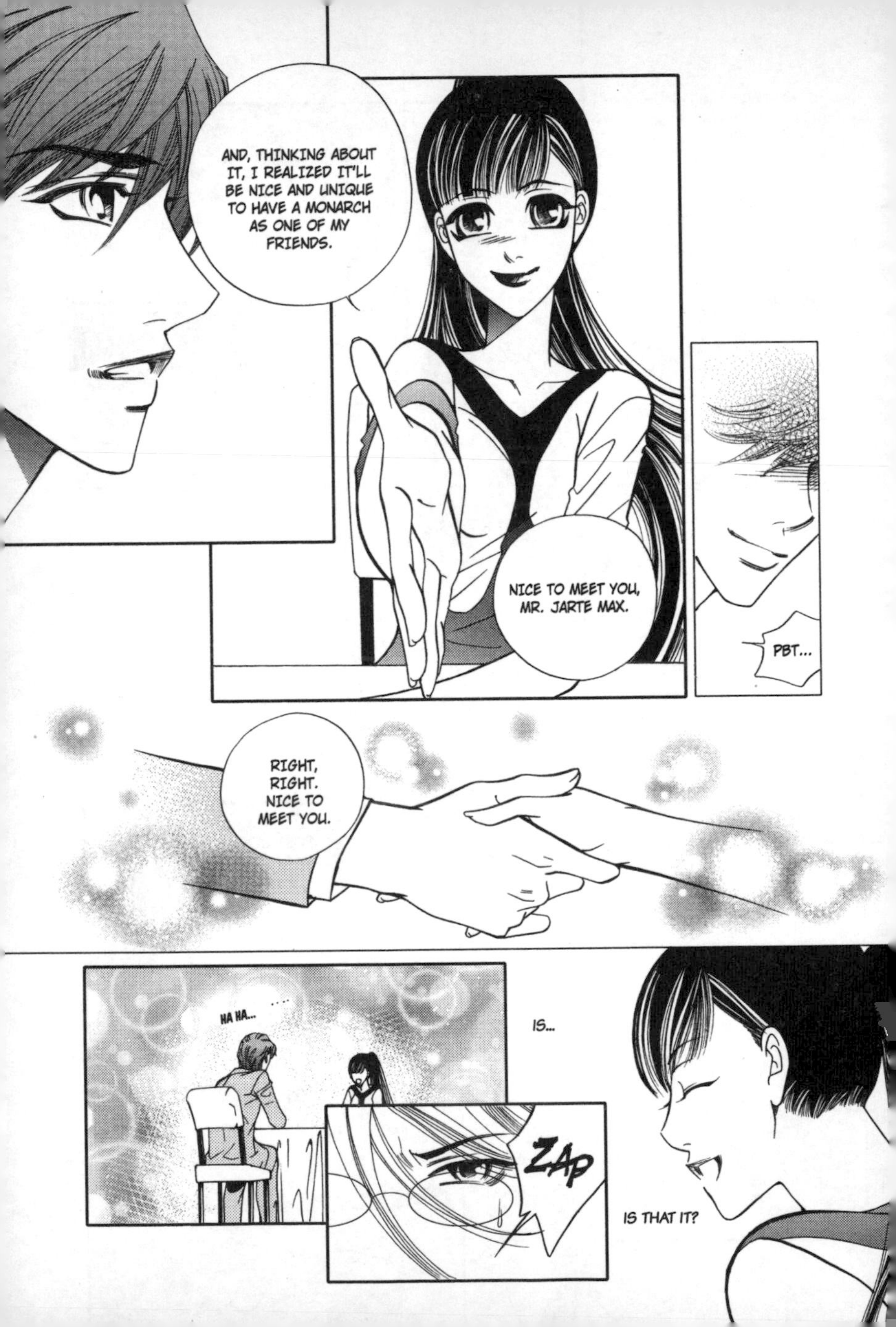
AND, THINKING ABOUT IT, I REALIZED IT'LL BE NICE AND UNIQUE TO HAVE A MONARCH AS ONE OF MY FRIENDS.
NICE TO MEET YOU, MR. JARTE MAX.
PBT...
RIGHT, RIGHT. NICE TO MEET YOU.
HA HA...
....
ZAP
IS...
IS THAT IT?

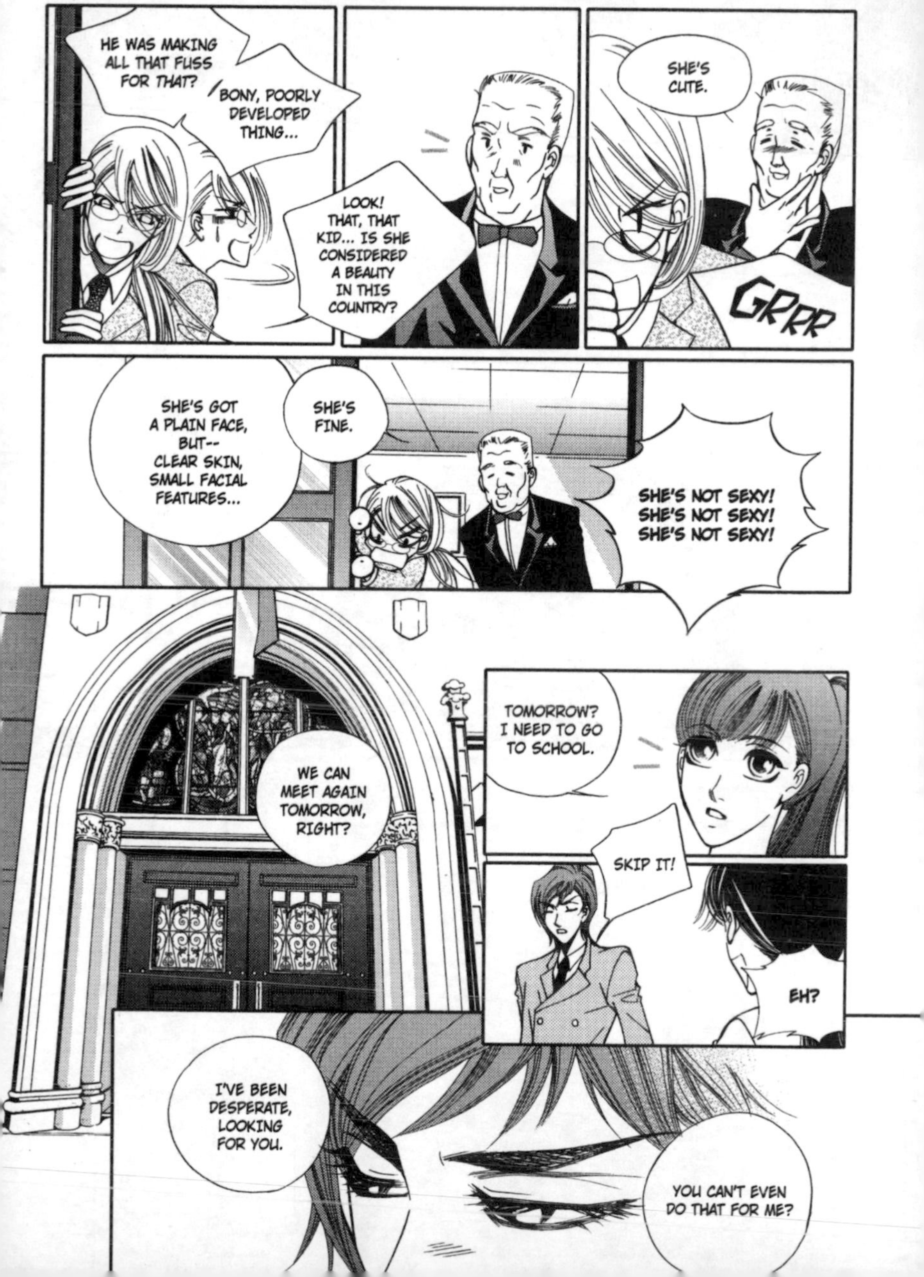
HE WAS MAKING ALL THAT FUSS FOR THAT?
BONY, POORLY DEVELOPED THING...
LOOK! THAT, THAT KID... IS SHE CONSIDERED A BEAUTY IN THIS COUNTRY?
SHE'S CUTE.
GRRR
SHE'S GOT A PLAIN FACE, BUT-- CLEAR SKIN, SMALL FACIAL FEATURES...
SHE'S FINE.
SHE'S NOT SEXY! SHE'S NOT SEXY! SHE'S NOT SEXY!
WE CAN MEET AGAIN TOMORROW, RIGHT?
TOMORROW? I NEED TO GO TO SCHOOL.
SKIP IT!
EH?
I'VE BEEN DESPERATE, LOOKING FOR YOU.
YOU CAN'T EVEN DO THAT FOR ME?

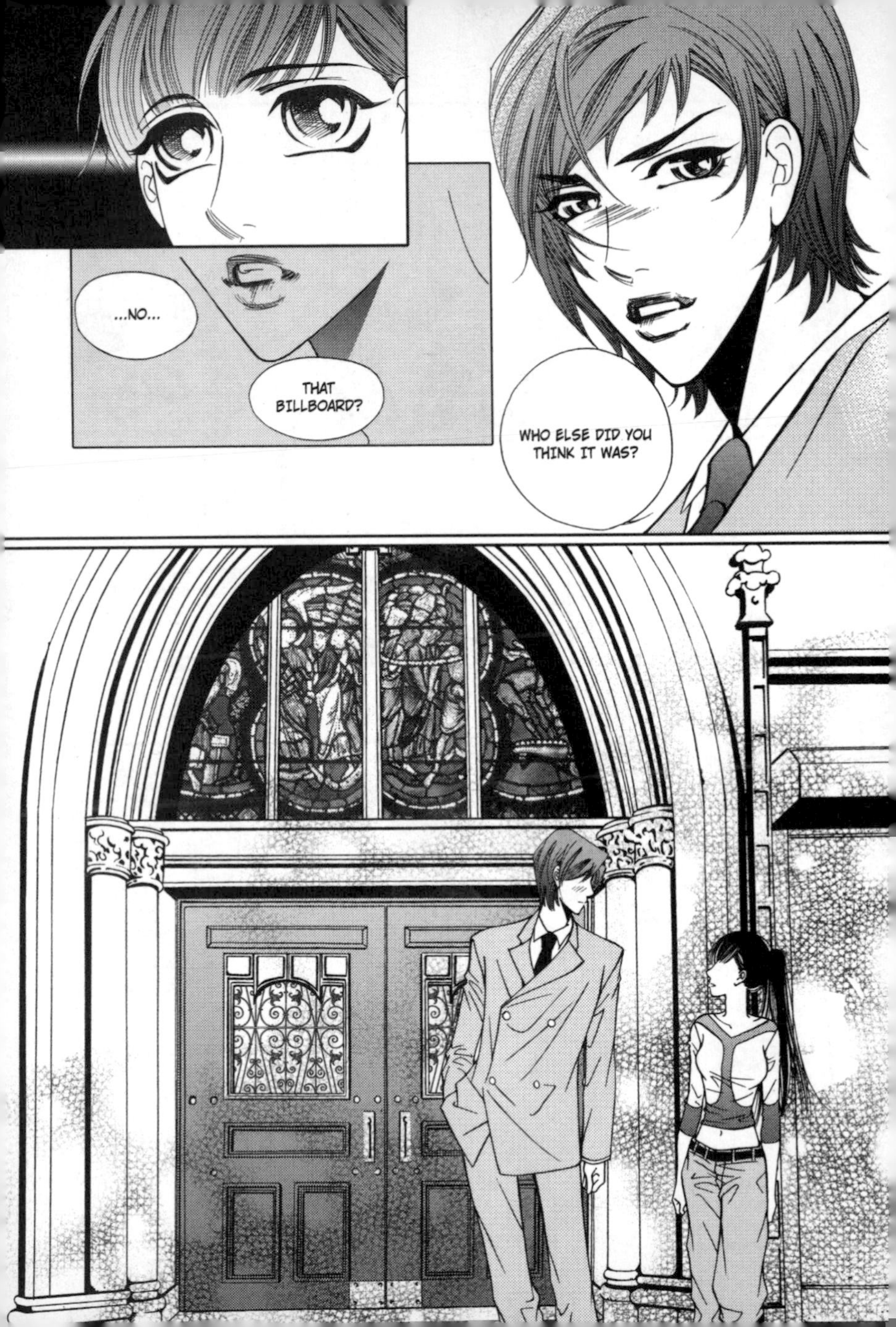
...NO...
THAT BILLBOARD?
WHO ELSE DID YOU THINK IT WAS?

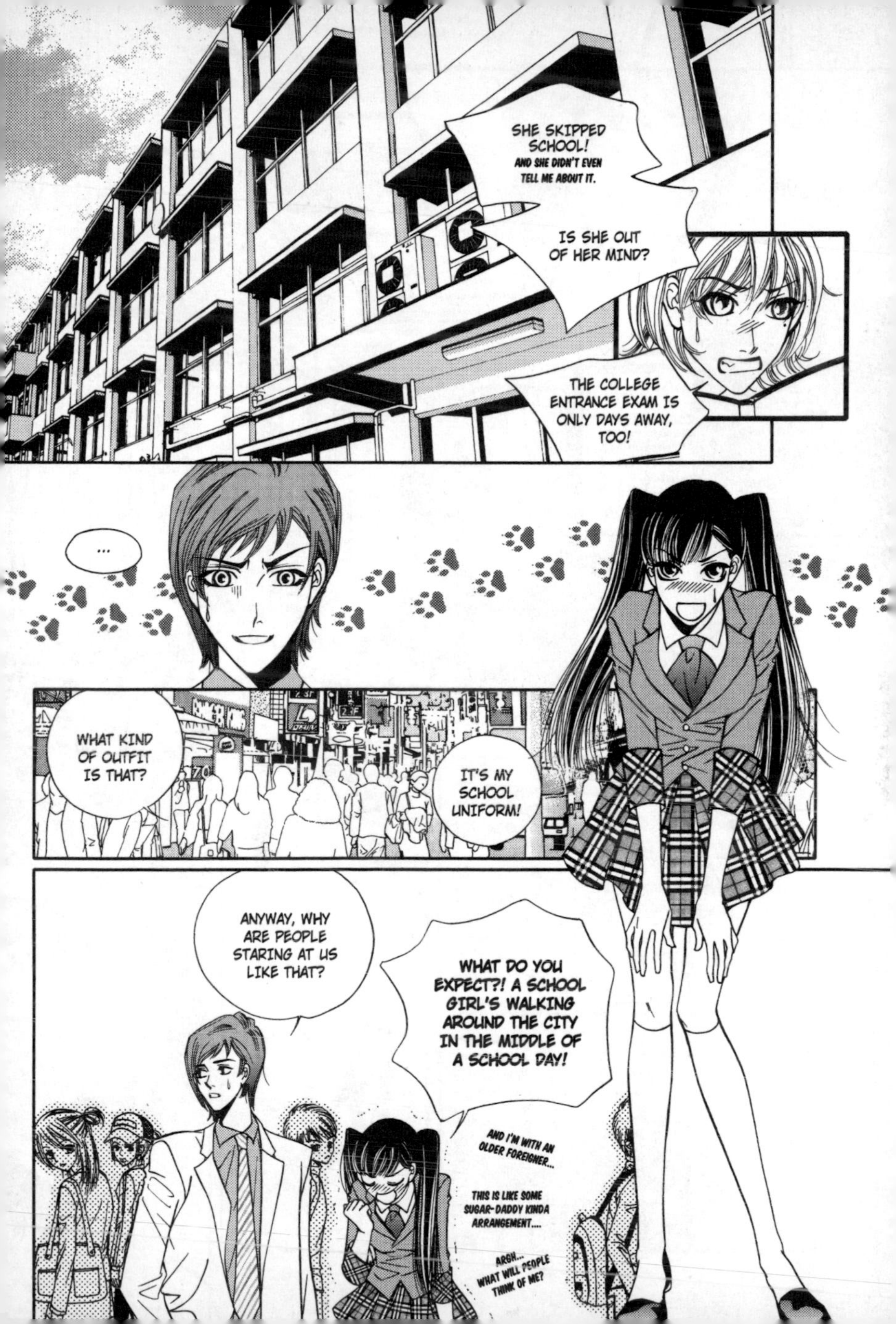
SHE SKIPPED SCHOOL!
AND SHE DIDN'T EVEN TELL ME ABOUT IT.
IS SHE OUT OF HER MIND?
THE COLLEGE ENTRANCE EXAM IS ONLY DAYS AWAY, TOO!
...
WHAT KIND OF OUTFIT IS THAT?
IT'S MY SCHOOL UNIFORM!
ANYWAY, WHY ARE PEOPLE STARING AT US LIKE THAT?
WHAT DO YOU EXPECT?! A SCHOOL GIRL'S WALKING AROUND THE CITY IN THE MIDDLE OF A SCHOOL DAY!
AND I'M WITH AN OLDER FOREIGNER...
THIS IS LIKE SOME SUGAR-DADDY KINDA ARRANGEMENT....
ARGH... WHAT WILL PEOPLE THINK OF ME?

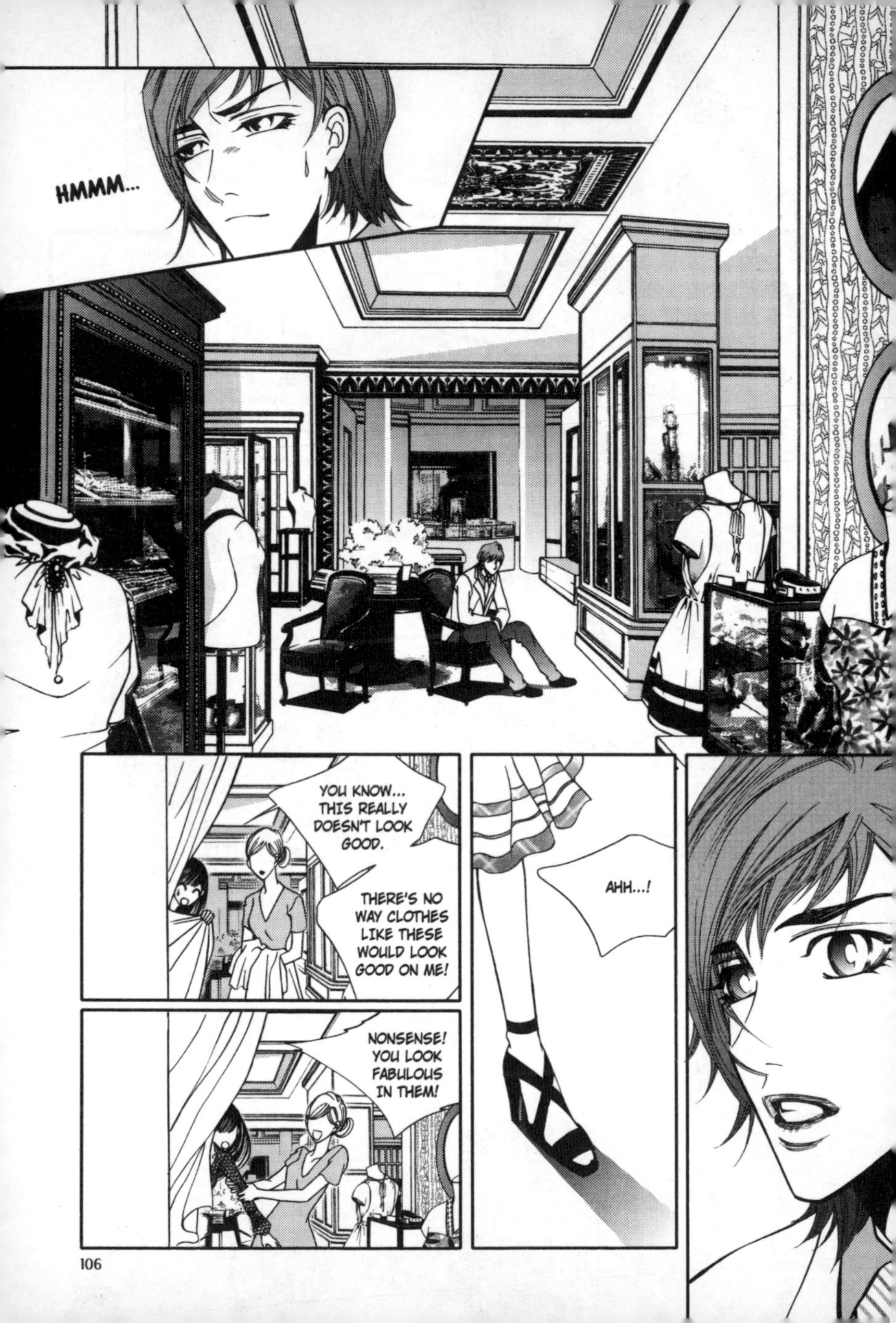
HMMM...
YOU KNOW... THIS REALLY DOESN'T LOOK GOOD.
THERE'S NO WAY CLOTHES LIKE THESE WOULD LOOK GOOD ON ME!
NONSENSE! YOU LOOK FABULOUS IN THEM!
AHH...!

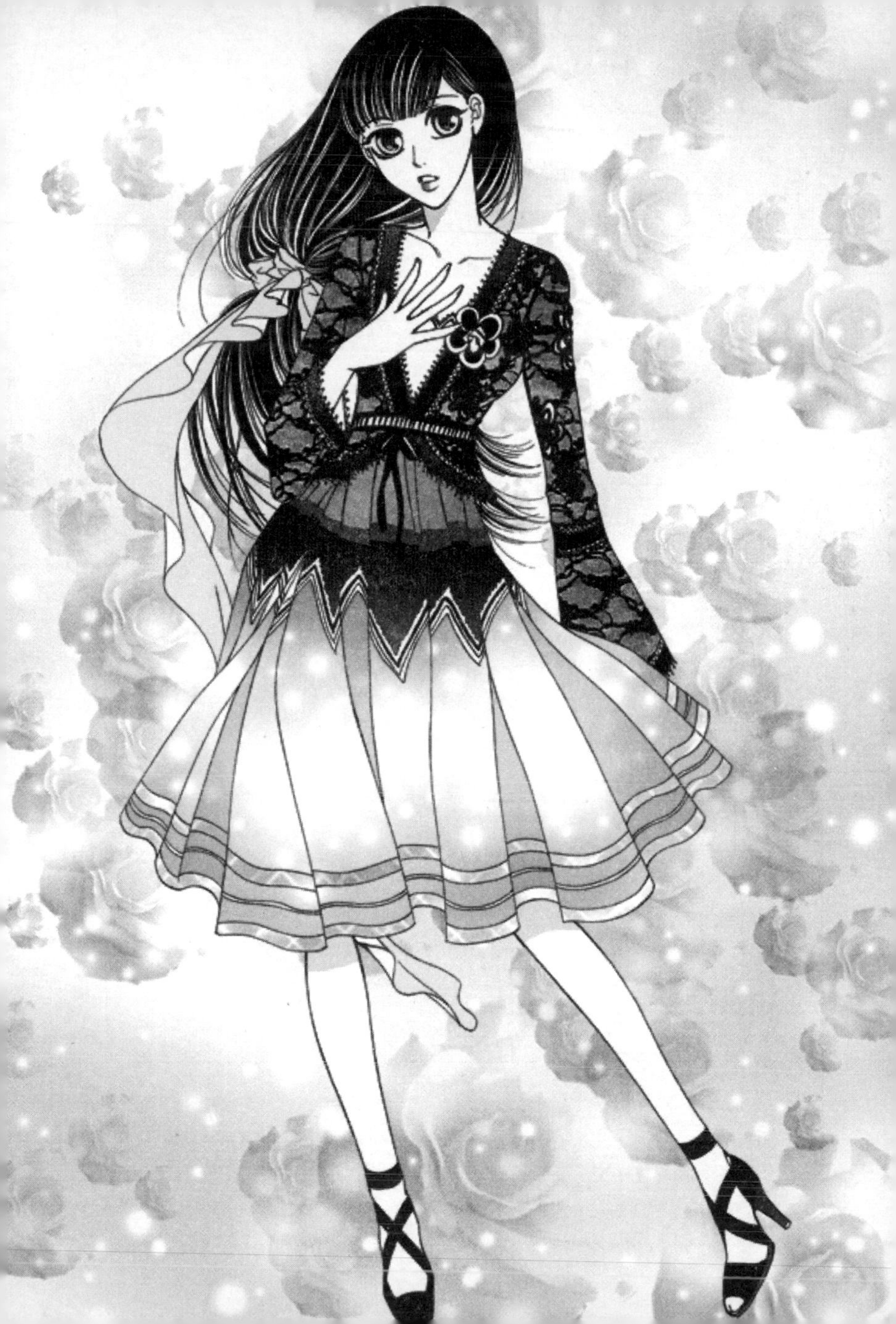

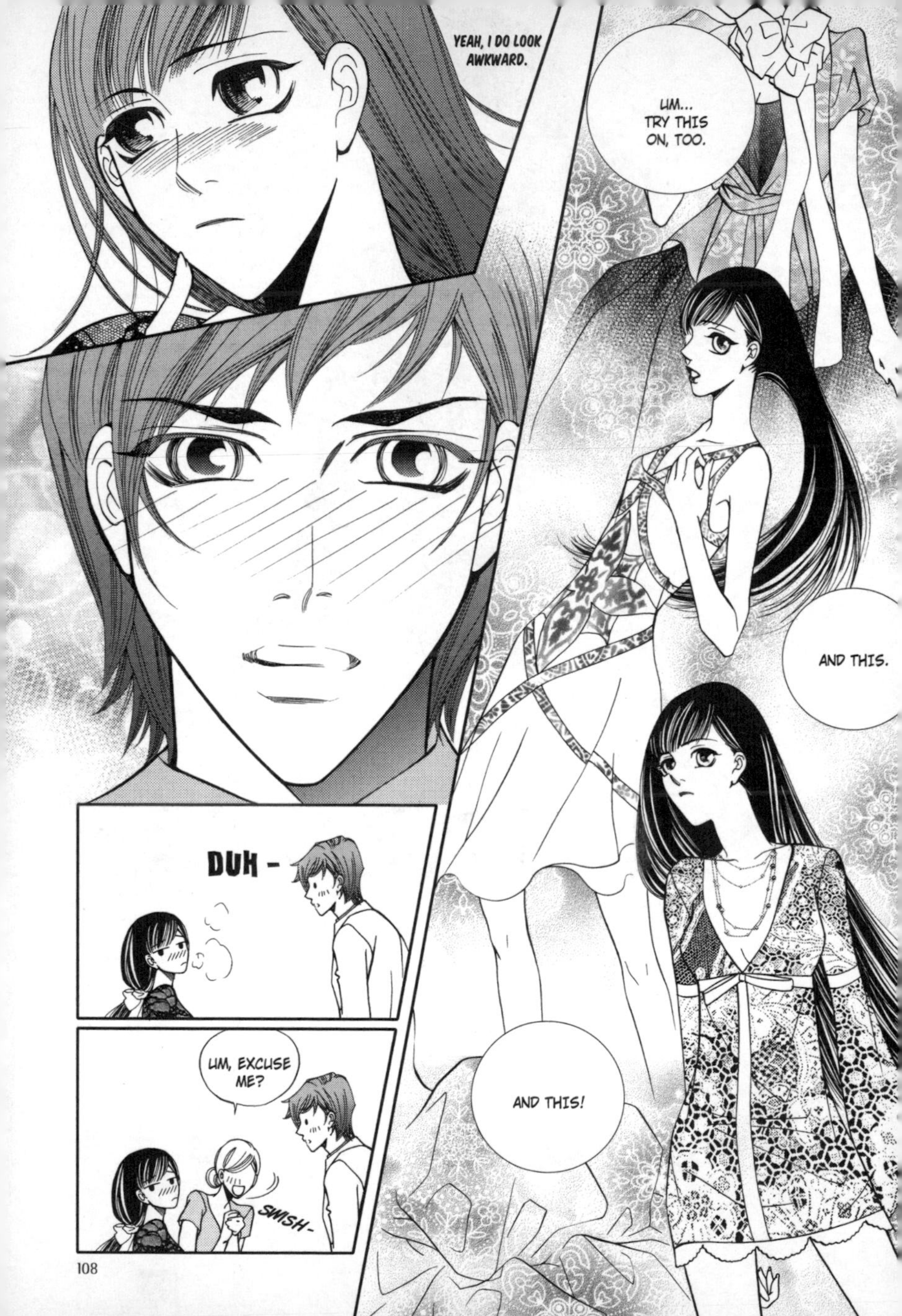
YEAH, I DO LOOK AWKWARD.
DUH -
UM, EXCUSE ME?
SWISH-
UM... TRY THIS ON, TOO.
AND THIS.
AND THIS!

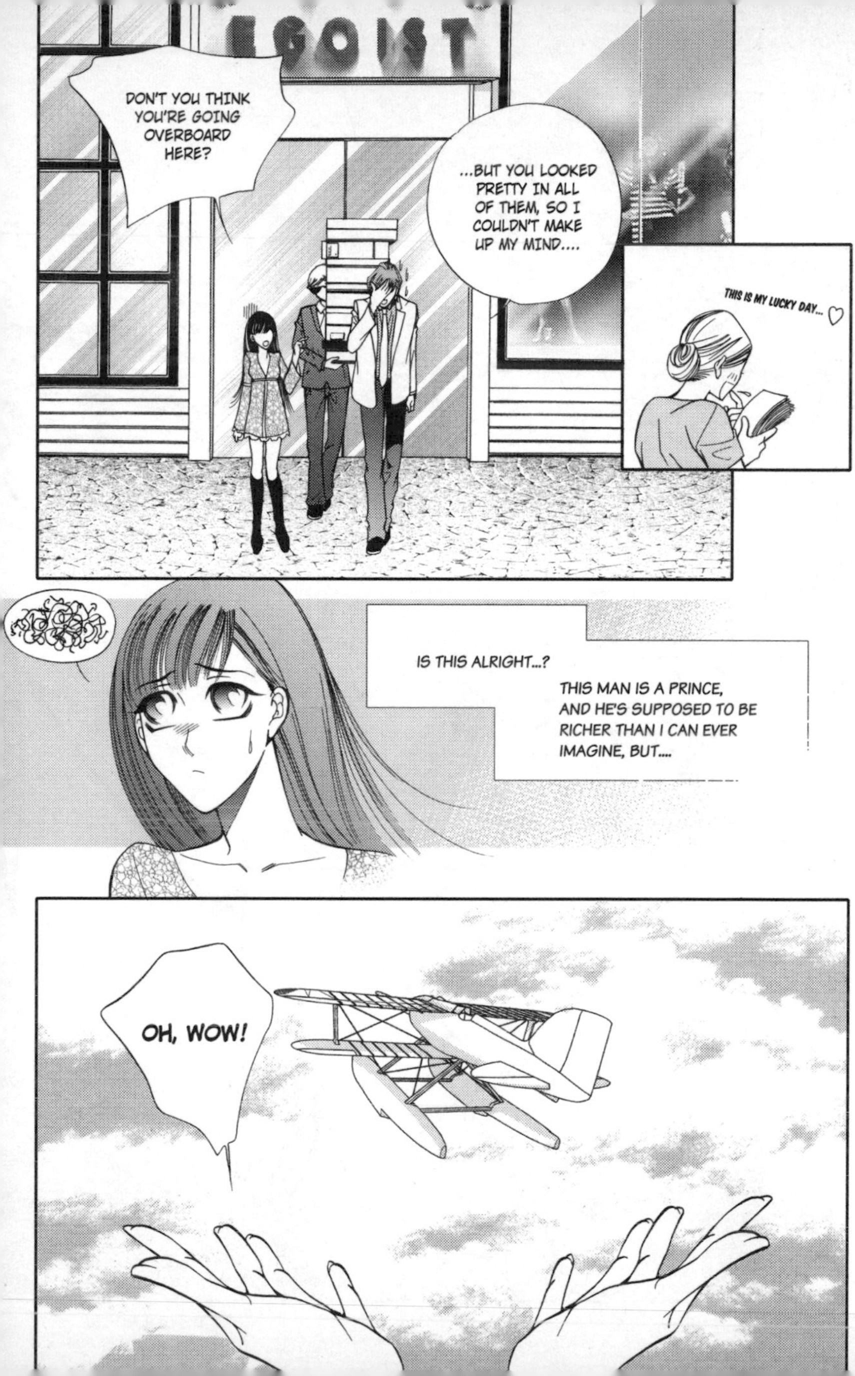
EGOIST
DON'T YOU THINK YOU'RE GOING OVERBOARD HERE?
...BUT YOU LOOKED PRETTY IN ALL OF THEM, SO I COULDN'T MAKE UP MY MIND....
THIS IS MY LUCKY DAY... ♡
IS THIS ALRIGHT...?
THIS MAN IS A PRINCE, AND HE'S SUPPOSED TO BE RICHER THAN I CAN EVER IMAGINE, BUT....
OH, WOW!

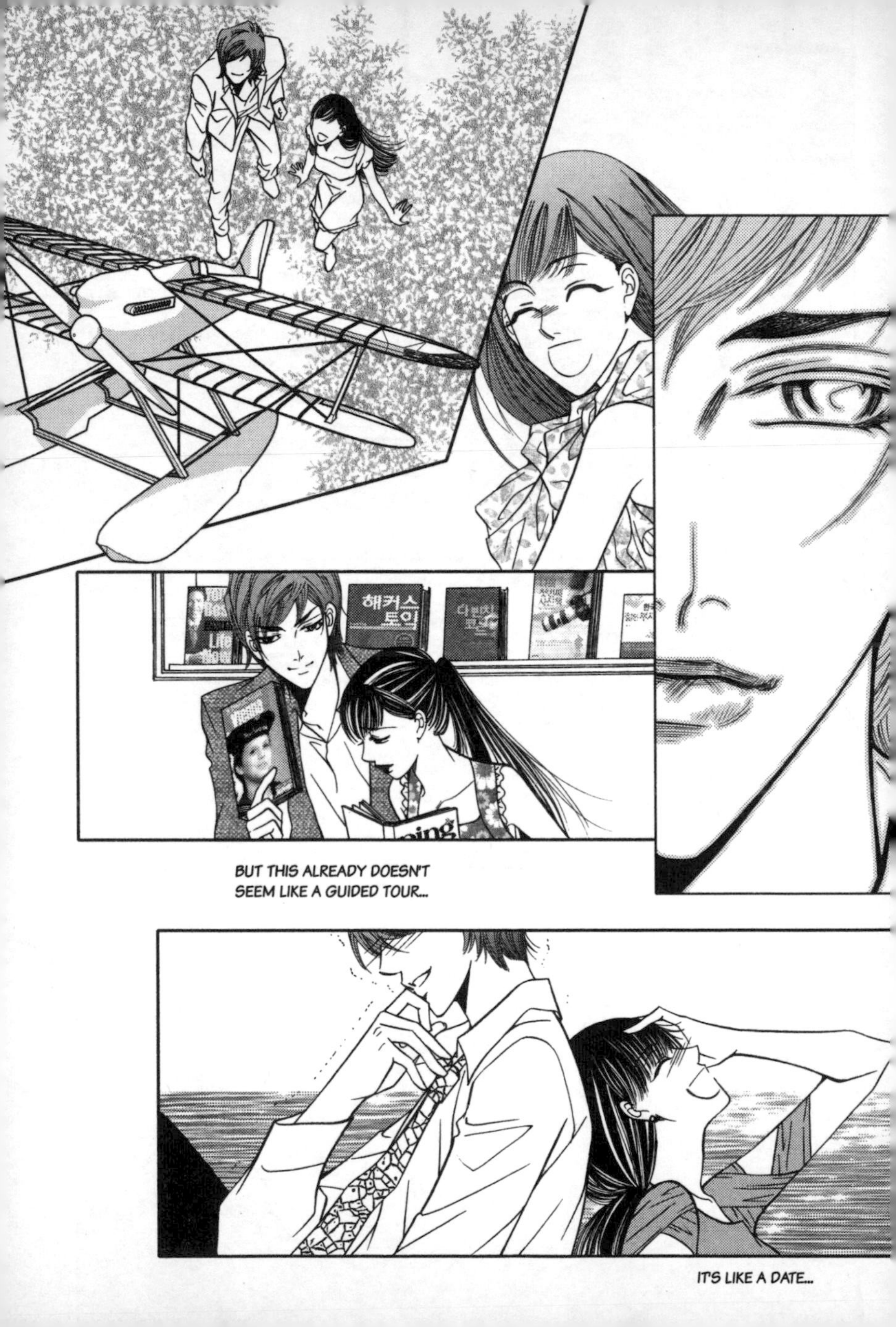
해커스
토익
BUT THIS ALREADY DOESN'T SEEM LIKE A GUIDED TOUR...
IT'S LIKE A DATE...

IS THIS ALRIGHT?

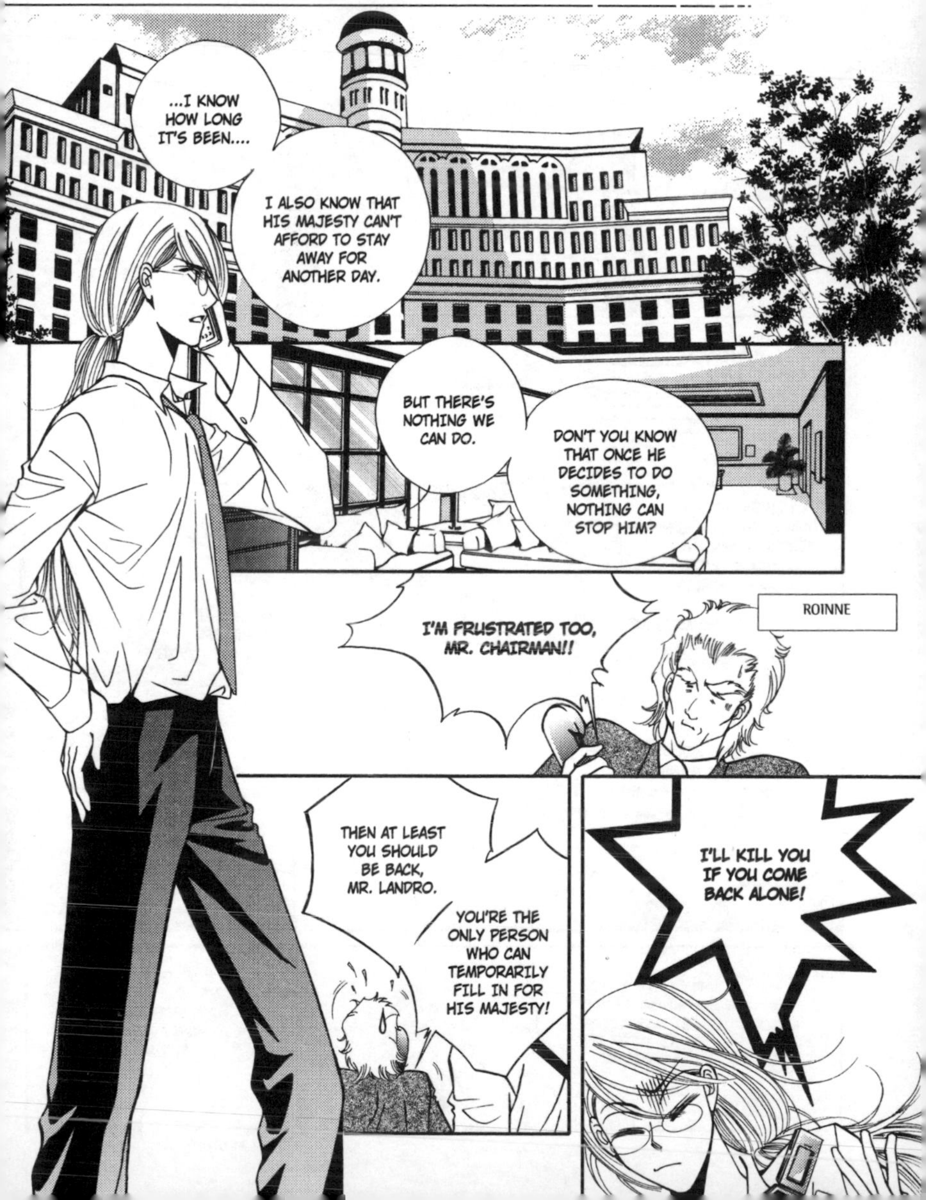
...I KNOW HOW LONG IT'S BEEN....
I ALSO KNOW THAT HIS MAJESTY CAN'T AFFORD TO STAY AWAY FOR ANOTHER DAY.
BUT THERE'S NOTHING WE CAN DO.
DON'T YOU KNOW THAT ONCE HE DECIDES TO DO SOMETHING, NOTHING CAN STOP HIM?
ROINNE
I'M FRUSTRATED TOO, MR. CHAIRMAN!!
THEN AT LEAST YOU SHOULD BE BACK, MR. LANDRO.
YOU'RE THE ONLY PERSON WHO CAN TEMPORARILY FILL IN FOR HIS MAJESTY!
I'LL KILL YOU IF YOU COME BACK ALONE!

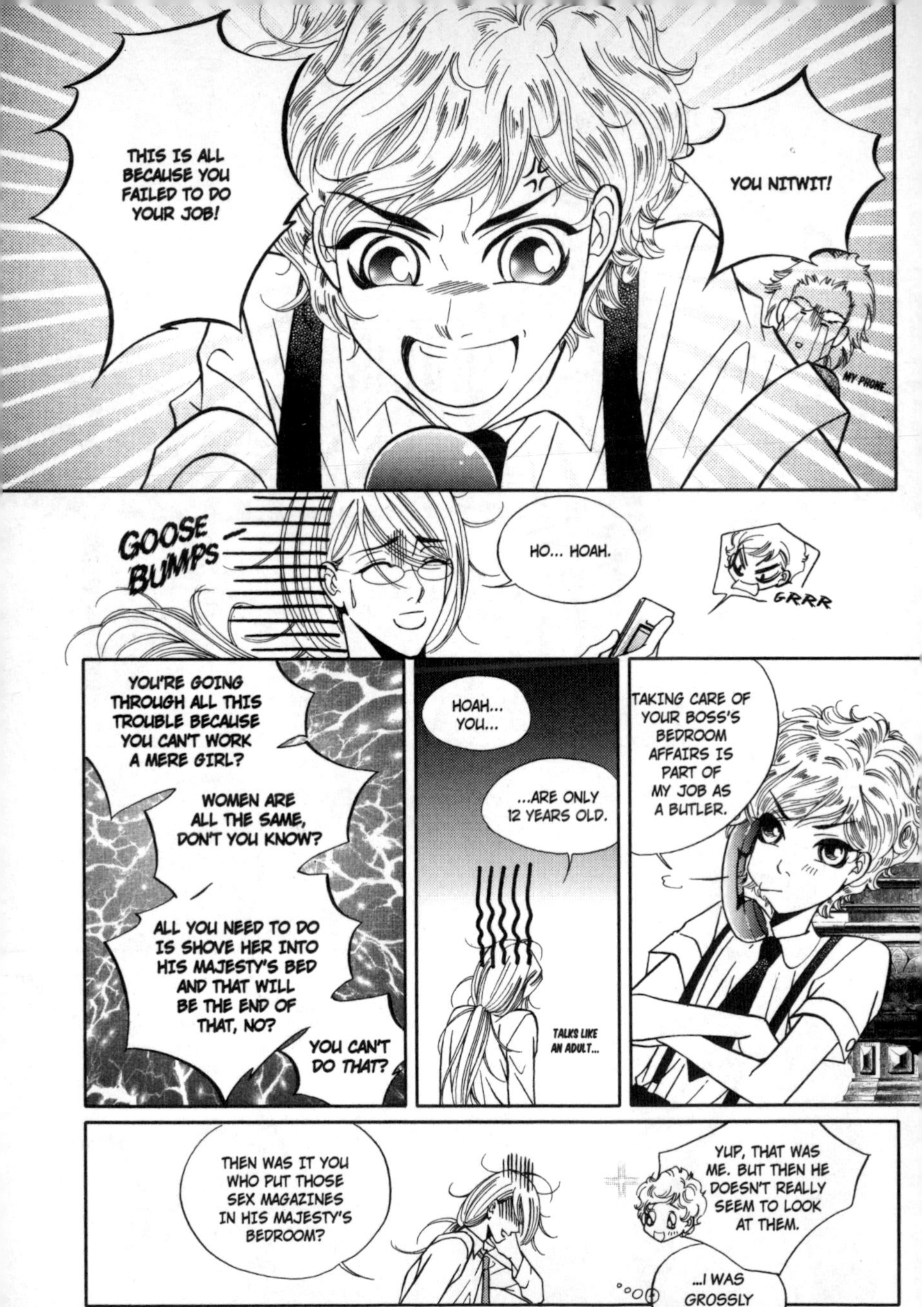
THIS IS ALL BECAUSE YOU FAILED TO DO YOUR JOB!
YOU NITWIT!
MY PHONE...
GOOSE BUMPS
HO... HOAH.
GRRR
YOU'RE GOING THROUGH ALL THIS TROUBLE BECAUSE YOU CAN'T WORK A MERE GIRL?
WOMEN ARE ALL THE SAME, DON'T YOU KNOW?
ALL YOU NEED TO DO IS SHOVE HER INTO HIS MAJESTY'S BED AND THAT WILL BE THE END OF THAT, NO?
YOU CAN'T DO THAT?
HOAH... YOU...
...ARE ONLY 12 YEARS OLD.
TALKS LIKE AN ADULT...
TAKING CARE OF YOUR BOSS'S BEDROOM AFFAIRS IS PART OF MY JOB AS A BUTLER.
THEN WAS IT YOU WHO PUT THOSE SEX MAGAZINES IN HIS MAJESTY'S BEDROOM?
YUP, THAT WAS ME. BUT THEN HE DOESN'T REALLY SEEM TO LOOK AT THEM.
...I WAS GROSSLY MISTAKEN.

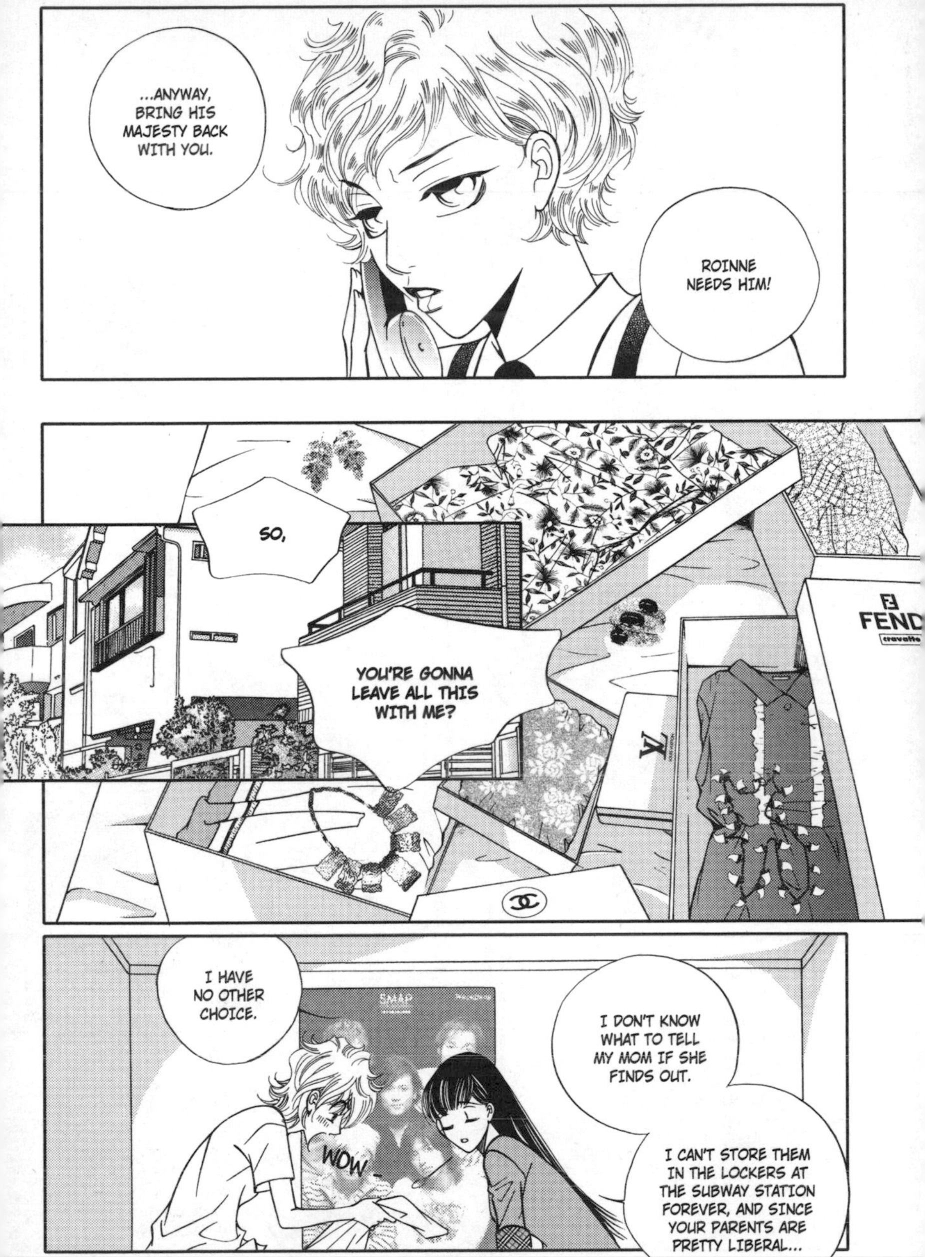
...ANYWAY, BRING HIS MAJESTY BACK WITH YOU.
ROINNE NEEDS HIM!
SO,
YOU'RE GONNA LEAVE ALL THIS WITH ME?
I HAVE NO OTHER CHOICE.
SMAP
WOW
I DON'T KNOW WHAT TO TELL MY MOM IF SHE FINDS OUT.
I CAN'T STORE THEM IN THE LOCKERS AT THE SUBWAY STATION FOREVER, AND SINCE YOUR PARENTS ARE PRETTY LIBERAL...

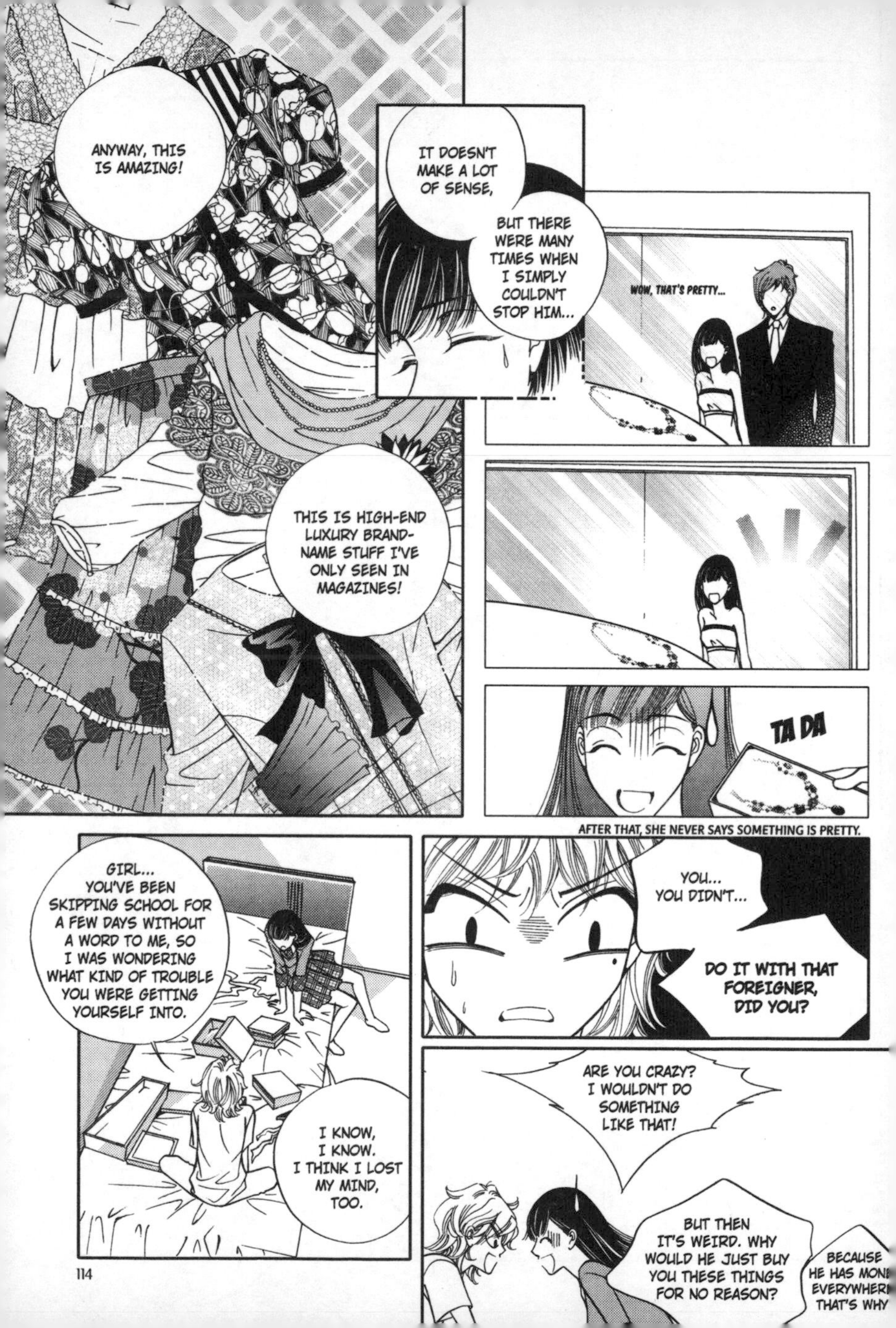

ANYWAY, THIS IS AMAZING!
THIS IS HIGH-END LUXURY BRAND-NAME STUFF I'VE ONLY SEEN IN MAGAZINES!
IT DOESN'T MAKE A LOT OF SENSE,
BUT THERE WERE MANY TIMES WHEN I SIMPLY COULDN'T STOP HIM...
WOW, THAT'S PRETTY...
TA DA
AFTER THAT, SHE NEVER SAYS SOMETHING IS PRETTY.
GIRL... YOU'VE BEEN SKIPPING SCHOOL FOR A FEW DAYS WITHOUT A WORD TO ME, SO I WAS WONDERING WHAT KIND OF TROUBLE YOU WERE GETTING YOURSELF INTO.
I KNOW, I KNOW. I THINK I LOST MY MIND, TOO.
YOU... YOU DIDN'T...
DO IT WITH THAT FOREIGNER, DID YOU?
ARE YOU CRAZY? I WOULDN'T DO SOMETHING LIKE THAT!
BUT THEN IT'S WEIRD. WHY WOULD HE JUST BUY YOU THESE THINGS FOR NO REASON?
BECAUSE HE HAS MONE EVERYWHER THAT'S WHY

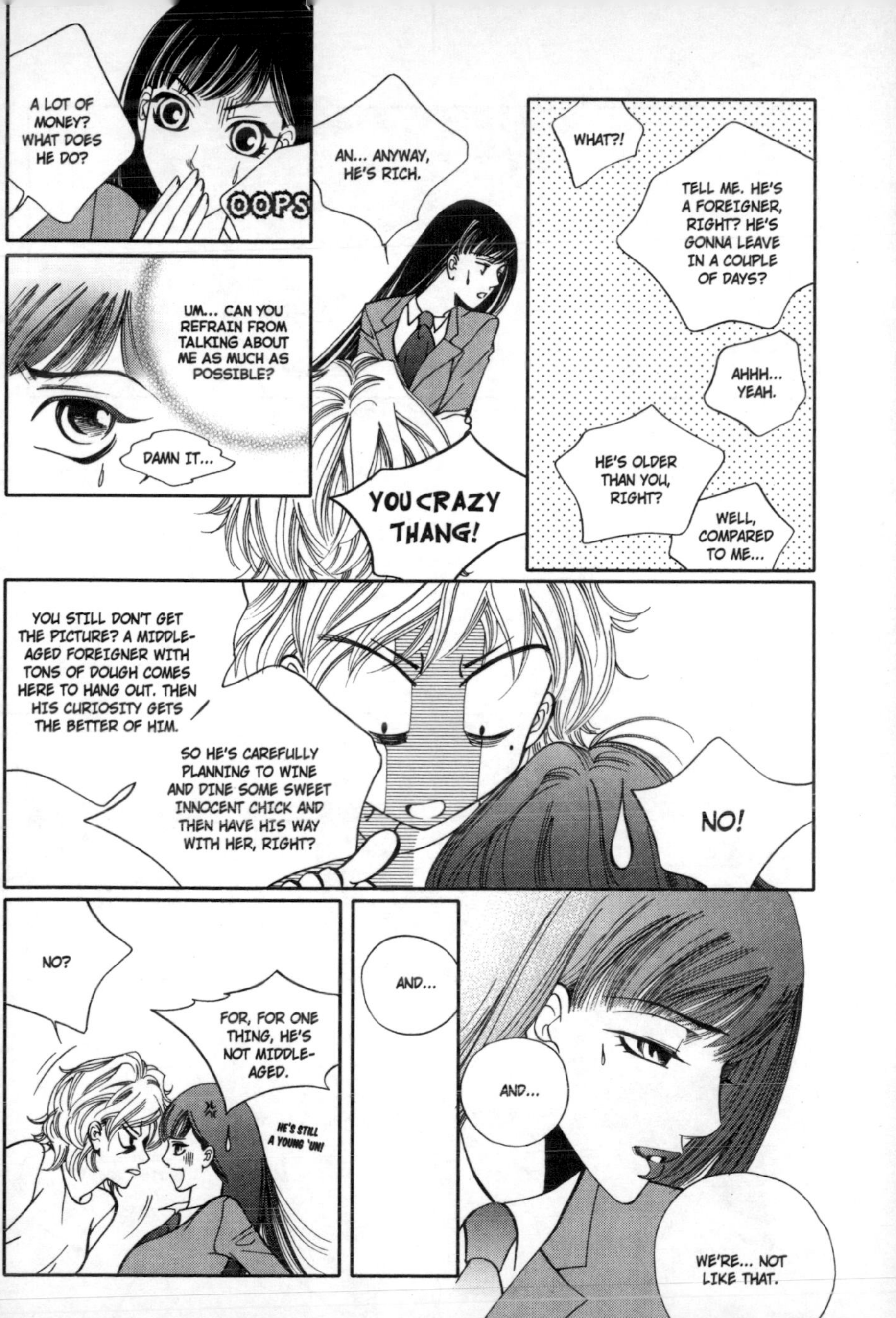
A LOT OF MONEY? WHAT DOES HE DO?
OOPS
UM... CAN YOU REFRAIN FROM TALKING ABOUT ME AS MUCH AS POSSIBLE?
DAMN IT...
AN... ANYWAY, HE'S RICH.
YOU CRAZY THANG!
WHAT?!
TELL ME. HE'S A FOREIGNER, RIGHT? HE'S GONNA LEAVE IN A COUPLE OF DAYS?
AHHH... YEAH.
HE'S OLDER THAN YOU, RIGHT?
WELL, COMPARED TO ME...
YOU STILL DON'T GET THE PICTURE? A MIDDLE-AGED FOREIGNER WITH TONS OF DOUGH COMES HERE TO HANG OUT. THEN HIS CURIOSITY GETS THE BETTER OF HIM.
SO HE'S CAREFULLY PLANNING TO WINE AND DINE SOME SWEET INNOCENT CHICK AND THEN HAVE HIS WAY WITH HER, RIGHT?
NO!
NO?
FOR, FOR ONE THING, HE'S NOT MIDDLE-AGED.
HE'S STILL A YOUNG 'UN!
AND...
AND...
WE'RE... NOT LIKE THAT.

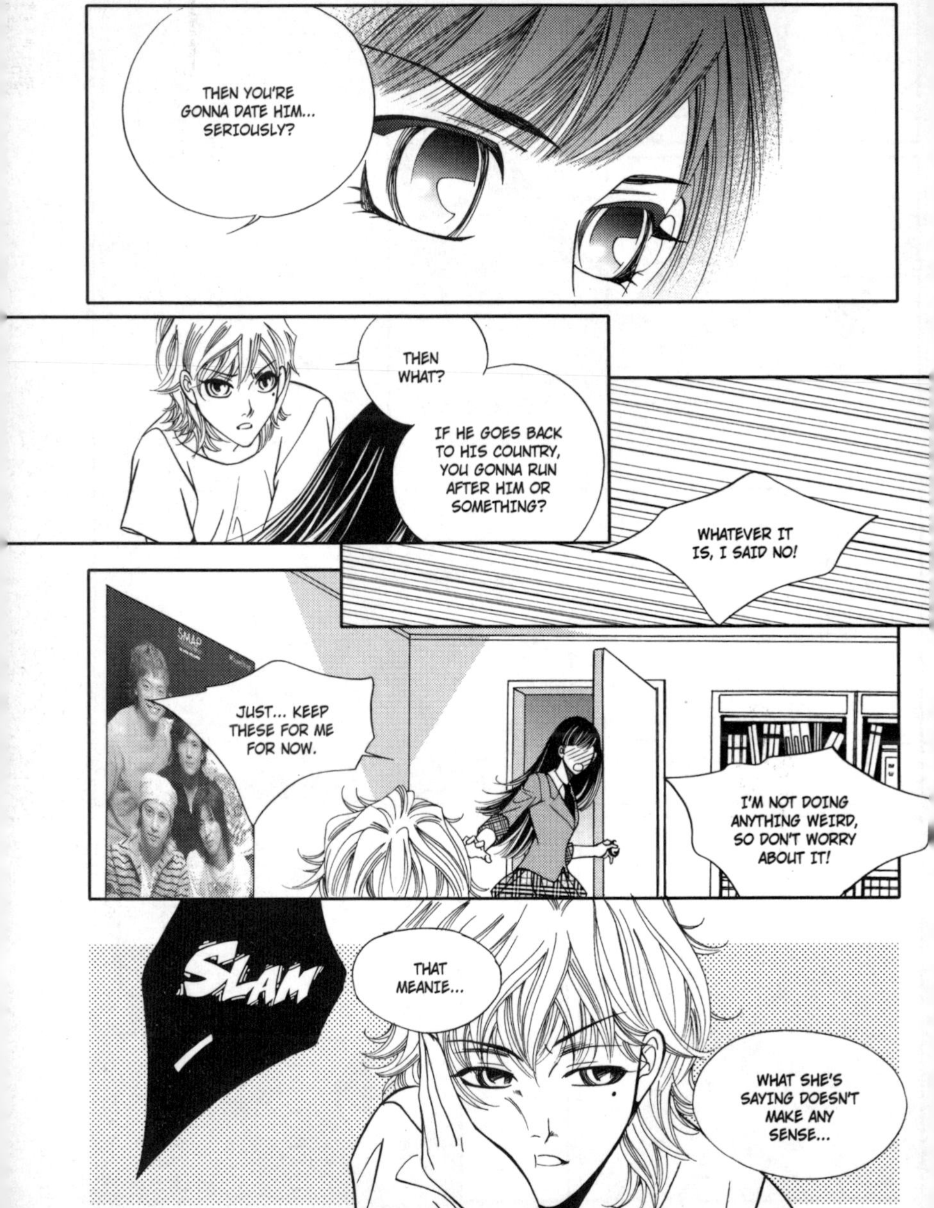
THEN YOU'RE GONNA DATE HIM... SERIOUSLY?
THEN WHAT?
IF HE GOES BACK TO HIS COUNTRY, YOU GONNA RUN AFTER HIM OR SOMETHING?
WHATEVER IT IS, I SAID NO!
JUST... KEEP THESE FOR ME FOR NOW.
I'M NOT DOING ANYTHING WEIRD, SO DON'T WORRY ABOUT IT!
SLAM
THAT MEANIE...
WHAT SHE'S SAYING DOESN'T MAKE ANY SENSE...

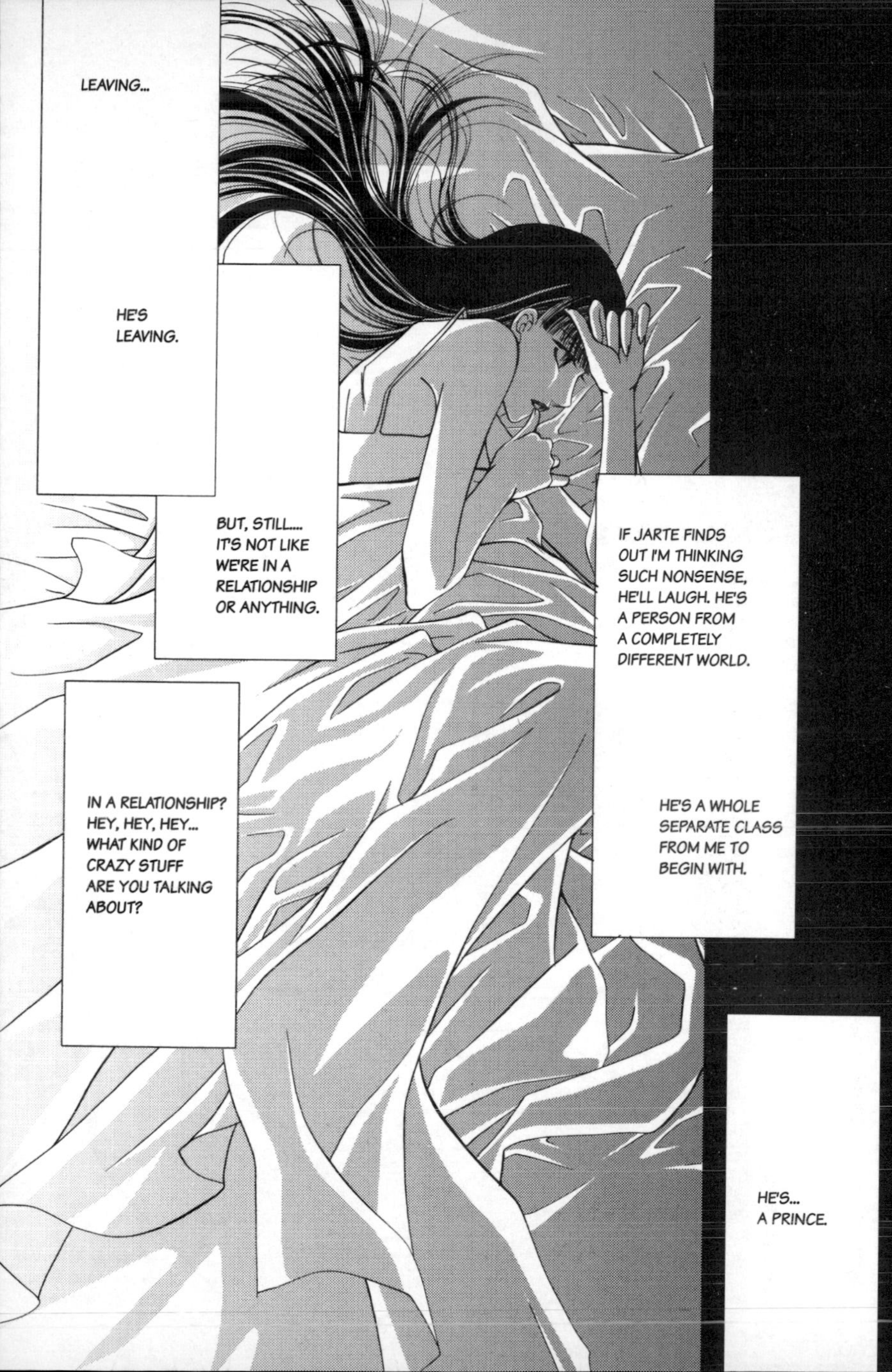
LEAVING...
HE'S LEAVING.
BUT, STILL.... IT'S NOT LIKE WE'RE IN A RELATIONSHIP OR ANYTHING.
IN A RELATIONSHIP? HEY, HEY, HEY... WHAT KIND OF CRAZY STUFF ARE YOU TALKING ABOUT?
IF JARTE FINDS OUT I'M THINKING SUCH NONSENSE, HE'LL LAUGH. HE'S A PERSON FROM A COMPLETELY DIFFERENT WORLD.
HE'S A WHOLE SEPARATE CLASS FROM ME TO BEGIN WITH.
HE'S... A PRINCE.

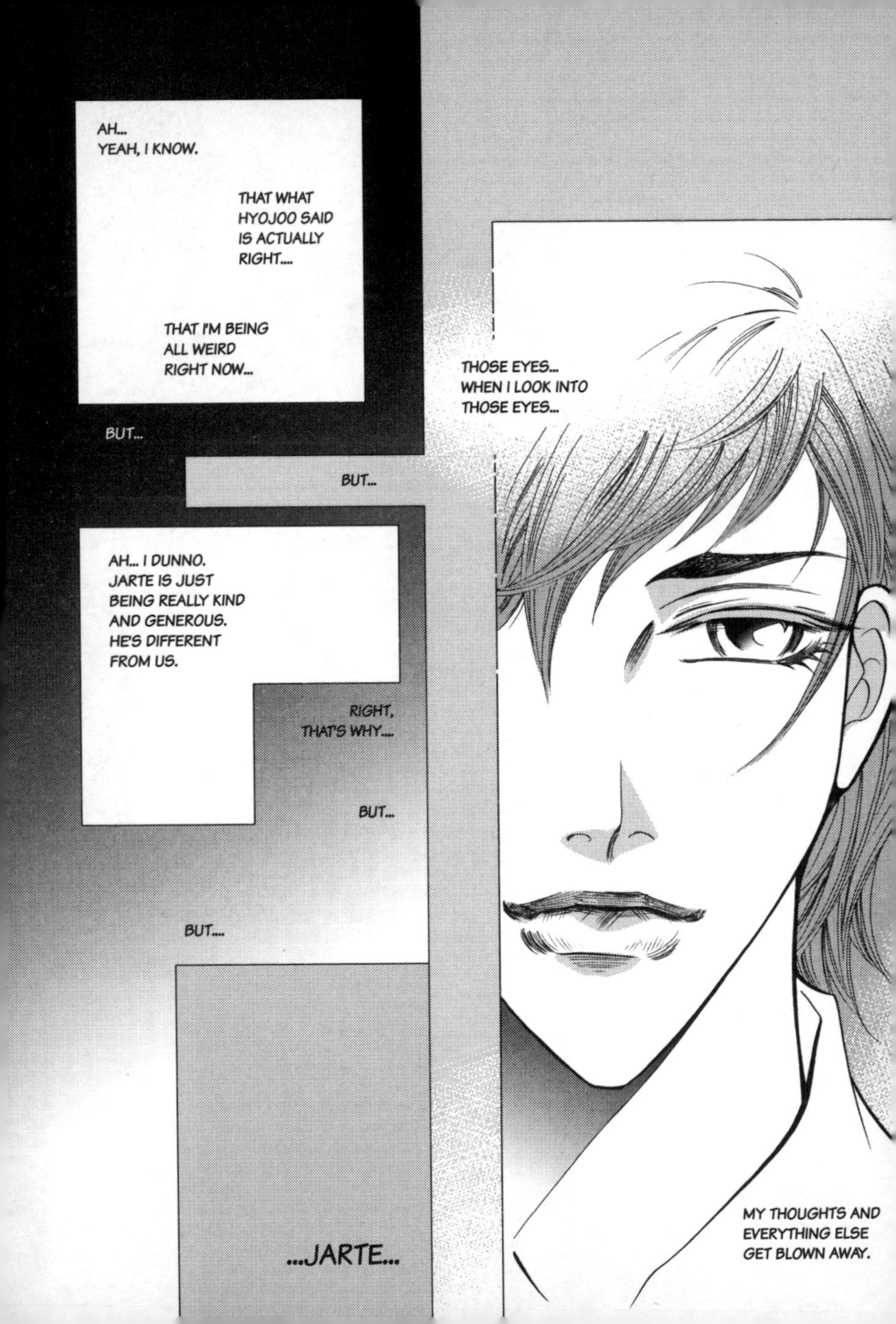
AH...
YEAH, I KNOW.
THAT WHAT HYOJOO SAID IS ACTUALLY RIGHT....
THAT I'M BEING ALL WEIRD RIGHT NOW...
BUT...
BUT...
AH... I DUNNO. JARTE IS JUST BEING REALLY KIND AND GENEROUS. HE'S DIFFERENT FROM US.
RIGHT, THAT'S WHY....
BUT...
BUT....
...JARTE...
THOSE EYES... WHEN I LOOK INTO THOSE EYES...
MY THOUGHTS AND EVERYTHING ELSE GET BLOWN AWAY.

HE'S SOMEONE WHO IS GOING TO LEAVE IN A FEW DAYS....

BUT...

BUT...

MOM, I'M SORRY....

I THINK....

JUST A COUPLE OF DAYS....

WILL BE OKAY, YOU KNOW.

I'M NOT GOING TO SCHOOL TOMORROW, EITHER.

HAAH...

HERE. THAT'S MY FRIEND'S HOUSE RIGHT UP THERE.

DROP ME OFF HERE. I CAN'T BE SEEN.

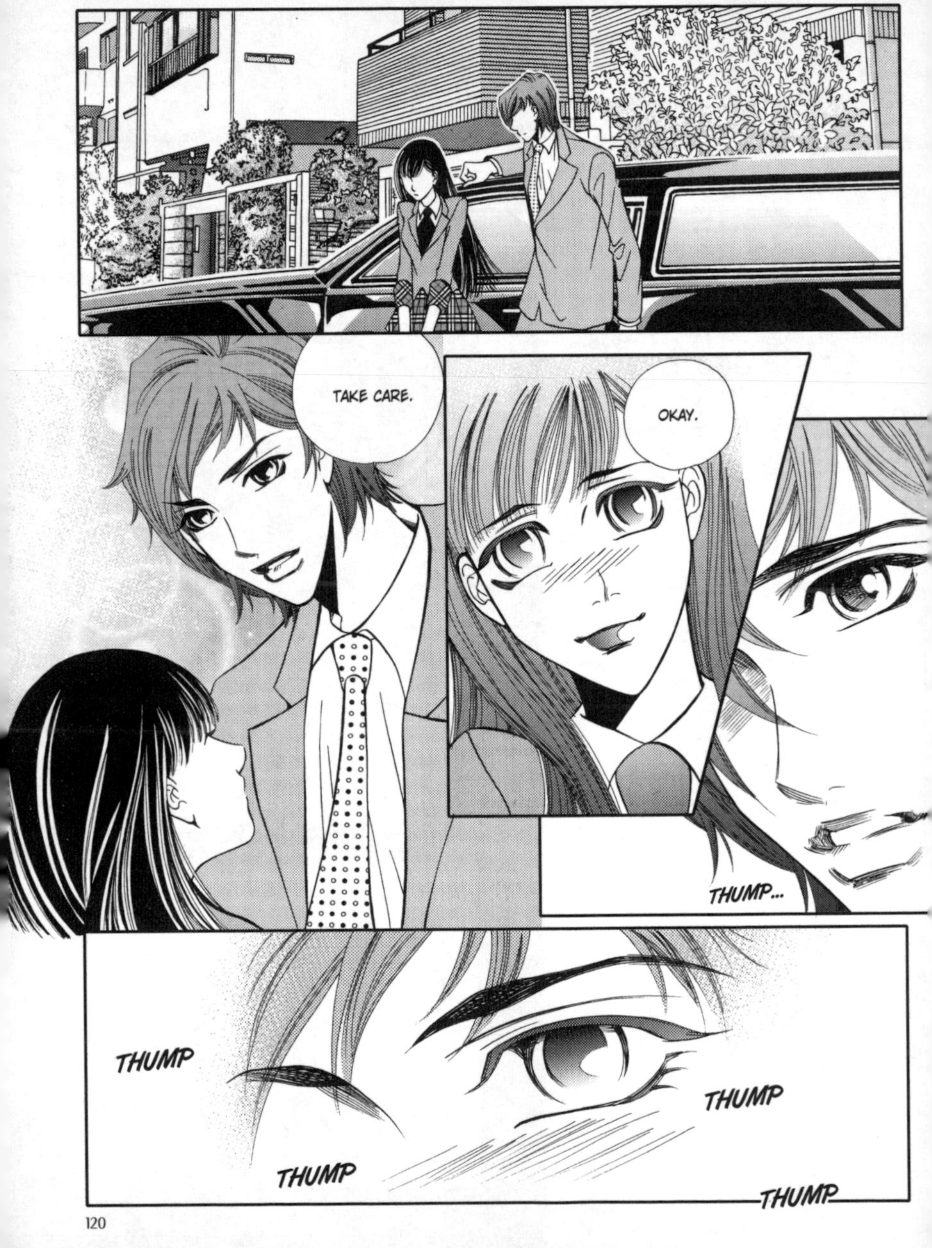
TAKE CARE.
OKAY.
THUMP...
THUMP
THUMP
THUMP
THUMP

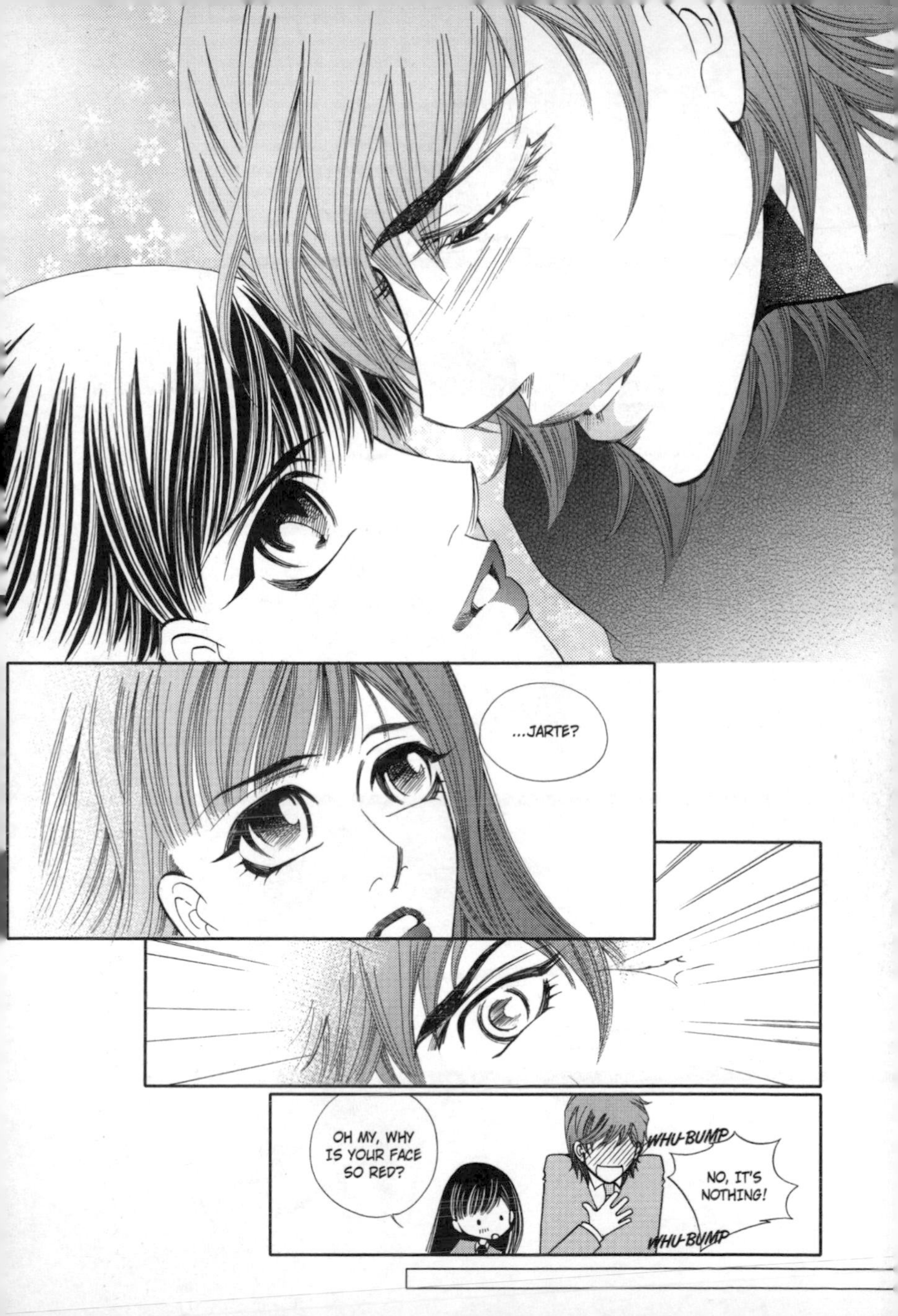
...JARTE?
OH MY, WHY IS YOUR FACE SO RED?
WHU-BUMP
NO, IT'S NOTHING!
WHU-BUMP

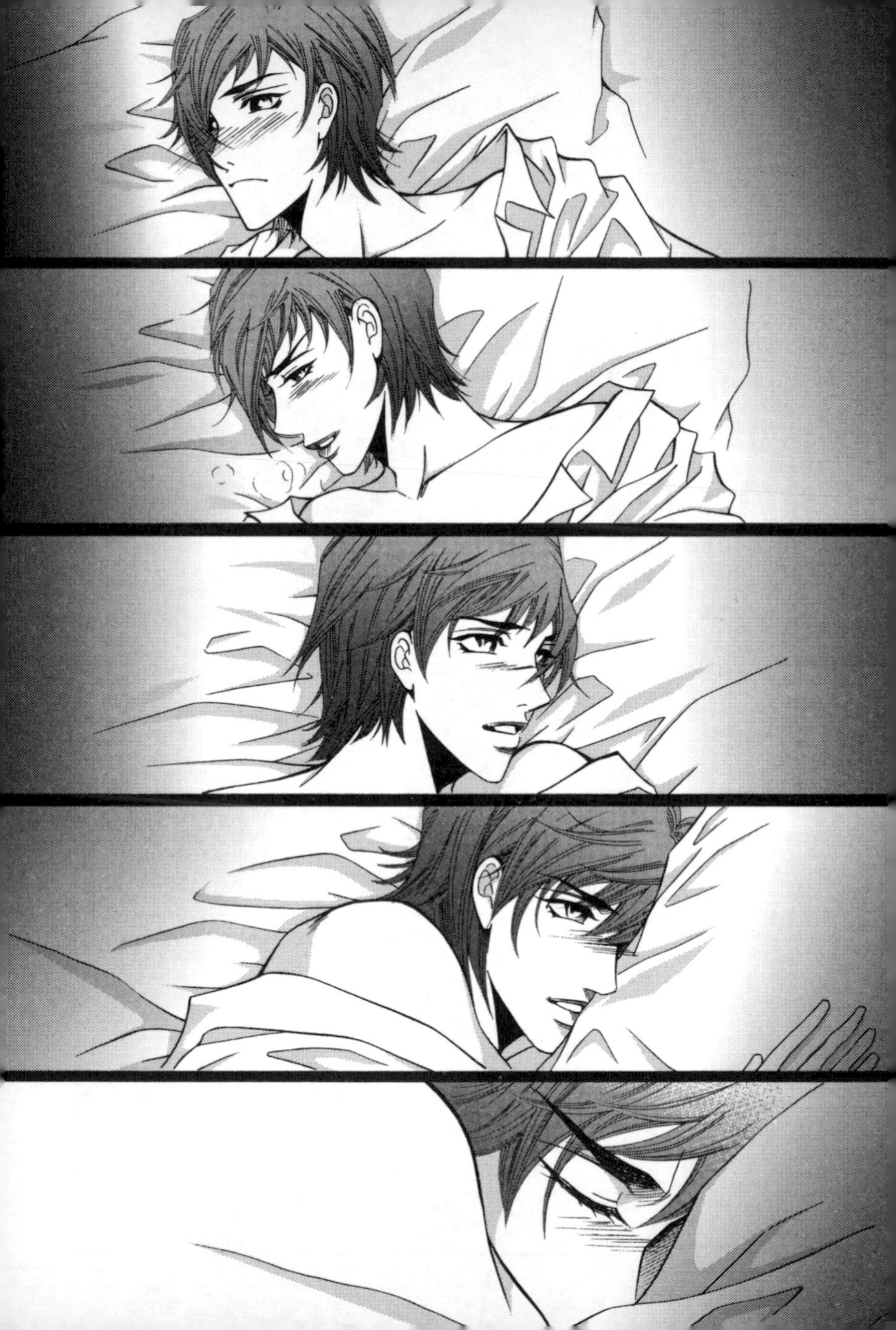

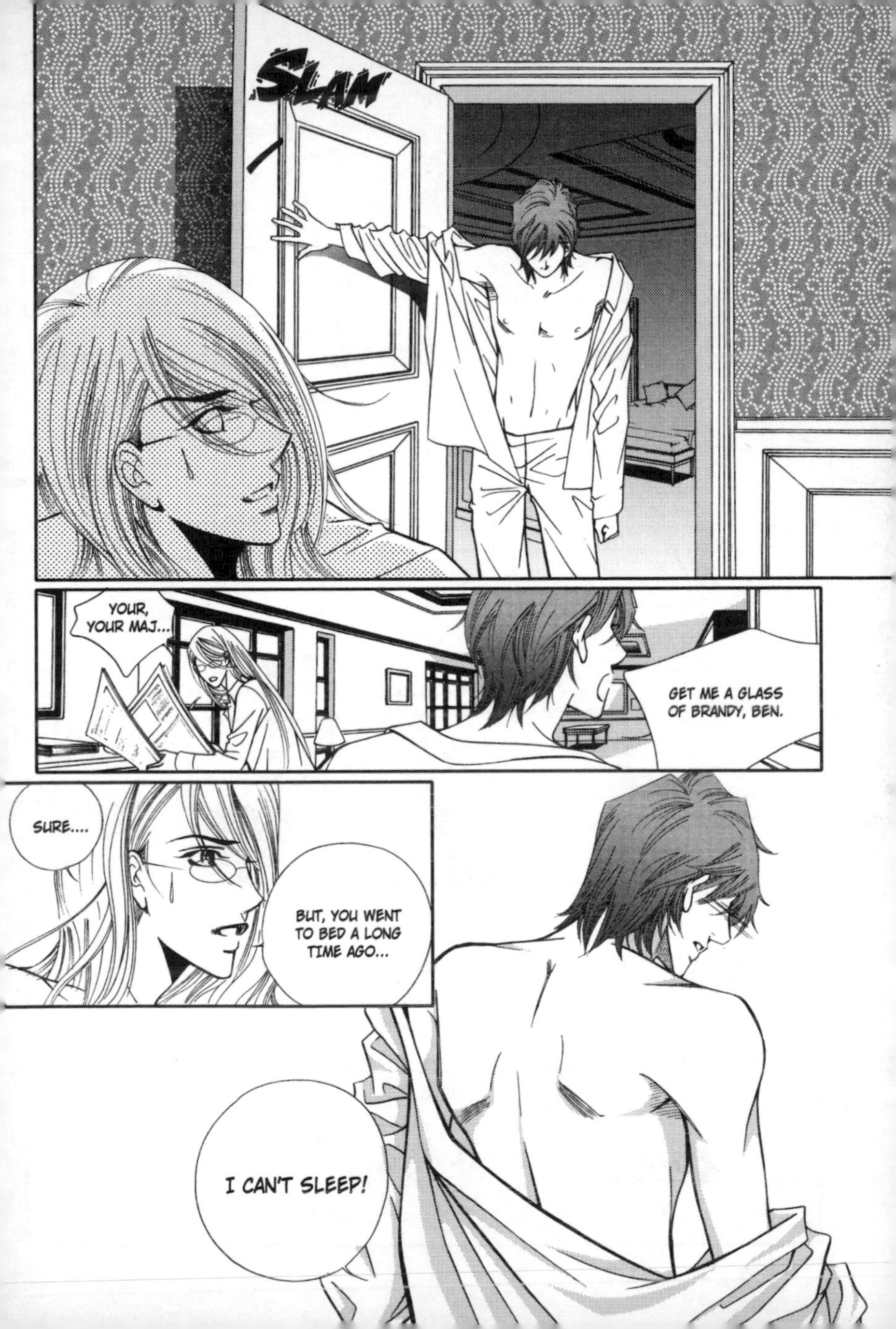
SLAM
YOUR, YOUR MAJ...
GET ME A GLASS OF BRANDY, BEN.
SURE....
BUT, YOU WENT TO BED A LONG TIME AGO...
I CAN'T SLEEP!

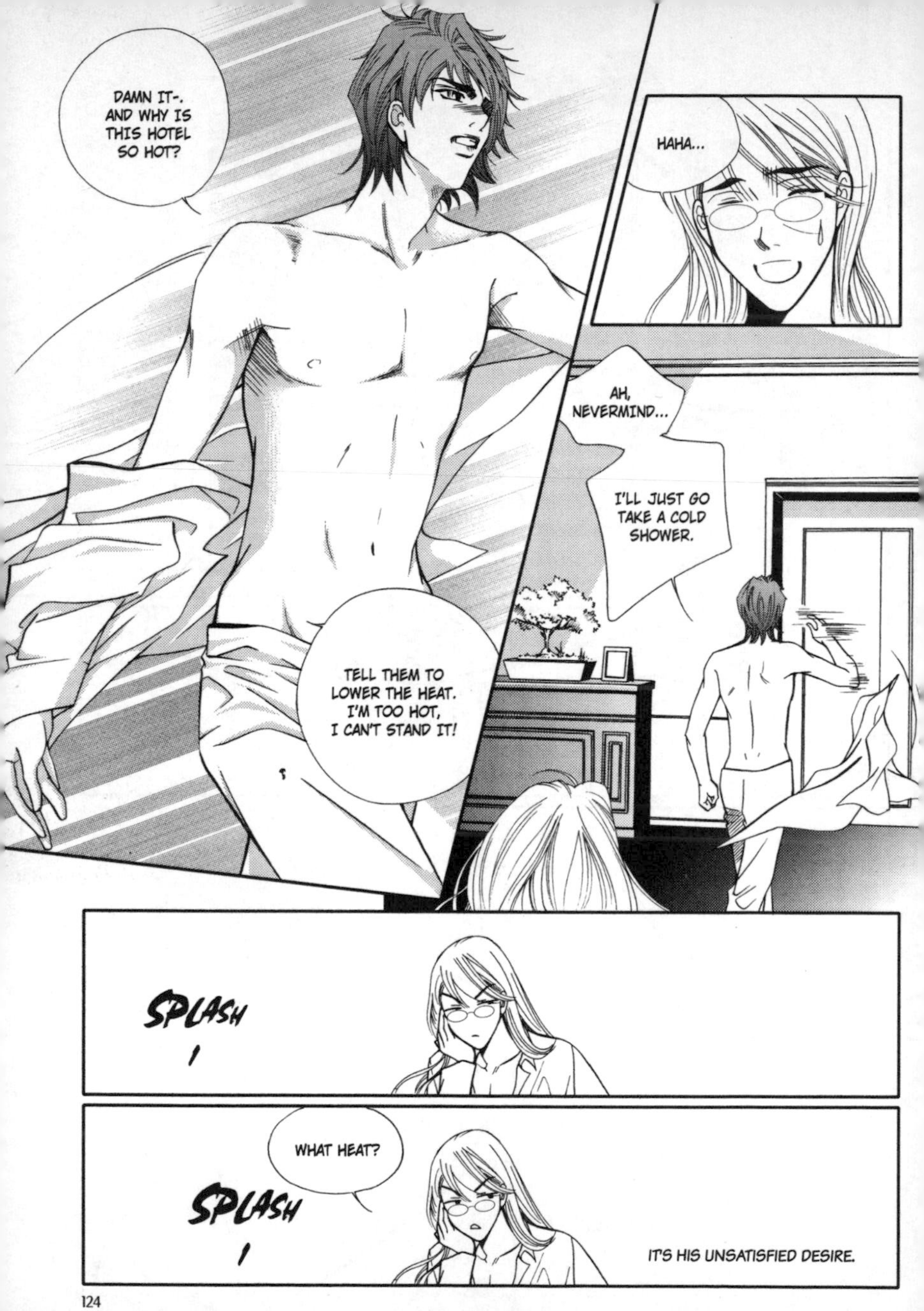
DAMN IT-. AND WHY IS THIS HOTEL SO HOT?
TELL THEM TO LOWER THE HEAT. I'M TOO HOT, I CAN'T STAND IT!
HAHA...
AH, NEVERMIND...
I'LL JUST GO TAKE A COLD SHOWER.
SPLASH
WHAT HEAT?
SPLASH
IT'S HIS UNSATISFIED DESIRE.

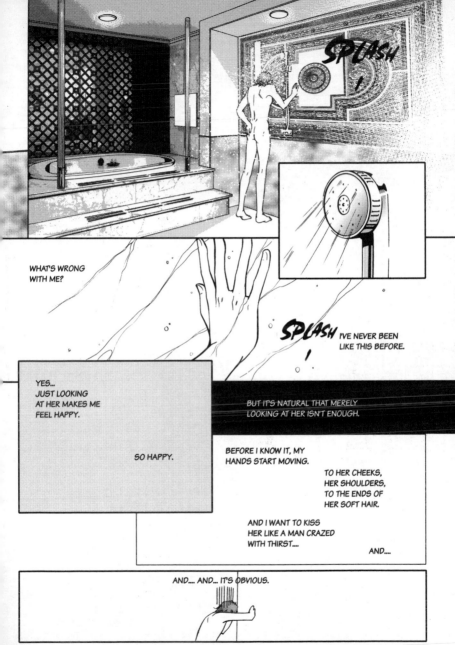

SPLASH

WHAT'S WRONG
WITH ME?

SPLASH I'VE NEVER BEEN
LIKE THIS BEFORE.

YES...
JUST LOOKING
AT HER MAKES ME
FEEL HAPPY.

BUT IT'S NATURAL THAT MERELY
LOOKING AT HER ISN'T ENOUGH.

SO HAPPY.

BEFORE I KNOW IT, MY
HANDS START MOVING.

TO HER CHEEKS,
HER SHOULDERS,
TO THE ENDS OF
HER SOFT HAIR.

AND I WANT TO KISS
HER LIKE A MAN CRAZED
WITH THIRST....

AND....

AND.... AND... IT'S OBVIOUS.

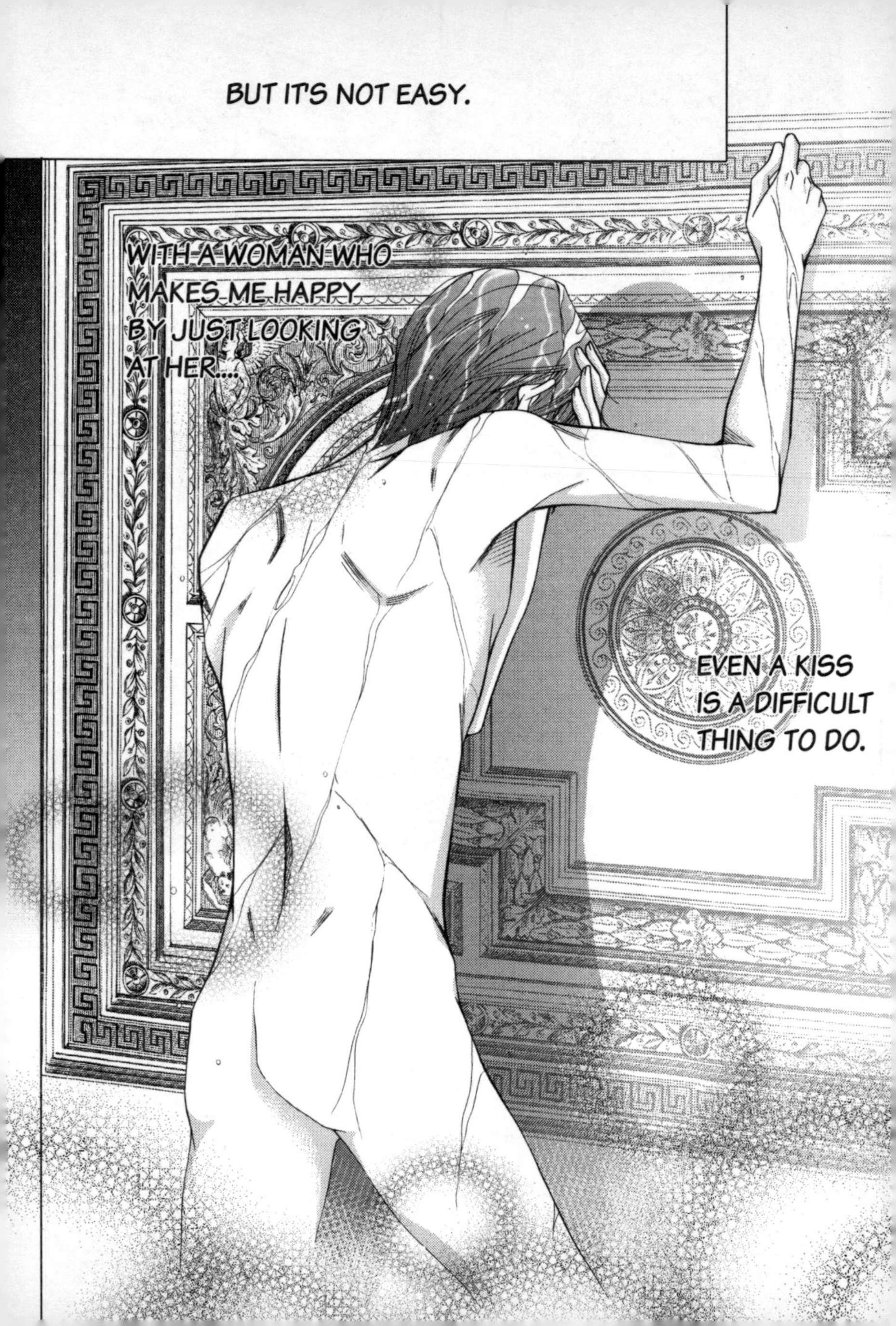
BUT IT'S NOT EASY.
WITH A WOMAN WHO MAKES ME HAPPY BY JUST LOOKING AT HER....
EVEN A KISS IS A DIFFICULT THING TO DO.

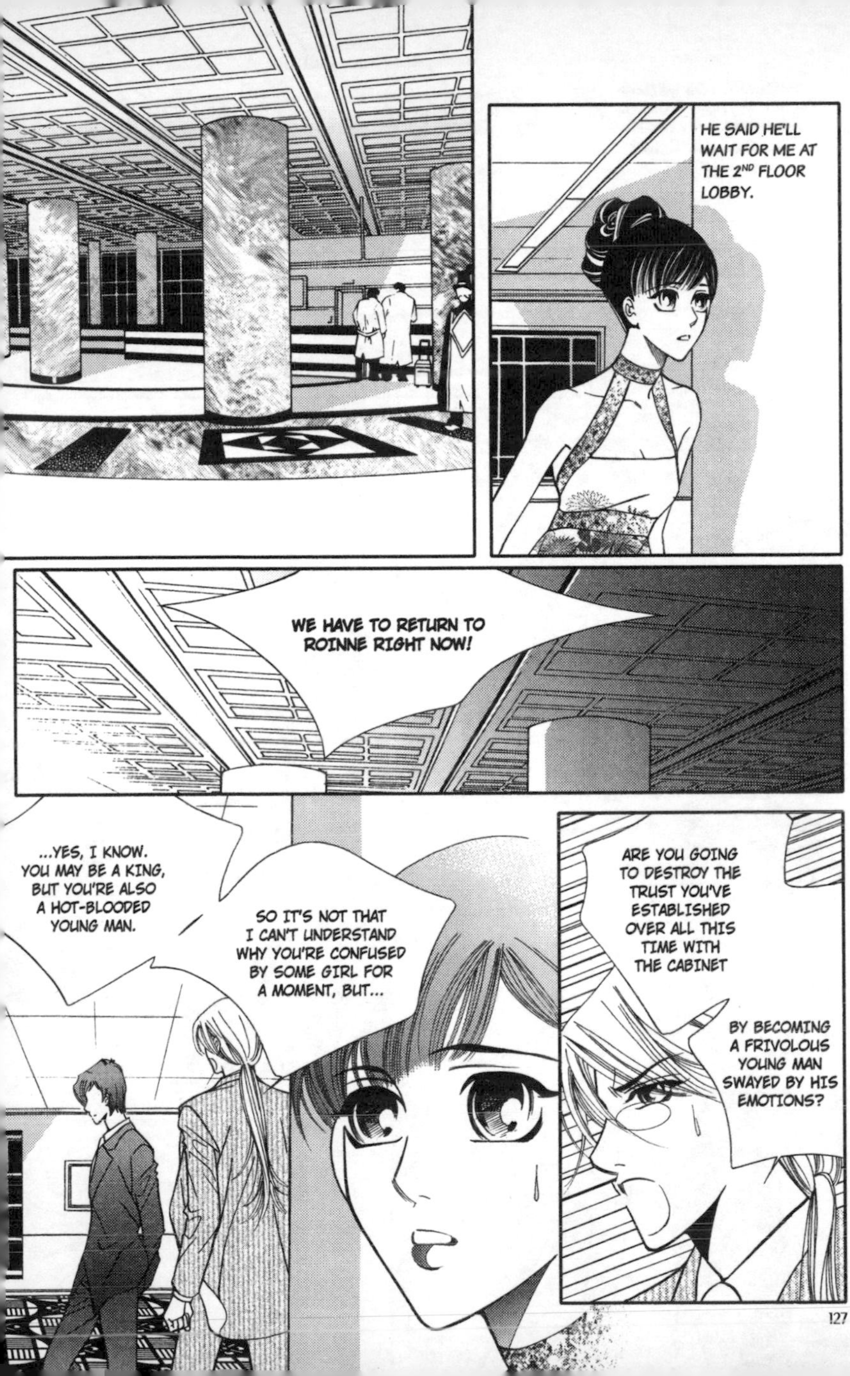
HE SAID HE'LL WAIT FOR ME AT THE 2ND FLOOR LOBBY.
WE HAVE TO RETURN TO ROINNE RIGHT NOW!
...YES, I KNOW. YOU MAY BE A KING, BUT YOU'RE ALSO A HOT-BLOODED YOUNG MAN.
SO IT'S NOT THAT I CAN'T UNDERSTAND WHY YOU'RE CONFUSED BY SOME GIRL FOR A MOMENT, BUT...
ARE YOU GOING TO DESTROY THE TRUST YOU'VE ESTABLISHED OVER ALL THIS TIME WITH THE CABINET
BY BECOMING A FRIVOLOUS YOUNG MAN SWAYED BY HIS EMOTIONS?

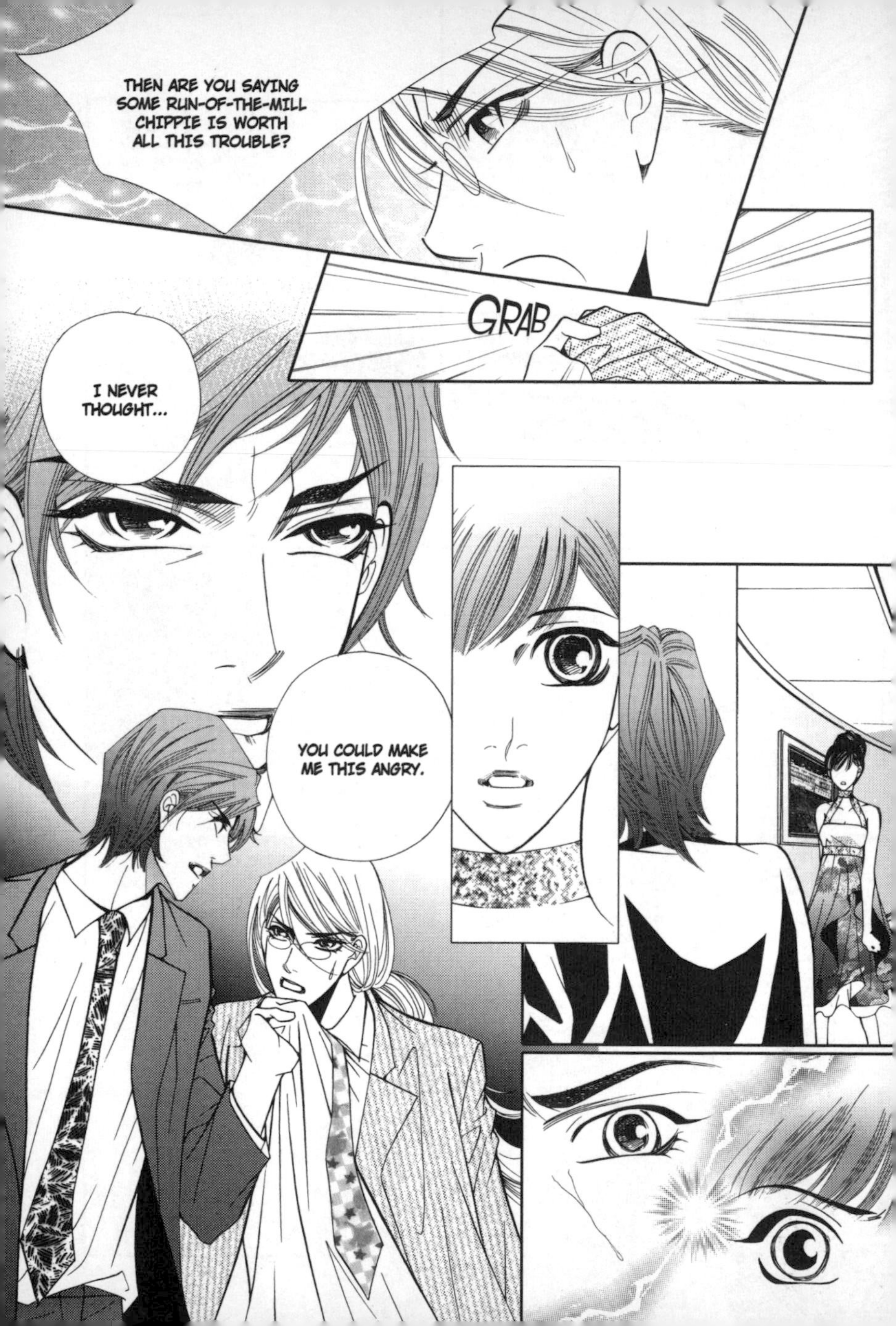
THEN ARE YOU SAYING SOME RUN-OF-THE-MILL CHIPPIE IS WORTH ALL THIS TROUBLE?
GRAB
I NEVER THOUGHT...
YOU COULD MAKE ME THIS ANGRY.

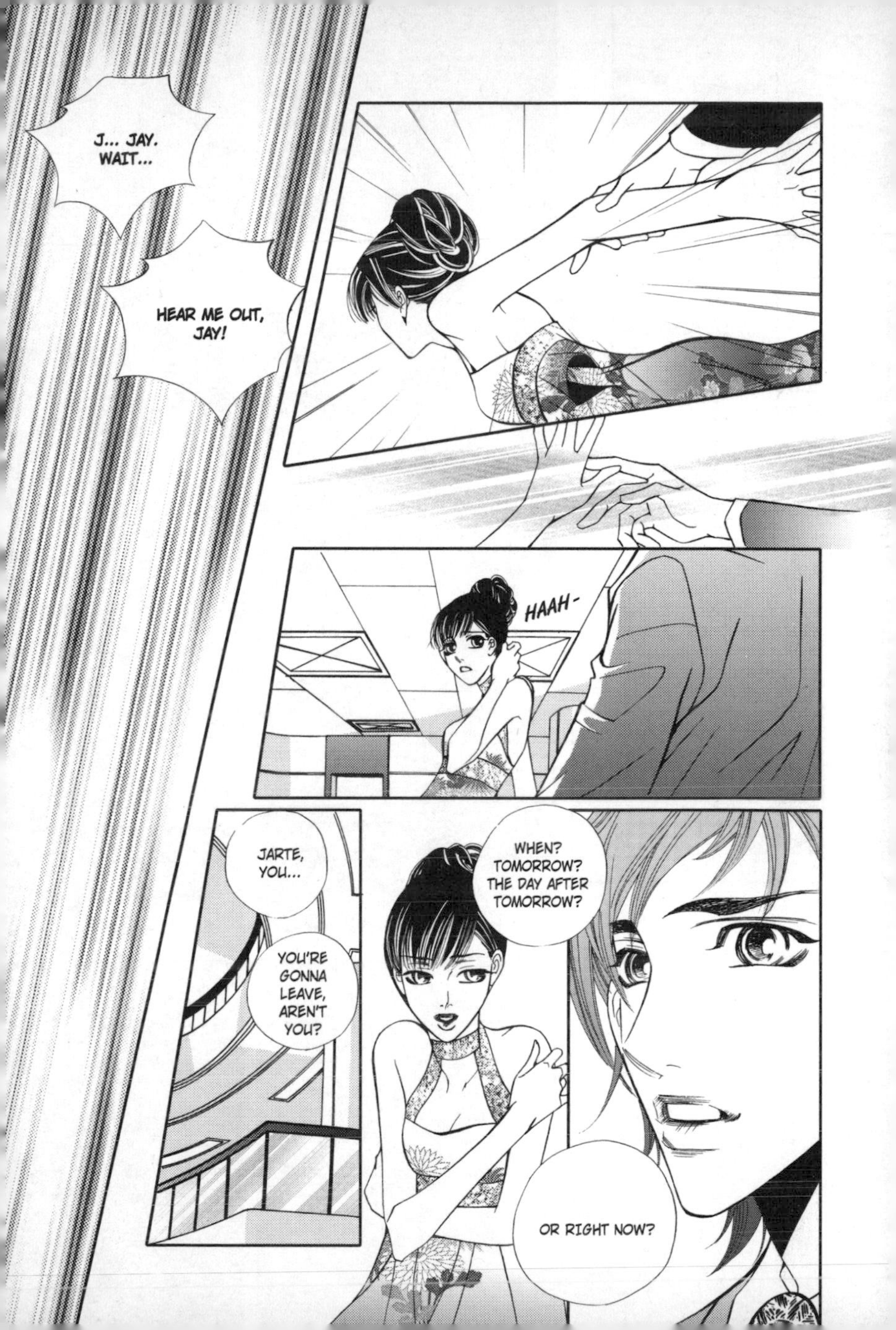
J... JAY. WAIT...
HEAR ME OUT, JAY!
HAAH-
JARTE, YOU...
YOU'RE GONNA LEAVE, AREN'T YOU?
WHEN? TOMORROW? THE DAY AFTER TOMORROW?
OR RIGHT NOW?

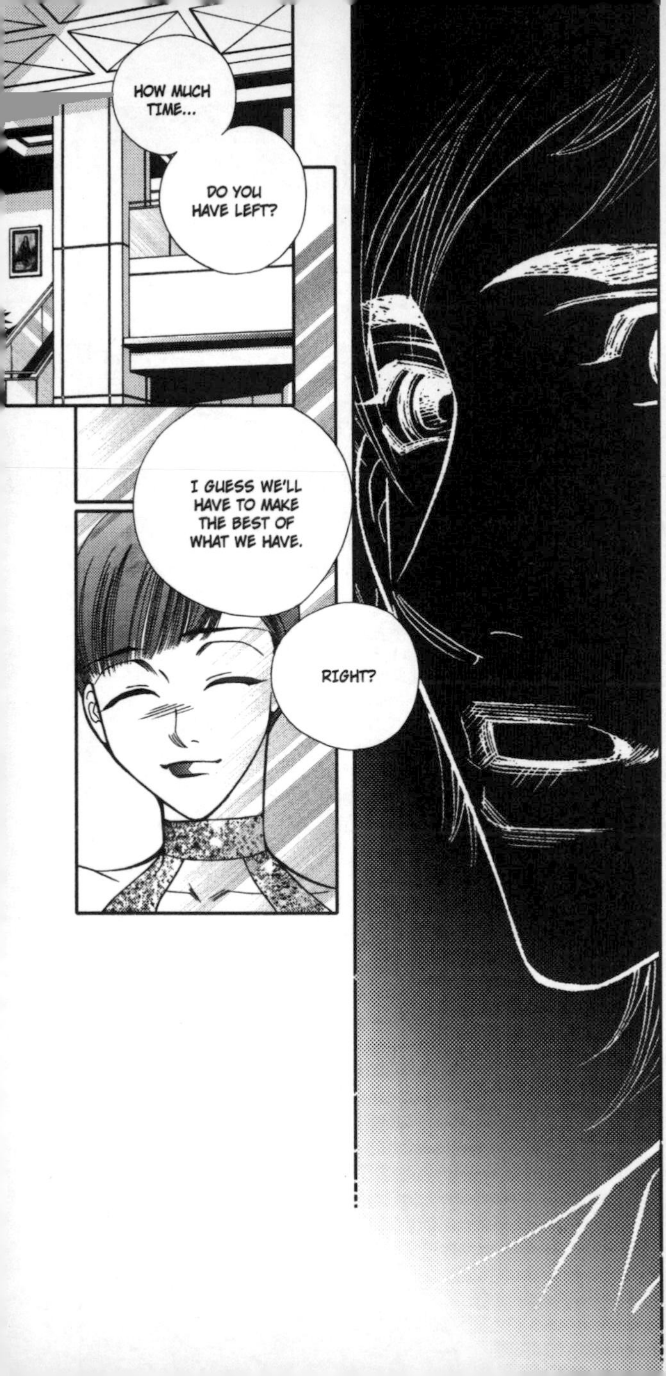
HOW MUCH TIME...
DO YOU HAVE LEFT?
I GUESS WE'LL HAVE TO MAKE THE BEST OF WHAT WE HAVE.
RIGHT?

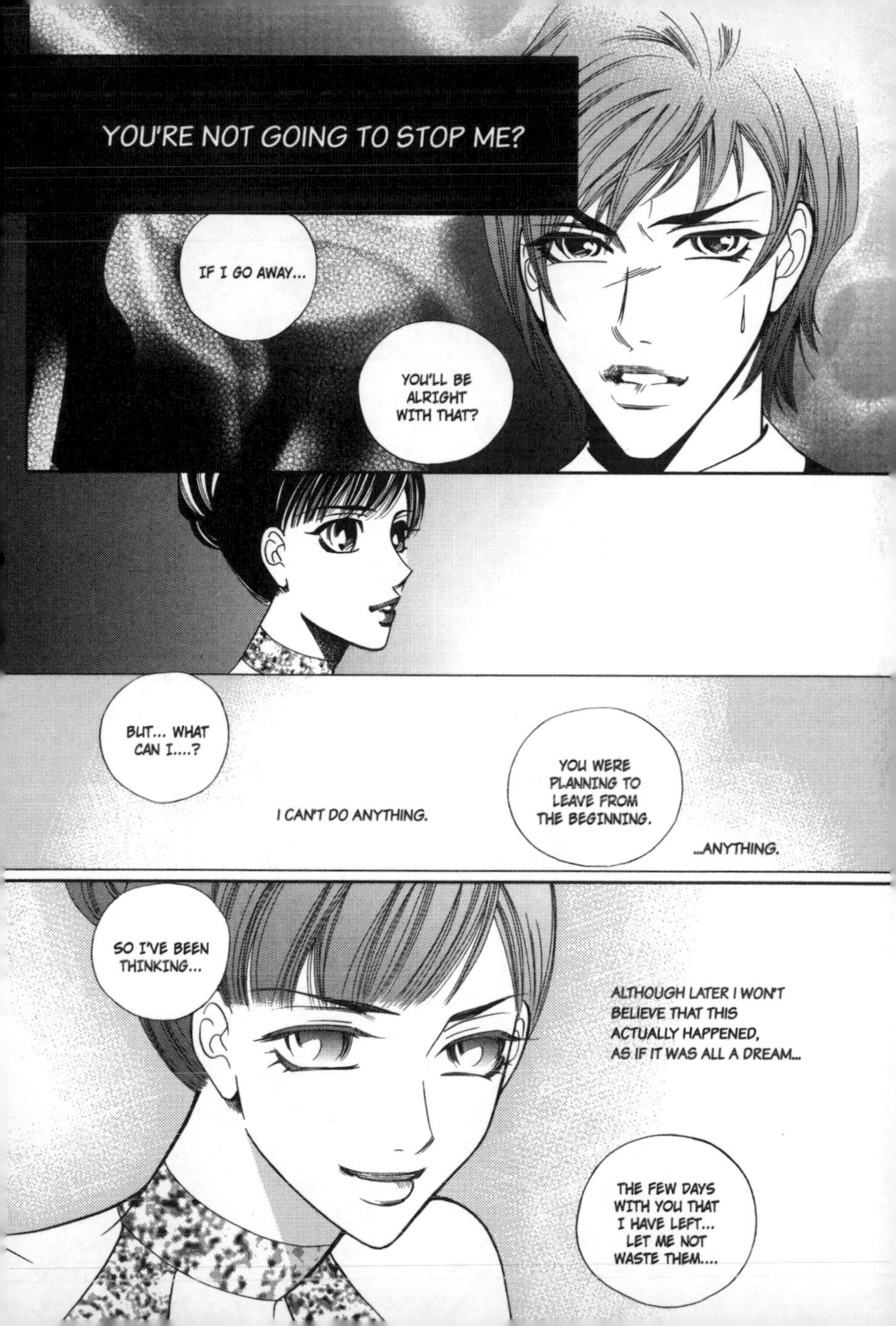
YOU'RE NOT GOING TO STOP ME?
IF I GO AWAY...
YOU'LL BE ALRIGHT WITH THAT?
BUT... WHAT CAN I....?
I CAN'T DO ANYTHING.
YOU WERE PLANNING TO LEAVE FROM THE BEGINNING.
...ANYTHING.
SO I'VE BEEN THINKING...
ALTHOUGH LATER I WON'T BELIEVE THAT THIS ACTUALLY HAPPENED, AS IF IT WAS ALL A DREAM...
THE FEW DAYS WITH YOU THAT I HAVE LEFT... LET ME NOT WASTE THEM....

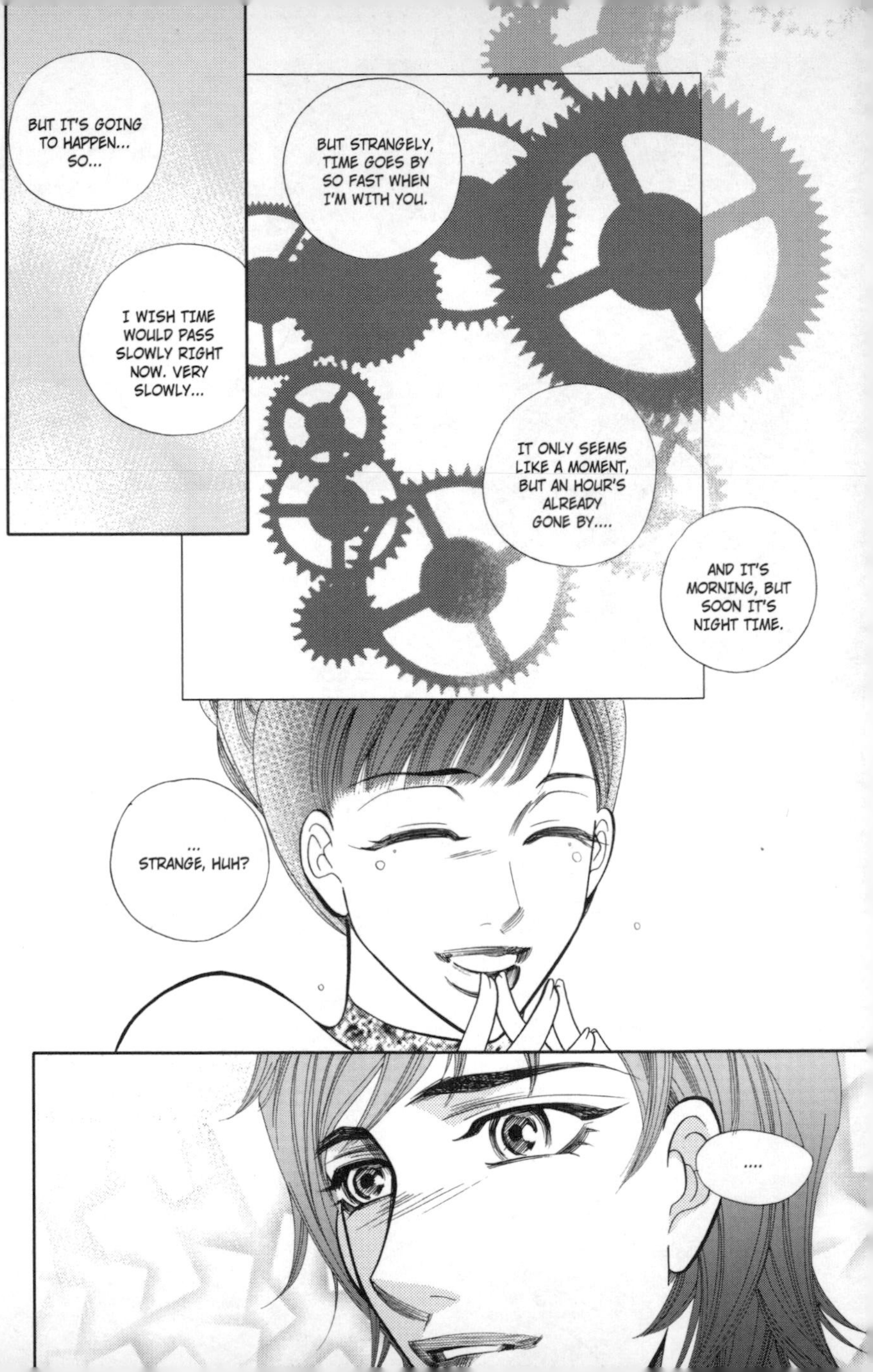
BUT IT'S GOING TO HAPPEN... SO...
I WISH TIME WOULD PASS SLOWLY RIGHT NOW. VERY SLOWLY...
BUT STRANGELY, TIME GOES BY SO FAST WHEN I'M WITH YOU.
IT ONLY SEEMS LIKE A MOMENT, BUT AN HOUR'S ALREADY GONE BY....
AND IT'S MORNING, BUT SOON IT'S NIGHT TIME.
... STRANGE, HUH?
....

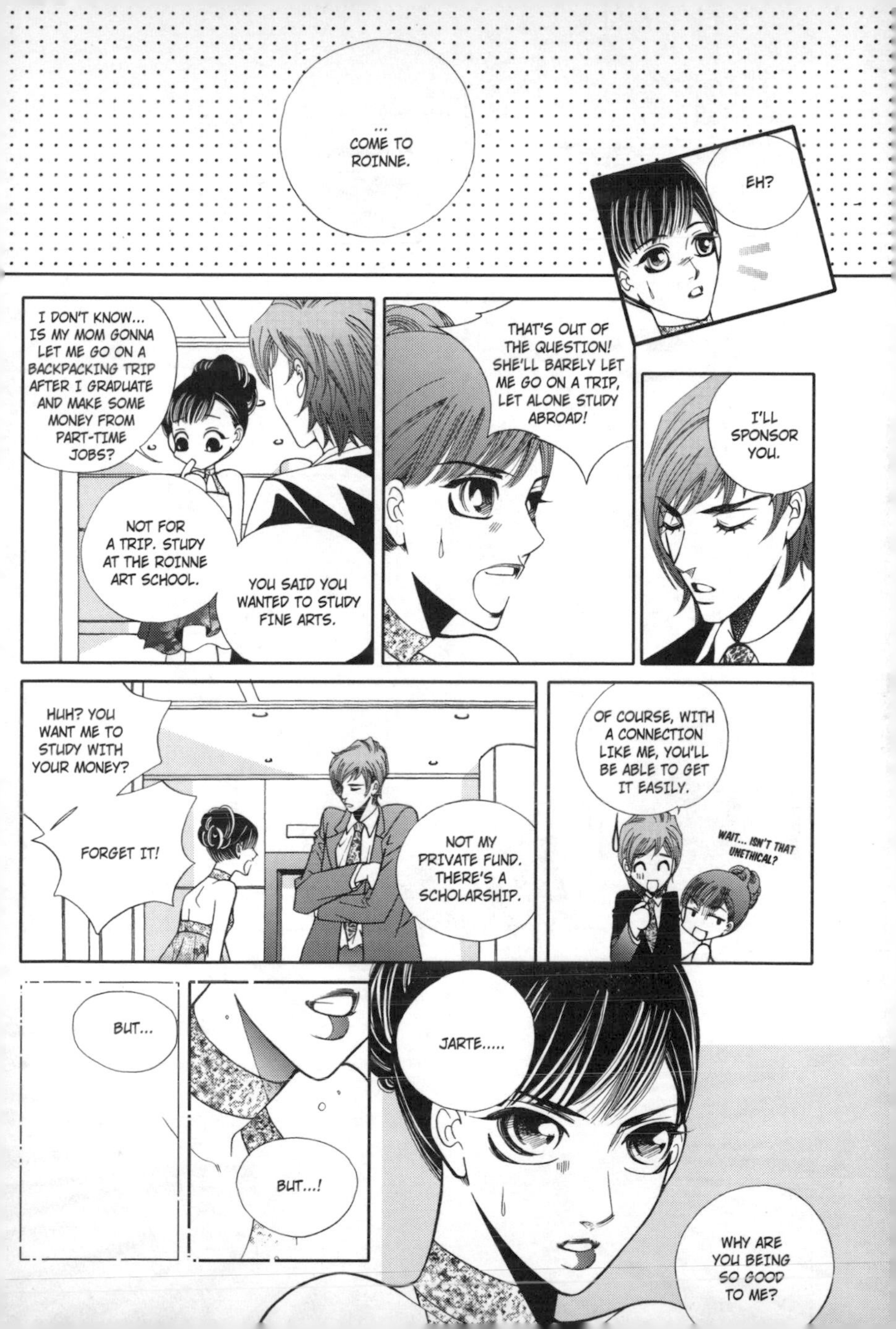

... COME TO ROINNE.
EH?
I DON'T KNOW... IS MY MOM GONNA LET ME GO ON A BACKPACKING TRIP AFTER I GRADUATE AND MAKE SOME MONEY FROM PART-TIME JOBS?
NOT FOR A TRIP. STUDY AT THE ROINNE ART SCHOOL.
YOU SAID YOU WANTED TO STUDY FINE ARTS.
THAT'S OUT OF THE QUESTION! SHE'LL BARELY LET ME GO ON A TRIP, LET ALONE STUDY ABROAD!
I'LL SPONSOR YOU.
HUH? YOU WANT ME TO STUDY WITH YOUR MONEY?
FORGET IT!
NOT MY PRIVATE FUND. THERE'S A SCHOLARSHIP.
OF COURSE, WITH A CONNECTION LIKE ME, YOU'LL BE ABLE TO GET IT EASILY.
WAIT... ISN'T THAT UNETHICAL?
BUT...
BUT...!
JARTE.....
WHY ARE YOU BEING SO GOOD TO ME?

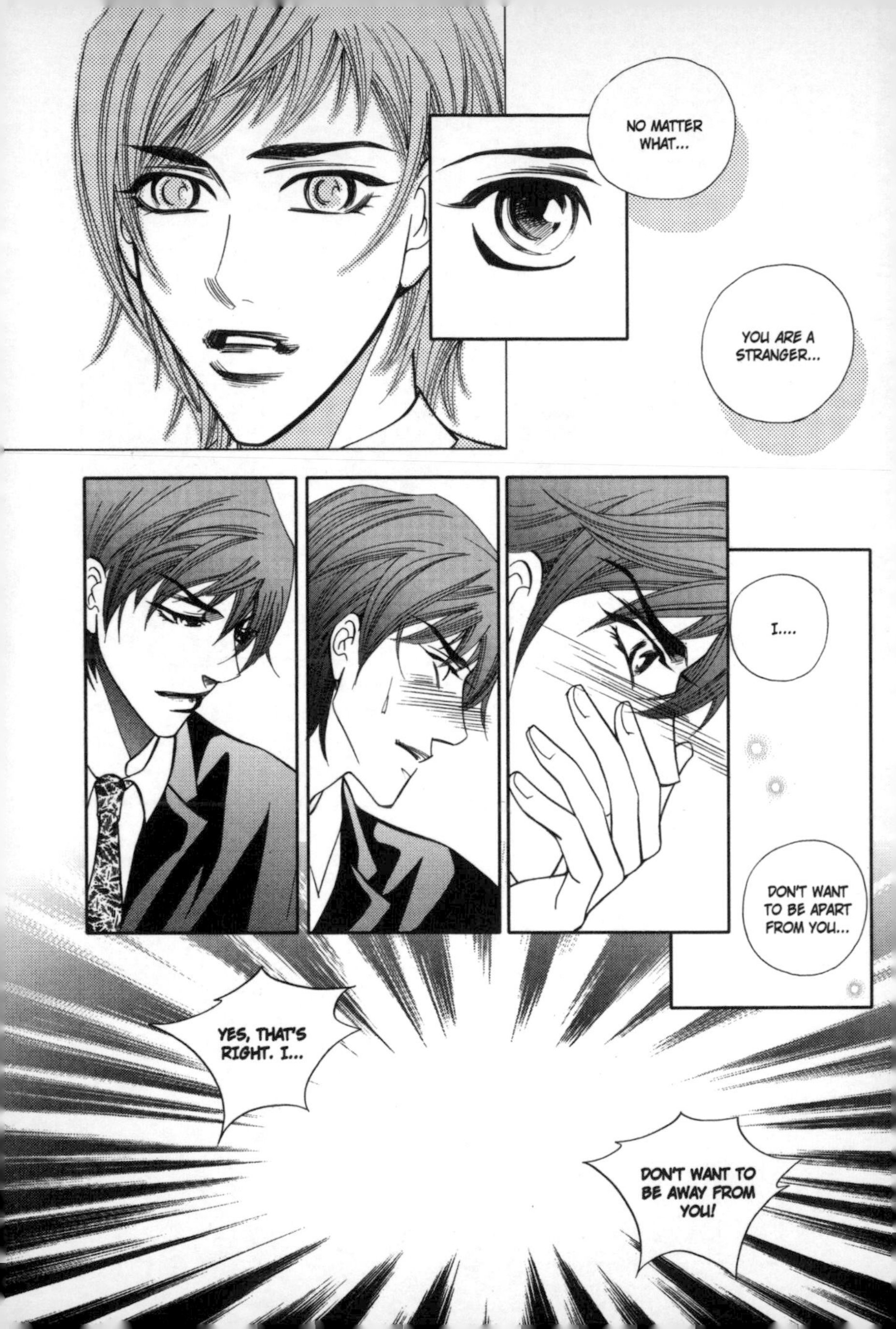
NO MATTER WHAT...
YOU ARE A STRANGER...
I....
DON'T WANT TO BE APART FROM YOU...
YES, THAT'S RIGHT. I...
DON'T WANT TO BE AWAY FROM YOU!

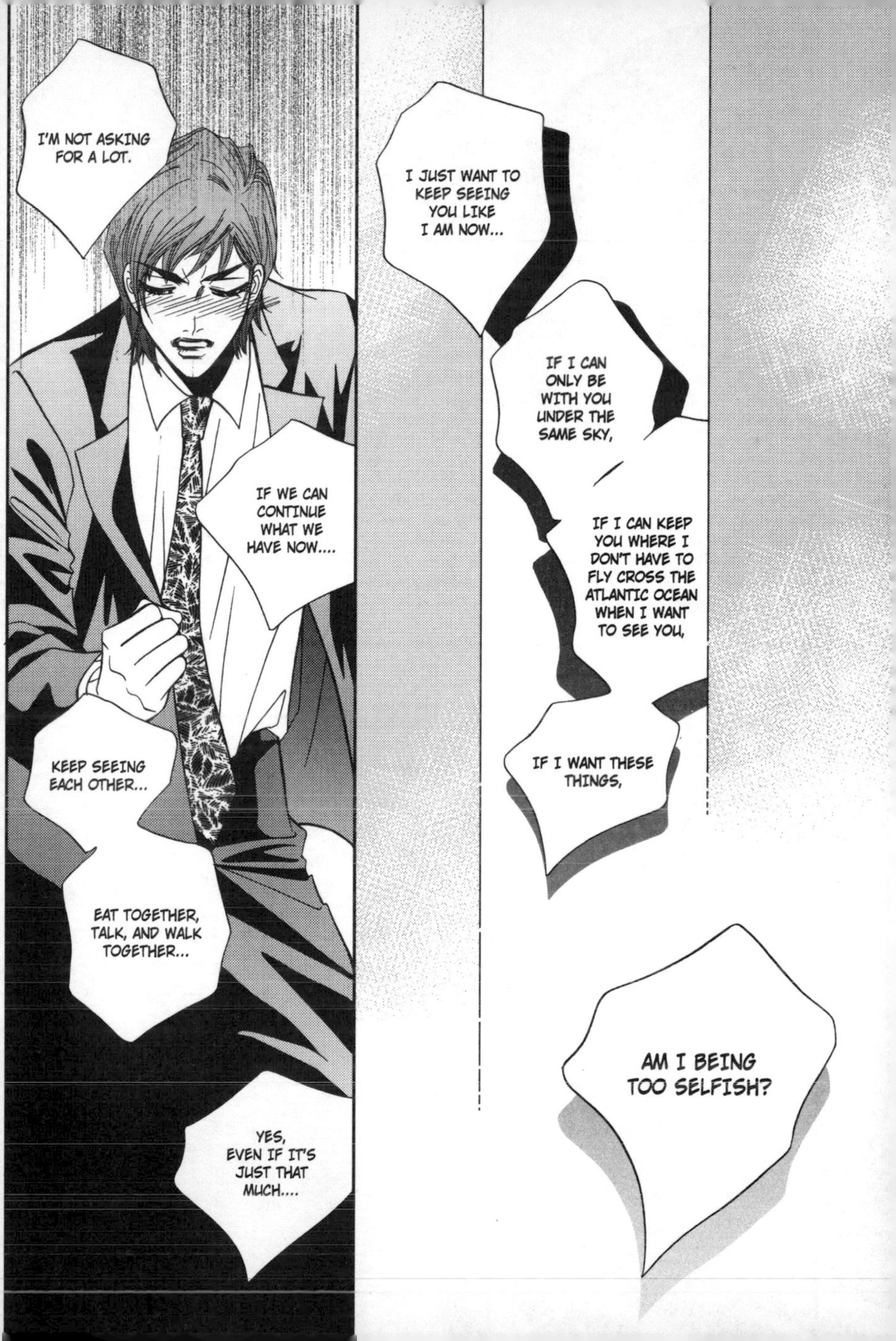
I'M NOT ASKING FOR A LOT.
IF WE CAN CONTINUE WHAT WE HAVE NOW....
KEEP SEEING EACH OTHER...
EAT TOGETHER, TALK, AND WALK TOGETHER...
YES, EVEN IF IT'S JUST THAT MUCH....
I JUST WANT TO KEEP SEEING YOU LIKE I AM NOW...
IF I CAN ONLY BE WITH YOU UNDER THE SAME SKY,
IF I CAN KEEP YOU WHERE I DON'T HAVE TO FLY CROSS THE ATLANTIC OCEAN WHEN I WANT TO SEE YOU,
IF I WANT THESE THINGS,
AM I BEING TOO SELFISH?

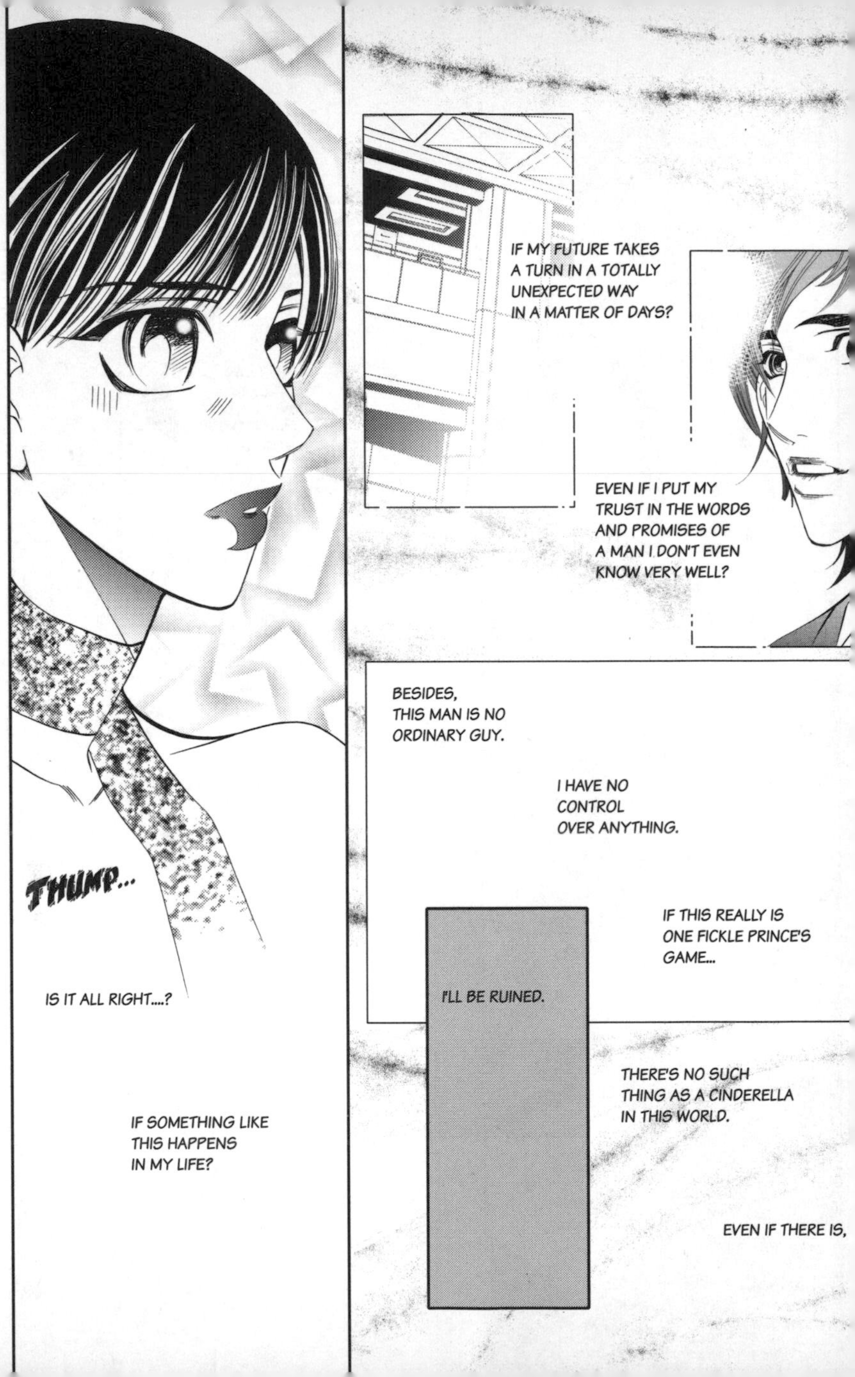
THUMP...
IS IT ALL RIGHT....?
IF SOMETHING LIKE THIS HAPPENS IN MY LIFE?
IF MY FUTURE TAKES A TURN IN A TOTALLY UNEXPECTED WAY IN A MATTER OF DAYS?
EVEN IF I PUT MY TRUST IN THE WORDS AND PROMISES OF A MAN I DON'T EVEN KNOW VERY WELL?
BESIDES, THIS MAN IS NO ORDINARY GUY.
I HAVE NO CONTROL OVER ANYTHING.
IF THIS REALLY IS ONE FICKLE PRINCE'S GAME...
I'LL BE RUINED.
THERE'S NO SUCH THING AS A CINDERELLA IN THIS WORLD.
EVEN IF THERE IS,

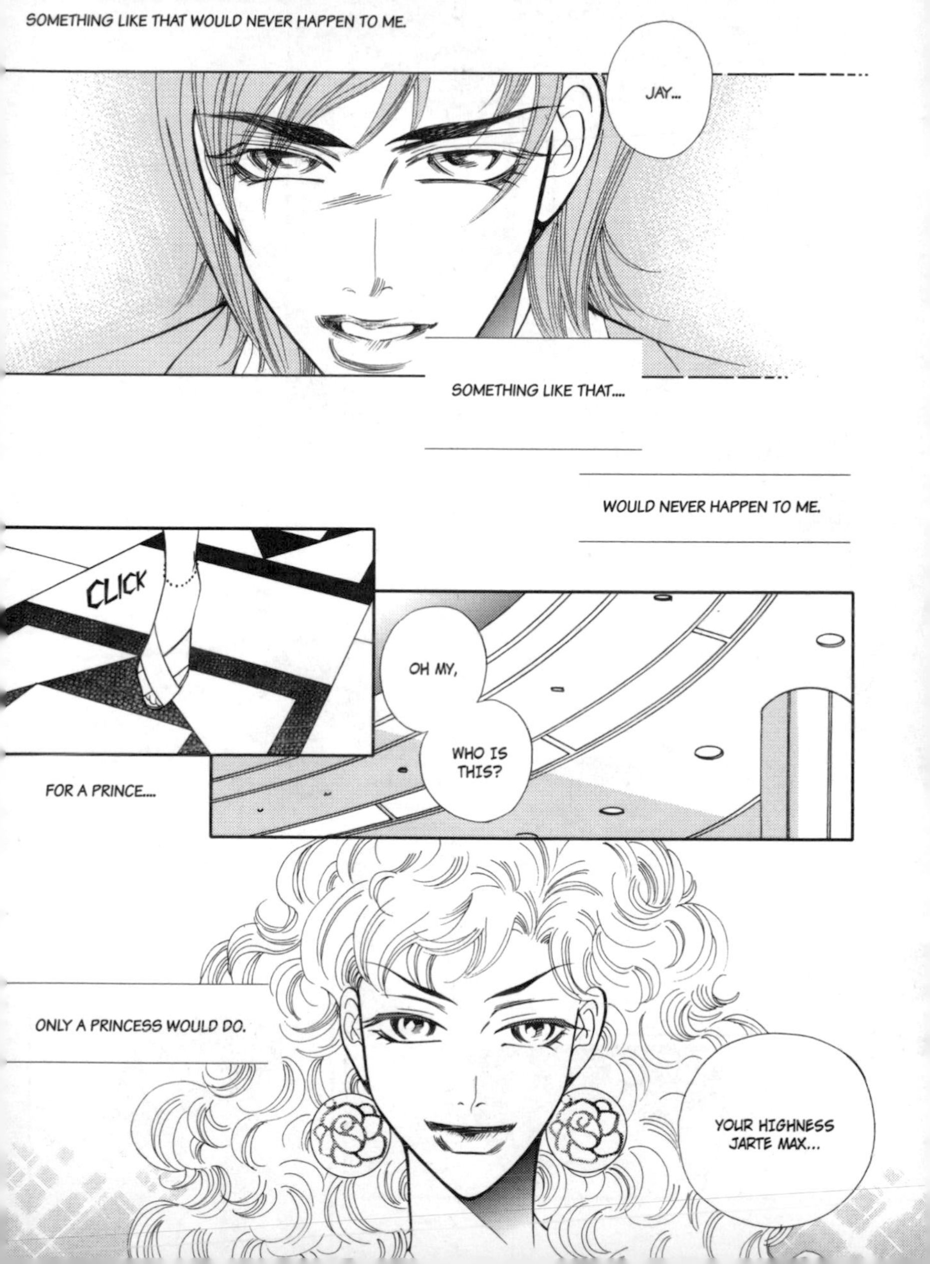
SOMETHING LIKE THAT WOULD NEVER HAPPEN TO ME.
JAY...
SOMETHING LIKE THAT....
WOULD NEVER HAPPEN TO ME.
CLICK
OH MY,
WHO IS THIS?
FOR A PRINCE....
ONLY A PRINCESS WOULD DO.
YOUR HIGHNESS JARTE MAX...

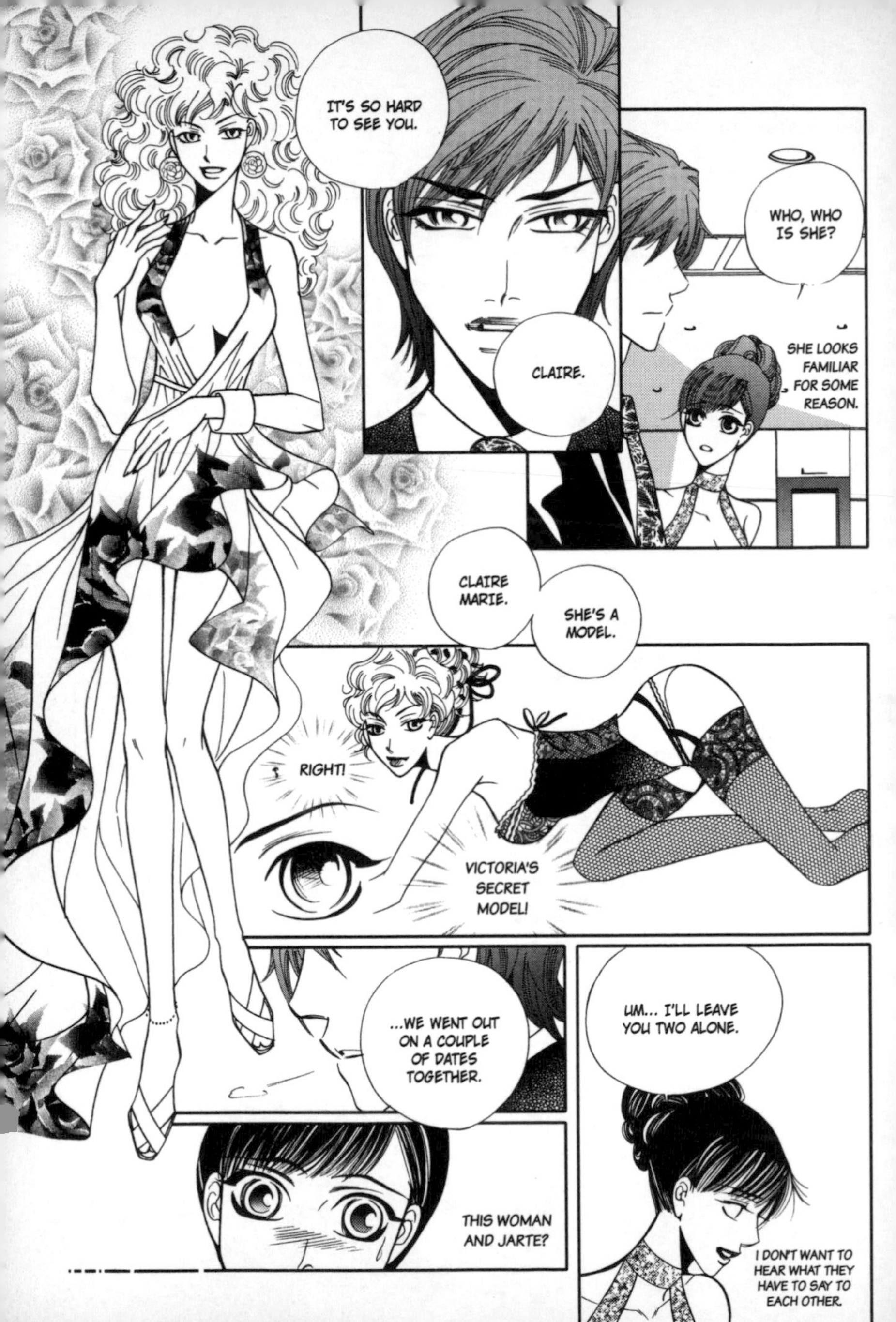
IT'S SO HARD TO SEE YOU.
CLAIRE.
WHO, WHO IS SHE?
SHE LOOKS FAMILIAR FOR SOME REASON.
CLAIRE MARIE.
SHE'S A MODEL.
RIGHT!
VICTORIA'S SECRET MODEL!
...WE WENT OUT ON A COUPLE OF DATES TOGETHER.
THIS WOMAN AND JARTE?
UM... I'LL LEAVE YOU TWO ALONE.
I DON'T WANT TO HEAR WHAT THEY HAVE TO SAY TO EACH OTHER.

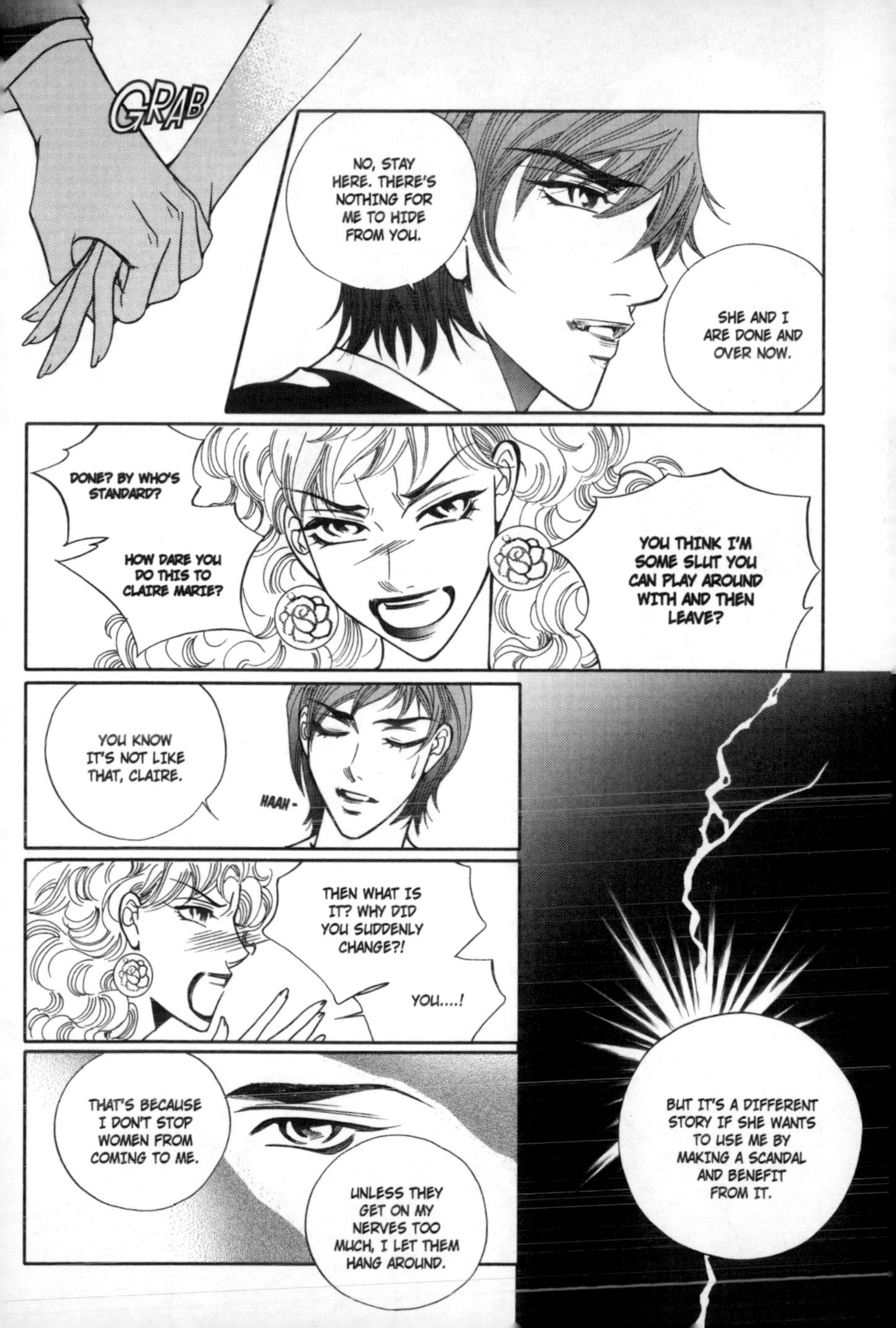
GRAB
NO, STAY HERE. THERE'S NOTHING FOR ME TO HIDE FROM YOU.
SHE AND I ARE DONE AND OVER NOW.
DONE? BY WHO'S STANDARD?
HOW DARE YOU DO THIS TO CLAIRE MARIE?
YOU THINK I'M SOME SLUT YOU CAN PLAY AROUND WITH AND THEN LEAVE?
YOU KNOW IT'S NOT LIKE THAT, CLAIRE.
HAAH-
THEN WHAT IS IT? WHY DID YOU SUDDENLY CHANGE?!
YOU....!
THAT'S BECAUSE I DON'T STOP WOMEN FROM COMING TO ME.
UNLESS THEY GET ON MY NERVES TOO MUCH, I LET THEM HANG AROUND.
BUT IT'S A DIFFERENT STORY IF SHE WANTS TO USE ME BY MAKING A SCANDAL AND BENEFIT FROM IT.

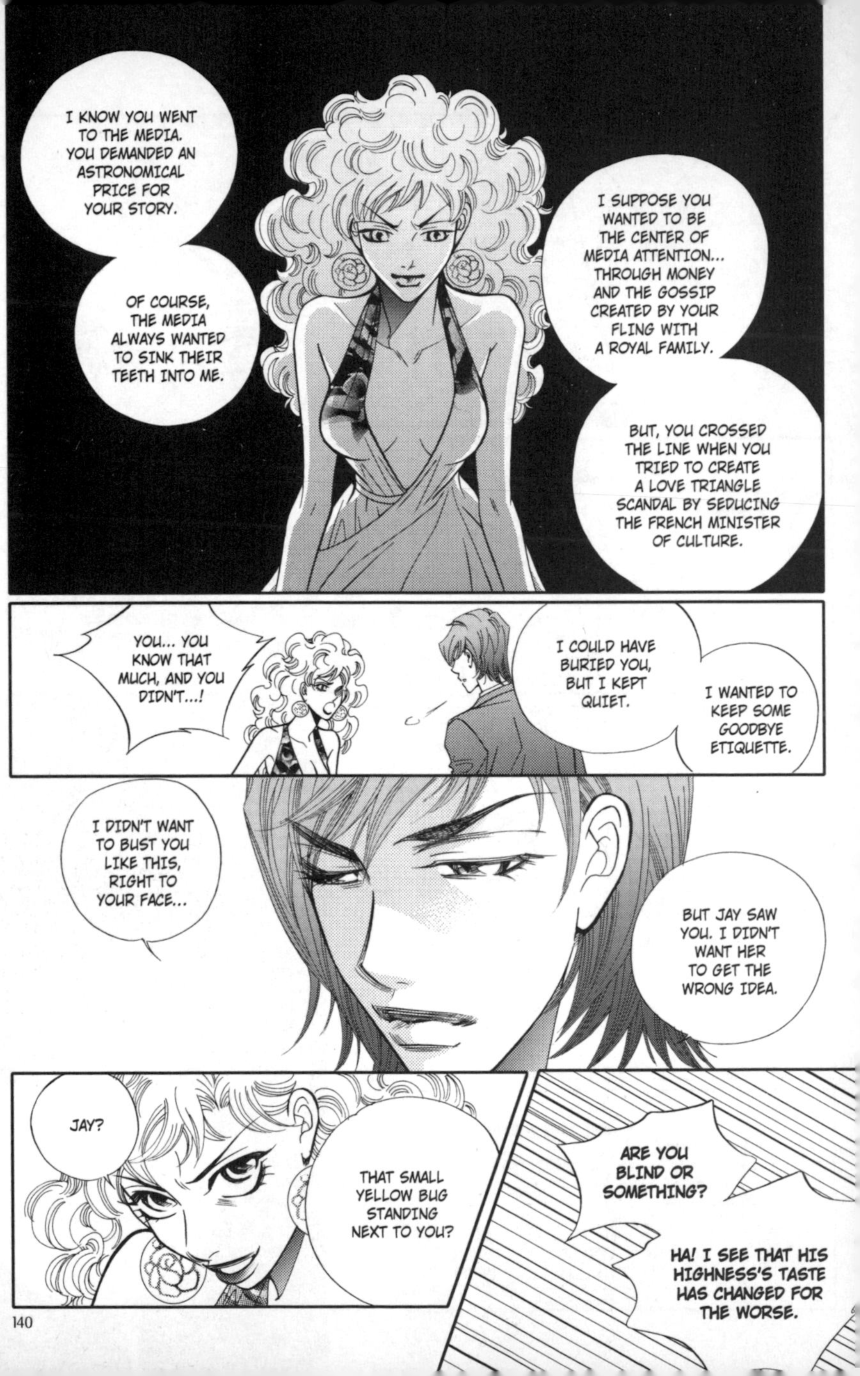
I KNOW YOU WENT TO THE MEDIA. YOU DEMANDED AN ASTRONOMICAL PRICE FOR YOUR STORY.
OF COURSE, THE MEDIA ALWAYS WANTED TO SINK THEIR TEETH INTO ME.
I SUPPOSE YOU WANTED TO BE THE CENTER OF MEDIA ATTENTION... THROUGH MONEY AND THE GOSSIP CREATED BY YOUR FLING WITH A ROYAL FAMILY.
BUT, YOU CROSSED THE LINE WHEN YOU TRIED TO CREATE A LOVE TRIANGLE SCANDAL BY SEDUCING THE FRENCH MINISTER OF CULTURE.
YOU... YOU KNOW THAT MUCH, AND YOU DIDN'T...!
I COULD HAVE BURIED YOU, BUT I KEPT QUIET.
I WANTED TO KEEP SOME GOODBYE ETIQUETTE.
I DIDN'T WANT TO BUST YOU LIKE THIS, RIGHT TO YOUR FACE...
BUT JAY SAW YOU. I DIDN'T WANT HER TO GET THE WRONG IDEA.
JAY?
THAT SMALL YELLOW BUG STANDING NEXT TO YOU?
ARE YOU BLIND OR SOMETHING?
HA! I SEE THAT HIS HIGHNESS'S TASTE HAS CHANGED FOR THE WORSE.

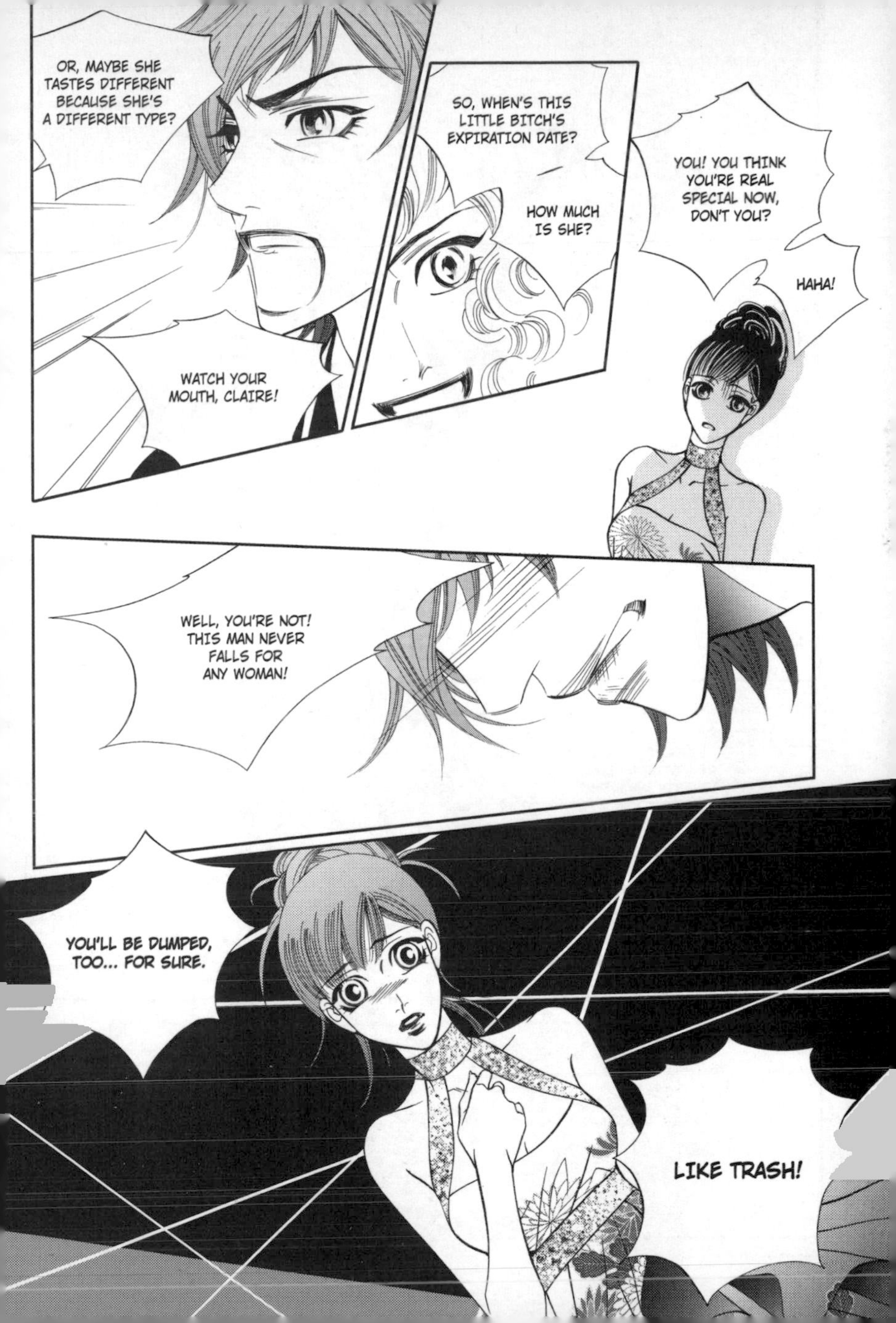
OR, MAYBE SHE TASTES DIFFERENT BECAUSE SHE'S A DIFFERENT TYPE?
WATCH YOUR MOUTH, CLAIRE!
SO, WHEN'S THIS LITTLE BITCH'S EXPIRATION DATE?
HOW MUCH IS SHE?
YOU! YOU THINK YOU'RE REAL SPECIAL NOW, DON'T YOU?
HAHA!
WELL, YOU'RE NOT! THIS MAN NEVER FALLS FOR ANY WOMAN!
YOU'LL BE DUMPED, TOO... FOR SURE.
LIKE TRASH!

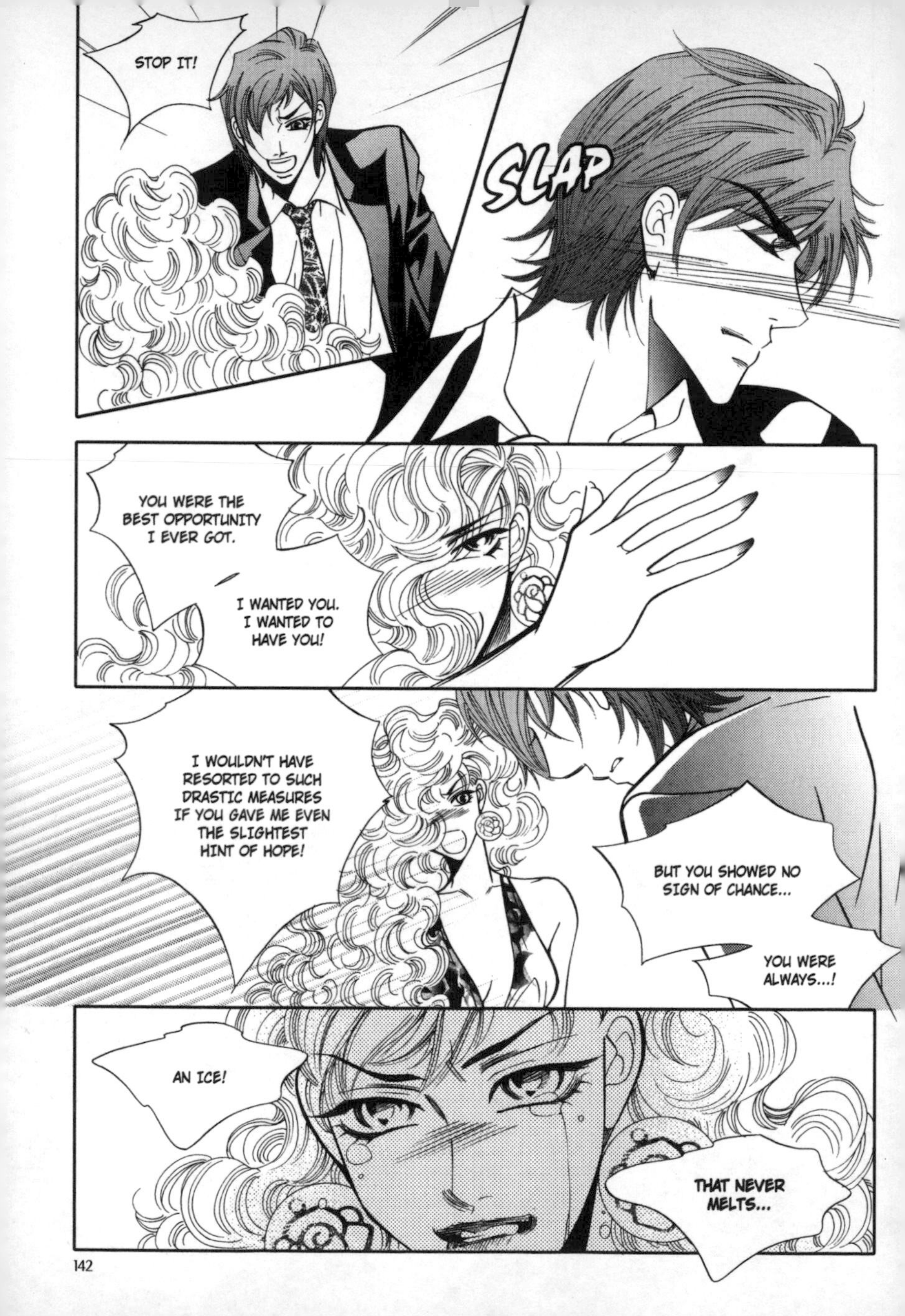
STOP IT!
SLAP
YOU WERE THE BEST OPPORTUNITY I EVER GOT.
I WANTED YOU. I WANTED TO HAVE YOU!
I WOULDN'T HAVE RESORTED TO SUCH DRASTIC MEASURES IF YOU GAVE ME EVEN THE SLIGHTEST HINT OF HOPE!
BUT YOU SHOWED NO SIGN OF CHANCE...
YOU WERE ALWAYS...!
AN ICE!
THAT NEVER MELTS...

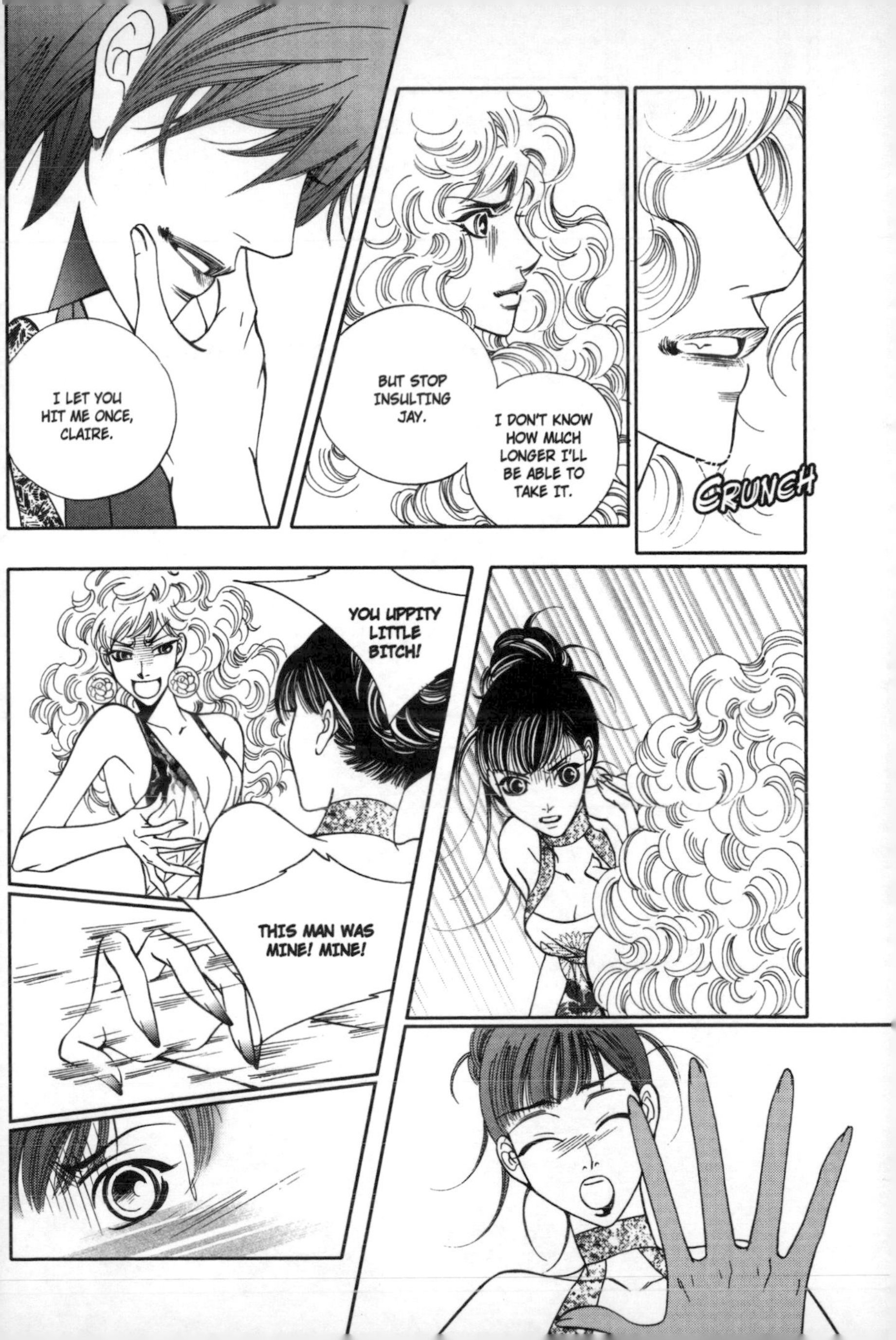
I LET YOU HIT ME ONCE, CLAIRE.
BUT STOP INSULTING JAY.
I DON'T KNOW HOW MUCH LONGER I'LL BE ABLE TO TAKE IT.
CRUNCH
YOU UPPITY LITTLE BITCH!
THIS MAN WAS MINE! MINE!

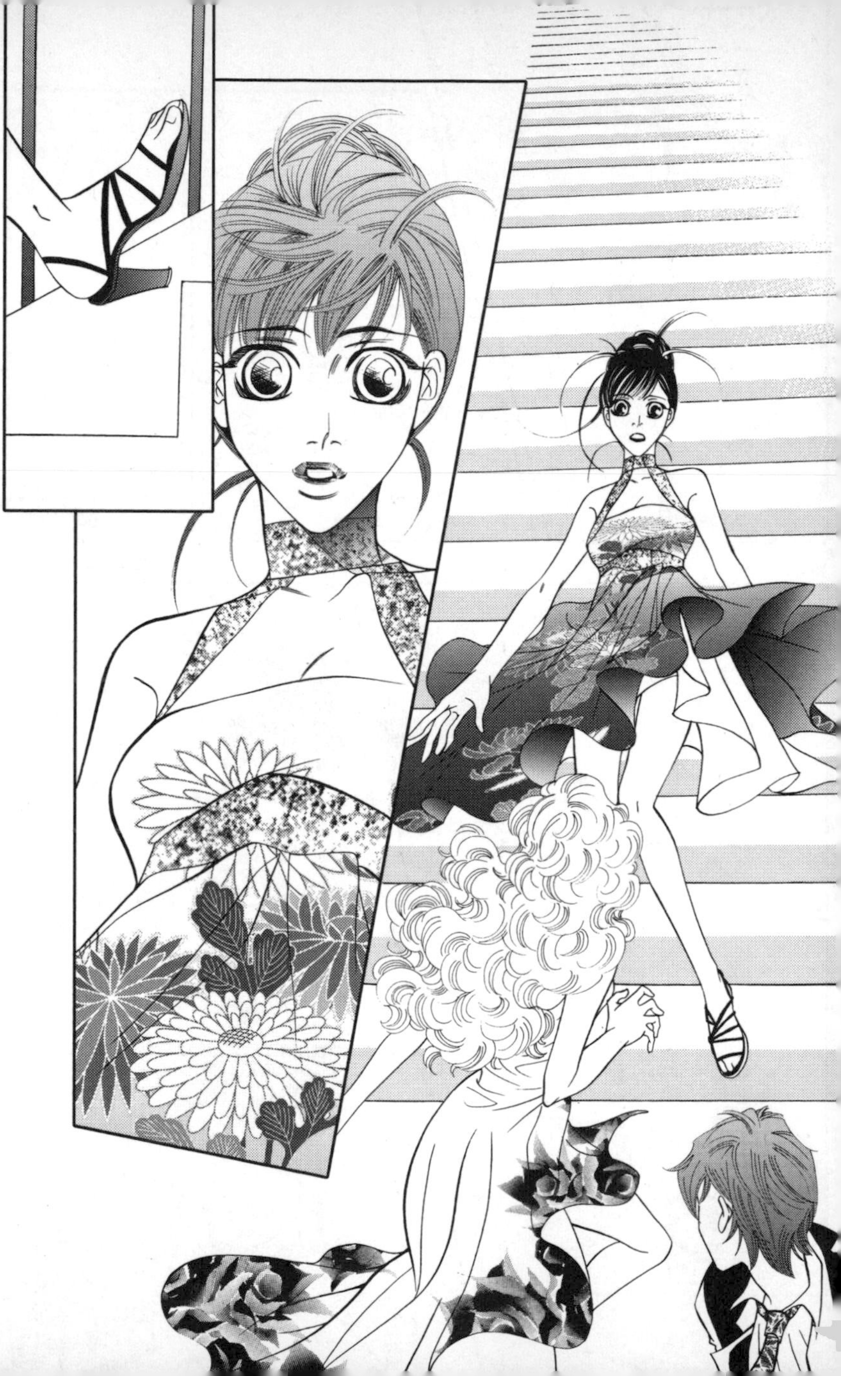

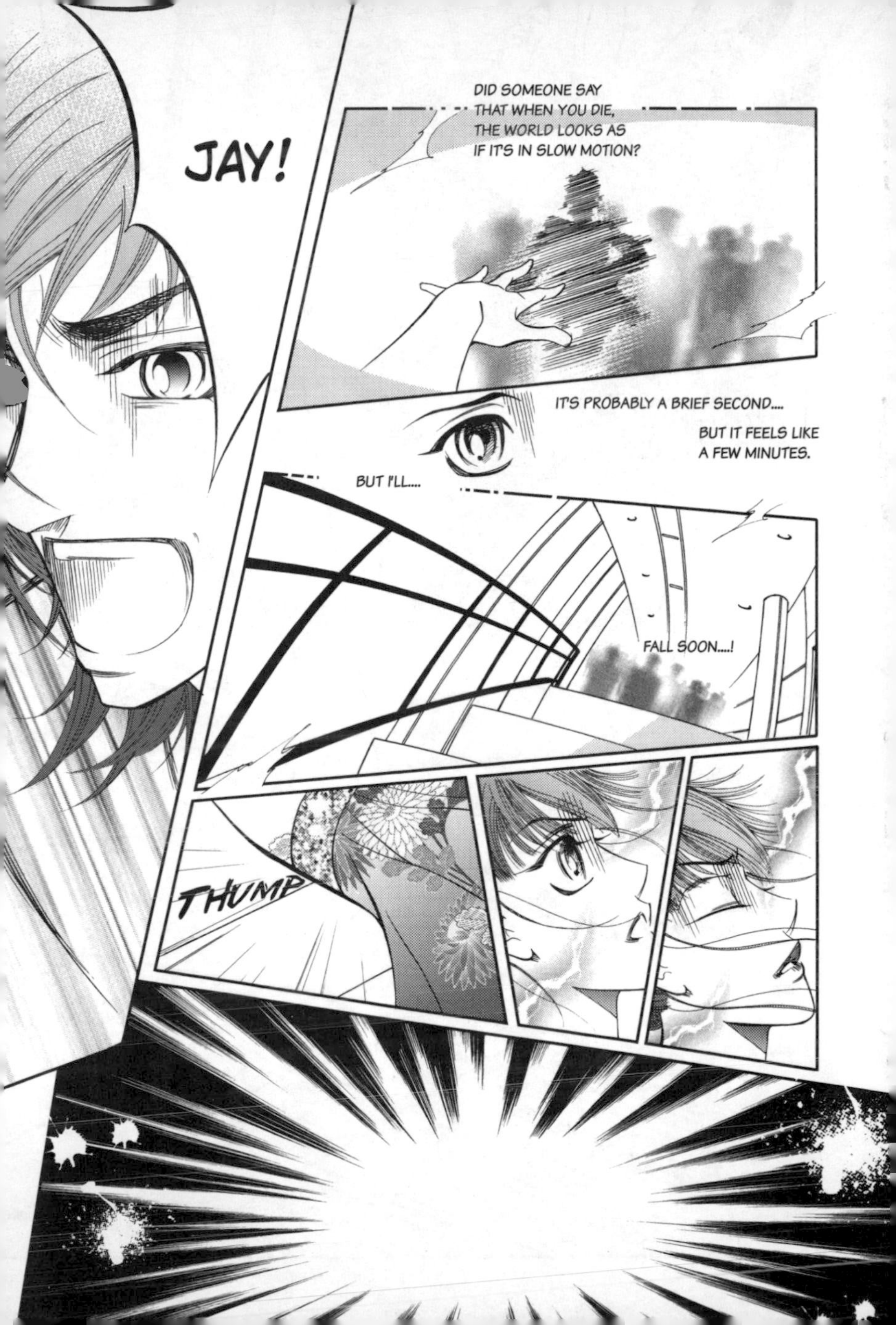
JAY!
DID SOMEONE SAY THAT WHEN YOU DIE, THE WORLD LOOKS AS IF IT'S IN SLOW MOTION?
IT'S PROBABLY A BRIEF SECOND....
BUT IT FEELS LIKE A FEW MINUTES.
BUT I'LL....
FALL SOON....!
THUMP

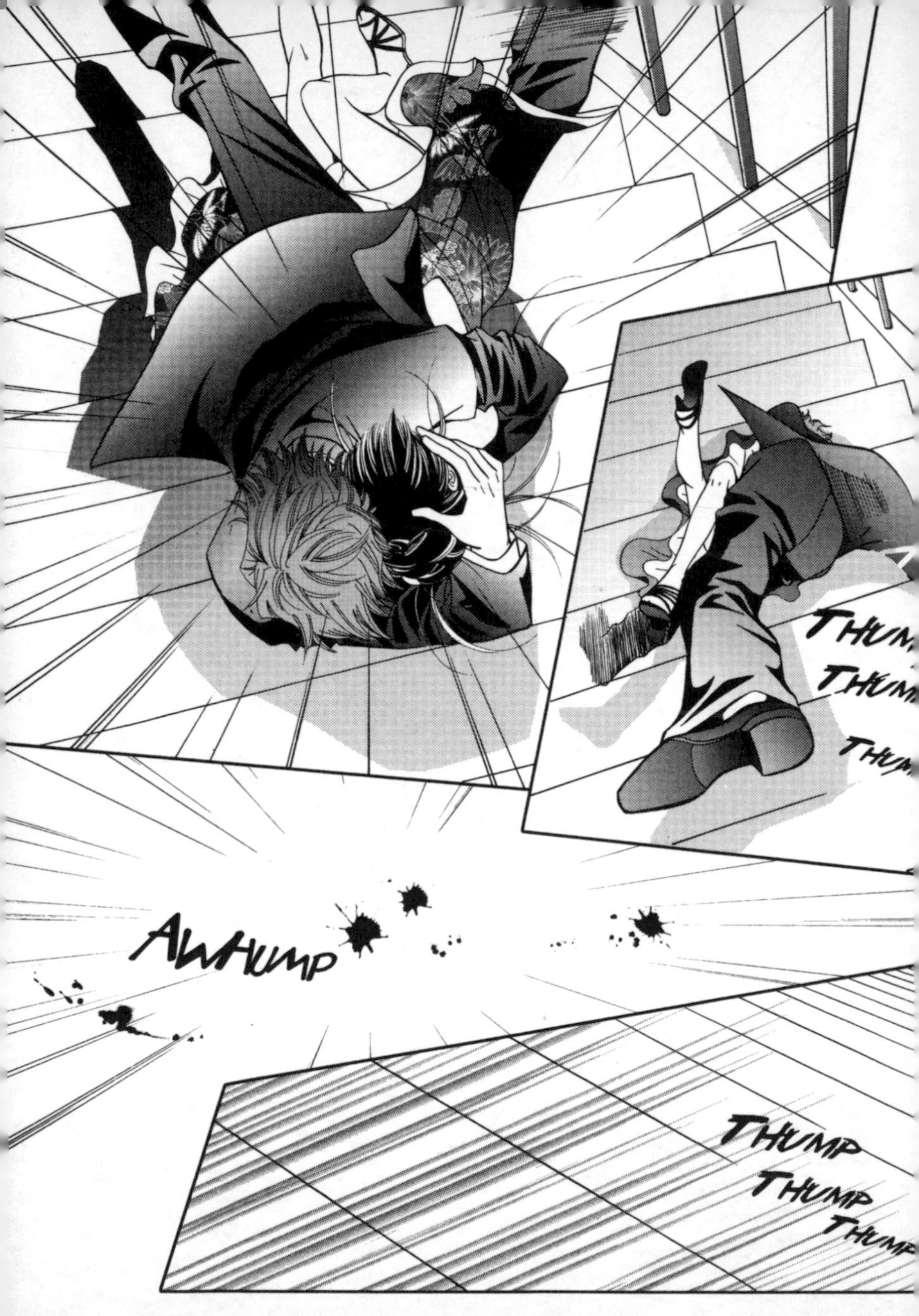
THUM
THUM
THUM
AWHUMP
THUMP
THUMP
THUMP

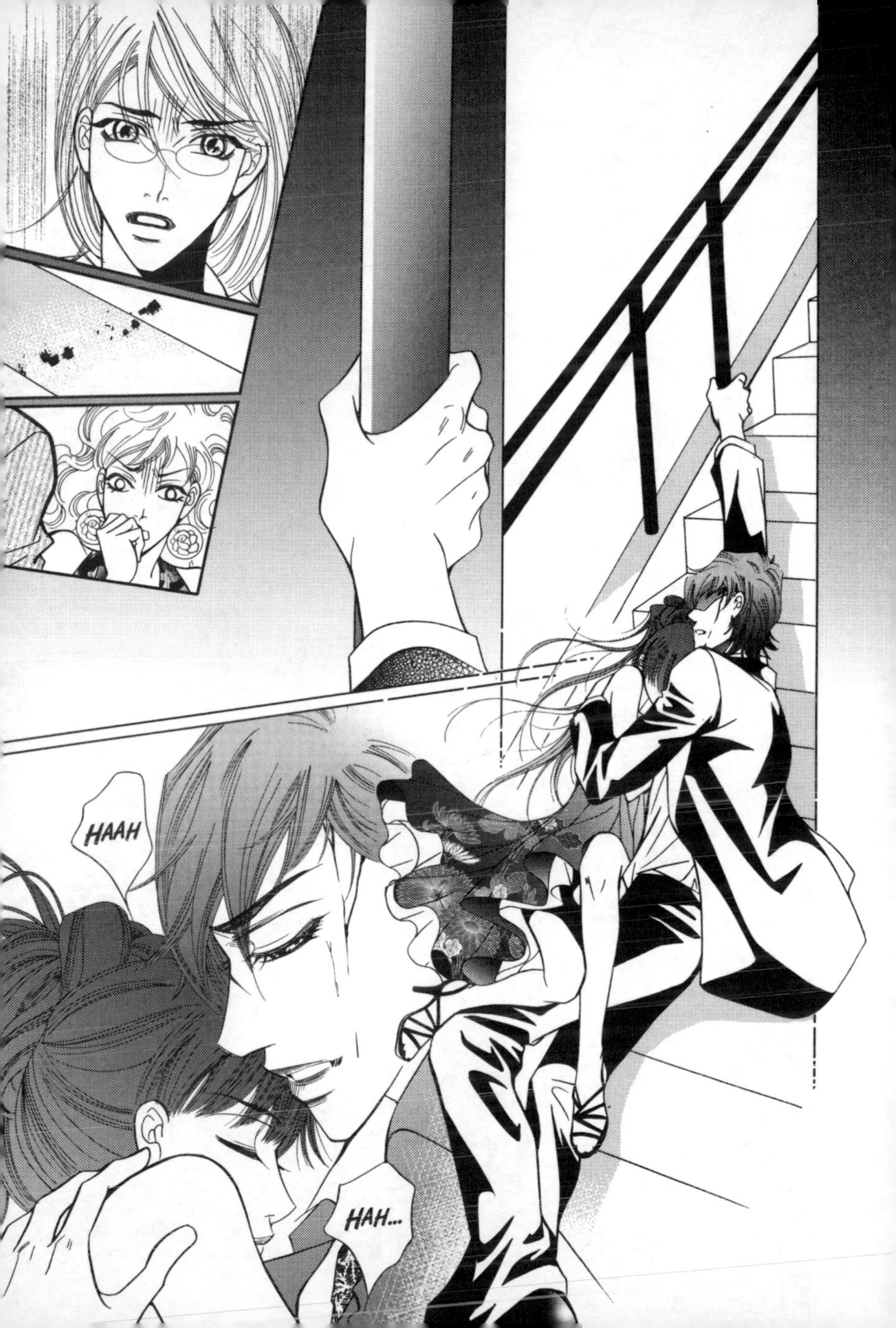
HAAH
HAH...

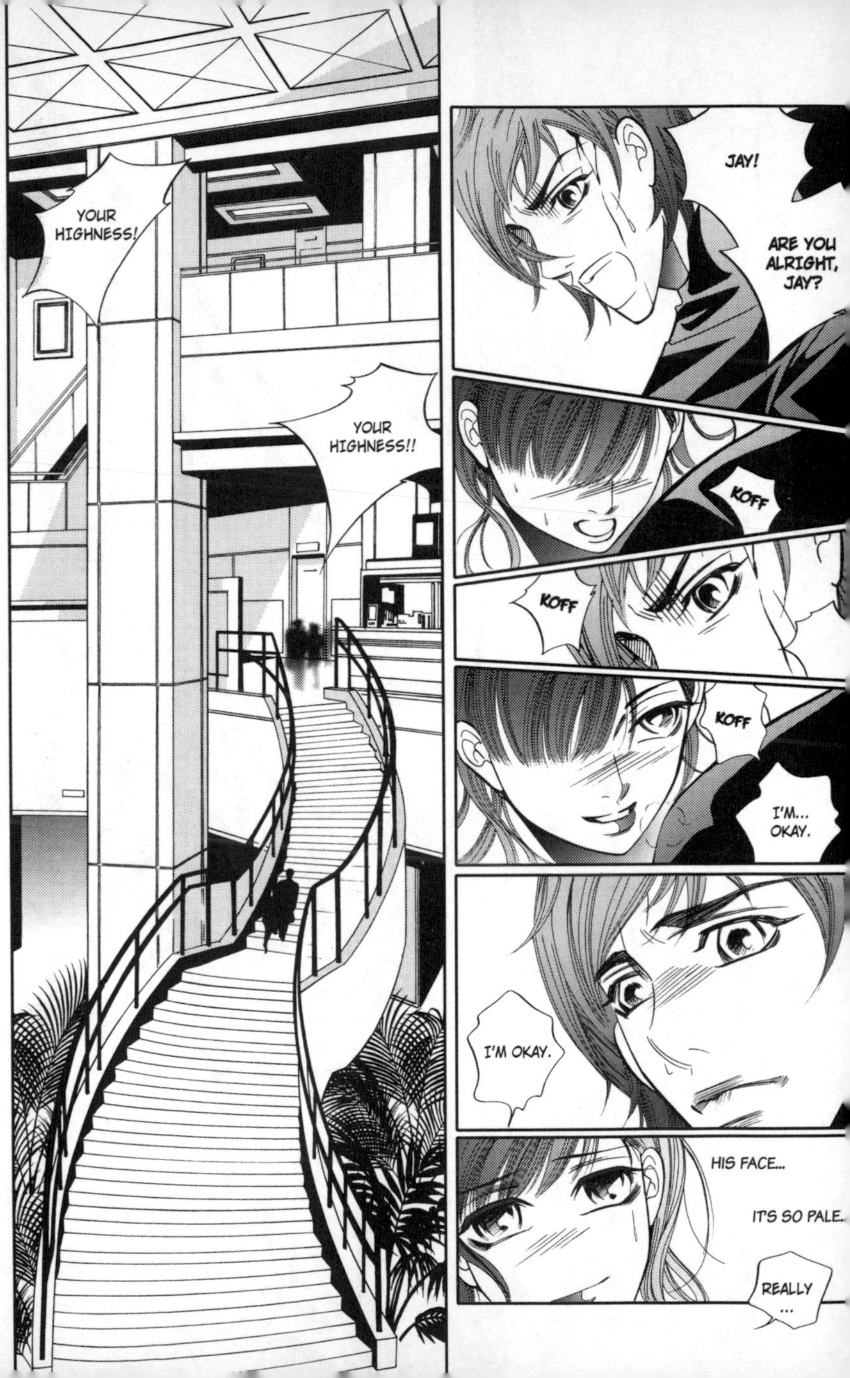
JAY!
ARE YOU ALRIGHT, JAY?
KOFF
KOFF
KOFF
I'M... OKAY.
I'M OKAY.
HIS FACE...
IT'S SO PALE.
REALLY ...
YOUR HIGHNESS!
YOUR HIGHNESS!!

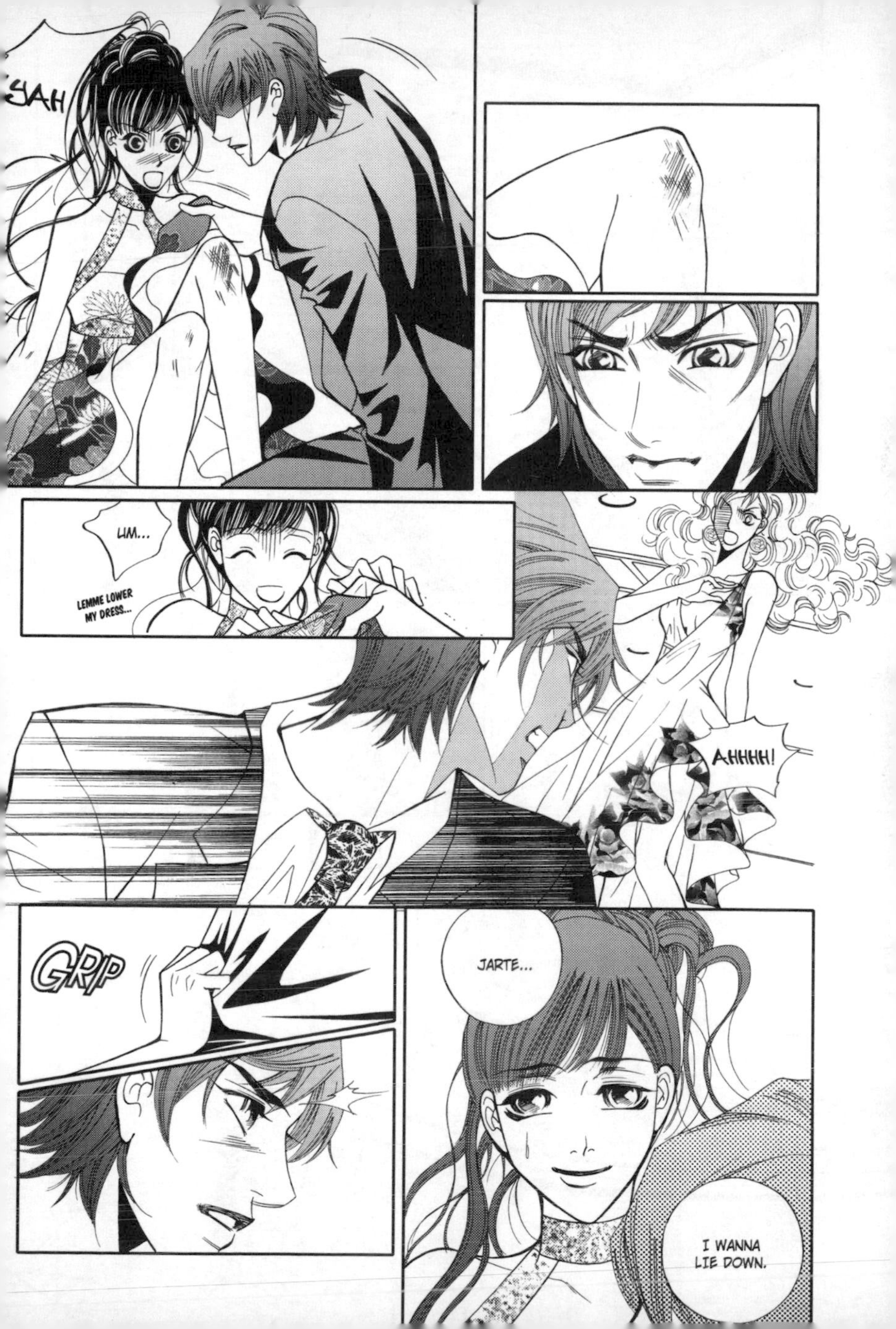
YAH
UM...
LEMME LOWER MY DRESS...
AHHHH!
GRIP
JARTE...
I WANNA LIE DOWN.

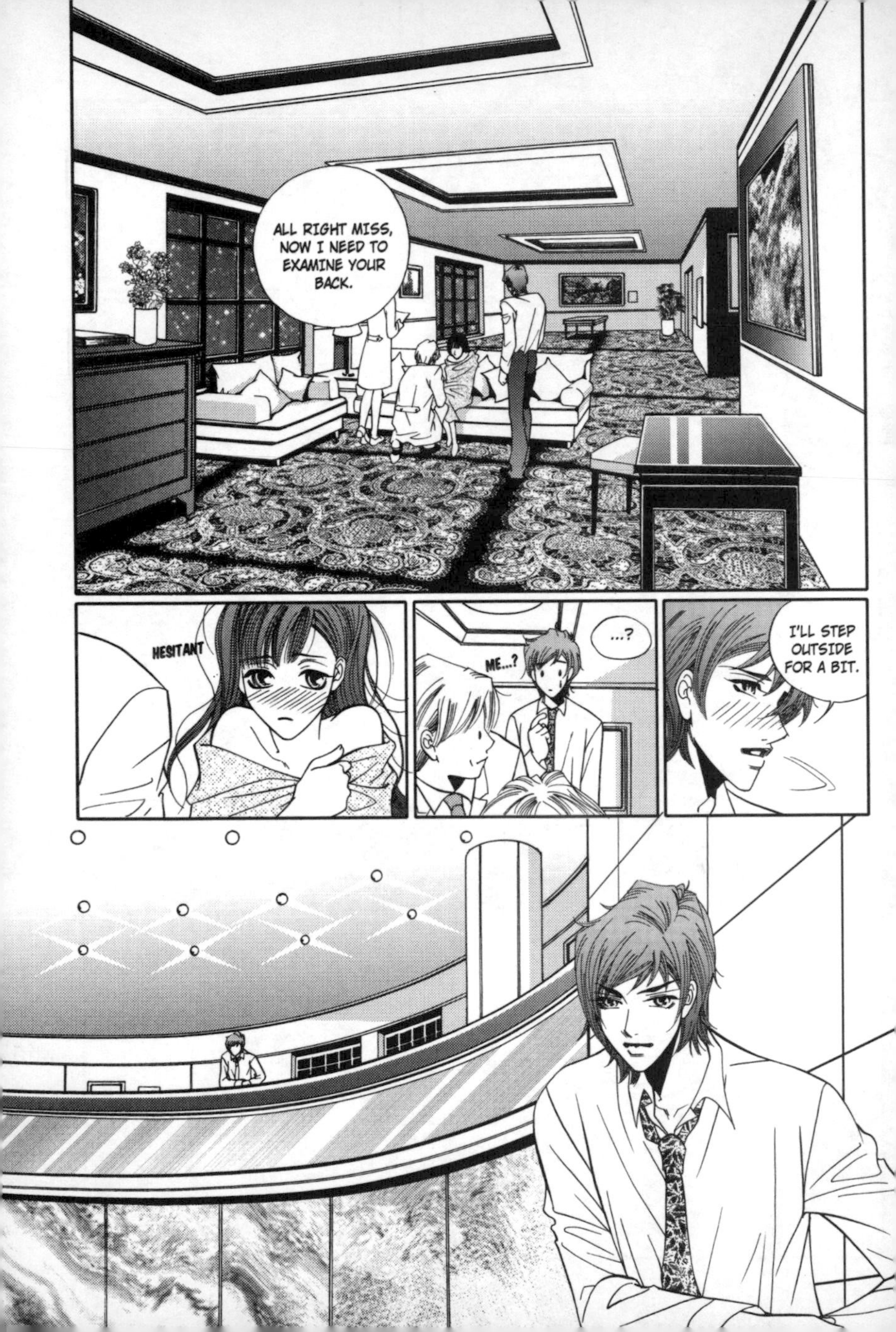
ALL RIGHT MISS, NOW I NEED TO EXAMINE YOUR BACK.
HESITANT
...?
ME...?
I'LL STEP OUTSIDE FOR A BIT.

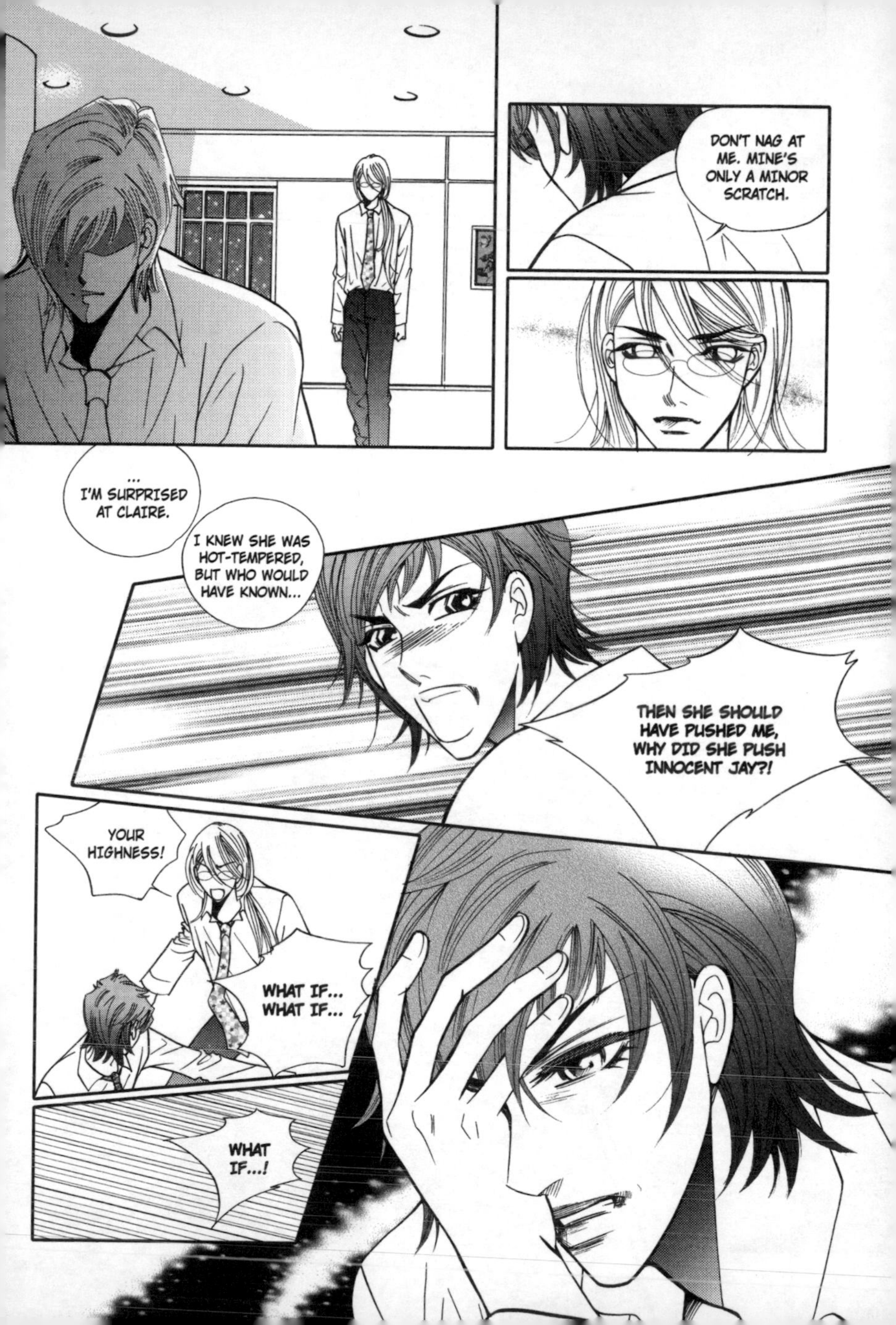
DON'T NAG AT ME. MINE'S ONLY A MINOR SCRATCH.
... I'M SURPRISED AT CLAIRE.
I KNEW SHE WAS HOT-TEMPERED, BUT WHO WOULD HAVE KNOWN...
THEN SHE SHOULD HAVE PUSHED ME, WHY DID SHE PUSH INNOCENT JAY?!
YOUR HIGHNESS!
WHAT IF... WHAT IF...
WHAT IF...!

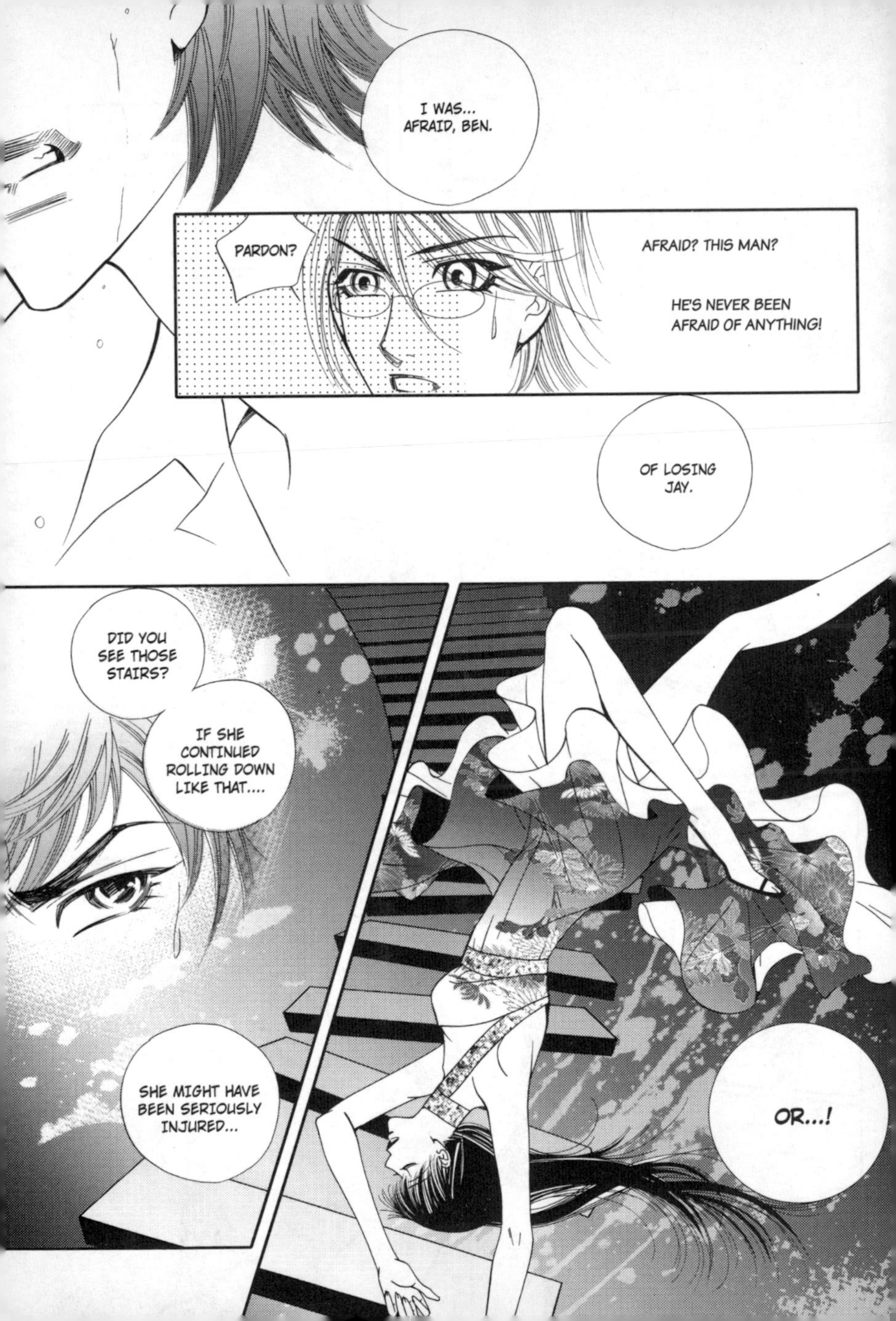
I WAS... AFRAID, BEN.
PARDON?
AFRAID? THIS MAN?
HE'S NEVER BEEN AFRAID OF ANYTHING!
OF LOSING JAY.
DID YOU SEE THOSE STAIRS?
IF SHE CONTINUED ROLLING DOWN LIKE THAT....
SHE MIGHT HAVE BEEN SERIOUSLY INJURED...
OR...!

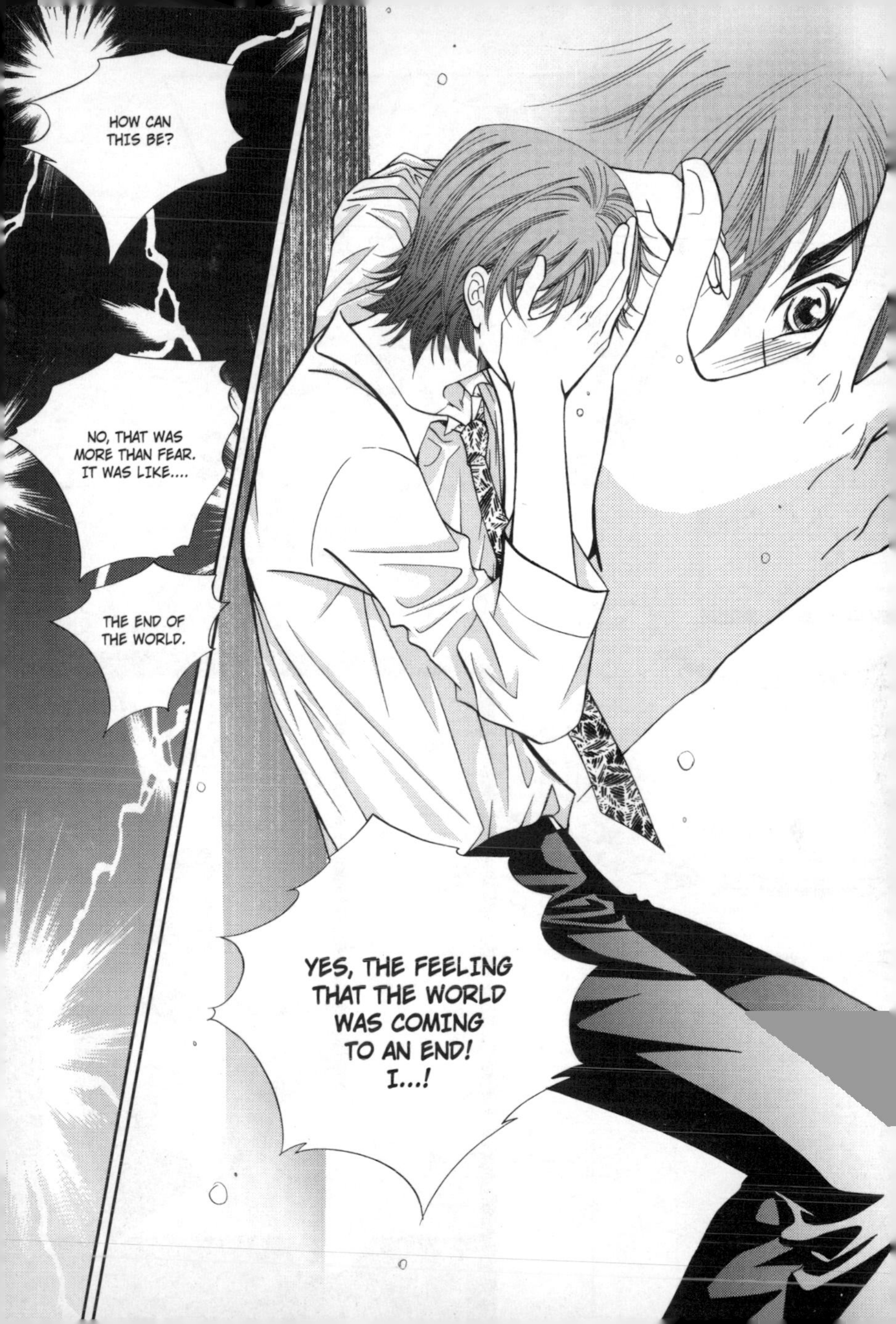
HOW CAN THIS BE?
NO, THAT WAS MORE THAN FEAR. IT WAS LIKE....
THE END OF THE WORLD.
YES, THE FEELING THAT THE WORLD WAS COMING TO AN END! I...!

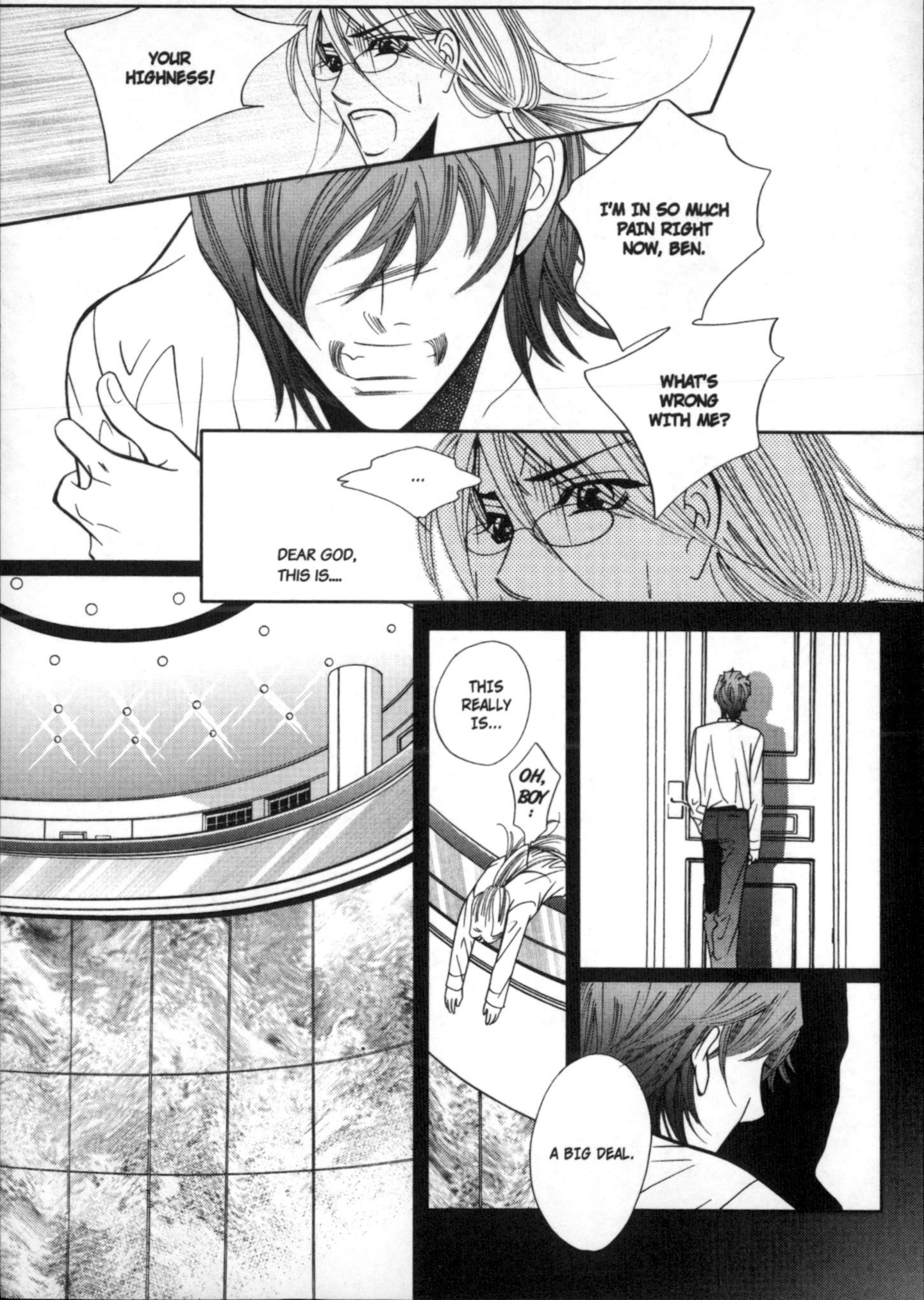
YOUR HIGHNESS!
I'M IN SO MUCH PAIN RIGHT NOW, BEN.
WHAT'S WRONG WITH ME?
...
DEAR GOD, THIS IS....
THIS REALLY IS...
OH, BOY
A BIG DEAL.

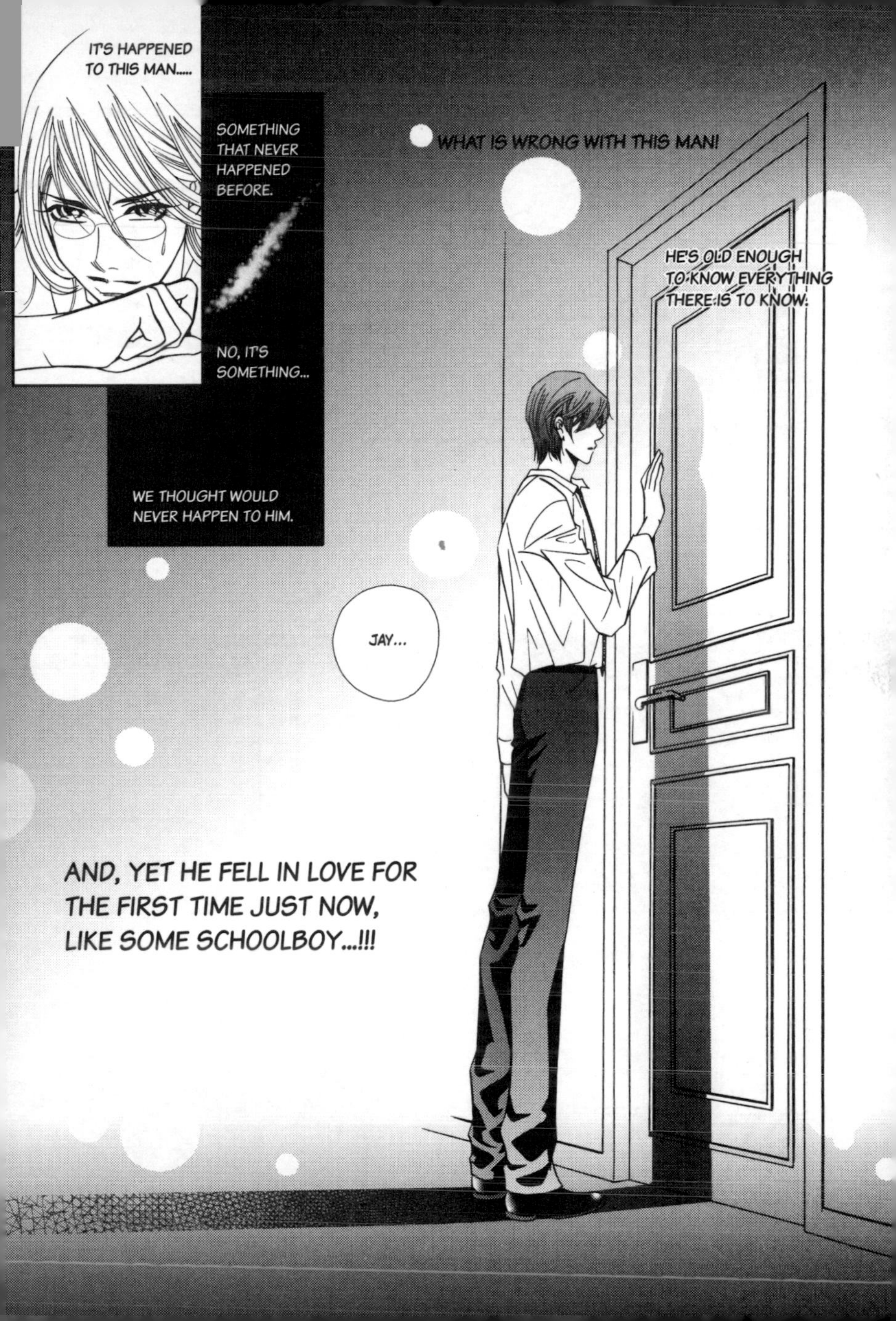

IT'S HAPPENED TO THIS MAN.....
SOMETHING THAT NEVER HAPPENED BEFORE.
NO, IT'S SOMETHING...
WE THOUGHT WOULD NEVER HAPPEN TO HIM.
WHAT IS WRONG WITH THIS MAN!
HE'S OLD ENOUGH TO KNOW EVERYTHING THERE IS TO KNOW.
JAY...
AND, YET HE FELL IN LOVE FOR THE FIRST TIME JUST NOW, LIKE SOME SCHOOLBOY...!!!

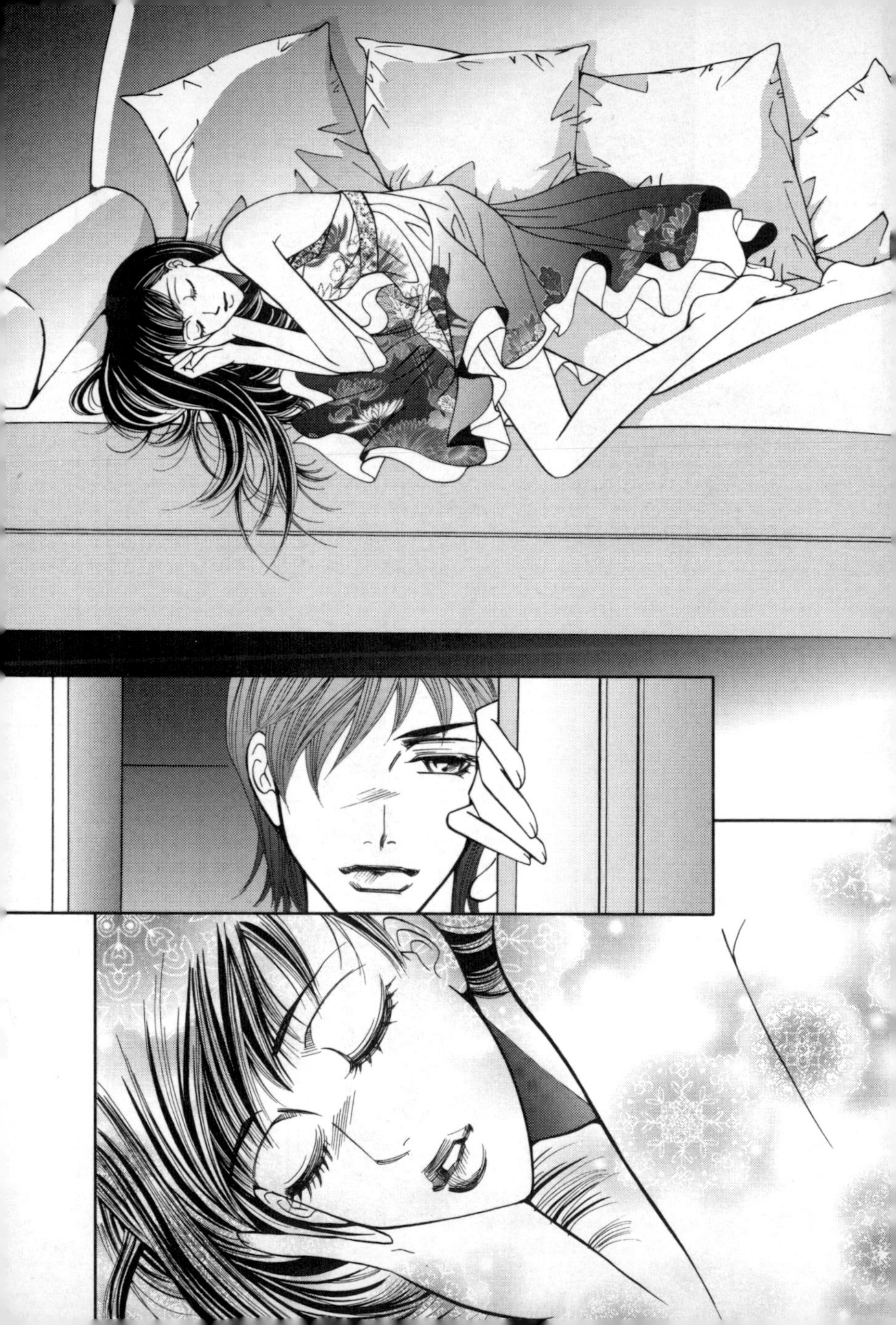

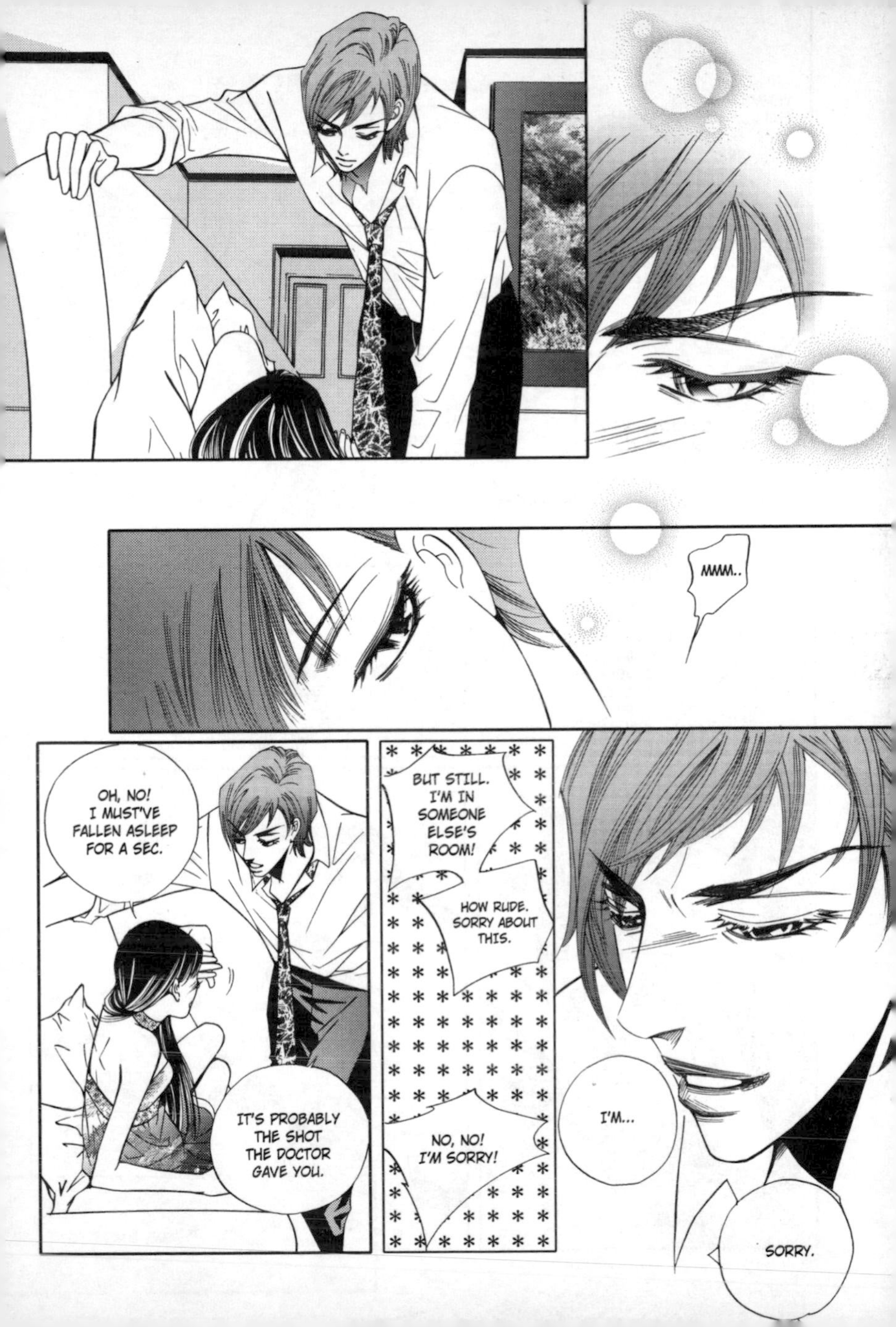
MMM..
OH, NO! I MUST'VE FALLEN ASLEEP FOR A SEC.
IT'S PROBABLY THE SHOT THE DOCTOR GAVE YOU.
BUT STILL. I'M IN SOMEONE ELSE'S ROOM!
HOW RUDE. SORRY ABOUT THIS.
NO, NO! I'M SORRY!
I'M...
SORRY.

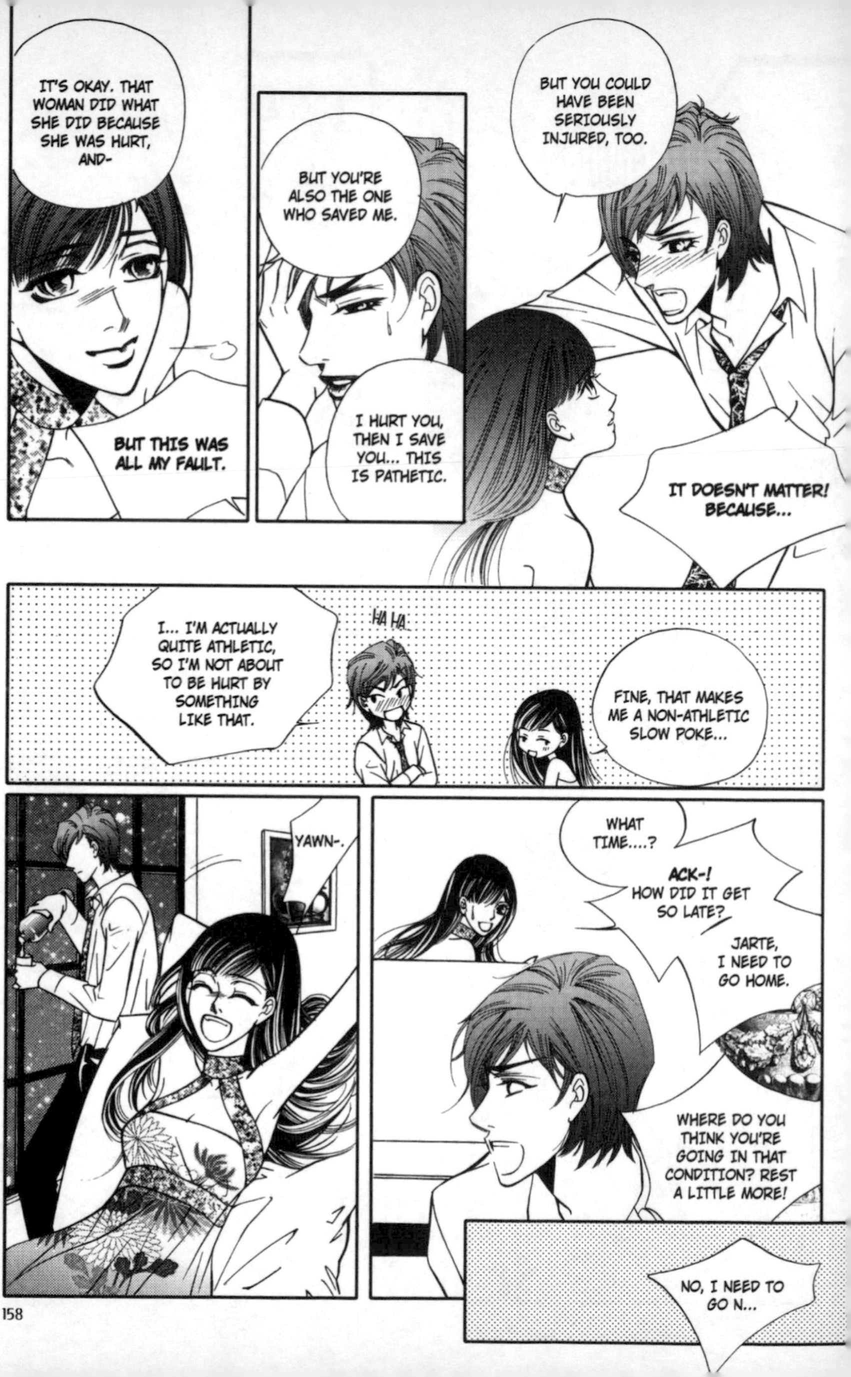
IT'S OKAY. THAT WOMAN DID WHAT SHE DID BECAUSE SHE WAS HURT, AND-
BUT THIS WAS ALL MY FAULT.
BUT YOU'RE ALSO THE ONE WHO SAVED ME.
I HURT YOU, THEN I SAVE YOU... THIS IS PATHETIC.
BUT YOU COULD HAVE BEEN SERIOUSLY INJURED, TOO.
IT DOESN'T MATTER! BECAUSE...
I... I'M ACTUALLY QUITE ATHLETIC, SO I'M NOT ABOUT TO BE HURT BY SOMETHING LIKE THAT.
HA HA
FINE, THAT MAKES ME A NON-ATHLETIC SLOW POKE...
YAWN-.
WHAT TIME....?
ACK-! HOW DID IT GET SO LATE?
JARTE, I NEED TO GO HOME.
WHERE DO YOU THINK YOU'RE GOING IN THAT CONDITION? REST A LITTLE MORE!
NO, I NEED TO GO N...

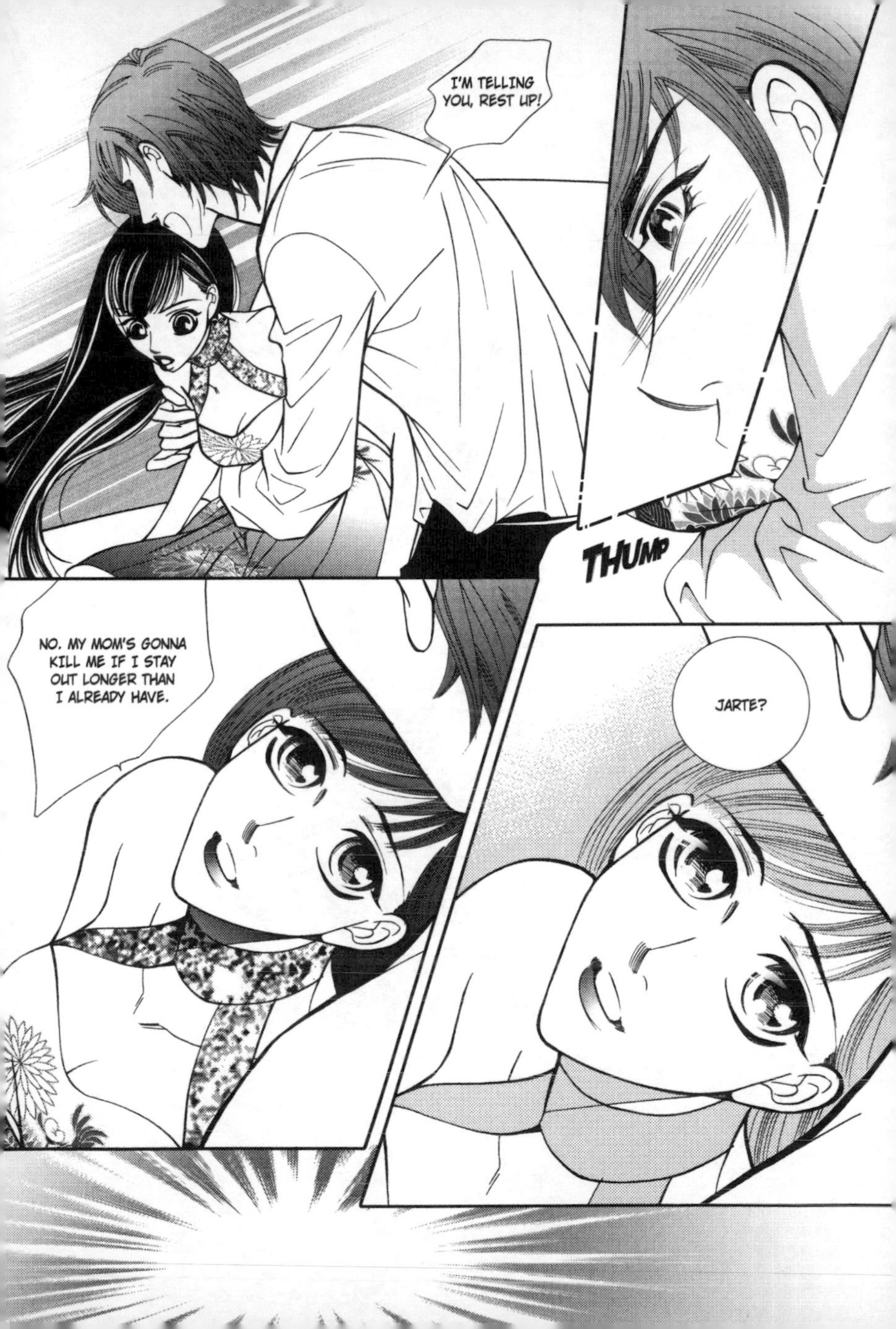
I'M TELLING YOU, REST UP!
THUMP
NO. MY MOM'S GONNA KILL ME IF I STAY OUT LONGER THAN I ALREADY HAVE.
JARTE?

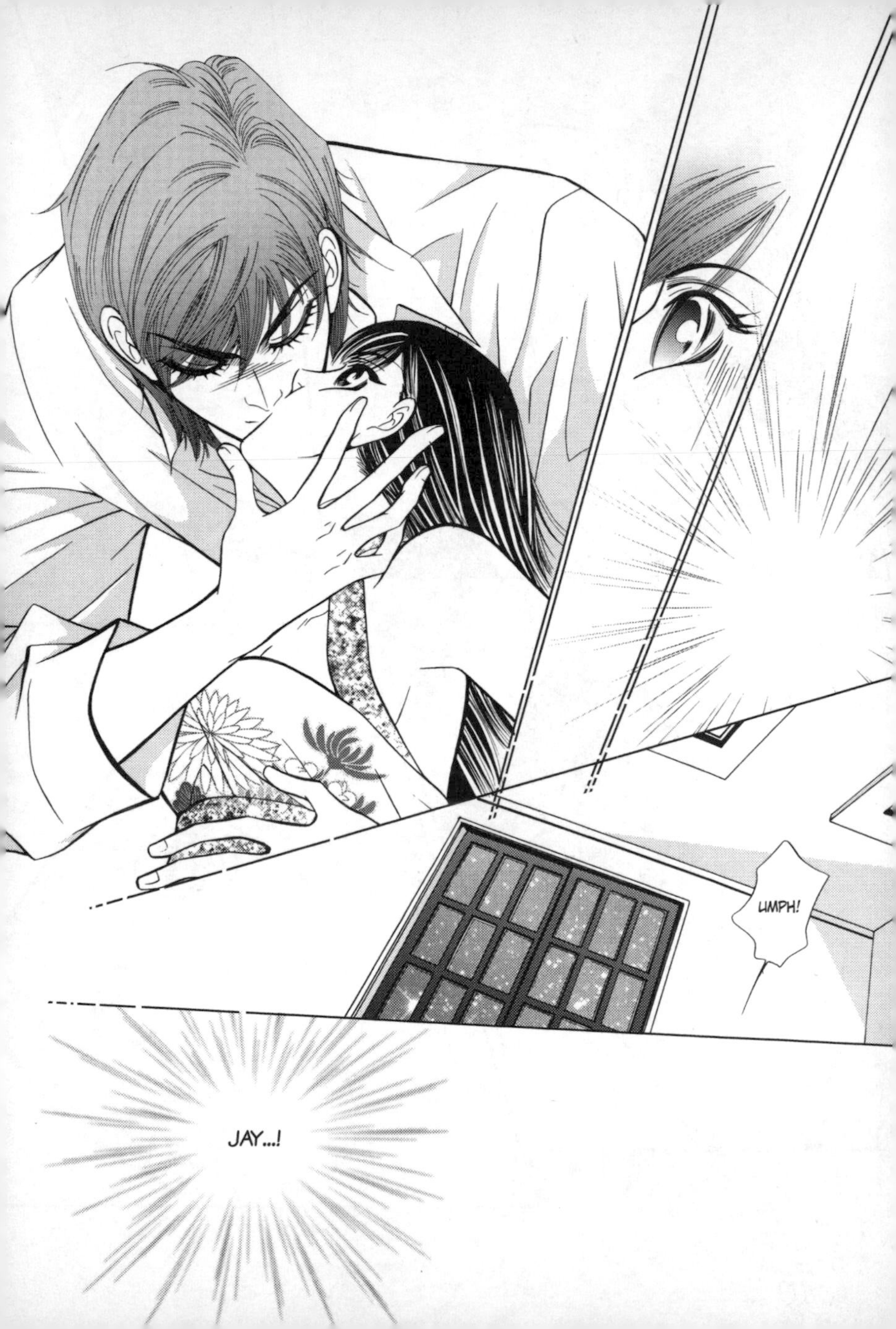
UMPH!
JAY...!

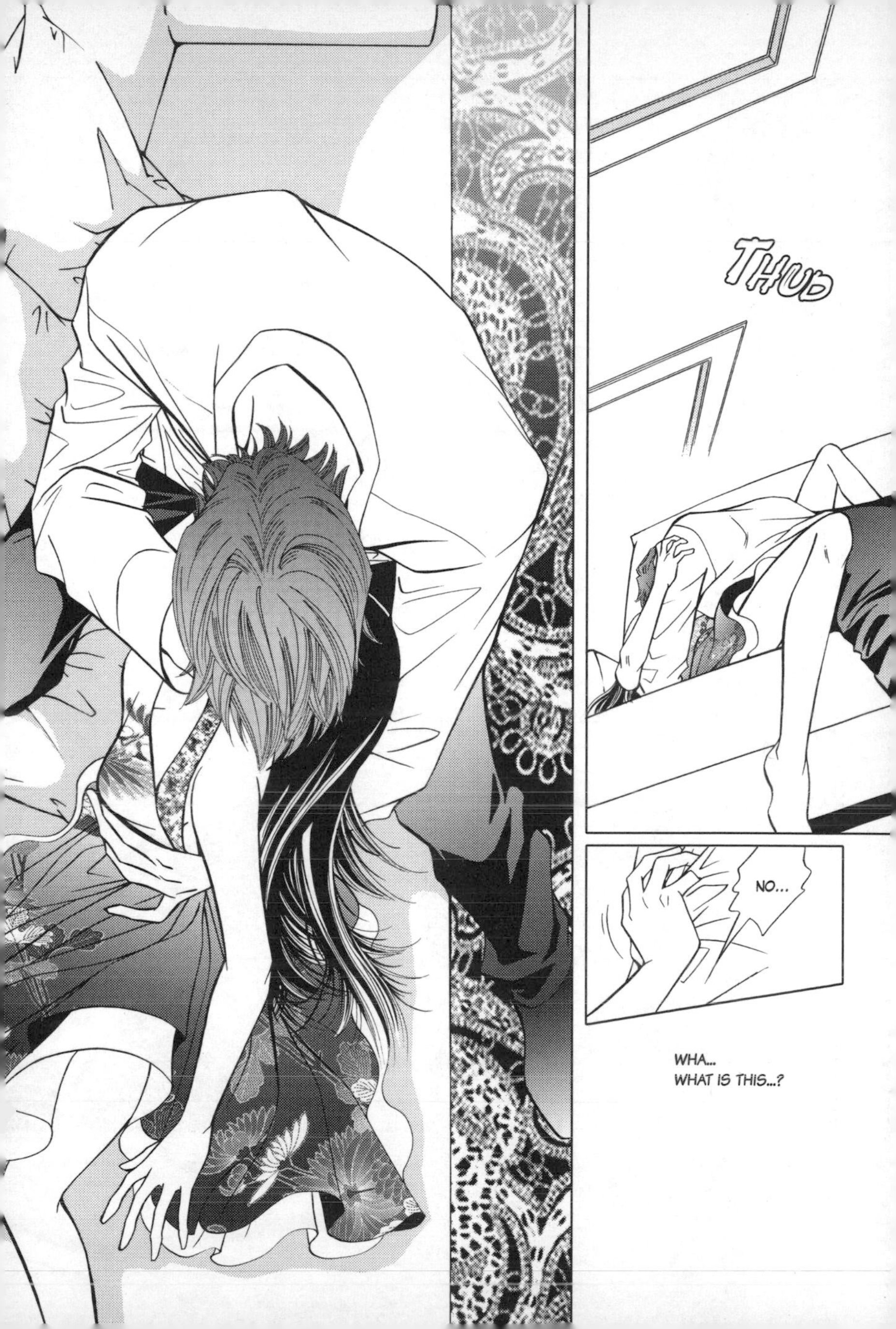
THUD
NO...
WHA...
WHAT IS THIS...?

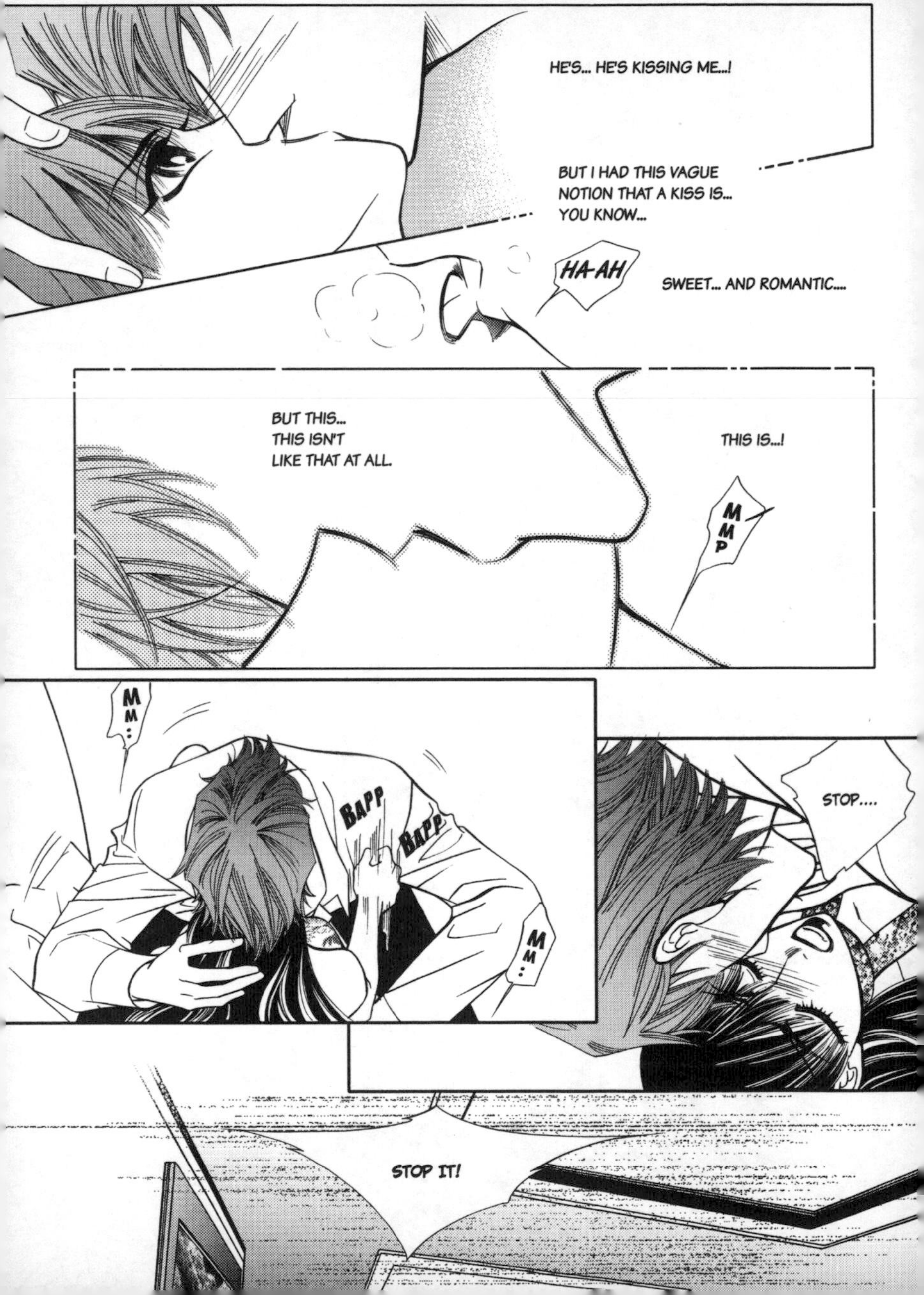
HE'S... HE'S KISSING ME...!
BUT I HAD THIS VAGUE NOTION THAT A KISS IS... YOU KNOW...
HA-AH
SWEET... AND ROMANTIC....
BUT THIS... THIS ISN'T LIKE THAT AT ALL.
THIS IS...!
MMP
MM...
BAPP
BAPP
MM...
STOP....
STOP IT!

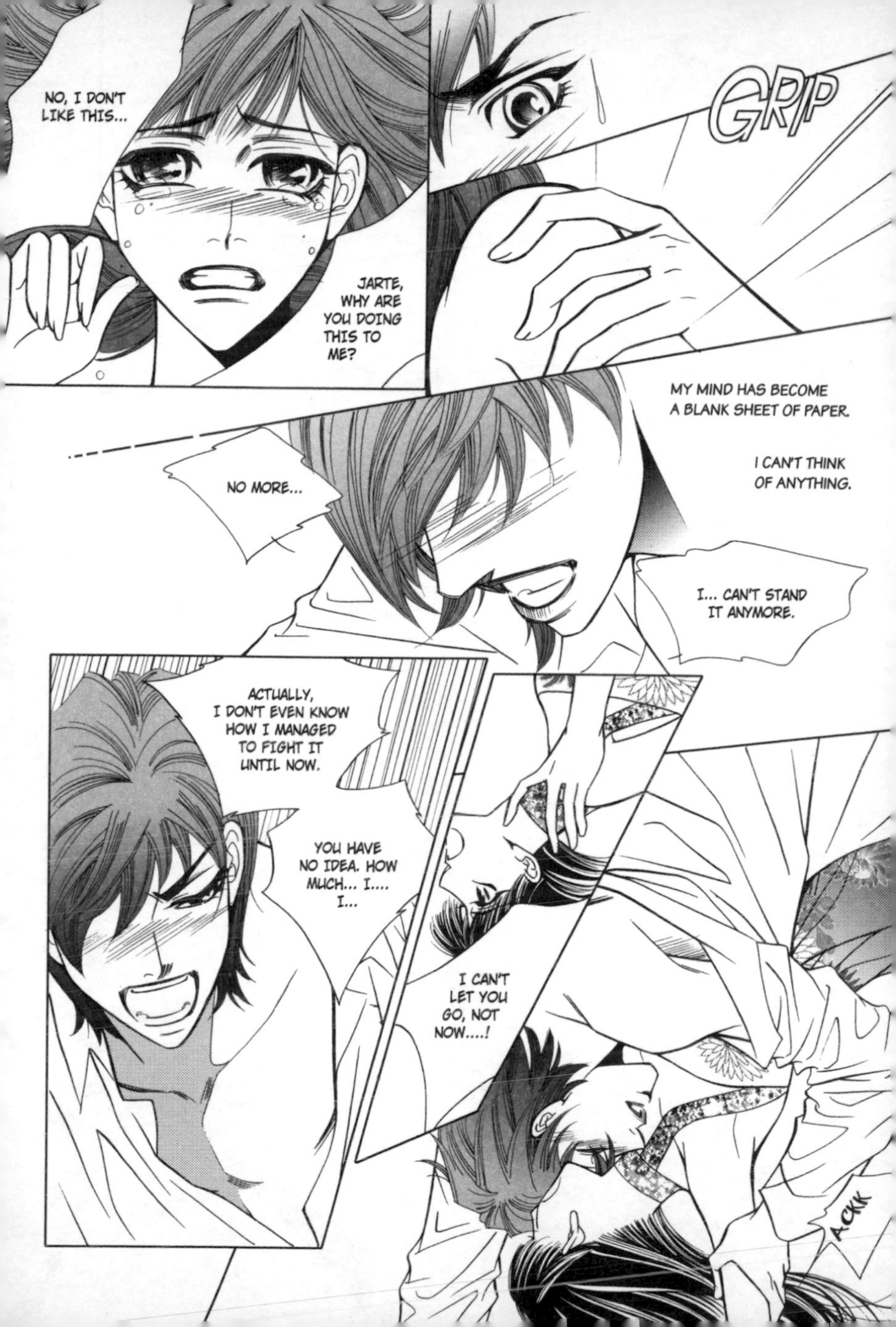
NO, I DON'T LIKE THIS...
JARTE, WHY ARE YOU DOING THIS TO ME?
GRIP
MY MIND HAS BECOME A BLANK SHEET OF PAPER.
I CAN'T THINK OF ANYTHING.
NO MORE...
I... CAN'T STAND IT ANYMORE.
ACTUALLY, I DON'T EVEN KNOW HOW I MANAGED TO FIGHT IT UNTIL NOW.
YOU HAVE NO IDEA. HOW MUCH... I.... I...
I CAN'T LET YOU GO, NOT NOW....!
ACKK

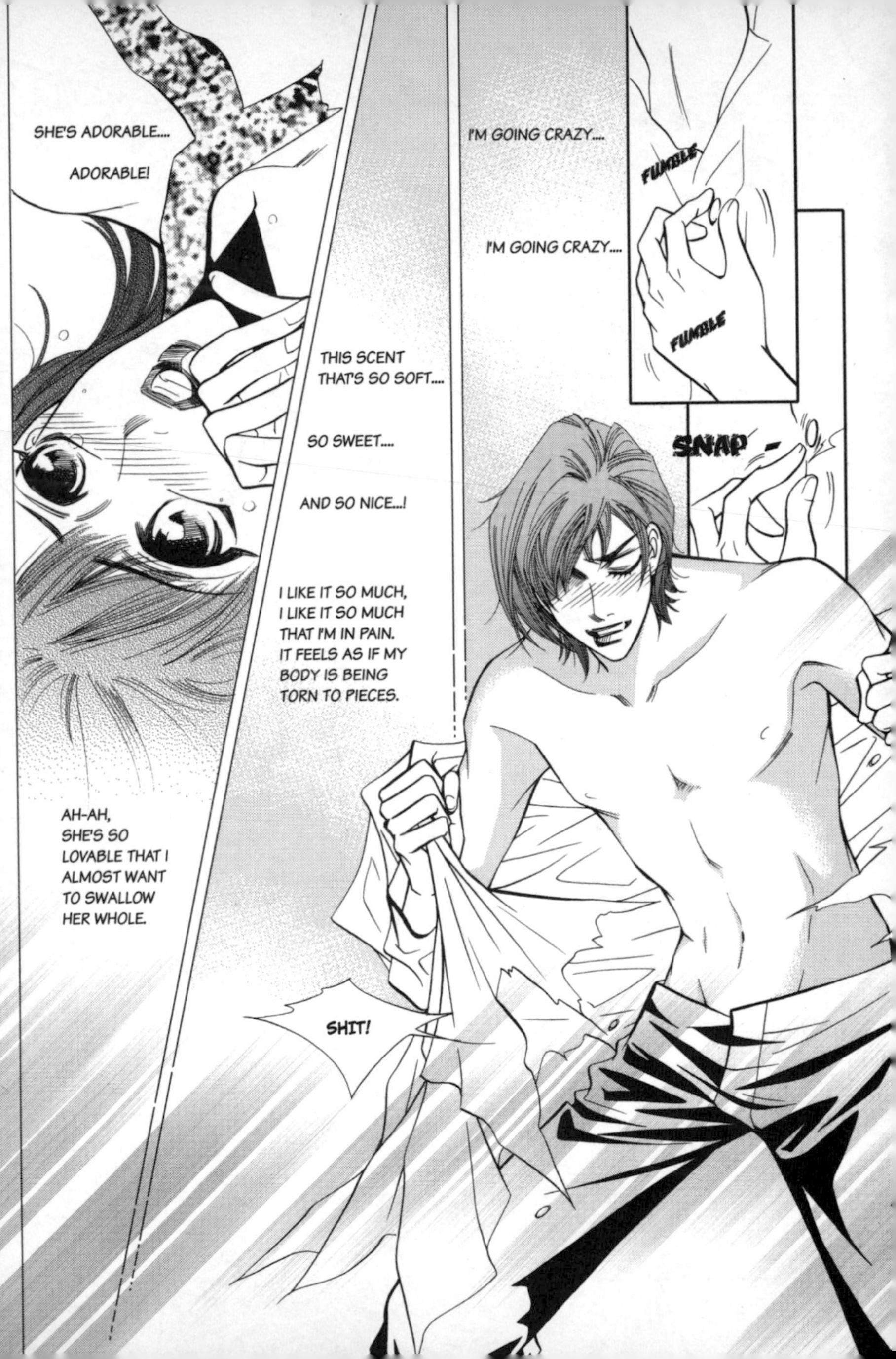
SHE'S ADORABLE....
ADORABLE!
AH-AH, SHE'S SO LOVABLE THAT I ALMOST WANT TO SWALLOW HER WHOLE.
THIS SCENT THAT'S SO SOFT....
SO SWEET....
AND SO NICE...!
I LIKE IT SO MUCH, I LIKE IT SO MUCH THAT I'M IN PAIN. IT FEELS AS IF MY BODY IS BEING TORN TO PIECES.
I'M GOING CRAZY....
FUMBLE
I'M GOING CRAZY....
FUMBLE
SNAP
SHIT!

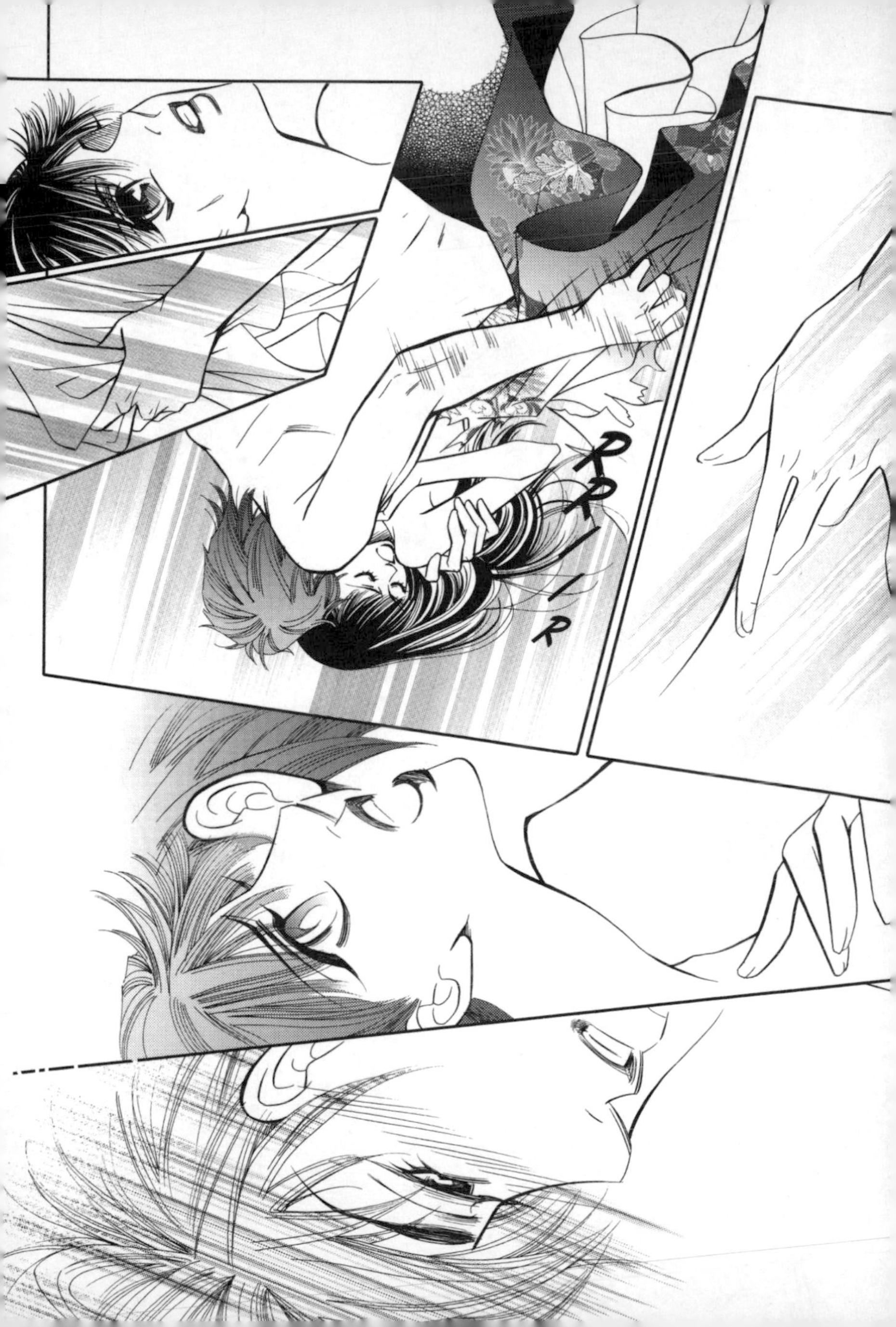
RRIIR

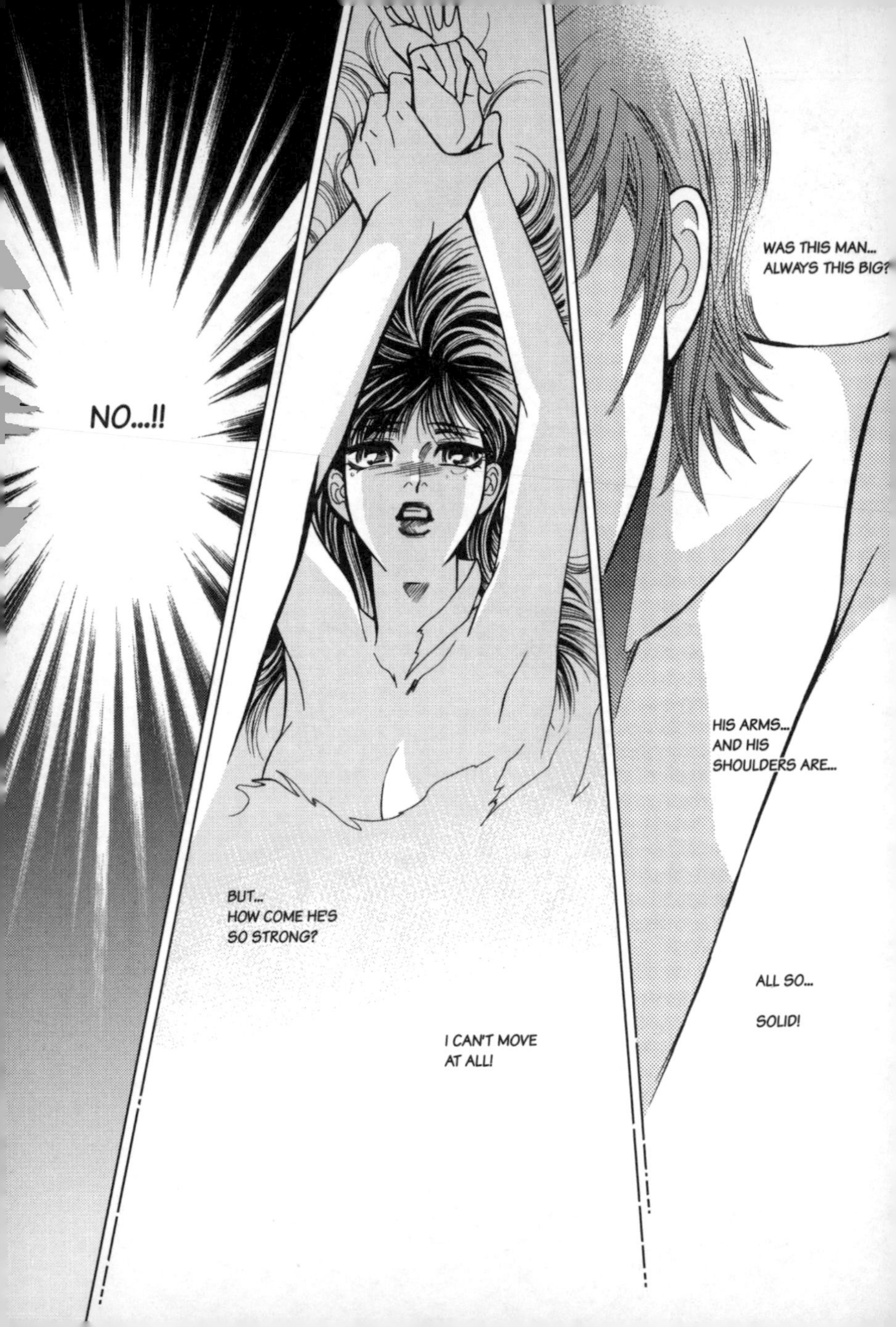
NO...!!
BUT... HOW COME HE'S SO STRONG?
I CAN'T MOVE AT ALL!
WAS THIS MAN... ALWAYS THIS BIG?
HIS ARMS... AND HIS SHOULDERS ARE...
ALL SO...
SOLID!

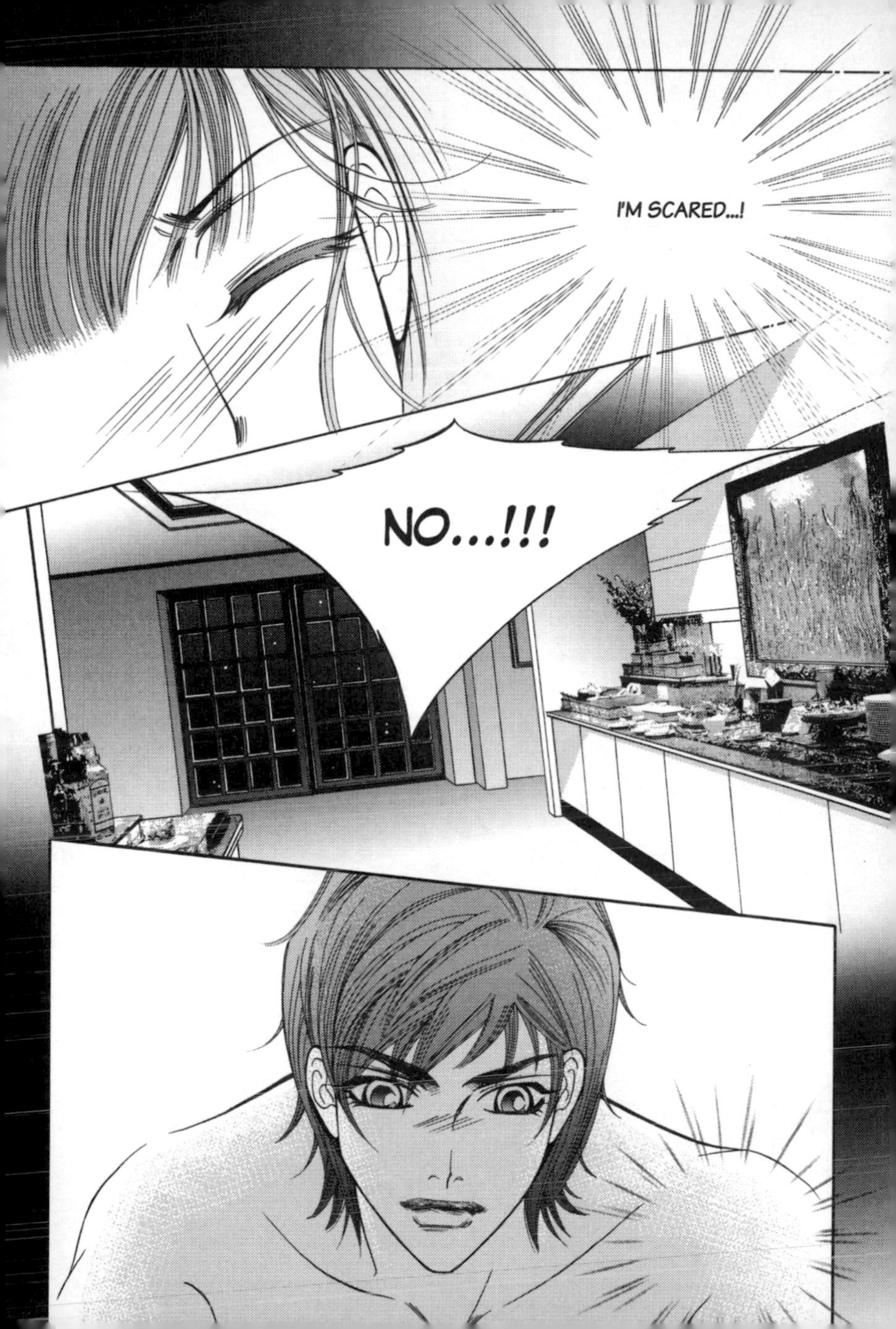
I'M SCARED...!
NO...!!!

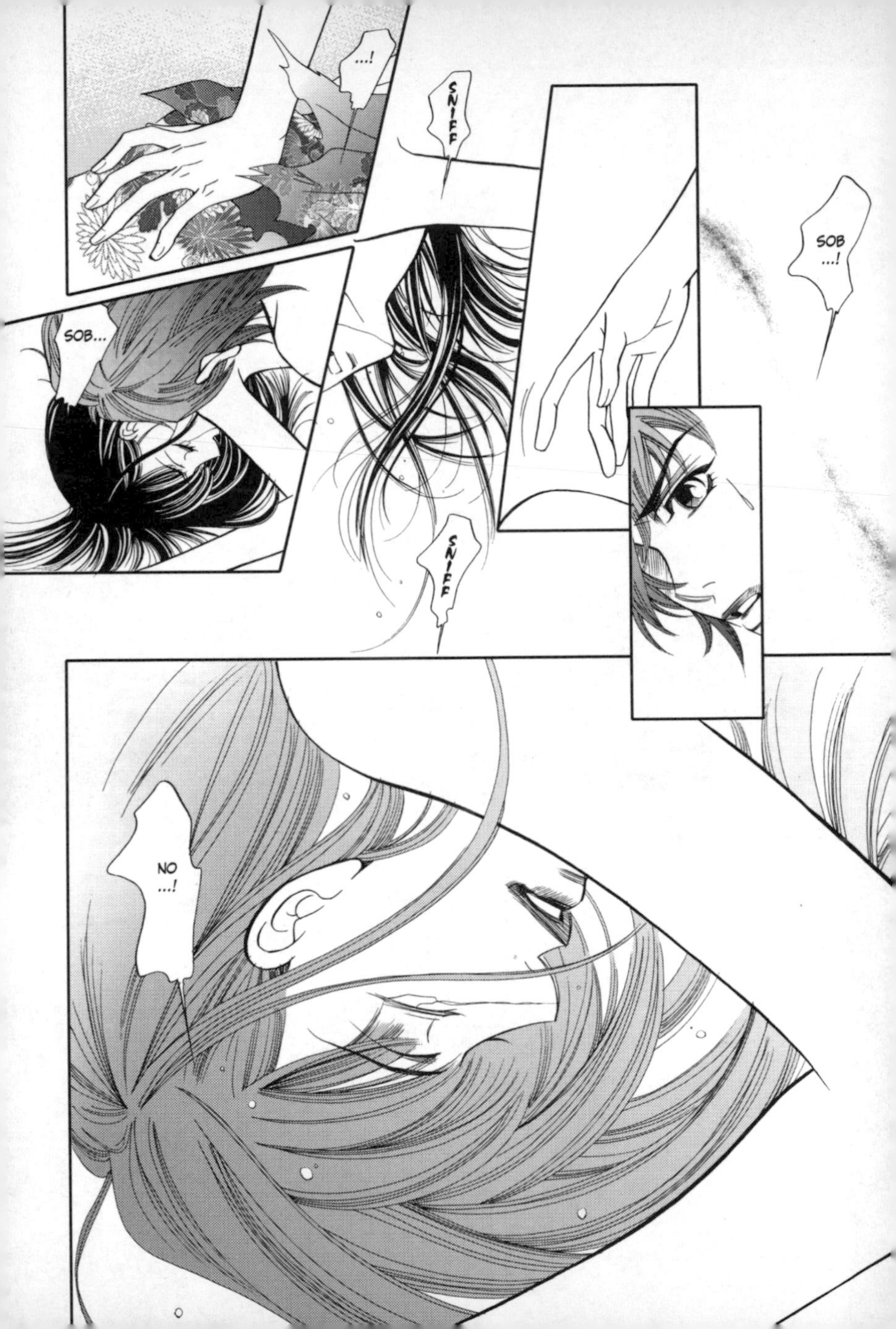
...!
SNIFF
SOB ...!
SOB...
SNIFF
NO ...!

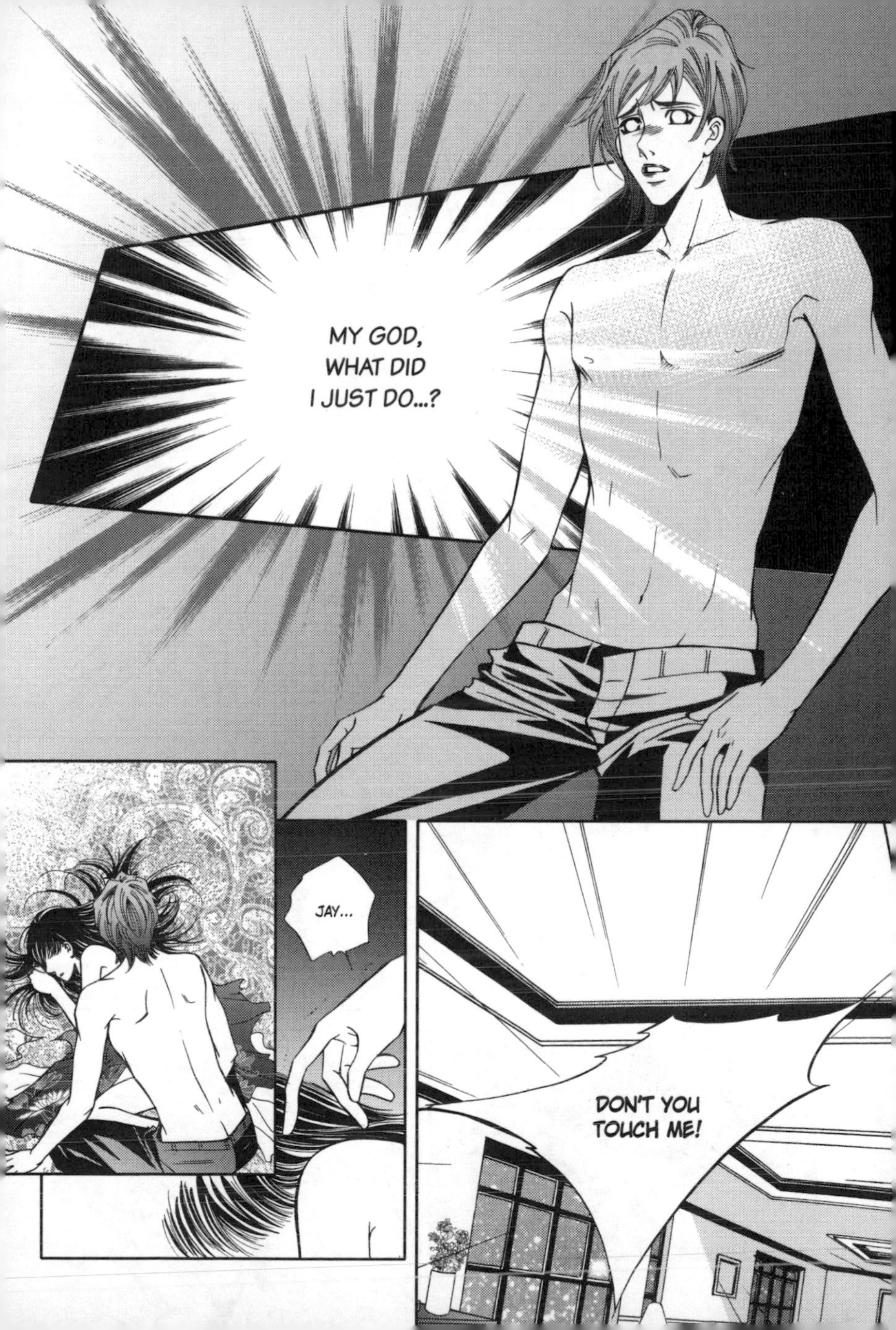
MY GOD, WHAT DID I JUST DO...?
JAY...
DON'T YOU TOUCH ME!

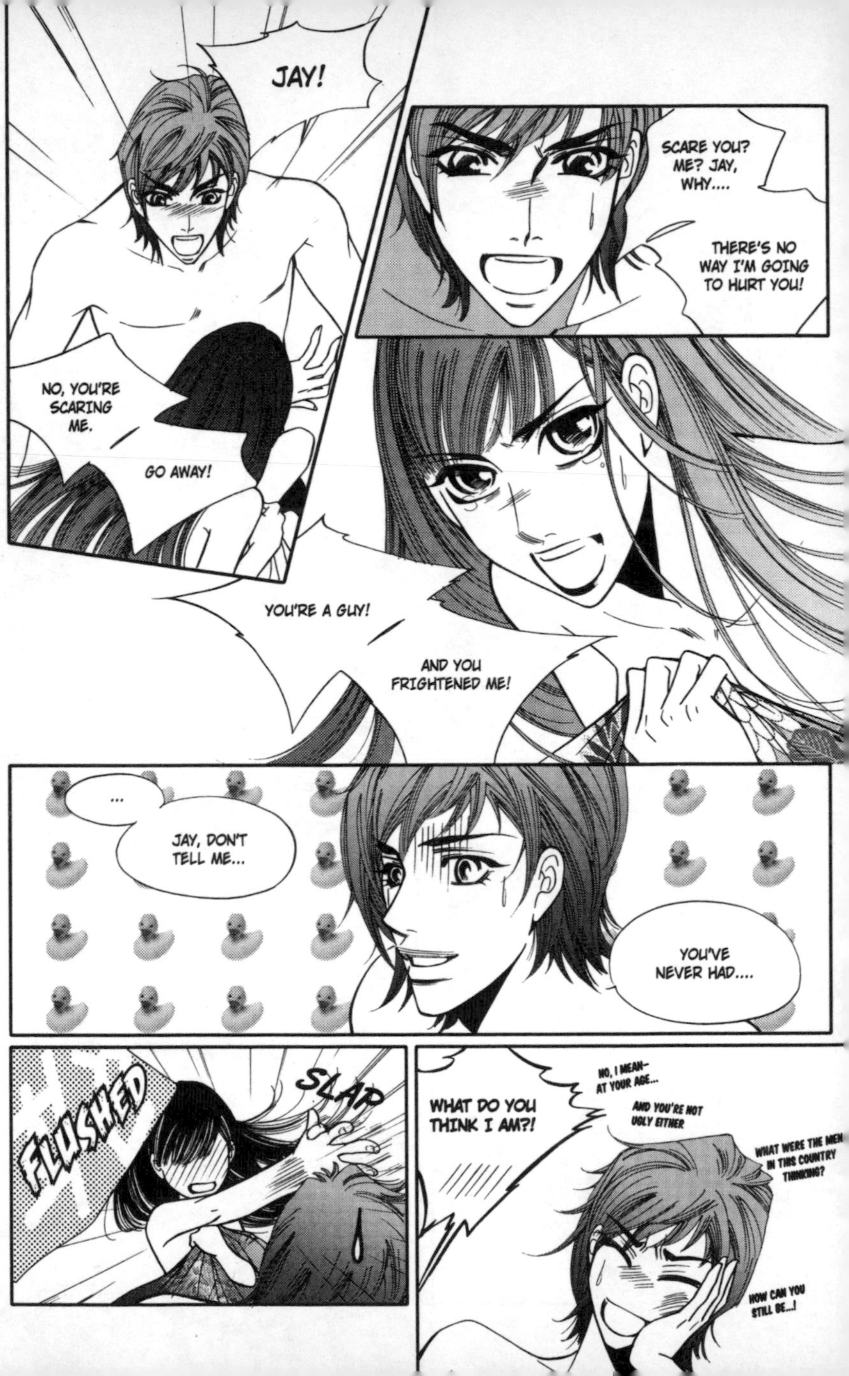
JAY!
NO, YOU'RE SCARING ME.
GO AWAY!
SCARE YOU? ME? JAY, WHY....
THERE'S NO WAY I'M GOING TO HURT YOU!
YOU'RE A GUY!
AND YOU FRIGHTENED ME!
...
JAY, DON'T TELL ME...
YOU'VE NEVER HAD....
FLUSHED
SLAP
WHAT DO YOU THINK I AM?!
NO, I MEAN- AT YOUR AGE...
AND YOU'RE NOT UGLY EITHER
WHAT WERE THE MEN IN THIS COUNTRY THINKING?
HOW CAN YOU STILL BE...!

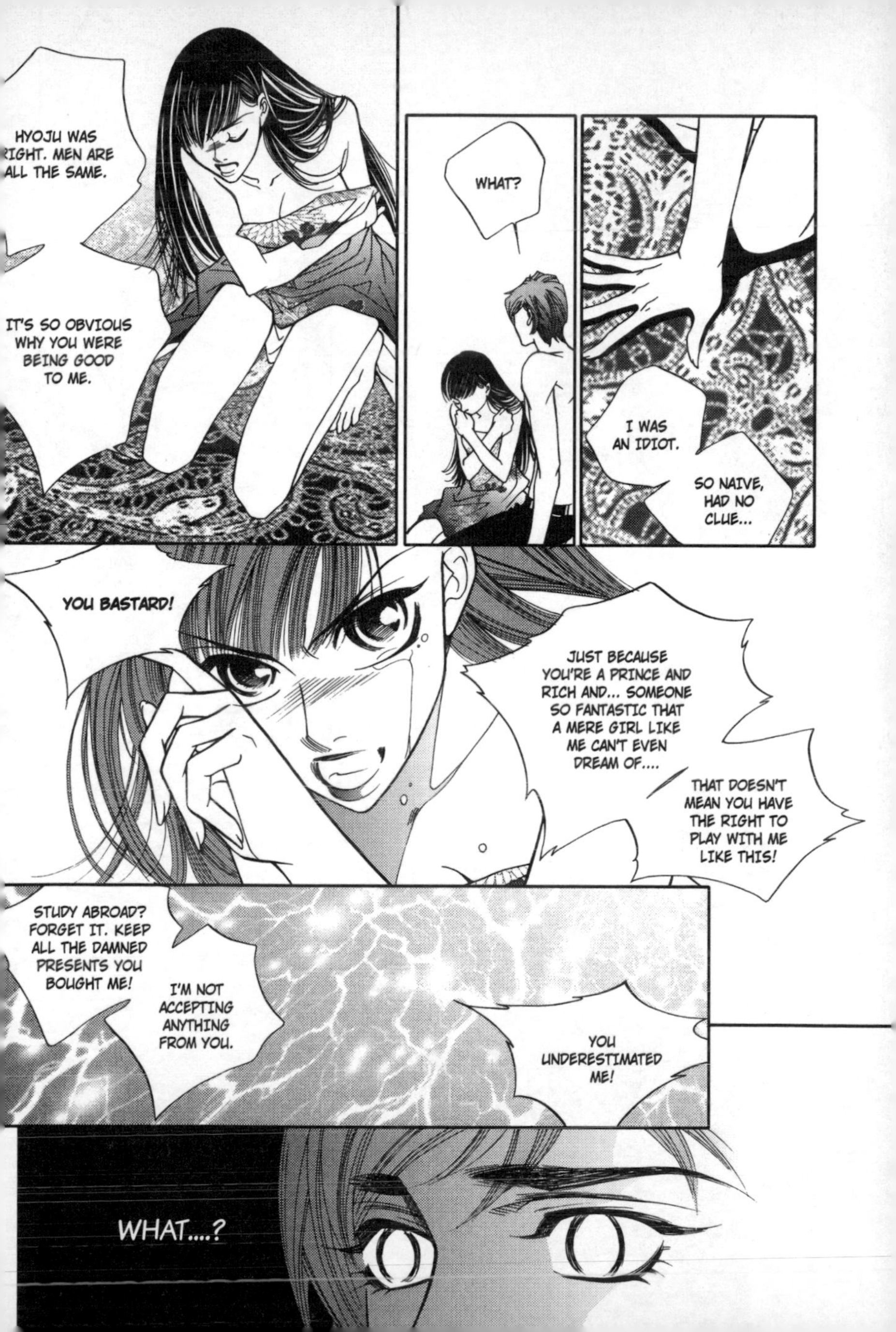
HYOJU WAS RIGHT. MEN ARE ALL THE SAME.
IT'S SO OBVIOUS WHY YOU WERE BEING GOOD TO ME.
WHAT?
I WAS AN IDIOT.
SO NAIVE, HAD NO CLUE...
YOU BASTARD!
JUST BECAUSE YOU'RE A PRINCE AND RICH AND... SOMEONE SO FANTASTIC THAT A MERE GIRL LIKE ME CAN'T EVEN DREAM OF....
THAT DOESN'T MEAN YOU HAVE THE RIGHT TO PLAY WITH ME LIKE THIS!
STUDY ABROAD? FORGET IT. KEEP ALL THE DAMNED PRESENTS YOU BOUGHT ME!
I'M NOT ACCEPTING ANYTHING FROM YOU.
YOU UNDERESTIMATED ME!
WHAT....?

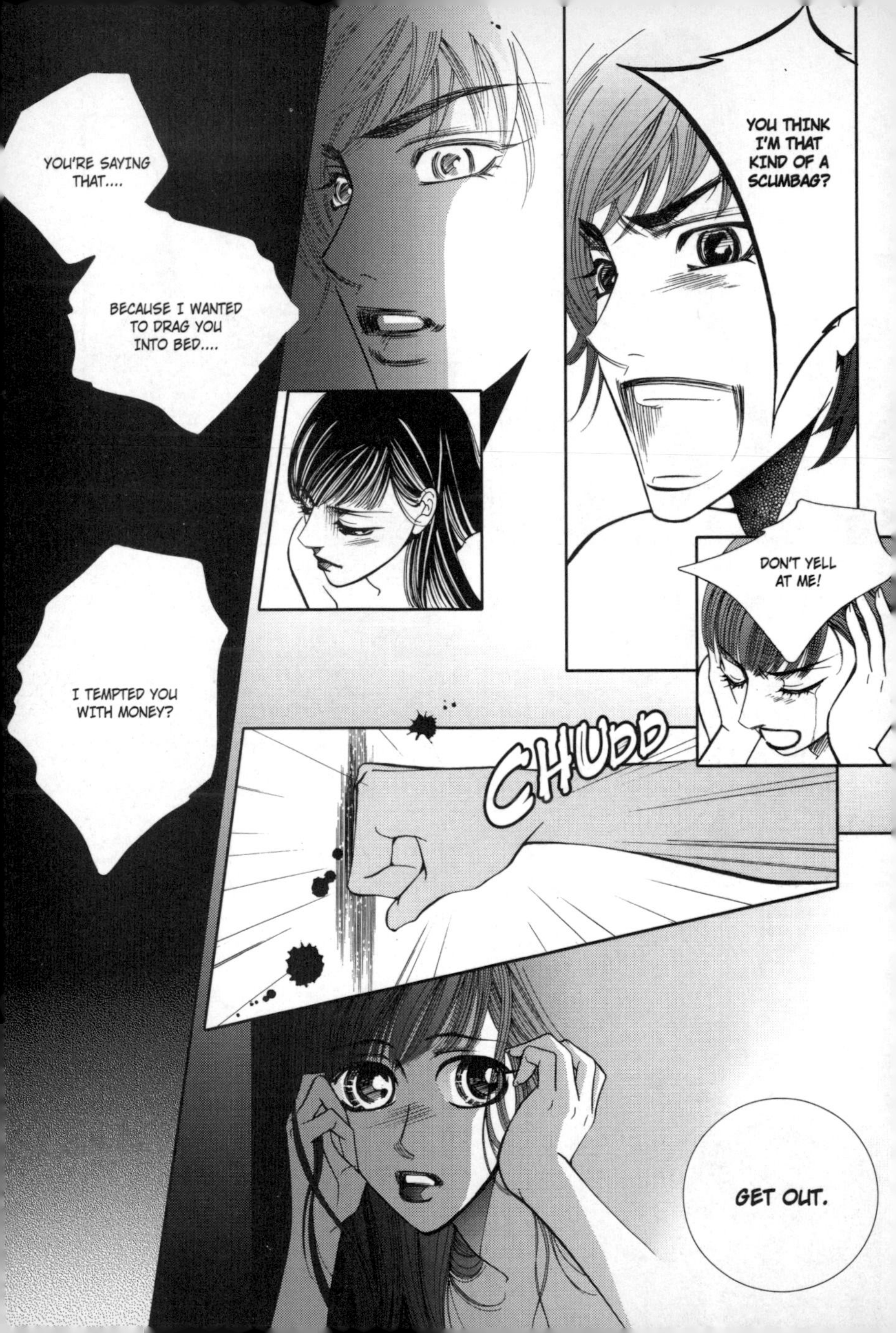
YOU'RE SAYING THAT....
BECAUSE I WANTED TO DRAG YOU INTO BED....
I TEMPTED YOU WITH MONEY?
YOU THINK I'M THAT KIND OF A SCUMBAG?
DON'T YELL AT ME!
CHUDD
GET OUT.

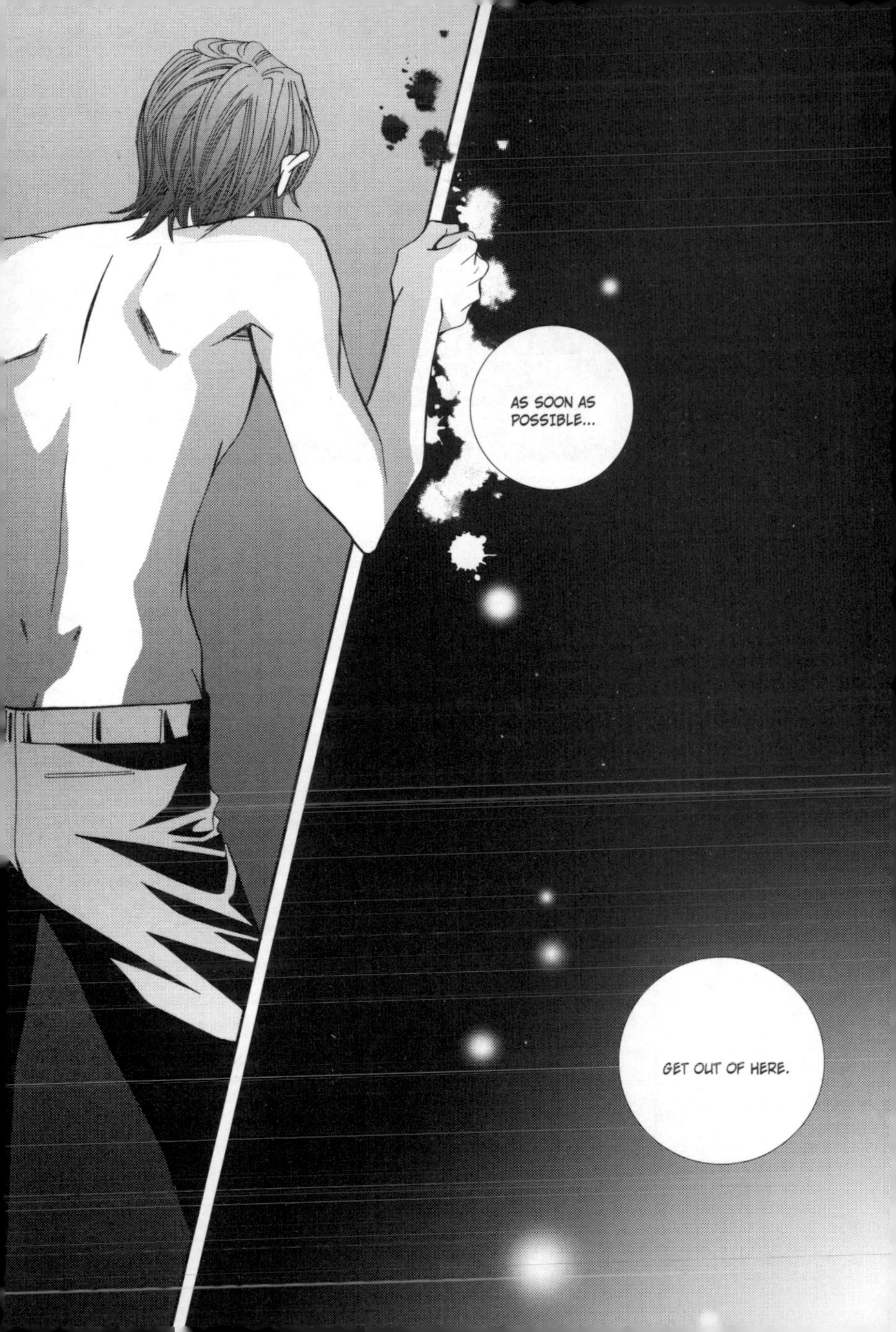
AS SOON AS POSSIBLE...
GET OUT OF HERE.

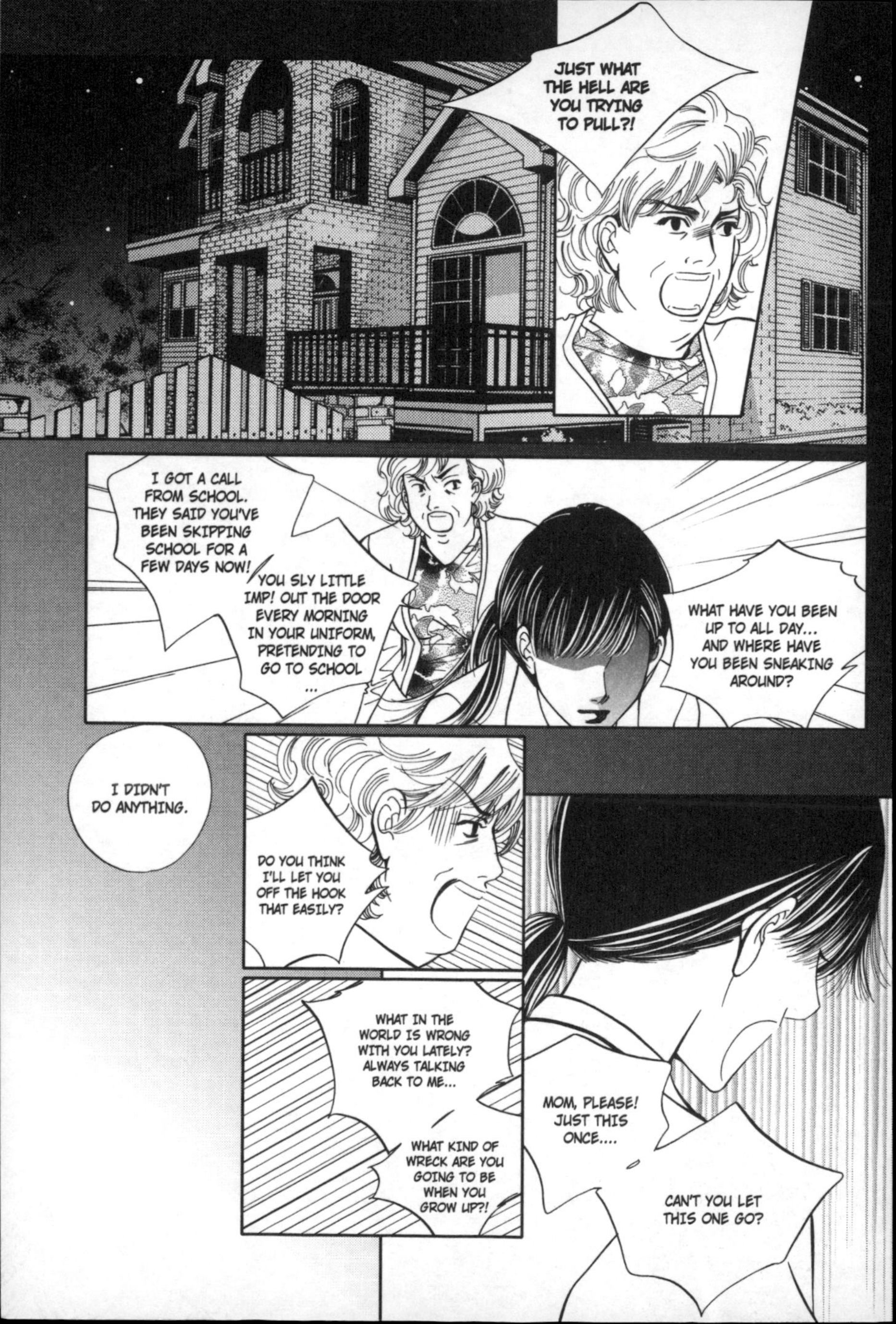
JUST WHAT THE HELL ARE YOU TRYING TO PULL?!
I GOT A CALL FROM SCHOOL. THEY SAID YOU'VE BEEN SKIPPING SCHOOL FOR A FEW DAYS NOW!
YOU SLY LITTLE IMP! OUT THE DOOR EVERY MORNING IN YOUR UNIFORM, PRETENDING TO GO TO SCHOOL ...
WHAT HAVE YOU BEEN UP TO ALL DAY... AND WHERE HAVE YOU BEEN SNEAKING AROUND?
I DIDN'T DO ANYTHING.
DO YOU THINK I'LL LET YOU OFF THE HOOK THAT EASILY?
WHAT IN THE WORLD IS WRONG WITH YOU LATELY? ALWAYS TALKING BACK TO ME...
WHAT KIND OF WRECK ARE YOU GOING TO BE WHEN YOU GROW UP?!
MOM, PLEASE! JUST THIS ONCE....
CAN'T YOU LET THIS ONE GO?

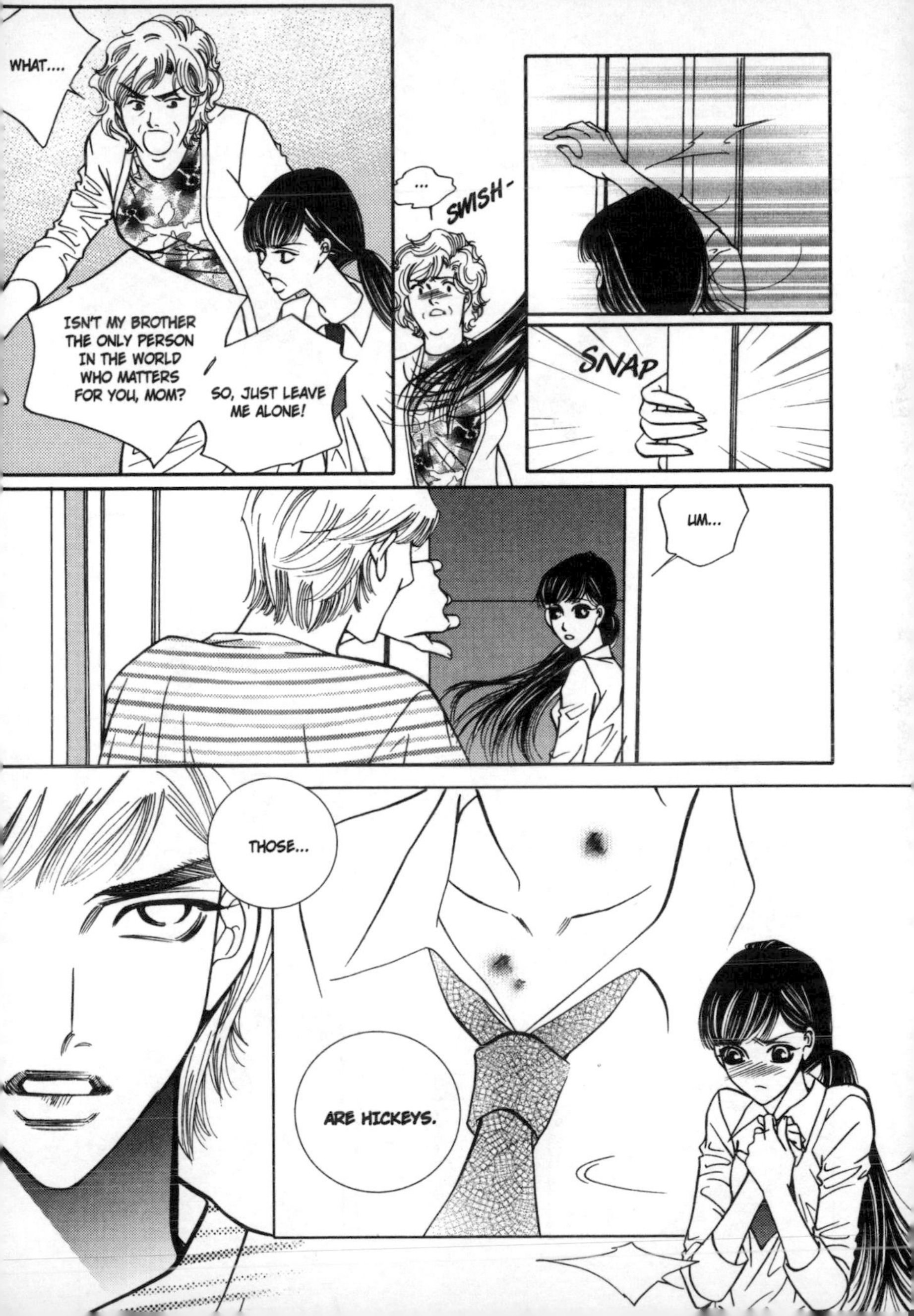
WHAT....
ISN'T MY BROTHER THE ONLY PERSON IN THE WORLD WHO MATTERS FOR YOU, MOM?
SO, JUST LEAVE ME ALONE!
...
SWISH-
SNAP
UM...
THOSE...
ARE HICKEYS.

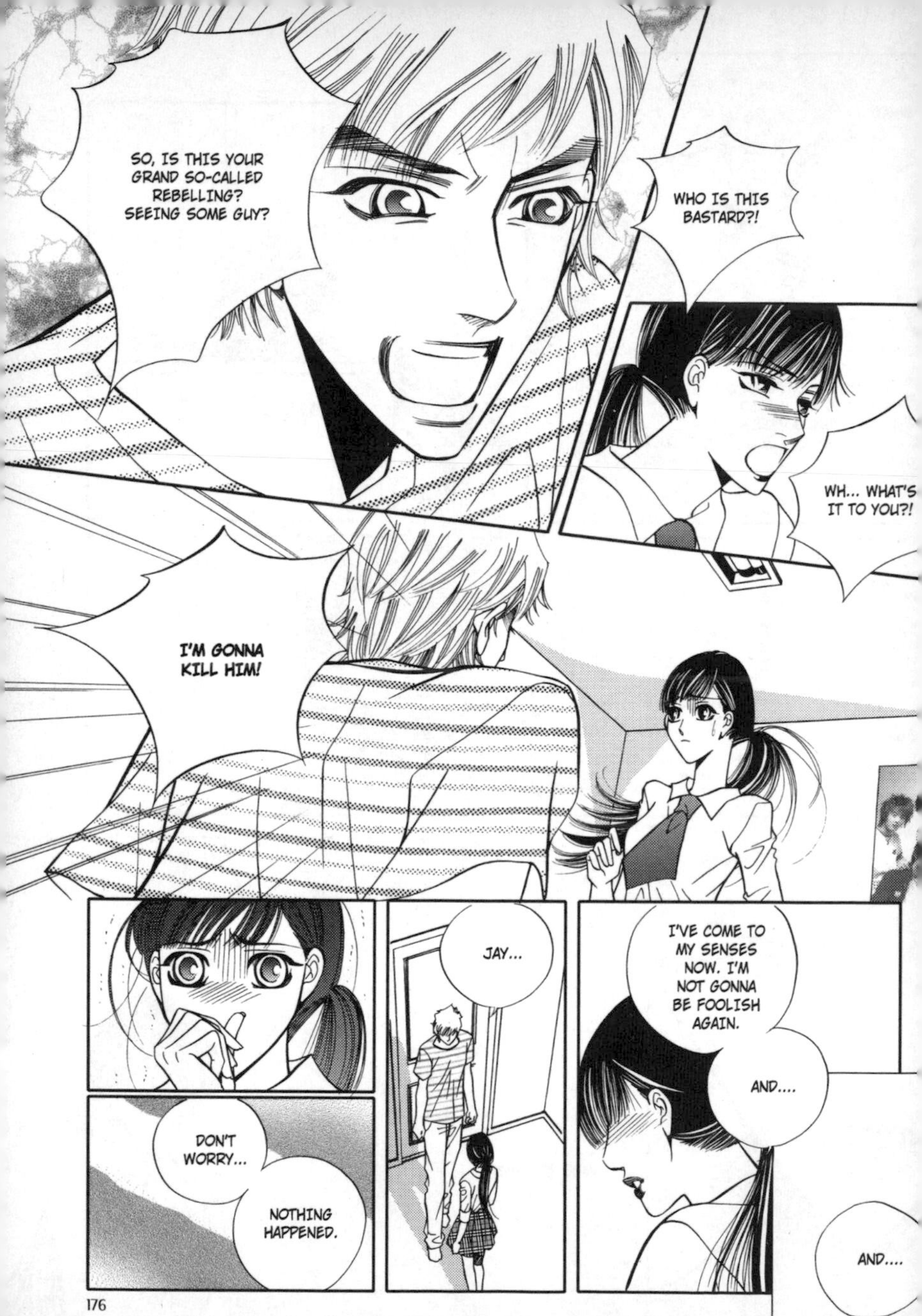
SO, IS THIS YOUR GRAND SO-CALLED REBELLING? SEEING SOME GUY?
WHO IS THIS BASTARD?!
WH... WHAT'S IT TO YOU?!
I'M GONNA KILL HIM!
DON'T WORRY...
NOTHING HAPPENED.
JAY...
I'VE COME TO MY SENSES NOW. I'M NOT GONNA BE FOOLISH AGAIN.
AND....
AND....

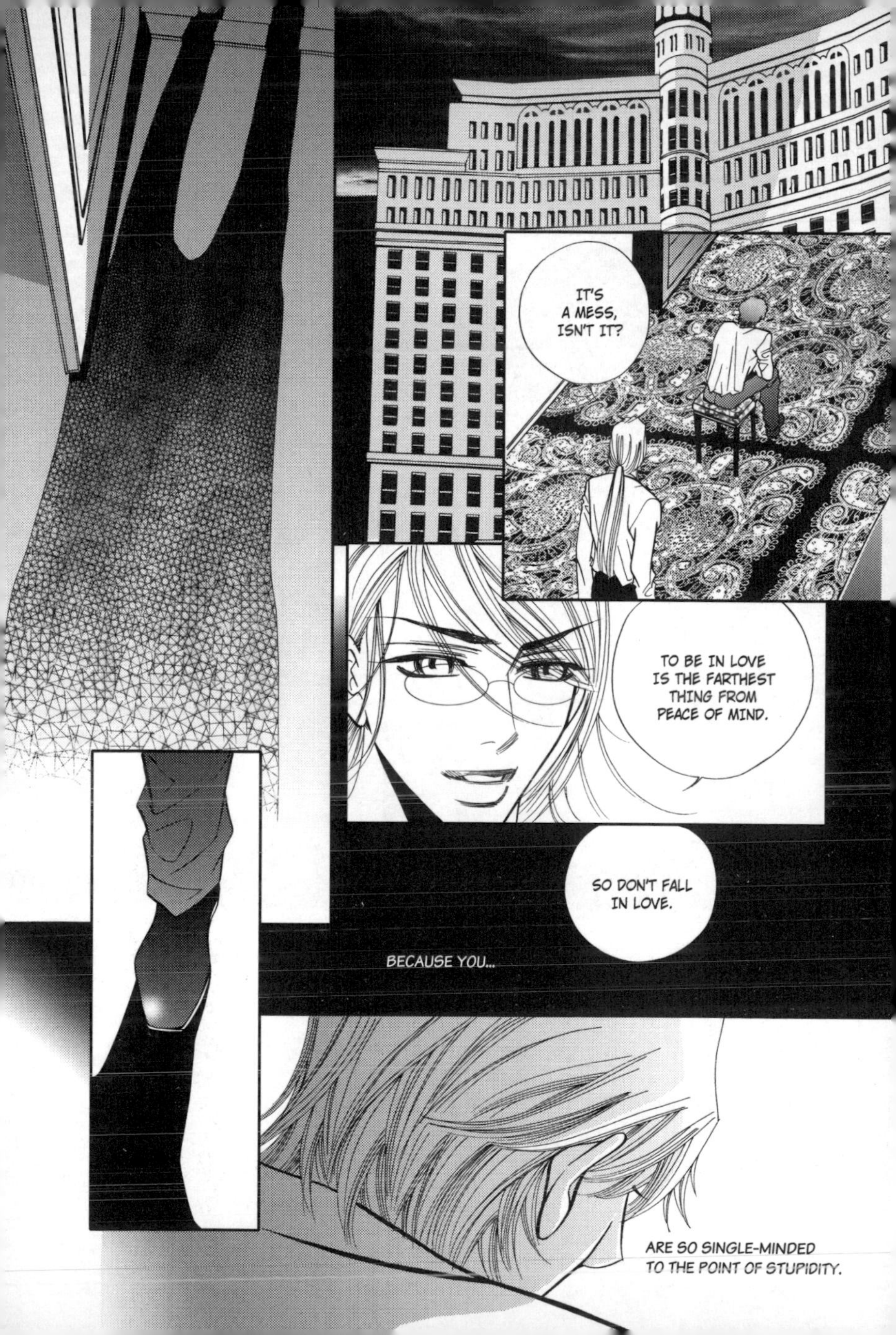
IT'S A MESS, ISN'T IT?
TO BE IN LOVE IS THE FARTHEST THING FROM PEACE OF MIND.
SO DON'T FALL IN LOVE.
BECAUSE YOU...
ARE SO SINGLE-MINDED TO THE POINT OF STUPIDITY.

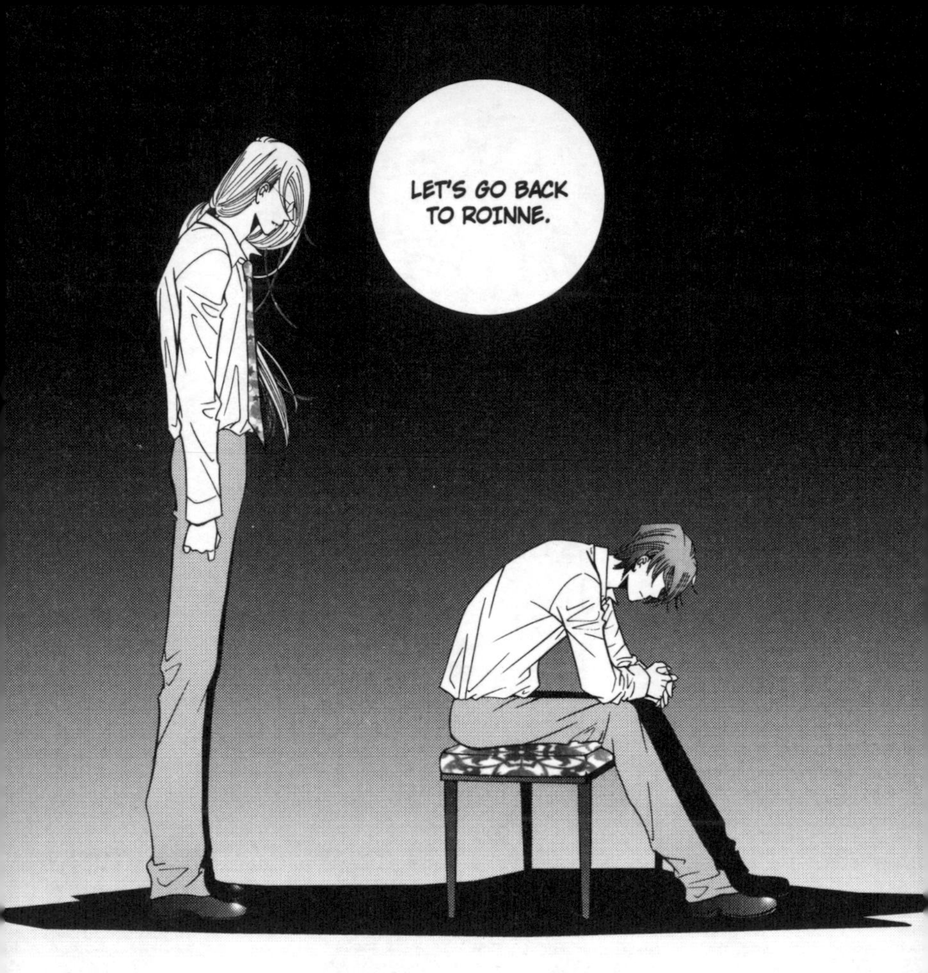
LET'S GO BACK TO ROINNE.

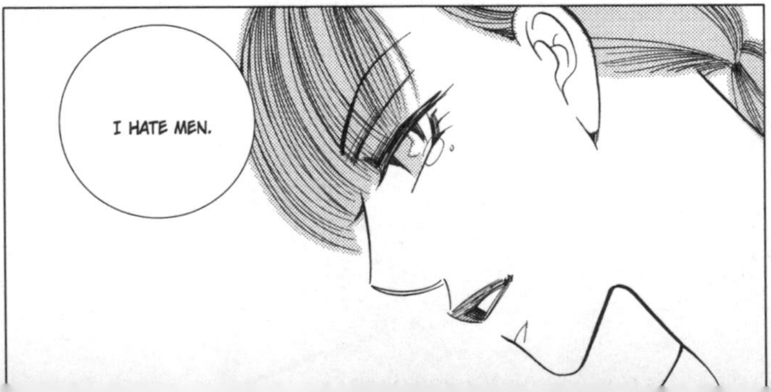
I HATE MEN.

BURSTS INTO MY LIFE AS HE PLEASES...

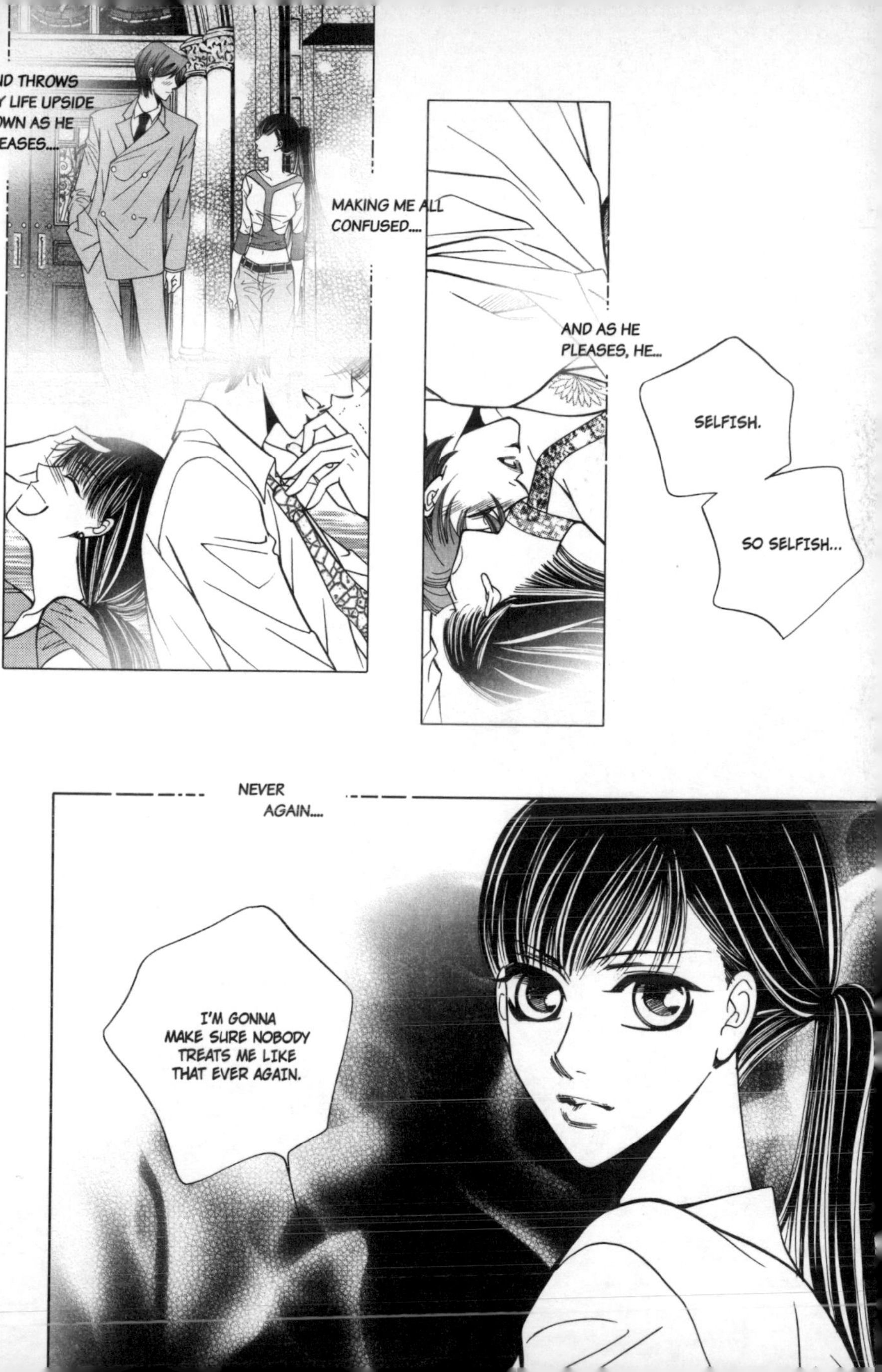
AND THROWS MY LIFE UPSIDE DOWN AS HE PLEASES....
MAKING ME ALL CONFUSED....
AND AS HE PLEASES, HE...
SELFISH.
SO SELFISH...
NEVER AGAIN....
I'M GONNA MAKE SURE NOBODY TREATS ME LIKE THAT EVER AGAIN.

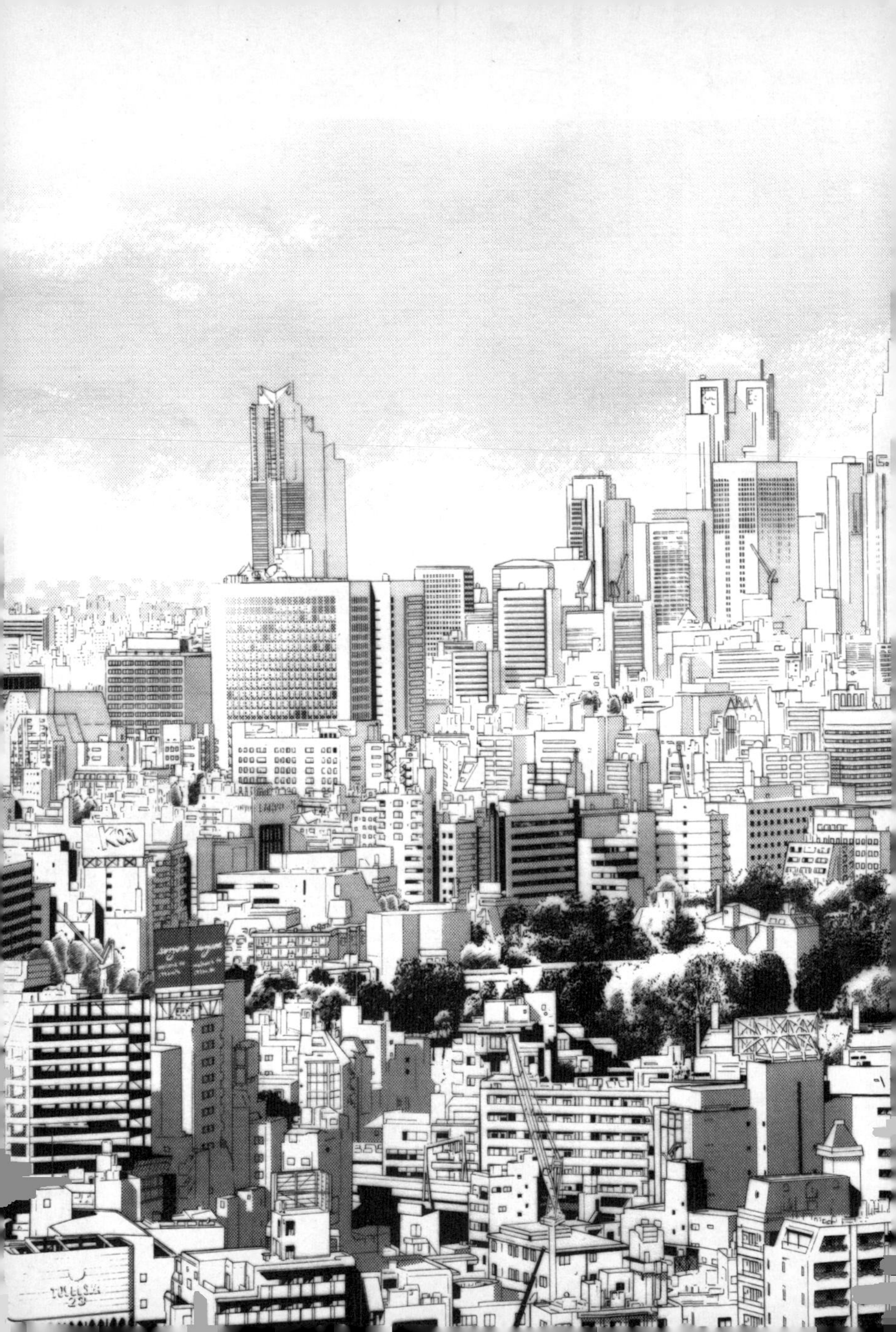

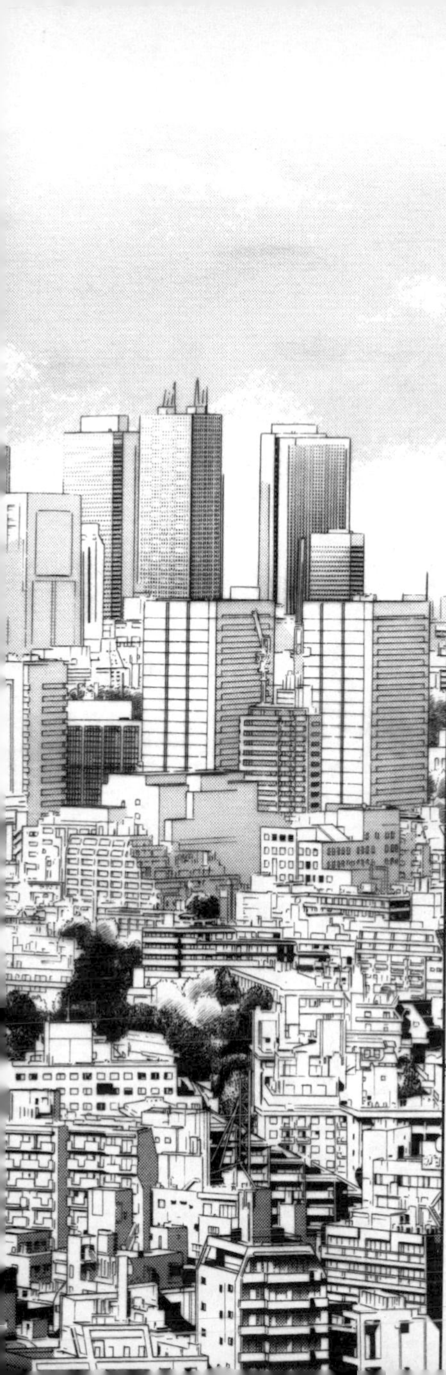

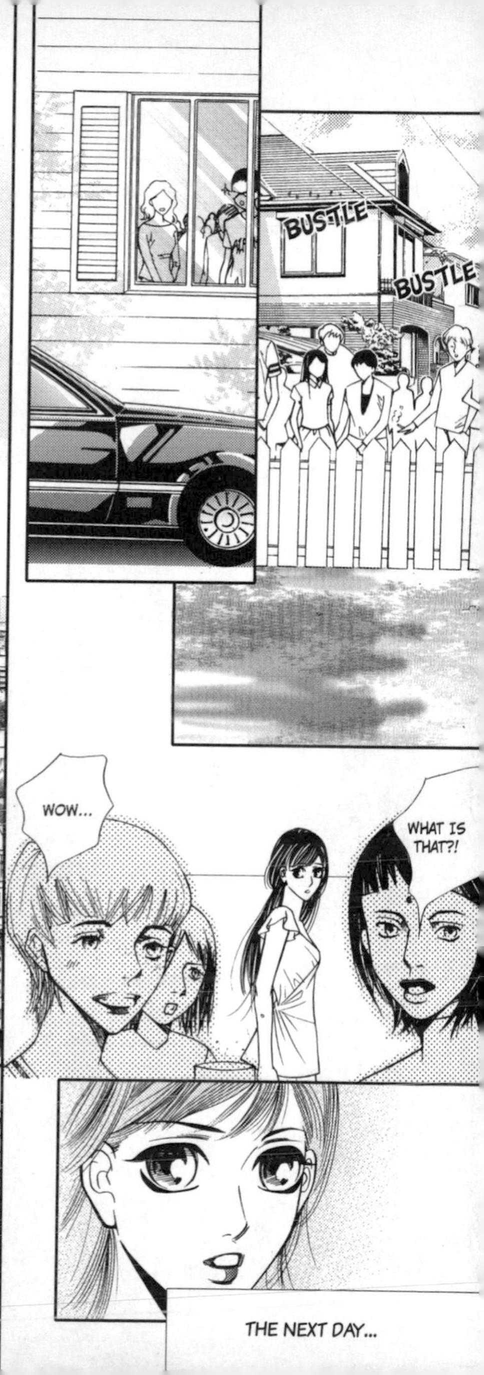
BUSTLE
BUSTLE
WOW...
WHAT IS THAT?!
THE NEXT DAY...

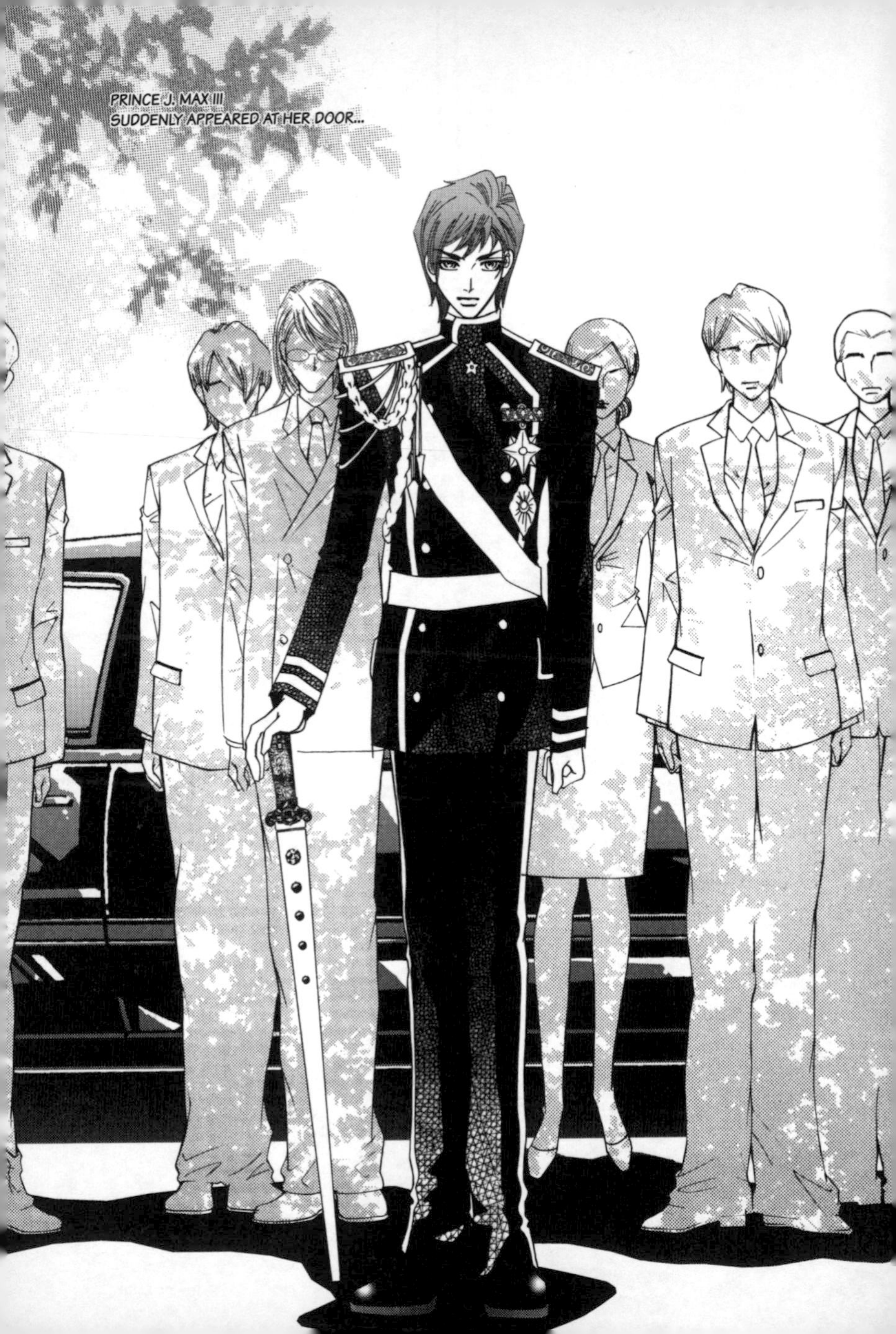
PRINCE J. MAX III
SUDDENLY APPEARED AT HER DOOR...

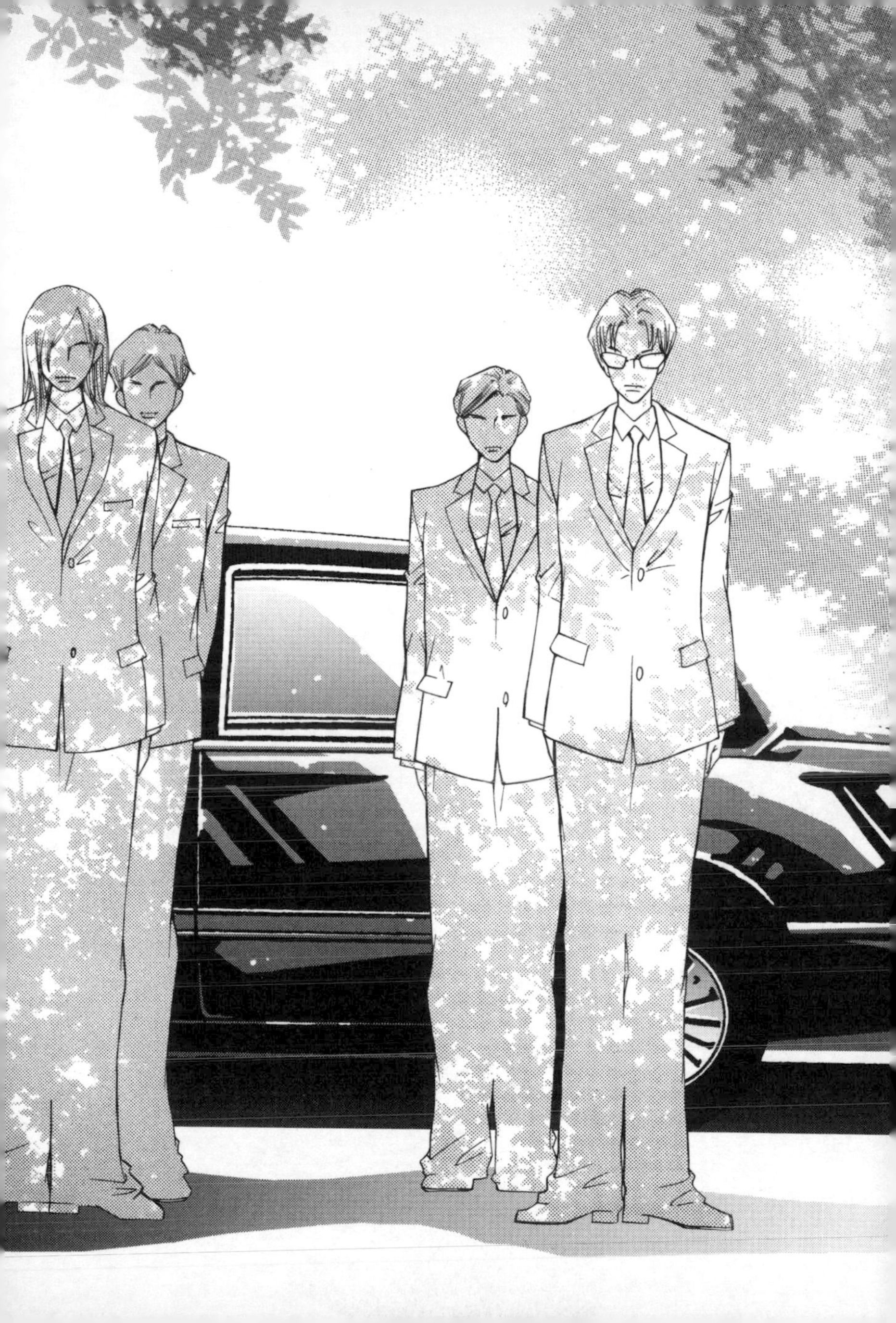

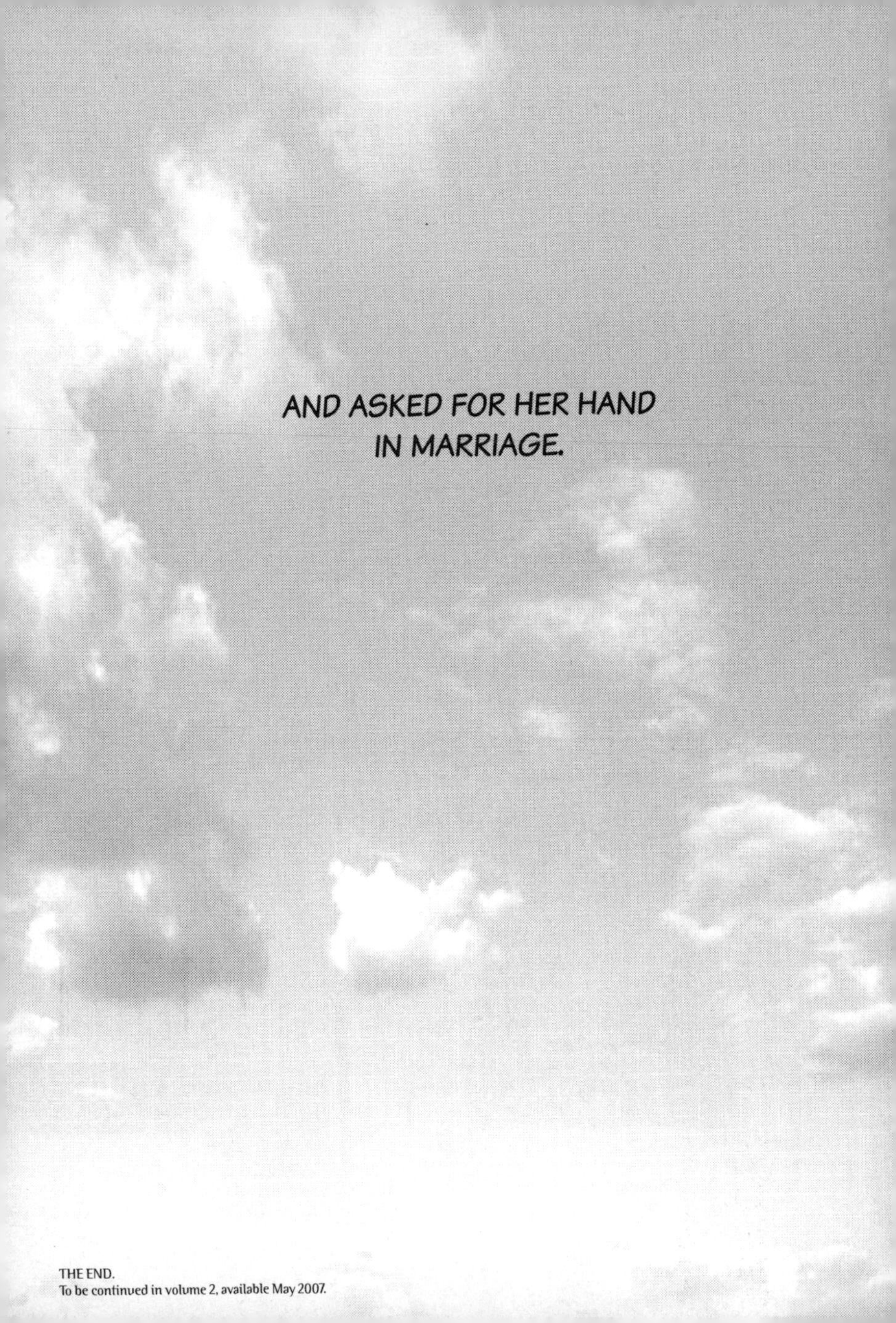
AND ASKED FOR HER HAND IN MARRIAGE.

THE END.
To be continued in volume 2, available May 2007.

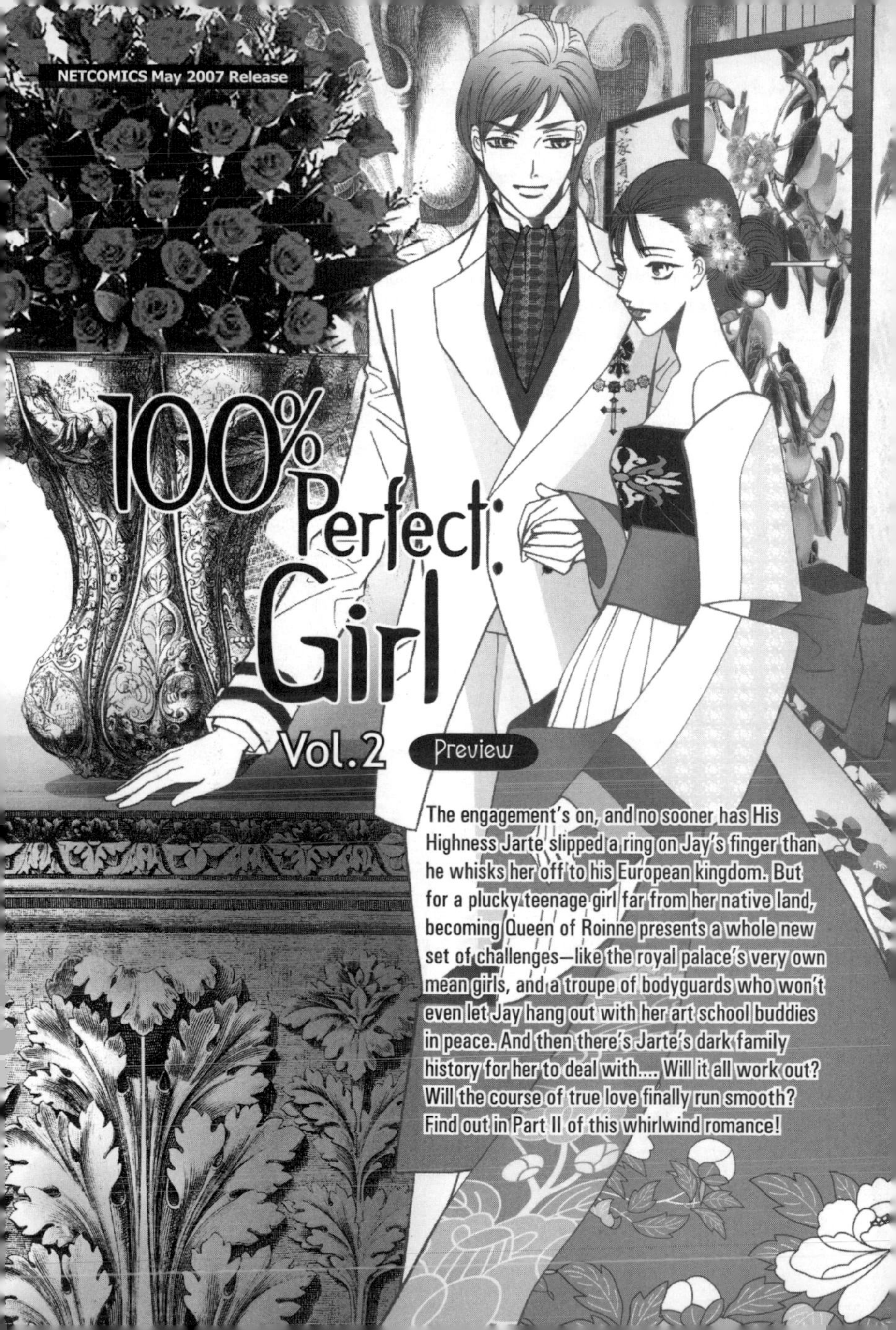
NETCOMICS May 2007 Release
100% Perfect Girl
Vol.2
Preview
The engagement's on, and no sooner has His Highness Jarte slipped a ring on Jay's finger than he whisks her off to his European kingdom. But for a plucky teenage girl far from her native land, becoming Queen of Roinne presents a whole new set of challenges—like the royal palace's very own mean girls, and a troupe of bodyguards who won't even let Jay hang out with her art school buddies in peace. And then there's Jarte's dark family history for her to deal with.... Will it all work out? Will the course of true love finally run smooth? Find out in Part II of this whirlwind romance!

WANN'S SIGNATURE SHORT STORIES

9 Faces of Love

Manhwa Novella Collection: Vol. 2

Presenting the second volume of NETCOMICS Manhwa Novella Collection
--an anthology of the most prominent Korean authors and their works
in which every page blazes with uniqueness and originality!
Volume 2 of this sensational, new series contains nine of the most
popular shorter works by Wann, the author of *Can't Lose You*.
Wann's colorful vignettes depict the most vexing of human emotions,
love, in all its guises:

- RETURN OF PRINCESS ROUANA
- BELIEVE YE YOUR EYES?
- A SHORT GAME ABOUT A CHANCE ENCOUNTER
- AUTOMATON
- A COLD
- PURPLE EYES
- LEUCADIAN
- MINT FLAVOR
- A FLYING LESSON

Roureville

New 2007

Vol. 1

by E.Hae

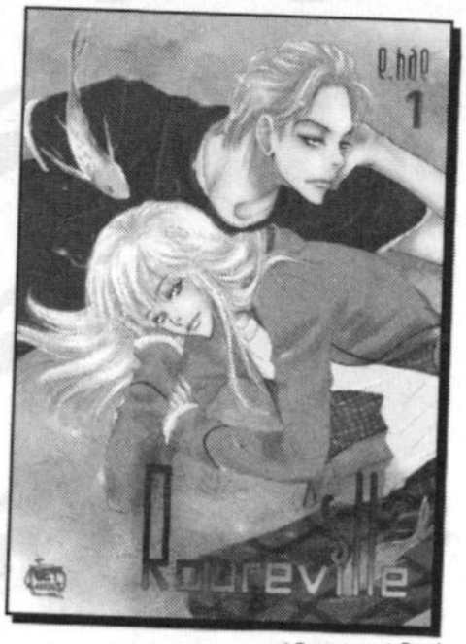
1
Roureville
*Cover not final

Evan Pryce is a celebrated New York Times reporter who has been ordered by his editor to cover an out-of-state story: "real" ghost sightings in a secluded village in the countryside. After ten days of driving by sleepy rural villages with zero results, our lost and exhausted New Yorker is just about ready to give up. But then suddenly, a road sign pointing to "Roureville" catches his eye. Little does he know that the end of his long road trip is just the beginning of an incredible tale.

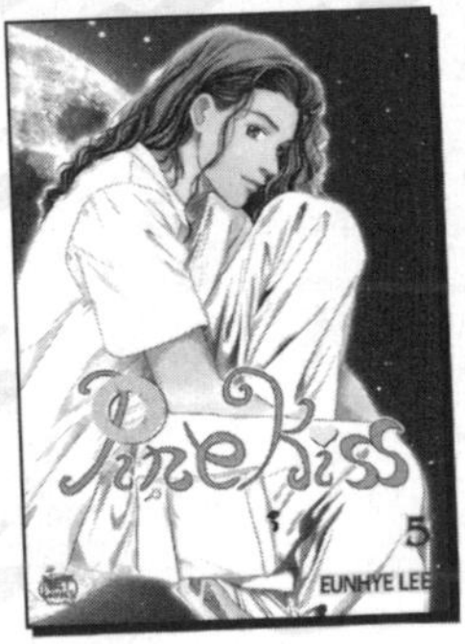
Pine Kiss
5
EUNHYE LEE

Pine Kiss

Vol. 5

by Eunhye Lee

Orion carries the unconscious Sebin home out of White Snake's sleazy grasp. Sebin's mother makes Orion a mysterious promise that she'll protect him with her life if Orion will do the same for Sebin. Meanwhile, street thugs assault Sanghyung and he's taken to the hospital unconscious and bleeding. That night, Orion receives a threatening letter from White Snake along with doctored photos that suggest intimacy between Orion and Sebin. And they could bring an end to Orion's career and his life.

Land of Silver Rain

Vol. 5

by Mira Lee

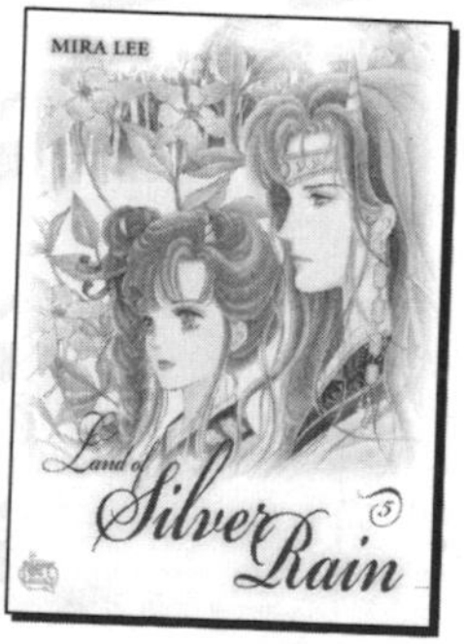
MIRA LEE
Land of Silver Rain
5

The 10th Sea Witch unfolds her evil plan to ensnare the life of Sirius, the Prince of Unicorns. Meanwhile, in the human world, Misty-Rain struggles with her school work, tormented by happy memory fragments of her younger life among the Dokebis. Sirius grows more popular at the expense of the jealous and arrogant Hanbit, but physically begins to deteriorate as the Witch's deadly potions take effect. Desperate to save his life, the Unicorn Kingdom sends deadly Griffons to retrieve their Prince and the only thing standing in their way is the life of Misty-Rain.

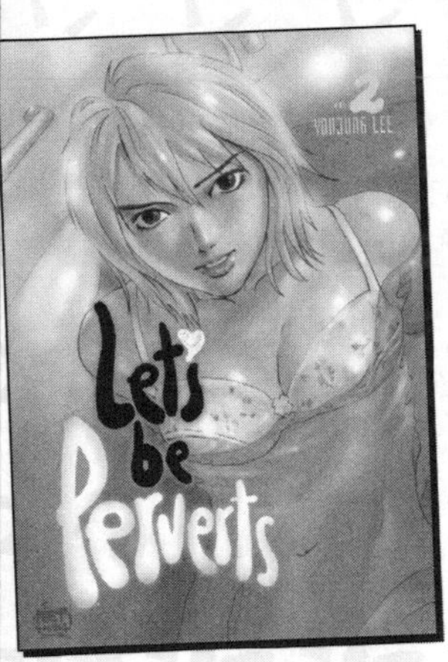
2
YOUJUNG LEE
Let's be Perverts

Let's be Perverts

by Youjung Lee

Vol. 2

In Volume 2 of *Let's Be Perverts,* Perverto is determined to forget about the devastating break-up with his first love so that he can attempt a healthy relationship with the beautiful tomboy Hongdan. But that's not an easy thing to do with both the perverted math teacher and Hongdan's ex-girlfriend, Gaheul, trying to steal her away from him. And as if that's not enough to deal with...Perverto also has to worry about a sadistic teacher who wants to cane him for sleeping in class, and a psychotic schoolmate who has vowed to rape a girl that rejected him. See who Hongdan chooses and find out just how perverted Perverto can be...

Emperor's Castle

by Sungmo Kim

Vol. 3

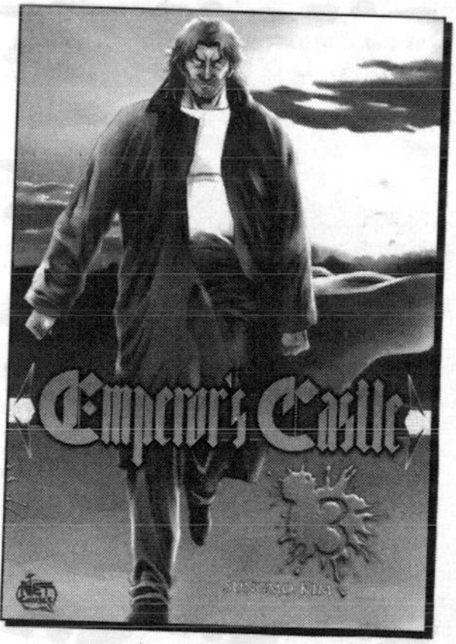
Emperor's Castle
3

After saving his son's life, Chunhoo realizes that he can't hide his powerful warrior aura even in the seedy red light district of Busan. The warden's pursuer, the Blood Demon Guhryong, tracks father and son like a bloodhound to their very doorstep. Fast on his heels, the Imperial assassins from Japan leave a trail of fear and violence in their wake. Chunhoo's former yakuza bosses, the Sochun Organization, want to guarantee the answer to that question by creating an unseen trap for them all. And their machinations won't stop until they provoke an apocalyptic battle between Japan's highest martial art Ki-Do-Ryu and the Shi-Nan-Joo style of Chunhoo. Sensing the approaching battles, Chunhoo gives his son Sugki a mysterious key that may change the fate of all.

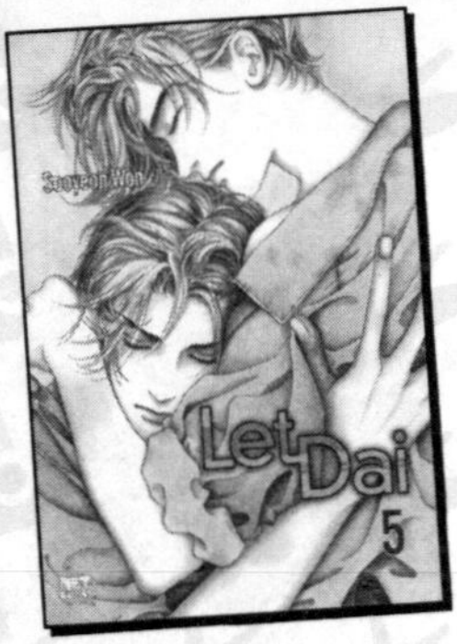
Sooyeon Won
Let Dai
5

Let Dai

by Sooyeon Won **Vol. 5**

Yooneun's fear for her sister's well-being has pushed her to ask Jaehee for help. But Jaehee has his own issues to deal with, and when Dai unexpectedly shows up in front of his house with a chauffered car, thoughts of Eunhyung are all but forgotten. Meanwhile, in another part of town, Yooneun is assaulted.. Fortunately, a knight in shining armor comes to her aid... but what she doesn't know is that her angel is closer to the devil than she thinks. And finally, Eunhyung has found friends who seem to understand the anguish raging inside.

Boy Princess

by Seyoung Kim **Vol. 5**

Jed snatches Nicole away onto a dangerous journey to visit the village of the mysterious apothecary. He desires to end their marriage and discourage Nicole's feelings for the sake of the boy's life, but he can't control his affections in the night. Elena seeks out her old love Martin. But, no matter how far Jed takes Nicole, the spies of the Crown Prince and the Queen keep close watch, ready to strike at any moment. If he can reach the village, Jed will learn a secret that will turn his world upside-down and shift the balance of powers in his kingdom.

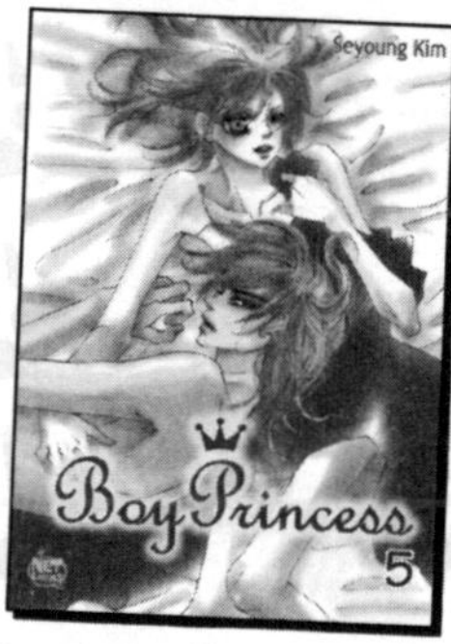
Seyoung Kim
Boy Princess
5

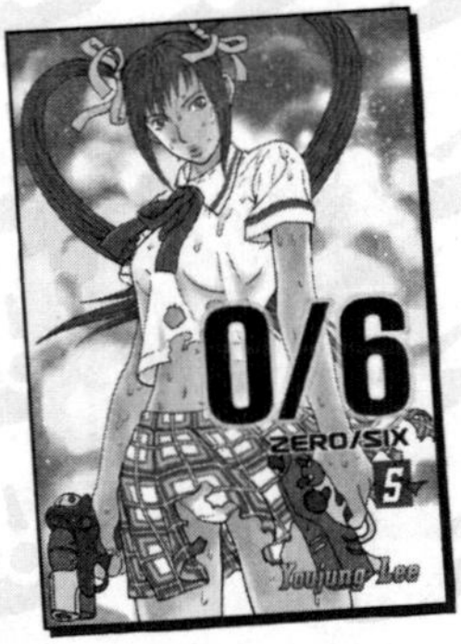
0/6
ZERO/SIX
5
Youjung Lee

0/6 (Zero/Six)

by Youjung Lee **Vol. 5**

The powerful automaton called Number One holds a young girl hostage and Moolchi must save her life by hunting him down within the halls of Ssangsan High School where it all began. However, Moolchi knows his power is limited. He ages drastically with every exertion. Faced with Moolchi's imminent death, Jong-E must come to terms with her automatic order to self-terminate should she fail in her mission to protect him. But hardened from his painful losses, Moolchi pushes her aid away. Who will stand triumphant? Moolchi or Number One? And will Jong-E share his fate?

Available now at your favorite bookstores.
Read them online at www.NETCOMICS.com!